Highly Recommended

New Edition

AF660897

OSWAAL BOOKS
LEARNING MADE SIMPLE

NCERT TEXTBOOK SOLUTIONS

CLASS 11

PHYSICS

Strictly based on Latest NCERT Textbook

Your Path to Academic Excellence:

1 **100% Updated** with Latest NCERT Textbook 2023-24

2 **Comprehensive Coverage** with All Concepts & Topics Covered

3 **Visual Learning Tools** with Concept Videos

4 **Extensive Revision Tools** with Crisp Revision Notes, Mind Maps & Mnemonics

5 **Complete Question Coverage** All Questions Fully Solved

1st EDITION

ISBN "9789359583143"

SYLLABUS COVERED

CENTRAL BOARD OF SECONDARY EDUCATION DELHI

PUBLISHED BY

OSWAAL BOOKS & LEARNING PVT. LTD.

1/11, Sahitya Kunj, M.G. Road,
Agra - 282002, (UP) India

1010, Cambourne Business Centre
Cambridge, Cambridgeshire
CB 236DP, United kingdom

0562-2857671

contact@oswaalbooks.com

www.OswaalBooks.com

Printed at Sahitya Bhawan C-17 Industrial Area, Agra

Contents

❑❑

PREFACE

"*Education is the passport to the future, for tomorrow belongs to those who prepare for it today.*" – Malcolm X

In the pursuit of academic excellence, the journey often begins with curiosity. As students embark on the path to success in the exams, the Oswaal NCERT Textbook Solutions Book for the academic year 2024-25 stands as an invaluable companion, illuminating the way forward.

Success in any exam goes beyond memorization; it involves developing a deep understanding of every concept. The NCERT textbooks provide the essential foundation. Introducing the Oswaal NCERT Textbook Solutions Book, a vital tool to unlock the full potential of every student.

Let's uncover what this book covers for you:

1) **Updated for 2024-25** – The books are 100% updated for the academic year 2024-25, adhering strictly to the latest NCERT guidelines.
2) **Comprehensive Coverage -** We cover all concepts and topics outlined in the most recent NCERT textbooks.
3) **Visual Learning Aids -** Explore theoretical concepts and concept videos that offer a brief description of the topic and help visualize complex concepts.
4) **Effective Revision Tools -** Benefit from crisp Revision Notes, Mind Maps, and Mnemonics designed to facilitate efficient and effective review.
5) **Complete Question Coverage -** All questions from the NCERT textbooks are covered in our solutions, providing a thorough grasp of the subject matter.

What sets this book apart is the expertise behind its creation. The solutions within are the result of the meticulous efforts of expert faculty, individuals with a profound understanding of the curriculum, and the dedication to maintaining the highest quality standards.

May this book be your guide, encouraging you to not just study but to explore and understand.

Wishing you a fulfilling and successful academic journey.

Team,

Oswaal Books

Order Form

ONE FOR ALL OLYMPIADS (Multicolour)

Classes 1 to 5

Mathematics, English, Reasoning, General Knowledge, Science & Cyber

ONE FOR ALL WORKBOOKS CONCEPT-WISE (Multicolour)

Classes 1 to 5

Mathematics, English, General Knowledge, Science

NCERT WORKBOOKS (Multicolour / B&W)

Classes 1 - 5

English, Hindi, Mathematics & EVS

ONE FOR ALL OLYMPIADS

Classes 6 to 8

Mathematics, English, Reasoning, General Knowledge, Science & Cyber

NCERT & CBSE One For All Workbook

Classes 6 to 8

Mathematics, English, Science, Social Science, Hindi & Sanskrit

CBSE WorkBook Classes 9 & 10

English Lang. & Literature, Science, Social Science & Mathematics

CBSE & NCERT Laboratory Manual

Classes 6 - 12

Mathematics, Science, Physics, Chemistry & Biology

CBSE QUESTION BANKS (CHAPTER-WISE & TOPIC-WISE SOLVED PAPERS)

Classes 9 & 10

Hindi-A, Hindi-B, English Lang. & Lit. (With NCERT Workbook), Science, Mathematics, Social Science, Computer Applications, Sanskrit & English Communicative (With CBSE Textbook),

Classes 11 & 12

Hindi Core, English Core, Mathematics, Chemistry, Applied Mathematics, Biology, Physics, Accountancy, Economics, Business Studies, Geography, History, Political Science, Computer Science, Entrepreneurship, Informatics Practices, Physical Education, Sociology (For Class 12th Only), Psychology (For Class 12th Only)

NCERT EXEMPLAR PROBLEMS-SOLUTIONS (Hindi & English Medium)

Classes 9 - 12

Science, Mathematics, Physics, Chemistry, Biology, Mathematics, गणित, भौतिक विज्ञान, रसायन विज्ञान, जीव विज्ञान

NCERT Textbook Solutions

Classes 6 - 12

Science, Mathematics, Physics, Chemistry, Biology

NCERT TEXTBOOK+EXEMPLAR

Classes 6 - 12

Science, Mathematics, Physics, Chemistry, Biology

CBSE 10 PREVIOUS YEARS' SOLVED PAPERS

Class 10

English Lang. & Lit, Science, Social Science, Sanskrit Mathematics Standard & Computer Applications

Class 12

Science Stream (PCM)-(Chemistry, Physics, Mathematics & English Core), Science Stream (PCB)-(Chemistry, Physics, English Core & Biology) Commerce Stream- (Economics, Accountancy, Business Studies, Mathematics & English Core), Humanities Stream- (Geography, History, Political Science & English Core)

CBSE RMT FLASH CARDS

Class 10

Mathematics, English Lang. & Lit., Social Science & Science

CBSE ONE FOR ALL

Classes 6 - 8

English, Hindi, Mathematics, Science, Social Science & Sanskrit

Classes 9 & 10

Mathematics, English Lang. & Lit., Social Science, Science, Hindi-A, Hindi-B, Mathematics (Stand.) & Mathematics Basic

Class 12

English Core, Physics, Chemistry, Mathematics, Biology, Accoutancy, Business Studies & Economics

CBSE LMP-Last Minute Preparation System

Class 10

Combined (English Lang. & Lit., Science, Mathematics Standard & Social Science)

Class 12

Science (Physics, Chemistry, Mathematics, Biology & English Core) **Commerce** (Accountancy, Business Studies, Economics, Mathematics & English Core) **Humanities** (History, Geography, Political Science & English Core)

CBSE SAMPLE QUESTION PAPERS

Classes 9 & 10

Hindi-A, Hindi-B, English Lang. & Lit., Computer Appl., English Communicative, Mathematics, Science, Social Science, Sanskrit & Samajik Vigyan (For Class 10th Only)

Classes 11 & 12

Hindi Core, English Core, Mathematics, Applied Mathematics, Physics, Chemistry, Biology, Accountancy, Economics, Business Studies, Geography, History, Political Science, Computer Science, Informatics Practices, Physical Education, Entrepreneurship (For Class 12th Only), Psychology (For Class 12th Only) & Sociology (For Class 12th Only)

CBSE 20 Combined Sample Question Papers

Classes 10 & 12

Science, Commerce & Humanities

Exam Preparation Books for Class 1 to 12 : CBSE, CISCE Boards & Karnataka Board | OLYMPIADS | JEE | NEET | CUET | NTSE | NDA | CDS | CAT | CTET | GATE | UPSC| RRB | BPSC | CLAT & AILET | UGC NET | NRA CET & more

We are available in all leading e-commerce platforms and all good bookstores.

OswaalBooks.com | amazon.in | Flipkart | meesho | JioMart | snapdeal | amazonkindle | Google Play Books

Positive Affirmations

An affirmation is a positive statement or phrase that individuals repeat to themselves with the intention of fostering a positive mindset, self-confidence, or personal development. The practice involves affirming desired beliefs or qualities, often in the present tense, to reinforce a positive self-image and encourage a more optimistic outlook.

" EMBRACE YOUR UNIQUENESS, NOURISH SELF-CARE, AND PRESS FORWARD RELENTLESSLY. TO ACHIEVE FLIGHT, UNLOAD THE BAGGAGE THAT SLOWS YOUR ASCENT."

I strongly trust in my vision and work deligently towards making it a reality.

I am capable of learning and growing everyday.

I am not defined by grades & test scores. My true worth lies in my character, compassion and positive impact I have on others.

I embrace my mistakes, learn from them and use them to fuel my growth & resilience.

I celebrate my quirks, for they make me beautifully unique.

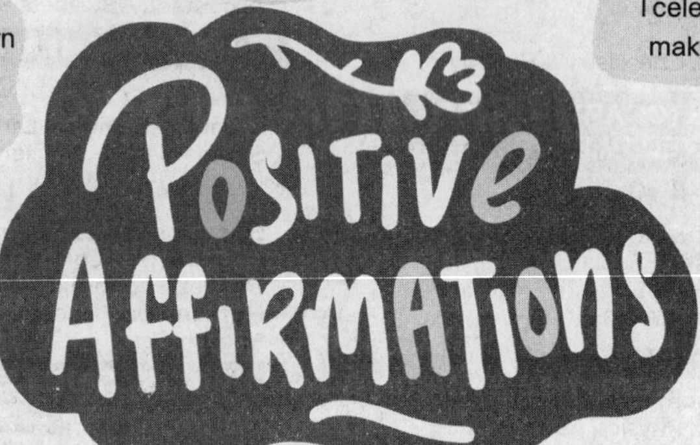

My voice matters and I believe in the power of my words to shape the world around me.

I am not the product of circumstances, I am the product of my own choices.

I face challenges with courage and determination.

I celebrate the achievements of others without diminishning my journey.

I believe that the twists & turns of my life lead me to an extraordinary destinations.

Exclusive School Books Suppliers

ANDHRA PRADESH
VIJAYAWADA Sri Vikas Book Centre, 9848571114, 9440715700,

ASSAM
WEST KAMENG Dutta Book Stall, 8729948473

KARNATAKA
BANGLORE Satish Agencies, 8861630123

GUJRAT
RAJKOT Royal Stationers, 9824207514

MAHARASHTRA
PUNE Madhusheela Books & Stationery, 7875899892

JALNA Anil Paper Mart, 9422722522, (02482) 230733

TAMIL NADU
CHENNAI Bookmark-IT, 7305151653

TELANGANA
HYDERABAD Sri Balaji Book Depot , 9676996199, (040) 27613300

WEST BENGAL
KOLKATA United Book House, 9831344622

Our Distributors

ANDHRA PRADESH
VISAKHAPATHAM JBD Educational, 9246632691, 9246633693, Sri Rajeshwari Book Link, 9848036014

VIJAYAWADA Akshaya Books Corner, 9666155555

ANDAMAN & NICOBAR ISLAND
PORTBLAIR Krishna Book Centre, 9474205570, Kumar Book Depot, 9932082455, Kumar Book Depot, 9932082455, Sree aditya Book Centre, 8332972720, 7013300914

ASSAM
GUWAHATI Book Emporium, 9675972993, 6000763186, Ashok Publication, 7896141127, Kayaan Enterprises, (0361) 2630443, Orchid Book house, 9864624209, Newco, 9864178188

BIHAR
PATNA Nova Publisher & Distributors, (0612) 2666404, Shri Durga Pustak Mandir, 9334477386, Sharda Pustak Bhandar, 9334259293, Vikas Book Depot, 9504780402, Alka Book Agency, 9835655005, Metro Book(E&C), Ishu Pustak Bhandar, 8294576789, Gyan Ganga Limited, 6203900312, Ishu Pustak Bhandar, (E & C), 9334186300/8294576789

MUZAFFARPUR Pustak Bhandar, 7870834225

CHATTISGARH
AMBIKAPUR Saini Brothers, 9425582561, M.P Department Stores, 9425254264

BOKARO Bokaro Student Friends Pvt. Ltd, Bokaro, 7277931285

BHILAI Anil Book Depot, 9425234260

DURG Bhagwati Bhawani Book Depot, 0788-2327620, 9827473100

KORBA Kitab Ghar, Korba (E & C), 9425226528

RAIPUR Shri Ramdev Traders, 9981761797, Gupta Pustak Mandir, 7974220323, Anil Publication, 9691618258/7999078802

RAIGARH Sindhu Book Deopt, 9981935763

DELHI
DELHI Mittal Books, (011) 23288887, 9899037390, Singhania Book & Stationer, 9212028238, AoneBooks, New Delhi, 8800497047, Radhey Book Depot, 9818314141, Batheja Super Store, 9871833924, Lov Dev & Sons, Delhi (E & C), 9811182352, Zombozone, 9871274082, LDS Marketing, 9811182352/9999353491

GUJARAT
AHMEDABAD Patel Book, 9898184248, 9824386112, 9825900335, Zaveri Agency, 9979897312, 9979890330, Hardik Book Agency, (ISC) 079-24110043, 9904659821

BHAVNAGAR Samir Book Stall, Bhavnagar (ISC) 9586305305

DAHOD Collegian Book Corner, 9925501981

VAPI Goutam Book Sellers, 9081790813

VALSAD Mahavir Stationers, 9429474177

NAVSARI College Store, (ISC) NO CALL 02637-258642, 9825099121

SURAT Shopping Point, 9824108663

VADODARA Umakant Book Sellers & Stationer, 9624920709

HARYANA
ROHTAK Manish Traders, 9812556687, Swami Kitab Ghar, 9355611088, Babu Ram Pradeep Kumar, 9813214692

REWARI Sanjay book depot, 9255447231

BALLABGARH Kashi Ram Kishan lal, 9289504004, 8920567245

HISAR Natraj Book Distributors, 7988917452

BHUNA Khurana Book Store, 9896572520

JAMMU
Sahitya Sangam, 9419190177

JHARKHAND
BOKARO Bokaro Student Friends, (0654) 2233094, 7360021503, Bharati Bhawan Agencies, 9431740797

RANCHI Crown Book Distributor & Publishers, (0651) 2213735, 9431173904, Pustak Mandir, 9431115138,

DUMKA Vidyarthi Pustak Bhandar, 9431310228

KARNATAKA
HUBLI Renuka Book Distributor, (0836) 2244124, Vidyamandir Book Distributors, 9980773976

BANGLORE Krishna book house, 9739847334, Hema Book Stores, 9986767000, Sapna Book House Pvt. Ltd., 9980513242, Hema Book World, (Chamrajpet) (ISC) 080-40905110, 9945731121

BELLERI Chatinya book centre, 9886064731

KERALA
ERNAKULAM Academic Book House, (0484) 2376613, H & C Store, 9864196344, Surya Book House, 9847124217, 9847238314

KOTTAYAM Book Centre, (0481) 2566992

TRIVANDRUM Academic Book House, (0471) 2333349, 9447063349, Ponni Book Stall, 9037591721

CALICUT Aman Book Stall, (0495) 2721282,

MADHYA PRADESH
CHHINDWARA Pustak Bhawan, (E & C), 8982150100

GWALIOR Agarwal Book Depot, 9425116210

INDORE Bhaiya Industries, 9893326853, Sushil Prakashan,(0731) 2503333, 2535892, 9425322330, Bhaiya Store, 9425318103, Arun Prakashan, 9424890785, Bhaiya Book Centre, 9424081874, Seva Suppliers, 9826451052

JABALPUR Vinay Pustak Sadan, 8962362667, Anand Books and Stationers, 9425323508

SAGAR Princi Book Depot, Sagar, 9977277011

KATNI Shri Mahavir Agency, 9425363412

UJJAIN Shreenath Book Depot, 9827544045

BHOPAL Gupta Brother, 9644482444

MAHARASHTRA
PUNE Natraj Book Depot, (020) 24485054, 9890054092, Vikas Book House, 9921331187, Pravin Sales, 9890683475, New Saraswati Granth Bhandar, 9422323859, Akshar Books & Stationary, 7385089789, Vardhaman Educational, 9860574354, Yash Book Centre, 9890156763, Pragati Book Centre, (ISC), 9850039311, Praveen Sales, Pragati Book Centre, Pune (E & C), 9850039311

AURANGABAD Shree Sainath Agencies, 7350294089, Maya Book Centre, (ISC), 9372360150

MUMBAI Vidyarthi Sales Agencies, 9819776110, New Student Agencies, 7045065799, Shivam Books & Stationery, 8619805332

JALGAON Sharma Book Depot & Stat. (ISC), 9421393040

LATUR Yash Book House, 9637936999, Shri Ganesh Pustakalay, 9730172188

KOLHAPUR Granth the Book World, 9922295522

NAGPUR Laxmi Pustakalay and Stationers, (0712) 2727354, Vijay Book Depot, 9860122094 Renuka Book distributor, 9765406133, Novelty Book Depot, 9657690220, Karamveer Book Depot, 9923966466, Arun Book & Stationers, 9423110953

NANDED Abhang Pustakalaya, 9823470756/9175940756

NASHIK Rahul Book Centre, 9970849681, New India Book House, 9623123458

DHULE Navjeevan Book Stall, 7020525561

YAVATMAL Shri Ganesh Pustkalaya, 9423131275

VASAI Prime Book Centre, Vasai, 9890293662

ODISHA
CUTTACK A. K. Mishra Agencies, 9437025991, 9437081319

BHUBANESHWAR M/s Pragnya, 8847888616, 9437943777, Padmalaya, 9437026922, Bidyashree, 9937017070, Books Godown, 7894281110

BARIPADA Trimurti Book World, 9437034735

KEONJHAR Students corner, 7008435418

PUNJAB
AMBALA Bharat Book Depot, 7988455354

PATIALA Goel Sons, 9463619978, Adarsh Enterprises, 9814347613

JALANDHAR Cheap Book Store, 9872223458, 9878258592, City Book Shop, 9417440753, Subhash Book Depot, 9876453625, Paramvir Enterprises, 9878626248

FEROZPUR Sita Ram book Depot, 9463039199, 7696141911

LUDHIANA Amit Book, 9815807871, Gupta Brothers, 9888200206, Bhatia Book Centre, 9815277131

CHANDIGARH Mohindra Book Depot, 9814920226

RAJASTHAN
AJMER Laxmi General Store, Ajmer, 0145- 2428942 9460652197

KOTA Vardhman Book Depot, 9571365020, 8003221190 Raj Traders, 9309232829

BHILWARA Nakoda Book Depot, (01482) 243653, 9214983594, Alankar Book Depot, 9414707462

JAIPUR Ravi Enterprises, 9829060694, Saraswati Book House, (0141) 2610823, 9829811155, Goyal Book Distt., 9460983939, 9414782130

UDAIPUR Sunil Book Store, 9828682260

JODHPUR Second Hand Book Stall, 9460004745

TRIPURA
AGARTALA Book Corner, 8794894165, 8984657146, Book Emporium, 9089230412

TAMIL NADU
COIMBATORE Majestic Book House, (0422) 2384333, CBSC Book Shop, 9585979752

CHENNAI Arraba Book Traders, (044) 25387868, 9841459105, M.R. Book Store (044) 25364596, Kalaimagal Store, (044) 5544072, 9940619404, Vijaya Stores, 9381037417, Bookmark It-Books & Stat. Store, 7305151653, M.K. Store, 9840030099, Tiger Books Pvt. Ltd., 9710447000, New Mylai Stationers, 9841313062, Prince Book House, Chennai, 0444-2053926, 9952068491, S K Publishers & Distributors, 9789865544, Dharma Book Shop, 8667227171

PUDUCHERRY Sri Lakshmi Book Seller, 7871555145

SALEM Pattu book centre, 9894816280

TRICHY P.R.Sons Book Seller, 9443370597, Rasi Publication, 9894816280

THENI Maya Book Centre, 9443929274

MADURAI Selvi Book Shoppe, 9843057435, Jayam Book Centre, 9894658036

VELLORE G.K book centre and collections, 9894517994

TELANGANA
HYDERABAD Sri Balaji Book Depot, (040) 27613300, 9866355473, Shah Book House, 9849564564 Vishal Book Distributors, 9246333166, Himalaya Book World, 7032578527

0808

Exclusive School Books Suppliers

	UTTARAKHAND
DEHRADUN	Inder Book Agencies, 9634045280, Amar Book Depot , 8130491477, Goyal Book Store, 9897318047, New National Book House, 9897830283/9720590054
MUSSORIE	Ram Saran Dass Chanda kiran, 0135-2632785, 9761344588
	UTTAR PRADESH
AGRA	Sparsh Book Agency, 9412257817, Om Pustak Mandir, (0562) 2464014, 9319117771, Sanjay Publication, 8126699922 Arti book centre, 8630128856, Panchsheel Books, 9412257962, Bhagwati Book Store, (E & C), 9149081912
ALLAHABAD	Mehrotra Book Agency, (0532) 2266865, 9415636890
AZAMGARH	Sasta Sahitya Bhandar, 9450029674
ALIGARH	K.B.C.L. Agarwal, 9897124960, Shaligram Agencies, 9412317800, New Vimal Books, 9997398868, T.I.C Book centre, 9808039570
BULANDSHAHAR	Rastogi Book Depot, 9837053462/9368978202
BALRAMPUR	Universal Book Center, 8933826726
BAREILLY	Siksha Prakashan, 9837829284
HARDOI	Mittal Pustak Kendra, 9838201466
DEORIA	Kanodia Book Depot, 9415277835
VARANASI	Gupta Books, 8707225564, Bookman & Company,9935194495/7668899901
MATHURA	Sapra Traders, 9410076716, Vijay Book House , 9897254292
FARRUKHABAD	Anurag Book Agencies, 8844007575
NAJIBABAD	Gupta News Agency, 8868932500, Gupta News Agency, (E & C), 8868932500
DHAMPUR	Ramkumar Mahaveer Prasad, 9411942550
GORAKHPUR	Central Book House, 9935454590, Friends & Co., 9450277154, Dinesh book depot, 9125818274, Friends & Co., 9450277154
JHANSI	Bhanu Book Depot, 9415031340
KANPUR	Radha News Agency, 8957247427, Raj Book Dist., 9235616506, H K Book Distributors, 9935146730, H K Book Distributors, 9506033137/9935146730
LUCKNOW	Vyapar Sadan, 7607102462, Om Book Depot, 7705871398, Azad Book Depot Pvt. Ltd., 7317000250, Book Sadan, 9839487327, Rama Book Depot(Retail), 7355078254, Ashirwad Book Depot, 9235501197, Book.com, 7458922755, Universal Books, 9450302161, Sheetla Book Agency, 9235832418, Vidyarthi Kendra Publisher & Distributor Pvt Ltd, (Gold), 9554967415, Tripathi Book House, 9415425943
MEERUT	Ideal Book Depot, (0121) 4059252, 9837066307
NOIDA	Prozo (Global Edu4 Share Pvt. Ltd), 9318395520, Goyal Books Overseas Pvt.Ltd., 1204655555 9873387003
PRAYAGRAJ	Kanhaiya Pustak Bhawan, 9415317109
MAWANA	Subhash Book Depot, 9760262264
	WEST BENGAL
KOLKATA	Oriental Publishers & Distributor (033) 40628367, Katha 'O' Kahini, (033) 22196313, 22419071, Saha Book House, (033), 22193671, 9333416484, United Book House, 9831344622, Bijay Pustak Bhandar, 8961260603, Shawan Books Distributors, 8336820363, Krishna Book House, 9123083874
RENUKOOT	Om Stationers, 7007326732
COOCH BEHAR	S.B. Book Distributor, Cooch behar, 9002670771
KHARAGPUR	Subhani Book Store, 9046891334
SILIGURI	Agarwal Book House, 9832038727, Modern Book Agency, 8145578772
DINAJPUR	Krishna Book House, 7031748945
MURSHIDABAD	New Book House, 8944876176

Entrance & Competition Distributors

	BIHAR
PATNA	Metro Books Corner, 9431647013, Alka Book Agency, 9835655005, Vikas Book Depot, 9504780402
	CHATTISGARH
KORBA	Kitab Ghar, 9425226528, Shri Ramdev Traders, 9981761797
	DELHI
DELHI	Singhania Book & Stationer, 9212028238, Radhey Book depot, 9818314141, The Book Shop, 9310262701, Mittal Books, 9899037390, Lov Dev & Sons, 9999353491
NEW DELHI	Anupam Sales, 9560504617, A ONE BOOKS, 8800497047
	HARYANA
AMBALA	Bharat Book Depot, 7988455354
	JHARKHAND
BOKARO	Bokaro Student Friends Pvt. Ltd, 7360021503
	MADHYA PRADESH
INDORE	Bhaiya Industries, 9109120101
CHHINDWARA	Pustak Bhawan, 9827255997
	MAHARASHTRA
NAGPUR	Laxmi Pustakalay and Stationers, (0712) 2727354
PUNE	Pragati Book Centre, 9850039311
MUMBAI	New Student Agencies LLP, 7045065799
	ODISHA
BARIPADA	Trimurti Book World, 9437034735
CUTTAK	A.K.Mishra Agencies, 9437025991
BHUBANESHWAR	M/s Pragnya, 9437943777
	PUNJAB
JALANDHAR	Cheap Book Store, 9872223458, 9878258592
	RAJASTHAN
KOTA	Vardhman Book Depot, 9571365020, Raj Traders, 9309232829
JAIPUR	Goyal Book Distributors, 9414782130
	UTTAR PRADESH
AGRA	BHAGWATI BOOK STORE, 9149081912, Sparsh Book Agency, 9412257817, Sanjay Publication, 8126699922
ALIGARH	New Vimal Books, 9997398868
ALLAHABAD	Mehrotra Book Agency, (532) 2266865, 9415636890
GORAKHPUR	Central Book House, 9935454590
KANPUR	Raj Book Dist, 9235616506
LUCKNOW	Azad Book Depot PVT LTD, 7317000250, Rama Book Depot(Retail), 7355078254 Ashirwad Book Depot , 9235501197, Book Sadan, 8318643277, Book.com , 7458922755, Sheetla Book Agency, 9235832418
PRAYAGRAJ	Format Center, 9335115561, Garg Brothers Trading & Services Pvt. Ltd., 7388100499
	UTTAR PRADESH
DEHRADUN	Inder Book Agancies, 9634045280
	WEST BENGAL
KOLKATA	Bijay Pustak Bhandar Pvt. Ltd., 8961260603, Saha Book House, 9674827254 United Book House, 9831344622, Techno World, 9830168159

0808

CHAPTER 1

UNITS AND MEASUREMENT

Introduction

- **Units:** It is the chosen standard of measurement of a quantity which has essentially the same nature as that of the quantity.
- **Fundamental Units:** The physical quantities which are independent of each other and which can represent remaining physical quantities are called fundamental physical quantities and their units are called fundamental units.

Seven Fundamental physical quantities in SI system of units are:

(a) Mass - *kg (Kilogram)*
(b) Length - *m (Meter)*
(c) Time - s *(Second)*
(d) Temperature - K (Kelvin)
(e) Electric current - A *(Ampere)*
(f) Luminous Intensity - cd (Candela)
(g) Amount of substance - mol *(Mole)*

Scan to know more about this topic

Units

- **Derived Units:** These are the units of measurement of all other physical quantities which can be obtained from fundamental units, e.g., Velocity - (m/s), Acceleration - (m/s^2), Pressure - (Pa), Force - (N) and so on.

The International System of Units

(a) **F. P. S. system:** Foot, Pound, Second.
(b) **C. G. S. system:** Centimetre, Gram, Second.
(c) **M. K. S. system:** Meter, Kilogram, Second.

Significant Figures

- The significant figures of a given number are those significant or important digits, which convey the meaning according to its accuracy. For example, 6.658 has four significant digits. These substantial figures provide precision to the numbers. They are also termed as significant digits.
- **Rules for significant figure:**

(a) All non-zero digits are significant. 198745 contains six significant digits.
(b) All zeros those occur between any two non-zero digits are significant. For example, 108.0097 contains seven significant digits.
(c) All zeros those are on the right of a decimal point and also to the left of a non-zero digit is never significant. For example, 0.00798 contained three significant digits.
(d) All zeros those are on the right of a decimal point are significant, only if, a non-zero digit does not follow them. For example, 20.00 contained four significant digits.
(e) All the zeros those are on right of the last non-zero digit, after the decimal point, are significant. For example, 0.0079800 contains five significant digits.
(f) All the zeros that are on the right of the last non-zero digit are significant if they come from a measurement. For example, 1090 m contains four significant digits.

Dimensional Analysis

- Dimensional analysis is the study of relationship between physical quantities and the fundamental quantities.
- Dimensional equation is the equation expressing of the relationship between physical quantities and the fundamental quantities.
- **Principle of homogeneity:** Dimensions of each term of a dimensional equation on both side should be same.

Scan to know more about this topic

Units

- **Conversion of units from one system to another:**
n_1 and n_2 be the magnitudes of a physical quantity in two systems respectively. General dimensions of the physical quantity be $[M^aL^bT^C]$. If dimensions in two system be $u_1 = [M_1^aL_1^bT_1^c]$ and $u_2 = [M_2^aL_2^bT_2^c]$ respectively then $n_1\,[M_1^aL_1^bT_1^c] = n_2\,[M_2^aL_2^bT_2^c]$
- Dimensional analysis used to derive formula of a physical quantity.
- Correctness of formula of a physical quantity may be checked using principle of homogeneity.
- **Limitations of dimensional analysis:**
  - Cannot provide information about dimensional constant.
  - Formula containing trigonometric functions, logarithmic functions, and exponential function cannot be derived.
  - Cannot provide information whether the quantity is a vector or a scalar.
  - If the physical quantity depends on more than three quantities then it becomes difficult to derive the formula.
  - It is not possible to find the formula correctly when the physical quantity is not related by multiplication of the other quantities.

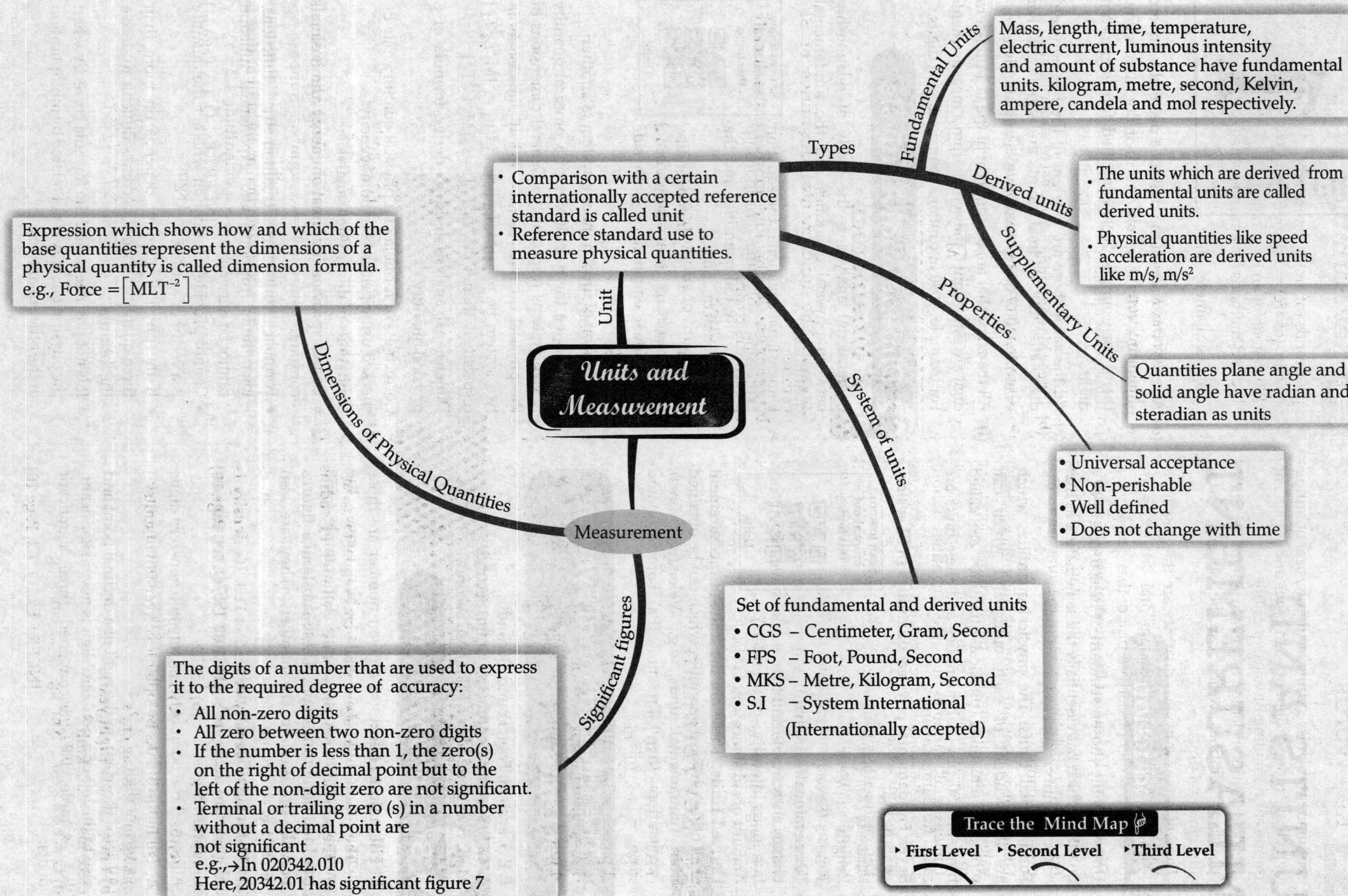
Units and Measurement
Unit
Comparison with a certain internationally accepted reference standard is called unit
Reference standard use to measure physical quantities.
Types
Fundamental Units
Mass, length, time, temperature, electric current, luminous intensity and amount of substance have fundamental units. kilogram, metre, second, Kelvin, ampere, candela and mol respectively.
Derived units
The units which are derived from fundamental units are called derived units.
Physical quantities like speed acceleration are derived units like m/s, m/s²
Supplementary Units
Quantities plane angle and solid angle have radian and steradian as units
Properties
Universal acceptance
Non-perishable
Well defined
Does not change with time
System of units
Set of fundamental and derived units
CGS – Centimeter, Gram, Second
FPS – Foot, Pound, Second
MKS – Metre, Kilogram, Second
S.I – System International (Internationally accepted)
Measurement
Dimensions of Physical Quantities
Expression which shows how and which of the base quantities represent the dimensions of a physical quantity is called dimension formula.
e.g., Force = [MLT⁻²]
Significant figures
The digits of a number that are used to express it to the required degree of accuracy:
All non-zero digits
All zero between two non-zero digits
If the number is less than 1, the zero(s) on the right of decimal point but to the left of the non-digit zero are not significant.
Terminal or trailing zero (s) in a number without a decimal point are not significant
e.g.,→In 020342.010
Here, 20342.01 has significant figure 7
Trace the Mind Map
First Level
Second Level
Third Level

Key Words

- **Fundamental Units :** Units of the physical quantities which are independent of each other and which can represent remaining physical quantities.
- **Derived Units :** Units of measurement of those physical quantities which can be obtained from fundamental units.
- **Dimensions of physical quantity** are the powers to which the symbols of fundamental quantities are raised to represent a derived unit of that quantity.
- **Dimensional formula of the given physical quantity** is the expression which shows how and which of the fundamental quantities represent the dimensions of a physical quantity.
- **Dimensional constants** are the quantities whose values are constant and they possess dimensions e.g., universal gravitational constant G etc.
- **Dimensional variables** are the quantities whose values are variable and they possess dimensions e.g., area, volume, etc.
- **Dimensionless constants** are the quantities whose value are constant but they do not possess dimensions e.g., mathematical constants– π, e and numbers.
- **Dimensionless variables** are the quantities whose values are variable and they do not have dimensions e.g., angle, strain, etc.

Key Formulae

- 1 AU = 1.496×10^{11} m.
- 1 ly = 9.46×10^{15} m.
- 1 parsec = 3.1×10^{16} m.
- 1 Å = 10^{-10} m; 1 nm = 10^{-9} m
  1 μm = 10^{-6} m, 1 mm = 10^{-3} m

Key Formulae

- 60 seconds (of arc) = 1 min (arc)
- 60 min. (of arc) = 1 degree (of arc)
- 180 degree (of arc) = π radian
- Indirect methods for long and small distances :

  Angular diameter (θ) = $\dfrac{d}{D}$

  d = diameter, D = distance, radius = *r*
- **Magnification :**

(a) Linear Magnification = $\dfrac{\text{Size of image}}{\text{Size of object}}$

(b) Linear Magnification = $\sqrt{\text{Areal Magnification}}$

- Conversion of one system of units into another

$$n_2 = \frac{n_1 u_1}{u_2} = n_1\left(\frac{M_1}{M_2}\right)^a\left(\frac{L_1}{L_2}\right)^b\left(\frac{T_1}{T_2}\right)^c$$

Mnemonics

Concept: The fundamental quantities of SI system:

Mnemonics: At the **l**ast **m**oment she **lu**ckily **c**aught the **t**rain.

Interpretation:

A - Amount of substance
t - Temperature (thermodynamic)
l - Length
m - Mass
lu - Luminous intensity
c - Current
t - Time

NCERT CORNER

Q. 1. Fill in the blanks:

(a) The volume of a cube of side 1 cm is equal to ..... m³.

(b) The surface area of a solid cylinder of radius 2.0 cm and height 10.0 cm is equal to ..... mm².

(c) A vehicle moving with a speed of 18 kmh⁻¹ covers .... m in 1 s.

(d) The relative density of lead is 11.3. Its density is .... g cm⁻³ or ...... kg m⁻³. [NCERT Ex., Q. 1.1, Page 10]

Ans. (a) 10^{-6} (b) 15072
(c) 5 (d) 11.3, 11300

Q. 2. Fill in the blanks by suitable conversion of units:

(a) 1 kg m^2s^{-2} = ...g cm^2s^{-2}

(b) 1 m = ... ly (light year)

(c) 3.0 ms^{-2} = ... kmh^{-2}

(d) G = 6.67×10^{-11} $Nm^2\ kg^{-2}$ = ... $cm^3\ s^{-2}\ g^{-1}$

[NCERT Ex., Q. 1.2, Page 10]

Ans. (a) 10^7 (b) 1.053×10^{-16}
(c) 3.888×10^4 (d) 6.67×10^{-8}

Q. 3. A calorie is a unit of heat or energy and it equals about 4.2 J, where 1 J = 1 kgm²s⁻². Suppose we employ a system of units in which the unit of mass equals α kg, the unit of length β m, the unit of time is γ s. Show that a calorie has a magnitude 4.2 $\gamma^{-1}\ \gamma^{-2}\ \gamma^2$ in terms of new units. [NCERT Ex., Q. 1.3, Page 11]

Ans. Given: 1 cal = 4.2 J = 4.2 kgm^2s^{-2}

So, $a = 1, b = 2, c = -2$

In S.I. system, $n_1 = 4.2$, $M_1 = 1$ kg, $L_1 = 1$ m,
$T_1 = 1$s, $n_2 = ?$, $M_2 = \gamma$ kg, $L_2 = \gamma$ m, $T_2 = \gamma$ s

From equations,

$$n_2 = n_1\left[\frac{M_1}{M_2}\right]^a\left[\frac{L_1}{L_2}\right]^b\left[\frac{T_1}{T_2}\right]^c$$

$$n_2 = 4.2\left[\frac{1\text{ kg}}{\alpha\text{ kg}}\right]^{1}\left[\frac{1\text{ m}}{\beta\text{m}}\right]^{2}\left[\frac{1\text{ s}}{\gamma\text{s}}\right]^{-2}$$

$\therefore n_2 = 4.2\,\gamma^{-1}\gamma^{-2}\gamma^{2}$ in new system.

Hence, proved.

Q. 4. Explain the statement clearly:

"To call a dimensional quantity 'large' or 'small' is meaningless without specifying a standard for comparison." In view of this, re-frame the following statements wherever necessary:

(a) Atoms are very small objects.

(b) A jet plane moves with great speed.

(c) The mass of Jupiter is very large.

(d) The air inside this room contains a large number of molecules.

(e) A proton is much more massive than an electron.

(f) The speed of sound is much smaller than the speed of light. [NCERT Ex., Q. 1.4, Page 11]

Ans. The physical quantities are called large or small in comparison to some standard units of measurement. So, statement is correct:

(a) As size of an atom is smaller than the sharp tip of pin.

(b) As a jet plane moves faster than a superfast train.

(c) As mass of Jupiter is very large as compared to the mass of Earth.

(d) As air inside the room contains more number of molecules than in one mole of air.

(e) Statement is true.

(f) Statement is true.

Q. 5. A new unit of length is chosen such that the speed of light in vacuum is unity. What is the distance between the Sun and the Earth in terms of the new unit if light takes 8 min and 20 s to cover this distance ? [NCERT Ex., Q. 1.5, Page 11]

Ans. Distance between Sun and Earth is

$= 3 \times 10^8$ m/s $\times$ 500 s $= 500 \times 3 \times 10^8$ m

As the speed of light in vacuum = 1 ms^{-1} (in new system). So, distance between Sun and Earth.

= 500 new units.

Q. 6. Which of the following is the most precise device for measuring length?

(a) A vernier callipers with 20 division on the sliding scale.

(b) A screw gauge of pitch 1 mm and 100 divisions on the circular scale.

(c) An optical instrument that can measure length to within a wavelength of light. [NCERT Ex., Q. 1.6, Page 11]

Ans. (a) Least count of vernier callipers

$$= \frac{1}{20} = 0.05\text{ mm} = 5 \times 10^{-5}\text{ m}$$

(b) Least count of screw gauge $= \dfrac{1\times10^{-3}}{100} = 1 \times 10^{-5}$ m

(c) Least count of optical instrument $= 5 \times 10^{-7}$ m.

$\therefore$ Optical instrument is most precise instrument.

Q. 7. A student measures the thickness of a human hair with the help of a microscope of magnification 100. He takes 20 readings and finds average width of the hair in the field of view of microscope is 3.5 mm. What is the thickness of the hair ? [NCERT Ex., Q. 1.7, Page 11]

Ans. Magnification,

$$\text{Real width} = \frac{\text{Observed width }(y)}{\text{magnification}} = \frac{3.5}{100} = 0.035\text{ mm}$$

Q. 8. Answer the following:

(a) You are given a thread and a metre scale. How will you estimate the diameter of the thread ?

(b) A screw gauge has a pitch of 1.0 mm and 200 divisions on the circular scale. Do you think it is possible to increase the accuracy of the screw gauge arbitrarily by increasing the number of divisions on the circular scale ?

(c) The mean diameter of a thin brass rod is to be measured by vernier callipers. Why is a set of 100 measurements of the diameter expected to yield a more reliable estimate than a set of 5 measurements only ? [NCERT Ex., Q. 1.8, Page 11]

Ans. (a) By winding the thread in close turns on a pencil and using the formula i.e.,

$$\text{Diameter} = \frac{\text{Average length}}{\text{No. of turns}}$$

(b) Yes, by increasing the number of divisions on circular scale as Least count $= \dfrac{\text{Pitch}}{\text{No. of divisions on circular scale}}$

(c) Random error is reduced on taking large number of observations.

Q. 9. The photograph of a house occupies an area of 1.75 cm^2 on a 35 mm slide. The slide is projected on to a screen and the area of the house on the screen is 1.55 m^2. What is the linear magnification of the projector, screen arrangement ? [NCERT Ex., Q. 1.9, Page 11]

Ans. Here size of an object = Area of object

$= 1.75\text{ cm}^2 = 1.75 \times 10^{-4}\text{ m}^2$

Size of the image = Area of the image = 1.55 m^2

$$\therefore \text{Areal magnification} = \frac{\text{Area of image}}{\text{Area of object}}$$

$$= \frac{1.55}{1.75\times10^{-4}} = 8.857\times 10^3$$

Linear magnification $= \sqrt{8857} = 94.1$

Q. 10. State the number of significant figure in:

(a) 0.007 m^2 **(b) 2.64 $\times$ 10^{24}**

(c) 0.2370 g cm^{-3} **(d) 6.320 J**

(e) 6.032 Nm^{-2} **(f) 0.0006032 m^2**

[NCERT Ex., Q. 1.10, Page 11]

Ans. (a) 1 (b) 3

(c) 4 (d) 4

(e) 4 (f) 4

Q. 11. The length, breadth and thickness of a metal piece are 4.234 m, 1.005 m and 2.01 cm respectively. Find its area and volume to correct significant figures. [NCERT Ex., Q. 1.11, Page 11]

Ans. $A = 2\,(l \times b + b \times t + t \times l)$

$= 2\,(4.234 \times 1.005 + 1.005 \times 0.0201 + 0.0201 \times 4.234)\text{ m}^2$

$= 2(4.25517 + 0.0202005 + 0.0851034)\text{ m}^2$

$= 2 \times 4.3604739\text{ m}^2 = 8.7209478\text{ m}^2$

$= 8.72\text{ m}^2$ (approximated to 3 significant figures)

Volume $= 4.234 \times 1.005 \times (2.01 \times 10^{-2})\text{ m}^3$

$= 8.55289 \times 10^{-2}\text{ m}^3 = 0.0855\text{ m}^3$.

Q. 12. The mass of a box measured by a grocer's balance is 2.3 kg. Two gold pieces of masses 20.15 g and 20.17 g are added to the box. What is (a) the total mass of the box,

(b) the difference in the mass of the pieces to corrects significant figures ? [NCERT Ex., Q. 1.12, Page 11]

Ans. Here mass of the box, $m = 2.30$ kg

Mass of one gold piece, $m_1 = 20.15$ g $= 0.02015$ kg

Mass of second gold piece, $m_2 = 2017$ g $= 0.02017$ k

(a) Total mass $= m + m_1 + m_2$

$= (2.300 + 0.02015 + 0.02017)$ kg

$= 2.34032$ kg.

As the least no. of significant figures in the mass of box is 2, so, maximum no. of significant figures in the result can be 2. Total mass = 2.3 kg.

(b) Difference in masses,

$$m = m_2 - m_1 = 20.17 - 20.15 = 0.02 \text{ g}$$

Since, there are two significant figures, so, the difference in masses to the correct significant figures is 0.02 g.

Q. 13. A famous relation in physics relates 'moving mass' m to the 'rest mass' m_0 of a particle in terms of its speed v and speed of light c. (This relation first arose as a consequence of special theory of relativity due to Albert Einstein). A boy recalls the relation almost correctly but forgets where to put the constant c. He writes $m = \dfrac{m_0}{(1-v^2)^{1/2}}$. Guess where to put the missing c. [NCERT Ex., Q. 1.13, Page 11]

Ans. From principle of homogeneity of dimensions, power of M, L and T on either side of the formula must be equal. In the given formula, on R.H.S., the denominator $(1 - v^2)^{1/2}$ must be dimensionless.

Hence, the correct formula is $\dfrac{m_0}{\left(1-\dfrac{v^2}{c^2}\right)^{\frac{1}{2}}}$.

Q. 14. The unit of length convenient on the atomic scale is known as an angstrom and is denoted by Å: 1 Å = 10^{-10} m. The size of the hydrogen atom is about 0.5 Å. What is the total atomic volume in m³ of a mole of hydrogen atoms ? [NCERT Ex., Q. 1.14, Page 12]

Ans. Here, $r = 0.5 \text{ Å} = 0.5 \times 10^{-10}$ m

V_1 = Volume of each hydrogen atom

$$= \frac{4}{3}\pi r^3 = \frac{4}{3} \times 3.14 \times (0.5 \times 10^{-10})^3$$

$$= 5.236 \times 10^{-31} \text{ m}^3$$

According to Avogadro's hypothesis, one mole of hydrogen contains

$$N = 6.023 \times 10^{23} \text{ atoms}$$

∴ Atomic volume of 1 mole of hydrogen atoms,

$$V = NV_1$$

$$V = 6.023 \times 10^{23} \times 5.236 \times 10^{-31}$$

$$= 3.154 \times 10^{-7} \text{ m}^3$$

$$= 3.154 \times 10^{-7} \text{ m}^3.$$

Q. 15. One mole of an ideal gas at Standard temperature and pressure occupies 22.4 L (molar volume). What is the ratio of molar volume to the atomic volume of a mole of hydrogen ? (Take the size of hydrogen molecule to be about 1 Å). Why is this ratio so large ? [NCERT Ex., Q. 1.15, Page 12]

Ans. Atomic volume $= \dfrac{4}{3}\pi R^3 \times N$

$$= \frac{4}{3}\pi(0.5 \times 10^{-10})^3 \times 6.023 \times 10^{23}$$

$$= 3.154 \times 10^{-7} \text{ m}^3.$$

Molar volume $= 22.4 \text{ L} = 22.4 \times 10^{-3} \text{ m}^3$

$$\frac{\text{Molar volume}}{\text{Atomic volume}} = \frac{22.4\times10^{-3}}{3.154\times10^{-7}} = 7.1 \times 10^4$$

The large value of the ratio shows that the inter molecular separation in a gas is much larger than the size of a molecule.

Q. 16. Explain this common observation clearly: If you look out of the window of a fast moving train, the nearby trees, houses etc. seem to move rapidly in a direction opposite to the train's motion, but the distant, objects (hill tops, the Moon, the stars etc.) seem to be stationary (In fact, since you are aware that you are moving, these distant objects seem to move with you). [NCERT Ex., Q. 1.16, Page 12]

Ans. The line joining the object to the eye is line of sight. If we move rapidly, the line of sight nearby tree changes its direction of motion rapidly. It means near objects make greater angle than distant objects. Thus, the trees appear to run in opposite direction. But in case of Moon, stars etc., this change is negligible, so they appear stationary.

Q. 17. The Sun is a hot plasma (ionized matter) with its inner core at a temperature exceeding 10^7 K and its outer surface at a temperature of about 6000 K. At these high temperatures, no substance remains in a solid or liquid phase. In what range do you expect the mass density of the Sun to be, in the range of densities of solids and liquids or gases ? Check if your guess is correct from the following data:

Mass of Sun = 2.0×10^{30} kg,

Radius of the Sun = 7.0×10^8 m

[NCERT Ex., Q. 1.17, Page 12]

Ans. Here, $M = 2 \times 10^{30}$ kg

$R = 7.0 \times 10^8$ m

∴ Mass density of Sun

$$= \frac{\text{Mass of sun}}{\text{Volume of sun}} = \frac{M}{V} = \frac{M}{\frac{4}{3}\pi R^3}$$

$$= \frac{2\times10^{30}}{\frac{4}{3}\times3.14\times(7\times10^8)^3} = \frac{3\times2\times10^{30}}{4\times3.14\times343\times10^{24}} \text{ kgm}^{-3}$$

$$= 1.39 \times 10^3 \text{ kg m}^{-3}$$

This density is the range of density of solids and not gases.

Explanation—The temperature of the inner core of the Sun exceeds 10^7 K while the temperature of the outer surface of the Sun is nearly 6000 K. At such extremely high temperature, no substance can exist either in a solid or in a liquid phase. So, the Sun is made of ionized matter, i.e., hot plasma. The high density of the plasma is due to the inward gravitational attraction on outer layers due to the inner layers of the Sun.

□□

CHAPTER 2

MOTION IN A STRAIGHT LINE

Motion and Velocity

➤ **Rest:** An object or a particle is said to be in the state of rest when it does not change its position with time w.r.t. same reference point.

Depending upon the position of observer, the state of rest of a particle is of two types:

(a) Absolute state of rest,

(b) Relative state of rest.

➤ **Motion:** An object or a particle is said to be in the state of motion when it changes its position with time w.r.t. same reference point.

The motion of an object can be either linear or curvilinear, circular or in a plane or in a space.

(a) Linear or Rectilinear or Translatory motion:

(i) It is the motion in which a particle moves along a straight line with respect to a point of reference.

(ii) A body is said to be in linear motion if every constituent particle of the body move along parallel straight line and covers same distance in the given time.

(b) Circular or Rotatory Motion:

(i) A motion in which a particle or a point mass body is moving in a circle.

(ii) In rotatory motion all its constituent particles move simultaneously along concentric circles.

(c) Oscillatory or Vibratory Motion:

(i) In oscillatory motion the body moves back & forth repeatedly in definite interval of time about a fixed point.

(ii) If the amplitude of oscillating body is very small, the motion is called vibratory motion.

➤ **Dimensional Motion**

(a) Motion in 1–D:

(i) It is that motion in which a particle moves in one particular direction with respect to a point of reference.

(ii) In 1–D, the particle or a body moves along a straight line or a well defined path. Therefore, one dimensional motion is sometimes known as linear motion.

(b) Motion in 2–D

(i) If two out of three coordinates specifying the position of the object change with respect to time, the motion is called 2–D motion.

(c) Motion in 3–D

(i) If all the three coordinates specifying the position of the object change with respect to time, the motion is called 3–D motion.

Scan to know more about this topic

Inertial or Non-Inertial frame

➤ **Path Length or Distance:**

(a) Path Length is defined as the actual path traversed by body during motion in a given interval of time.

(b) Distance is a scalar quantity.

(c) The S.I. unit of distance is metre and C.G.S. unit is centimeter.

(d) The value of distance traversed by a moving body can never be zero or negative.

➤ **Displacement:**

(a) Displacement of a body in a given time is defined as the change in the position of the body in a particular direction during that time. It may also defined as the shortest distance between initial and final position of the object.

(b) Displacement is a vector quantity as it possesses both magnitude and direction.

(c) The unit of displacement is same as that of path length.

(d) The value of displacement can be positive, zero or negative.

(e) The value of displacement can never be greater than the distance travelled.

(f) When a moving body returns to its starting point, then its effective displacement is zero.

➤ **Difference between Distance & Displacement:**

S. No.	Distance	Displacement
1.	Actual path traversed by object in given time.	Shortest distance between initial & final positions of object in given time.
2.	Scalar quantity.	Vector quantity.
3.	It cannot be zero or negative, it will be always positive.	It can be positive, negative or zero.
4.	It is either equal or greater than displacement but never less than displacement.	It is either equal or less than distance but never greater than distance.
5.	It can have many values depending upon path followed between two positions.	It has unique value.
6.	Between two positions of an object, it tells type of path followed.	It does not tell type of path followed.

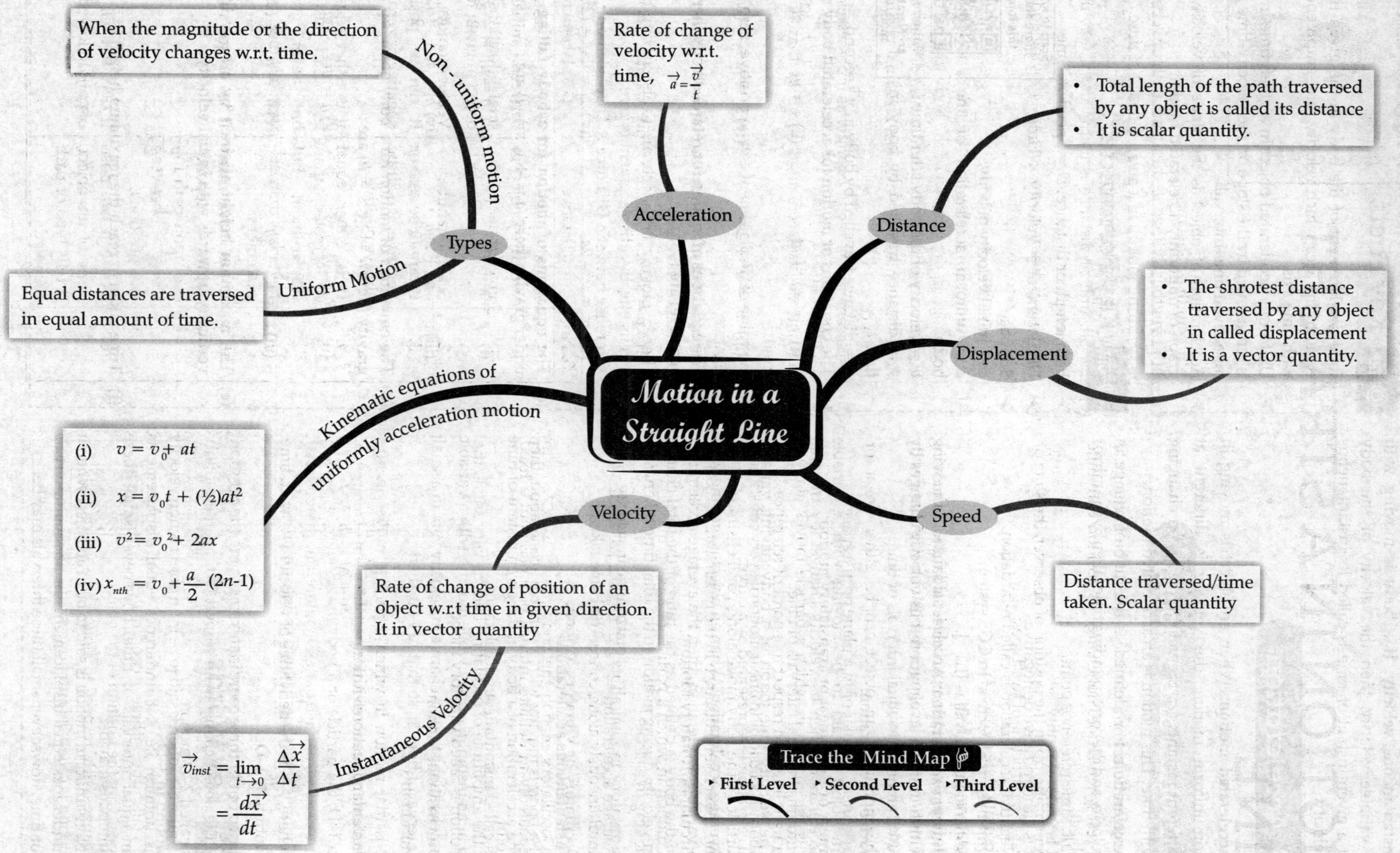
Motion in a Straight Line
Types
Non - uniform motion
When the magnitude or the direction of velocity changes w.r.t. time.
Uniform Motion
Equal distances are traversed in equal amount of time.
Acceleration
Rate of change of velocity w.r.t. time, $\vec{a} = \frac{\vec{v}}{t}$
Distance
• Total length of the path traversed by any object is called its distance
• It is scalar quantity.
Displacement
• The shrotest distance traversed by any object in called displacement
• It is a vector quantity.
Speed
Distance traversed/time taken. Scalar quantity
Velocity
Rate of change of position of an object w.r.t time in given direction. It in vector quantity
Instantaneous Velocity
$\vec{v}_{inst} = \lim_{t \to 0} \frac{\Delta \vec{x}}{\Delta t} = \frac{d\vec{x}}{dt}$
Kinematic equations of uniformly acceleration motion
(i) $v = v_0 + at$
(ii) $x = v_0 t + (½)at^2$
(iii) $v^2 = v_0^2 + 2ax$
(iv) $x_{nth} = v_0 + \frac{a}{2}(2n-1)$
Trace the Mind Map
First Level
Second Level
Third Level

- **Instantaneous velocity:** If a body is moving with a variable velocity, then the velocity of the body at a given instant of time is called its instantaneous velocity.

Acceleration

- **Accelerated motion:** When an object is moving in non-uniform motion, the velocity is different at different instants *i.e.*, the velocity keeps on changing with time. This motion is an accelerated motion.
- **Acceleration:** It is defined as the ratio of change in velocity and the corresponding time taken by the mirror object;

(a) It is vector quantity.
(b) It is either positive or negative.
(c) Negative acceleration is called retardation.
(d) Unit-m/s^2 in SI & cm/s^2 in CGS system.
(e) Dimensional formula– $[LT^{-2}]$.

(i) Uniform acceleration: An object is said to be moving with a uniform acceleration if its velocity changes by equal amounts in equal intervals of time.

(ii) Variable acceleration:

(a) An object is said to be moving with a variable acceleration when its velocity changes by unequal amounts in equal intervals of time.

(b) The velocity time graph of a body having variable acceleration is represented by a curve.

(iii) Average acceleration: When an object is moving with a variable acceleration, then the average acceleration of the body is defined as the ratio of the total change in velocity during motion to the total time taken, *i.e.*,

$$\text{Average acceleration} = \frac{\text{Total change in velocity}}{\text{Total time taken}}$$

(iv) Instantaneous acceleration:

(a) If a body is moving with a variable acceleration, then the acceleration of a body at the given instant of time is called instantaneous acceleration.

(b) If at an instant t, a body while moving with a variable acceleration shows a change in velocity $\Delta \vec{v}$ in a small interval of time Δt, so that $\Delta t \to 0$, then

$$\text{Instantaneous acceleration} = \underset{\Delta t \to 0}{\text{Lt}} \frac{\Delta \vec{v}}{\Delta t} = \frac{d\vec{v}}{dt}$$

where, $\frac{d\vec{v}}{dt}$ is the derivative of velocity $(\vec{v})$ w.r.t. time.

Key Words

- Uniform motion is said to be in an object when velocity is uniform i.e., it undergoes equal displacements in equal intervals of time, howsoever small these intervals may be.
- Non–uniform motion is said to be in an object when it undergoes equal displacements in unequal intervals of time, howsoever small these intervals may be.

Key Facts

- Total displacement of the body in the given time is equal to the area which velocity time-graph encloses with time axis.
- Uniformly accelerated object in a given time-interval is represented by the slope on the velocity-time graph for a given time-interval.
- Acceleration of object is the slope of velocity-time graph of uniformly accelerated motion.

Key Formulae

- Path length or distance, D = Speed × Time
- Displacement = Velocity × Time
- Suppose
  u = initial velocity of body,
  a = uniform acceleration of the body,
  v = velocity of the body after time t,
  s = distance travelled by body in time t,
  s_n = distance travelled by body in n^{th} second.

Scan to know more about this topic

Uniformaly accelerated motion

(a) The equations of motion for accelerated body are :

(i) $v = u + at$ (ii) $s = ut + \frac{1}{2}at^2$

(iii) $v^2 = u^2 + 2as$ (iv) $s_n = u + \frac{a}{2}(2n-1)$

(b) The equations of motion for retarded body (here, *a* is negative) are :

(i) $v = u - at$ (ii) $s = ut - \frac{1}{2}at^2$

(iii) $v^2 = u^2 - 2as$ (iv) $s_n = u - \frac{a}{2}(2n-1)$

(c) The equations of motion for a body falling down under gravity (here, $a = +g$, $s = h$) are :

(i) $v = u + gt$ (ii) $h = ut + \frac{1}{2}gt^2$

(iii) $v^2 = u^2 + 2gh$ (iv) $h_n = u + \frac{g}{2}(2n-1)$

(d) The equations of motion for a body going up under gravity (here $a = -g$, $s = h$) are :

(i) $v = u - gt$ (ii) $h = ut - \frac{1}{2}gt^2$

(iii) $v^2 = u^2 - 2gh$ (iv) $h_n = u - \frac{g}{2}(2n-1)$

(e) The maximum height attained by a body thrown vertically upwards with initial velocity *u* is

$$h_{max} = \frac{u^2}{2g}$$

(f) Time taken to reach the maximum height is

$$t = \frac{u}{g}$$

Key Formulae

(g) Total time taken by body in going up and coming down,

$$T = 2t = \frac{2u}{g}$$

(h) The initial velocity of body in order to attain height *h* is,

$$u = \sqrt{2gh}$$

Mnemonics

Concept: Motion In A Straight Line
Mnemonics: Delhi to **V**adodara via **T**undla **A**gra.
Interpretation: **D**isplacement/time = **V**elocity
Velocity / **t**ime = **A**cceleration

NCERT CORNER

Q. 1. In which of the following examples of motion, can the body be considered approximately a point object:

(a) a railway carriage moving without jerks between two stations.

(b) a monkey sitting on top of a man cycling smoothly on a circular track.

(c) a spinning cricket ball turns sharply on hitting the ground.

(d) a tumbling beaker slipped off the edge of a table.

[NCERT Ex., Q. 2.1, Page 24]

Ans. (a) Since, the motion of the train between two distant stations is smooth throughout, so keeping in view the long distance covered between the two stations in reasonable duration of time, the size of the train is neglected and it is considered as a point object.

(b) The distance covered by the monkey in reasonable duration of time is more so the monkey is considered as a point object. (Since its size is smaller.)

(c) Since, the turning of the ball is not smooth but sharp so the distance covered by it in reasonable duration of time is not large so this ball cannot be treated as a point object.

(d) Since, the beaker is tumbling and then it slips off, so the distance covered by it in reasonable duration of time is not large. Thus, it is not treated as a point object.

Q. 2 The position time $(x-t)$ graphs for two children A and B returning from their school O to their homes P and Q respectively are shown in fig. Choose the correct entries in the brackets below:

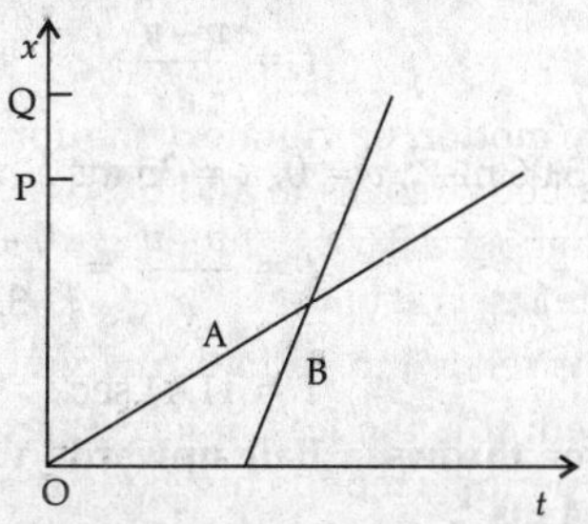

(a) (A/B) lives closer to the school than (B/A)
(b) (A/B) starts from the school earlier than (B/A)
(c) (A/B) walks faster than (B/A)
(d) A and B reach home at the (same/different) time.
(e) (A/B) overtakes (B/A) on the road (once/twice).

[NCERT Ex., Q. 2.2, Page 24]

Ans.

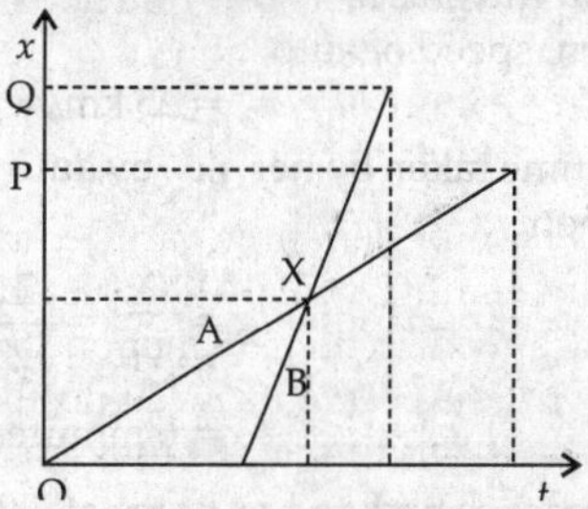

(a) A lives closer to the school than B, because B has to cover longer distance [$OP < OQ$].

(b) A starts from the school earlier than B because $t = 0$ for A but B has some finite value of time.

(c) A and B reach home at different time.

(d) B walks faster than A since, the slope of $(x-t)$ curve for B is greater than that of A.

(e) B overtakes A on the road once (at X, i.e., the point of intersection).

Q. 3. A woman starts from her home at 9.00 a.m., walks with a speed of 5 kmh^{-1} on a straight road up to her office 2.5 km away, stays at the office up to 5.00 p.m. and returns home by an auto with a speed of 25 kmh^{-1}. Choose suitable scales and plot the *x-t* graph of the motion. **[NCERT Ex., Q. 2.3, Page 24]**

Ans. *x-t* graph of the motion of woman is shown in given figure.

Let v_1 = speed of woman while going to office = 5 kmh^{-1}

x = Distance covered by her

= 2.5 km

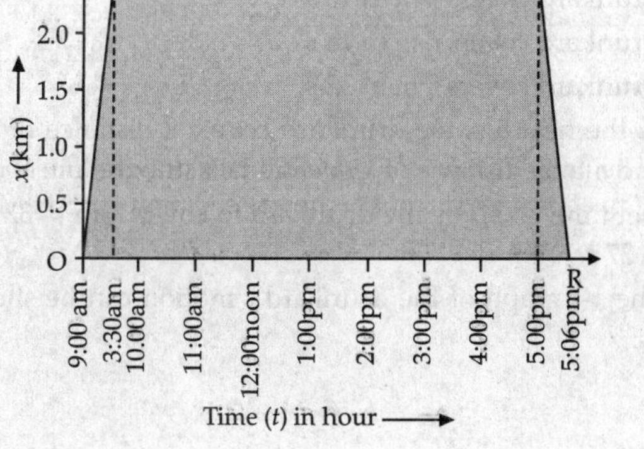

If t_1 = time taken to reach office, then it can be calculated by using the formula

$$x = v_1 t_1$$

$$\Rightarrow \quad t_1 = \frac{x}{v_1}$$

Hence, $$t_1 = \frac{25}{3} = \frac{1}{2}\text{ h} = 30 \text{ minutes.}$$

When O is regarded as origin for both time and distance, then at t = 9.00 a.m., x = 0, and at t = 9.30 a.m., x = 2.5 km and she reaches in her office. So, OP represents x-t graph of the motion when the woman walks from her home to office.

When she stays at her office from 9.30 a.m. to 5.00 p.m., she is at rest and her stay is represented by the straight line PQ in the graph.

On return, speed of auto,

$$v_2 = 25 \text{ km/h.}$$

Let, t_2 = time taken by her, i.e., by auto from office to her home, then

$$t_2 = \frac{x}{v_1} = \frac{2.5}{25} = \frac{1}{10}\text{ hour}$$

$$= 6 \text{ minutes.}$$

So, she reaches back to her home at 5.06 p.m.

Her motion on the return journey is shown by QR part of the graph.

Scale taken

Time on x-axis, 1 division = 1 hour.

Distance on y-axis, 1 division = 0.5 km.

Q. 4. A drunkard walking in a narrow lane takes 5 steps forward and 3 steps backward, followed again by 5 steps forward and 3 steps backward, and so on. Each step is 1 m long and requires 1 s. Plot the x-t graph of his motion. Determine graphically and otherwise how long the drunkard takes to fall in a pit 13 m away from the start.

Ans. Distance covered with 1 step = 1 m

Time taken = 1 s

Time taken to move first 5 m forward = 5 s

Time taken to move 3 m backward = 3 s

Net distance covered = 5 − 3 = 2 m

Net time taken to cover 2 m = 8 s

Drunkard covers 2 m in 8 s.

Drunkard covers 4 m in 16 s.

Drunkard covers 6 m in 24 s.

Drunkard covers 8 m in 32 s.

In the next 5 s, the drunkard covers a distance of 5 m and a total distance of 13 m and falls into the pit.

Net time taken by the drunkard to cover 13m = 32 + 5 = 37 s

The x-t graph of the drunkard's motion can be shown as:

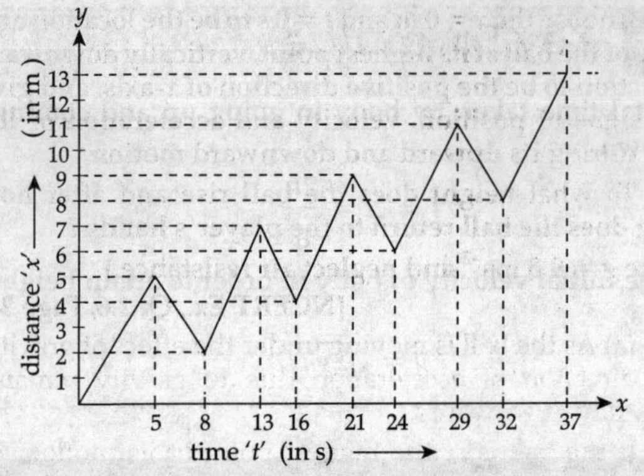

Q. 5. A car moving along a straight highway with speed of 126 kmh^{-1} is brought to a stop within a distance of 200 m. What is the retardation of the car (assumed uniform) and how long does it take for the car to stop ? [NCERT Ex., Q. 2.5, Page 24]

Ans. Initial velocity of car,

$$u = 126 \text{ kmh}^{-1}$$

$$= 126 \times \frac{5}{18}\text{ ms}^{-1}$$

$$= 35 \text{ ms}^{-1} \qquad \text{...(i)}$$

Since, the car finally comes to rest, $v = 0$

Distance covered, s = 200 m, a = ?, t = ?

From equation of motion

$$v^2 = u^2 - 2as$$

or, $$a = \frac{v^2 - u^2}{2s} \qquad \text{...(ii)}$$

Substituting the values from eq. (i) in eq. (ii)

$$a = \frac{0-(35)^2}{2\times 200} = -\frac{35\times 35}{400}$$

$$= -\frac{49}{16}\text{ ms}^{-2}$$

$$= -3.06 \text{ ms}^{-2}$$

Negative sign shows that acceleration is negative which is called retardation, i.e., car is uniformly retarded at $-a$ = 3.06 ms^{-2}.

To find t, let us use the relation

$$v = u + at$$

$$\therefore \quad t = \frac{v-u}{a}$$

Here, a = − 3.06 ms^{-2}, v = 0, u = 35 ms^{-1}.

$$\therefore \quad t = \frac{v-u}{a} = \frac{0-35}{-3.06} = 11.44 \text{ s}$$

$$\therefore \quad t = 11.44 \text{ sec.}$$

Q. 6. A player throws a ball upwards with an initial speed of 29.4 ms^{-1}.

(a) What is the direction of acceleration during the upward motion of the ball ?

(b) What are the velocity and acceleration of the ball at the highest point of its motion ?

(c) Choose the $x = 0$ m and $t = 0$ s to be the location and time of the ball at its highest point, vertically downward direction to be the positive direction of x-axis, and give the signs of position, velocity and acceleration of the ball during its upward and downward motion.

(d) To what height does the ball rise and after how long does the ball return to the player's hands ?

(Take $g = 9.8$ ms^{-2} and neglect air resistance.)

[NCERT Ex., Q. 2.6, Page 24]

Ans. (a) As the ball is moving under the effect of gravity, the direction of acceleration due to gravity remains vertically downwards.

(b) If the ball is at the highest point of its motion, its velocity becomes zero and the acceleration is equal to the acceleration due to gravity = 9.8 ms^{-2} in vertically downward direction.

(c) The highest point is chosen as the location for $x = 0$ and $t = 0$ and vertically downward direction to be the positive direction of x-axis.

For upward motion, sign of position is positive, sign of velocity is negative and the sign of acceleration is positive, i.e., $v < 0, a > 0$.

For downward motion, sign of position is positive, sign of velocity is positive and the sign of acceleration is also positive, i.e., $v > 0, a > 0$.

(d) Suppose, t = time taken by the ball to reach the highest point.

H = height of the highest point from the ground.

During vertically upward motion of the ball,

$\therefore$ Initial velocity,

$$u = 29.4 \text{ ms}^{-2},$$
$$g = 9.8 \text{ ms}^{-2},$$

Final velocity $\quad v = 0, h = H = ?, t = ?$

Applying the relation,

$$v^2 = u^2 - 2gh$$
$$v^2 - u^2 = -2gh$$
$$0^2 - (29.4)^2 = -2 \times 9.8\,H$$

or
$$H = \frac{29.4 \times 29.4}{2 \times 9.8} = 44.1 \text{ m}$$

During upward motion,

$$v = u - g\,t$$
$$0 = 29.4 + 9.8 \times t$$
$$\therefore \quad t = \frac{29.4}{9.8} = 3 \text{ s}.$$

i.e., time of ascent = 3 s.

It is also known that when the object moves under the effect of gravity alone, the time of ascent is always equal to the time of descent.

$\therefore$ Total time after which the ball returns to the player's hand = $2t = 2 \times 3 = 6$ s.

Q. 7. Read each statement below carefully and state with reasons and examples, if it is correct or wrong. A particle in one-dimensional motion

(a) with zero speed at an instant may have non-zero acceleration at that instant.

(b) with zero speed may have non-zero velocity.

(c) with constant speed must have zero acceleration.

(d)with positive value of acceleration must be speeding up. **[NCERT Ex., Q. 2.7, Page 24]**

Ans. (a) Correct. Example, if a ball is in vertically upward motion, i.e., thrown vertically upward, then it will be of zero speed at the highest point and an acceleration of 9.8 ms^{-2} in downward direction.

(b) Incorrect, because speed is the magnitude of velocity.

(c) Incorrect, change in direction of velocity also produces acceleration.

(d) Incorrect Example, if we take the positive direction of acceleration due to gravity downwards, a ball dropped of a tower will gain speed continuously.

Q. 8 A ball is dropped from a height of 90 m on a floor. At each collision with the floor, the ball loses one tenth of its speed. Plot the speed – time graph of its motion between $t = 0$ to 12 s. **[NCERT Ex., Q. 2.8, Page 25]**

Ans. Given, $h = 90$ m, $u = 0$, $g = 10$ m/s^2,

$$t_1 = \sqrt{\frac{2h}{g}} = \sqrt{\frac{2 \times 90}{10}} = 3\sqrt{2} = 4.24 \text{ s.}$$
$$v_1 = \sqrt{2gh} = \sqrt{2 \times 10 \times 90}$$
$$= 30\sqrt{2} \text{ m/s} = 42.43 \text{ m/s.}$$

In each collision, ball loses one tenth of its speed,

$$\therefore u_2 = \frac{9}{10} v_1 = \frac{9}{10} \times 30\sqrt{2}$$
$$= 27\sqrt{2}$$
$$= 38.2 \text{ m/s}$$

Time taken to reach highest point

$$t_2 = \frac{u_2}{g} = \frac{27\sqrt{2}}{10}$$
$$= 3.82 \text{ s.}$$

It will take same time to reach the ground i.e.,

$$t_3 = 3.82\text{s.}$$

Final velocity will be same as the initial velocity i.e., 38.2 m/s.

Now,

$$u_3 = \frac{9}{10} u_2$$
$$= \frac{9}{10} \times 38.2$$
$$= 34.37 \text{ m/s.}$$

Total time lapsed $= t_1 + t_2 + t_3$

$$= 4.24 + 3.82 + 3.82$$
$$= 11.88 \text{ s}$$

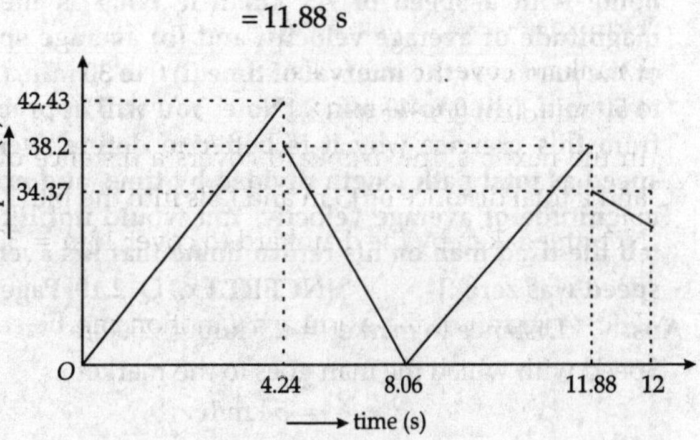

Q. 9. Explain clearly, with examples, the distinction between: (a) magnitude of displacement (sometimes called distance) over an interval of time, and the total length of path covered by a particle over the same interval; (b) magnitude of average velocity over an interval of time, and the average speed over the same interval. [Average speed of a particle over an interval of time is defined as the total path length divided by the time interval]. Show in both (a) and (b) that the second quantity is either greater than or equal to the first. When is the equality sign true? [For simplicity, consider one-dimensional motion only].

[NCERT Ex., Q. 2.9, Page 25]

Ans. **(a)** The magnitude of displacement over an interval of time is the shortest distance between the initial and final positions of the particle whereas the total length of path covered by a particle over the same interval is the actual path length covered by the particle in a given interval of time.

Example: If a particle moves from point A to point B and then, comes back to a point C, taking a total time (t), then the magnitude of displacement of the particle is AC whereas the total length of the path is AB + BC.

The magnitude of displacement over an interval of time can never be greater than the total length of the path. However, both quantities may be equal to each other in some cases.

(b) Magnitude of average velocity

$$= \frac{\text{Magnitude of displacement}}{\text{Time interval}}$$

For the given particle,

$$\text{Average velocity} = \frac{AC}{t}$$

$$\text{Average speed} = \frac{\text{Total length of path}}{\text{Time interval}}$$

$$= \frac{(AB+BC)}{t}$$

Since, $(AB + BC) > AC$, average speed is greater than the magnitude of average velocity. The two quantities will be equal if the particle continues to move along a straight line.

Q. 10. A man walks on a straight road from his home to a market 2.5 km away with a speed of 5 km h-1. Finding the market closed, he instantly turns and walks back home with a speed of 7.5 km h-1. What is the (a) magnitude of average velocity, and (b) average speed of the man over the interval of time (i) 0 to 30 min, (ii) 0 to 50 min, (iii) 0 to 40 min ? [Note: You will appreciate from this exercise why it is better to define average speed as total path length divided by time, and not as magnitude of average velocity. You would not like to tell the tired man on his return home that his average speed was zero !] **[NCERT Ex., Q. 2.10, Page 25]**

Ans. Distance to market = 2.5 km. = 2500 m

Speed with which the man goes to the market

= 5 km/h

$$= \frac{5\times10^3}{3600} = \frac{25}{18}\ \text{m/s}$$

Speed with which the man comes back from the market

$$= 7.5\ \text{km/h} = \frac{7.5\times10^3}{3600}$$

$$= \frac{75}{36}\ \text{m/s or}\ \frac{25}{12}\ \text{m/s}$$

(a) Average velocity = 0

Since, the displacement is zero

(b) (i) The initial speed of man is 5 km/s and the distance to the market is 2.5 km

Therefore, time taken to reach the market

$$= \frac{2.5}{5} = \frac{1}{2}\ \text{hour or 30 minutes}$$

Average speed of man over 0 to 30 mins. = 5 km/h

(ii) The speed of man after 30 minutes = 7.5 km/h

$$\text{Distance covered by man in 50 – 30 mins.} = \frac{7.5\times20}{60}$$

= 2.5 km

Total distance covered by man in 50 min.

= 2.5 km + 2.5 km = 5 km

Average speed of man in 50 mins.

$$\text{Vavg} = \frac{\text{Distance travelled}}{\text{time}}$$

$$= \frac{5\times50}{60} = 6\ \text{km/h}$$

(iii) The speed of man after 30 minutes = 7.5 km/h

$$\text{Distance covered by man in 40 – 30 mins.} = \frac{7.5\times10}{60}$$

= 1.25 km

Total distance covered by man in 40 min.

= 2.5 km + 1.25 km

= 3.75 km

Average speed of man in 40 mins.

$$\text{Vavg} = \frac{\text{Distance travelled}}{\text{time}}$$

$$= \frac{3.75\times40}{60} = 5.625\ \text{km/h}$$

Q. 11. In Q. 9 and Q. 10, we have carefully distinguished between average speed and magnitude of average velocity. No such distinction is necessary when we consider instantaneous speed and magnitude of velocity ? The instantaneous speed is always equal to the magnitude of instantaneous velocity. Why ?

[NCERT Ex., Q. 2.11, Page 25]

Ans. Instantaneous velocity is given by the first derivative of distance with respect to time i.e., here the time interval '*dt*' is so small that it is assumed that an object does not change its direction of motion. As a result both the total path length and magnitude of displacement become equal in this interval of time. Therefore, instantaneous speed is always equal to instantaneous velocity.

Q. 12. Look at the graphs (a) to (d) (fig.) carefully and state with reasons which of the following cannot possibly represent one dimensional motion of a particle.

[NCERT Ex., Q. 2.12, Page 24]

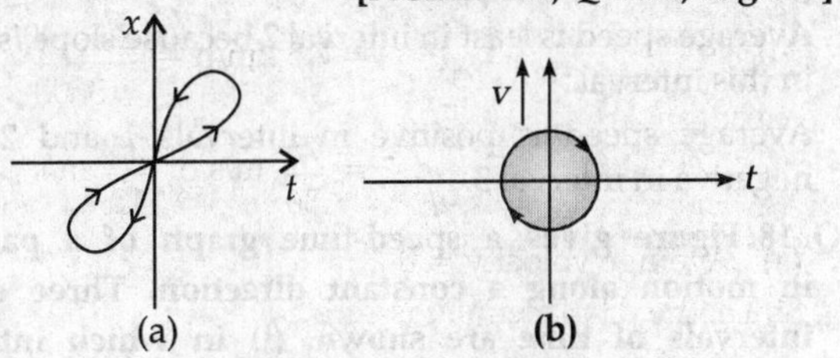

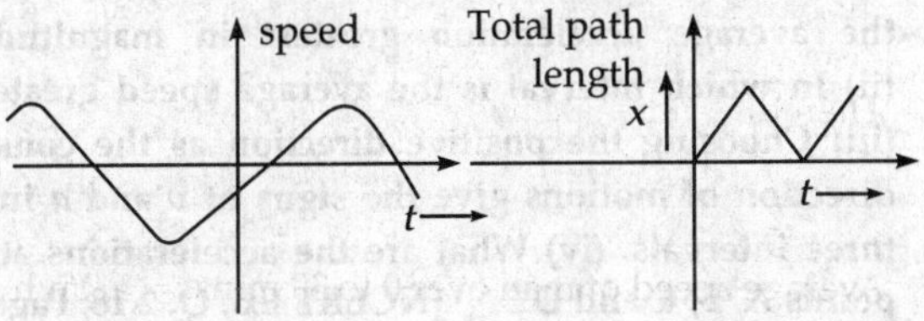

Ans. Graph (a) does not represent one dimensional motion of particle because the particle has two different positions at the same instant which is not the case of one dimensional motion.

Graph (b) does not represent one dimensional motion because at the same instant a particle cannot have positive and negative velocity if the motion is one dimensional.

Graph (c) does not represent one dimensional motion because speed cannot be negative as shown in graph.

Graph (d) also does not represent one dimensional motion of the particle because here the total path length is shown to decrease with time which is not possible in one dimensional motion.

Q. 13. Figure shows the x-t plot of one-dimensional motion of a particle. Is it correct to say from the graph that the particle moves in a straight line for t < 0 and on a parabolic path for t > 0 ? If not, suggest a suitable physical context for this graph.

[NCERT Ex., Q. 2.3, Page 25]

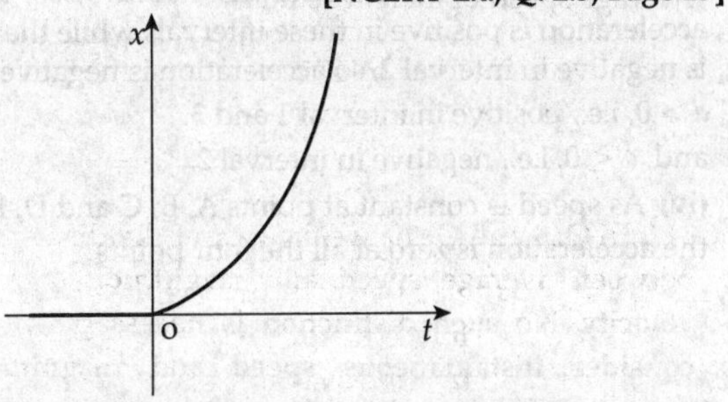

Ans. No, because the *x-t* graph does not represent the trajectory of the path followed by a particles. From the graph, a suitable physical context can be the particle dropped from the top of the tower at $t = 0$ and $x = 0$

Q. 14. A police van moving on a highway with a speed of 30 km h-1 fires a bullet at a thief's car speeding away in the same direction with a speed of 192 km h^{-1}. If the muzzle speed of the bullet is 150 m s^{-1}, with what speed does the bullet hit the thief's car ? (Note: Obtain that speed which is relevant for damaging the thief's car).

[NCERT Ex., Q. 2.14, Page 25]

Ans. Speed of the police van, $vp = 30$ km/h

$$= \frac{30 \times 10^3}{3600}$$

$$= 8.33 \text{ m/s}$$

Muzzle speed of the bullet, $vb = 150$ m/s

Speed of thief's car, $vt = 192$ km/h

$$= \frac{192 \times 10^3}{3600} = 53.33 \text{ m/s}$$

The resultant speed of the bullet, being fired from a moving van $= 150 + 8.33 = 158.33$ m/s

Since both the vehicles are moving in the same direction, the velocity with which the bullet hits the thief's car is:

$$Vbt = vb - vt$$

$$158.33 - 53.33 = 105 \text{ m/s}$$

Q. 15. Suggest a suitable physical situation for each of the following graphs:

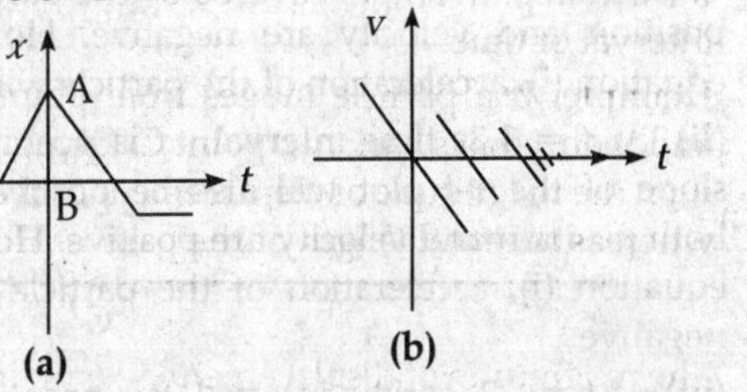

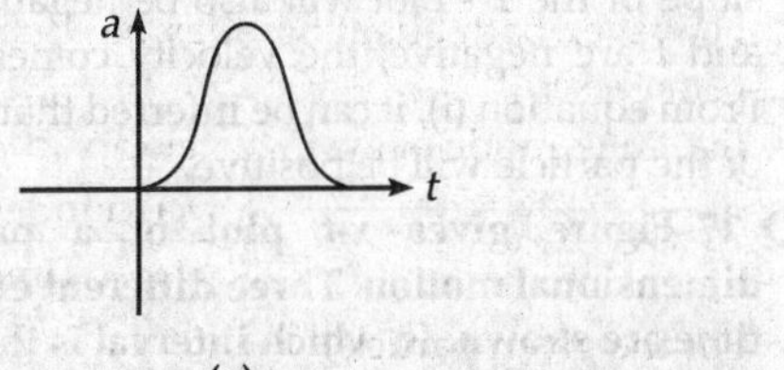

(c)

[NCERT Ex., Q. 2.15, Page 26]

Ans. **(a)** A ball at rest on a smooth floor is kicked, OP, shows it at rest position, at R the ball rebounds from the wall. RQ represents the bounced ball with reduced speed because the slope of RQ is less than that of PR. (The slope of *x-t* graph gives the speed of the moving body), ST shows the rest position of the ball.

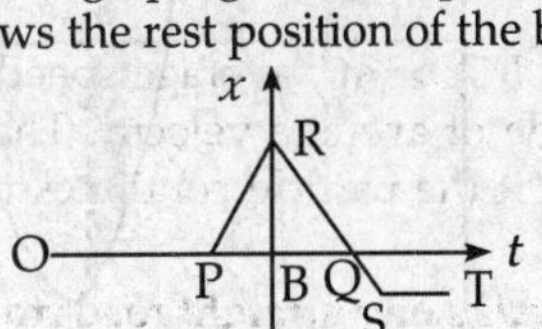

(b) The graph shows the case of a ball thrown up with some initial velocity and rebounding from the floor with reduced speed after each hit every time on the floor, i.e., after every bounce.

(c) It is the acceleration-time graph. The graph represents a uniformly moving cricket ball turned back after hitting the bat for a very short time interval.

Q. 16. Figure gives the x-t plot of a particle executing one-dimensional simple harmonic motion.

(You will learn about this motion in more detail in Chapter 14). Give the signs of position, velocity and acceleration variables of the particle at $t = 0.3$ s, 1.2 s, –1.2 s. **[NCERT Ex., Q. 2.16, Page 26]**

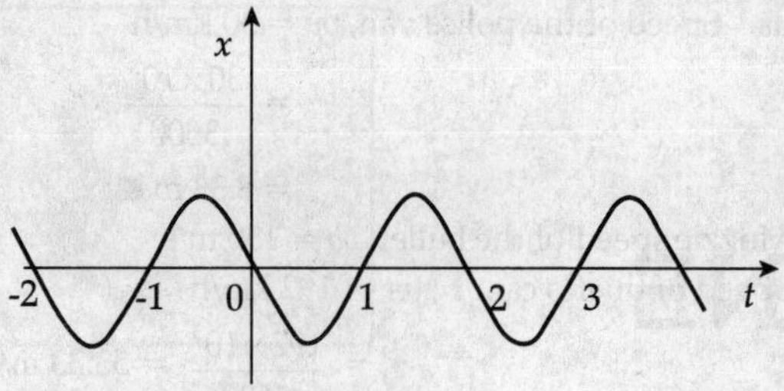

Ans. Negative, Negative, Positive
Positive, Positive, Negative
Negative, Positive, Positive

For simple harmonic motion (SHM) of a particle, the relation of acceleration (a) with angular frequency (ω) as

$$a \propto -\omega^2 x \quad ...(i)$$

(i) At t = 0.3s time interval, x is negative. Thus, the slope of the x-t plot will be positive. Therefore, both position and velocity are negative. However, using equation (i), acceleration of the particle will be positive.

(ii) At t = 1.2s time interval, x is positive. Thus, the slope of the x-t plot will also be positive. Therefore, both position and velocity are positive. However, using equation (i), acceleration of the particle comes to be negative.

(iii) At t = – 1.2s time interval, x is negative. Thus, the slope of the x-t plot will also be negative. Since both x and t are negative, the velocity comes to be positive. From equation (i), it can be inferred that the acceleration of the particle will be positive.

Q. 17. Figure gives *x-t* plot of a particle in one-dimensional motion. Three different equal intervals of time are shown. In which interval is the average speed greatest, and in which is it the least? Give the sign of average velocity for each interval.

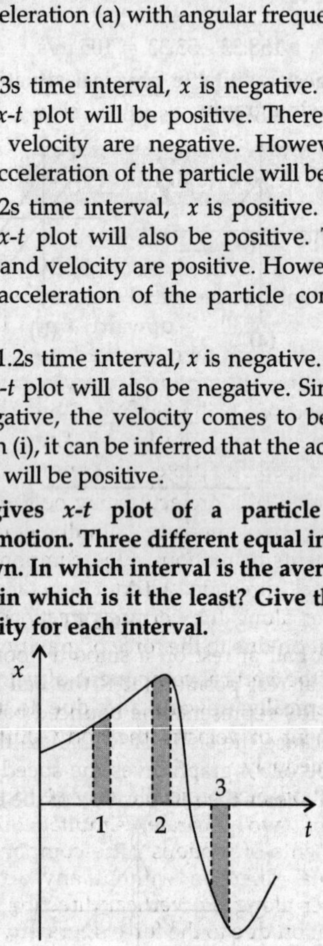

[NCERT Ex., Q. 2.17, Page 26]

Ans. Average speed in small interval of time is equal to slope of x-t graph in same interval.

Average speed is greatest in interval 3 because slope is greatest in this interval.

Average speed is least in interval 2 because slope is least in this interval.

Average speed is positive in intervals 1 and 2 and negative in interval 3.

Q. 18. Figure gives a speed-time graph of a particle in motion along a constant direction. Three equal intervals of time are shown. (i) In which interval the average acceleration greatest in magnitude ? (ii) In which interval is the average speed greatest ? (iii) Choosing the positive direction as the constant direction of motions give the signs of *v* and *a* in the three intervals. (iv) What are the accelerations at the points A, B, C and D ? [NCERT Ex., Q. 2.18, Page 26]

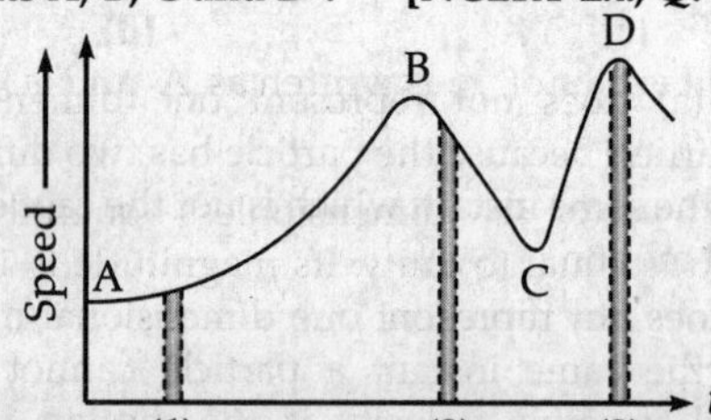

Ans. **(i)** The magnitude of the average acceleration is given by $a_{av} = \dfrac{\text{Change in speed}}{\text{Time interval}}$

i.e., average acceleration in a small interval of time is equal to the slope of v-t graph in that time interval.

As the slope of v-t graph is maximum in the interval 2 as compared to intervals 1 and 3, hence the magnitude of average acceleration is greatest in interval 2.

(ii) The average speed is greatest in the interval 3 as peak D is at maximum on speed axis.

(iii) $v > 0$, i.e., positive in all the three intervals.

The slope is positive in intervals 1 and 3, so 'a', i.e. acceleration is positive in these intervals while the slope is negative in interval 2, so acceleration is negative in it.

$a > 0$, i.e., positive in interval 1 and 3.

and, $a < 0$, i.e., negative in interval 2.

(iv) As speed is constant at points A, B, C and D, hence the acceleration is zero at all the four points.

□□

CHAPTER 3

MOTION IN A PLANE

Scalars and Vectors

Scalar: A physical quantity which has only magnitude and no direction is called a scalar quantity or scalar.

Vector: A physical quantity which constitutes of magnitude as well as direction is called a vector quantity or vector. If it follows law of vector addition too.

➤ **Unit vector:**

(i) A unit vector of $\vec{A}$ is written as $\hat{A}$ and is given by $\hat{A} = \vec{A}/|\vec{A}|$

(ii) A unit vector is dimensionless quantity of magnitude equal to unity. Its magnitude is 1 and it can have any direction.

(iii) In cartesian co-ordinates, $\hat{i}, \hat{j}, \hat{k}$ are the unit vectors along x, y and z-axes, respectively.

➤ **Polar vectors:** These are those vectors which have a linear directional effect. For example, force, linear momentum, linear velocity etc.

Scan to know more about this topic

Vector and scalar

➤ **Axial vectors or rotational vectors:** These vectors represent rotational effect. They are always directed along the axis of rotation in accordance with right hand screw rule. Angular velocity, torque, angular momentum etc. are few examples of axial vectors.

➤ **Some vector laws:**

(1) General law for addition of vector: It states that the vectors to be added are arranged in such a way so that the head of first vector coincides with the tail of second vector, whose head coincides with tail of third vector and so on then resultant vector is represented in magnitude and direction by the line starting from tail of first vector to head of last vector.

(2) Triangle Law: It states that if two vectors acting on a particle at the same time are represented in magnitude and direction by the two sides of a triangle taken in one order, their resultant vector is represented in magnitude and direction by the third side of triangle taken in opposite order.

(3) Parallelogram Law: It states that if two vectors acting on a particle at the same time be represented in magnitude and direction by the two adjacent sides of a parallelogram drawn from a point, their resultant vector is represented in magnitude and direction by the diagonal of the parallelogram drawn from the same point.

➤ **Lami's Theorem:** It states that if three forces acting at a point are in equilibrium, then each force is proportional to the sine of the angle between the other two forces, *i.e.*,

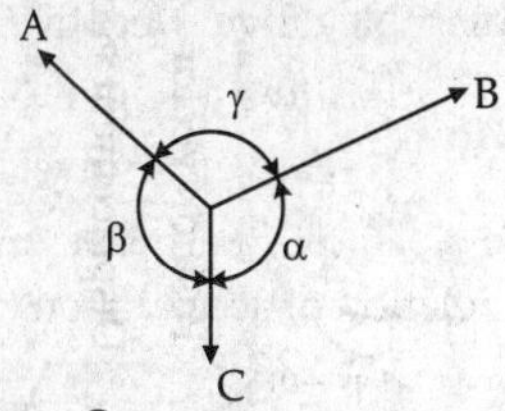

$$\frac{A}{\sin\alpha} = \frac{B}{\sin\beta} = \frac{C}{\sin\gamma}$$

Projectile Motion

➤ **Projectile:**

Scan to know more about this topic

Projectile motion

(a) Projectile is defined as a body thrown with some initial velocity except vertically upward or downward and then allowed to move under the action of gravity alone, without being propelled by an engine or fuel or any source. The path followed by a projectile is known as its **trajectory**.

(b) The motion of a projectile may be thought of as the result of two separate, simultaneously occurring components of motions. One component is along a horizontal direction without any acceleration and the other along the vertical direction with constant acceleration due to the force of gravity.

(c) Due to the vertical component of velocity, the body rises vertically upward and due to the horizontal component of velocity the body shifts horizontally simultaneously.

➤ The motion of a projectile may be thought of as the result of two separate, simultaneously occurring components of motions. One component is along a horizontal direction without any acceleration and the other along the vertical direction with constant acceleration due to the force of gravity.

➤ Due to the vertical component of velocity, the body rises vertically upward and due to the horizontal component of velocity the body shifts horizontally simultaneously.

➤ **Centripetal force:**

(a) It is the force required to move the body in circular path with a constant angular velocity.

(b) The centripetal force acts on the particle along the radius which is directed towards the centre of circular path.

(c) The centripetal force does not increase the kinetic energy and angular momentum of the particle moving in a circular path, therefore the work done by the centripetal force is zero.

(d) The centripetal force is provided in different ways, in different types of circular motions.

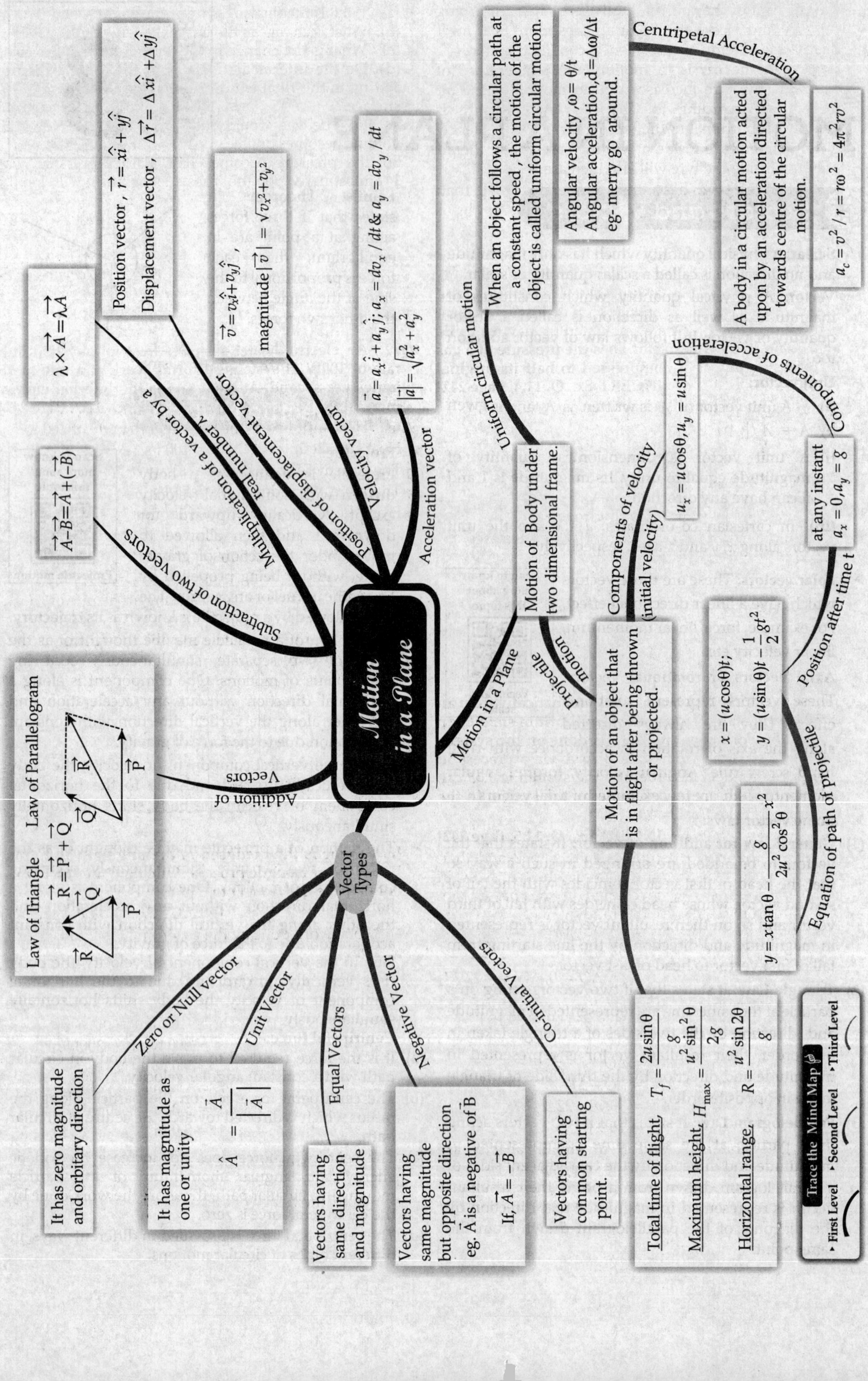

Motion in a Plane
Vector Types
Zero or Null vector
It has zero magnitude and orbitary direction
Unit Vector
It has magnitude as one or unity
$\hat{A} = \frac{\vec{A}}{|\vec{A}|}$
Equal Vectors
Vectors having same direction and magnitude
Negative Vector
Vectors having same magnitude but opposite direction eg. $\vec{A}$ is a negative of $\vec{B}$
If, $\vec{A} = -\vec{B}$
Co-initial Vectors
Vectors having common starting point.
Addition of Vectors
Law of Triangle
$\vec{R} = \vec{P} + \vec{Q}$
Law of Parallelogram
$\vec{R} = \vec{P} + \vec{Q}$
Subtraction of two vectors
$\vec{A} - \vec{B} = \vec{A} + (-\vec{B})$
Multiplication of a vector by a real number λ
$\lambda \times \vec{A} = \lambda\vec{A}$
Position of displacement vector
Position vector , $\vec{r} = x\hat{i} + y\hat{j}$
Displacement vector , $\Delta\vec{r} = \Delta x\hat{i} + \Delta y\hat{j}$
Velocity vector
$\vec{v} = v_x\hat{i} + v_y\hat{j}$,
magnitude $|\vec{v}| = \sqrt{v_x^2 + v_y^2}$
Acceleration vector
$\vec{a} = a_x\hat{i} + a_y\hat{j}$; $a_x = dv_x / dt$ & $a_y = dv_y / dt$
$|\vec{a}| = \sqrt{a_x^2 + a_y^2}$
Motion in a Plane
Motion of Body under two dimensional frame.
Uniform circular motion
When an object follows a circular path at a constant speed , the motion of the object is called uniform circular motion.
Angular velocity ,ω= θ/t
Angular acceleration,α=Δω/Δt
eg- merry go around.
Centripetal Acceleration
A body in a circular motion acted upon by an acceleration directed towards centre of the circular motion.
$a_c = v^2 / r = r\omega^2 = 4\pi^2 r\upsilon^2$
Projectile motion
Motion of an object that is in flight after being thrown or projected.
Components of velocity (initial velocity)
$u_x = u\cos\theta, u_y = u\sin\theta$
Components of acceleration
at any instant
$a_x = 0, a_y = g$
Position after time t
$x = (u\cos\theta)t$;
$y = (u\sin\theta)t - \frac{1}{2}gt^2$
Equation of path of projectile
$y = x\tan\theta - \frac{g}{2u^2\cos^2\theta}x^2$
Total time of flight, $T_f = \frac{2u\sin\theta}{g}$
Maximum height, $H_{max} = \frac{u^2\sin^2\theta}{2g}$
Horizontal range, $R = \frac{u^2\sin 2\theta}{g}$
Trace the Mind Map
First Level
Second Level
Third Level

Key Words

- **Modulus of vector** is the magnitude of vector.
- **Equal vectors** are those vectors which have equal magnitude and same direction.
- **Negative vector** of a given vector is a vector of same magnitude but acting in a direction opposite to that of given vector.
- **Co-initial vectors** are those vectors which have common initial point.
- **Collinear vectors** are those vectors which are having equal or unequal magnitudes and are acting along parallel straight lines.
- **Coplanar vectors** are those vectors which are acting in the same plane.
- **Localized vector** is that vector whose initial point is fixed.
- **Non-Localized vector** is that vector whose initial point is not fixed.
- **Zero or Null vector** is that vector which has zero magnitude and an arbitrary direction and represented by 0.
- **Displacement vector** is that vector which tells how much and in which direction an object has changed its position in a given interval of time.
- **Resultant vector** is defined as that single vector which produces the same effect as is produced by two or more individual vectors together.
- **Equilibrate vector** is a single vector which balances two or more vectors acting on a body at the same time.
- **Angular displacement** of the object moving around a circular path is defined as the angle traced out by radius vector at the centre of circular path in given time. It is vector quantity.
- **Angular velocity** of an object in circular motion is defined as the time rate of change of its angular displacement.
- **Angular acceleration** of an object in circular motion is defined as the time rate of change of its angular velocity.
- **Uniform circular motion** is the motion when a point object is moving on a circular path with a constant speed.

Key Formulae

- $\vec{R} = \vec{A} + \vec{B}$

$$R = \sqrt{A^2 + B^2 + 2AB\cos\theta}$$

$$\tan\beta = \frac{B\sin\theta}{A + B\cos\theta}$$; β = angle of $\vec{R}$ with $\vec{A}$.

- $\vec{R} = \vec{A} - \vec{B} = \vec{A} + (-\vec{B})$

$$R = \sqrt{A^2 + B^2 - 2AB\cos\theta}$$

$$\tan\beta = \frac{B\sin(180°)}{A + B\cos(180°)} = \frac{B\sin\theta}{A - B\cos\theta}$$

- $\vec{A} = A_x\hat{i} + A_y\hat{j}$ and $A_x = A\cos\theta$, $A_y = A\sin\theta$ (in 2D)

- $\vec{A} = A_x\hat{i} + A_y\hat{j} + A_z\hat{k}$, $\vec{B} = B_x\hat{i} + B_y\hat{j} + B_z\hat{k}$ (in 3D)

$$|\vec{A}| = \sqrt{A_x^2 + A_y^2 + A_z^2}, \quad |\vec{B}| = \sqrt{B_x^2 + B_y^2 + B_z^2}$$

- $\vec{A} + \vec{B} = (A_x + B_x)\hat{i} + (A_y + B_y)\hat{j} + (A_z + B_z)\hat{k}$

- Unit Vector or $\hat{A}$ is

$$\hat{A} = \frac{\vec{A}}{|A|} = \frac{A_x\hat{i} + A_y\hat{j} + A_z\hat{k}}{\sqrt{A_x^2 + A_y^2 + A_z^2}}$$

- $\vec{A}.\vec{B} = AB\cos\theta$

$$\vec{A}.\vec{B} = \vec{B}.\vec{A}$$

- If two vectors are parallel to each other i.e., $\theta = 0°$

$$\vec{A}.\vec{B} = AB\cos 0° = AB$$

$$\hat{i}.\hat{i} = \hat{j}.\hat{j} = \hat{k}.\hat{k} = 1$$

- If two vectors are perpendicular to each other i.e., $\theta = 90°$.

$$\vec{A}.\vec{B} = AB\cos 90° = 0$$

$$\hat{i}.\hat{j} = \hat{j}.\hat{k} = \hat{k}.\hat{j} = 0$$

- If two vectors are parallel to each other i.e., $\theta = 0°$

- $\vec{A} \times \vec{B} = AB\sin 0°\, \hat{n} = \vec{0}$.

$$\vec{A} \times \vec{B} = -\vec{B} \times \vec{A}$$

- If two vectors are perpendicular to each other *i.e.*, $\theta = 90°$

$$\vec{A} \times \vec{B} = AB\sin 90° = AB$$

Scan to know more about this topic

Scalars and Vectors

- Trick to remember Cross product

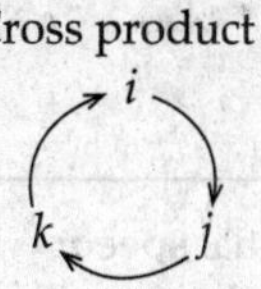

$$\hat{i}\times\hat{j} = \hat{k},\ \hat{j}\times\hat{k} = \hat{i},\ \hat{k}\times\hat{i} = \hat{j}$$

and $\hat{i}\times\hat{k} = -\hat{j},\ \hat{k}\times\hat{j} = -\hat{i},\ \hat{j}\times\hat{i} = -\hat{k}$

- Area of triangle $= \frac{1}{2}|\vec{A}\times\vec{B}|$

- Area of parallelogram $= |\vec{A}\times\vec{B}|$

- Unit vector perpendicular to $\vec{A}$ & $\vec{B}$

$$\hat{n} = \frac{\vec{A}\times\vec{B}}{|\vec{A}\times\vec{B}|}$$

where, $\vec{A} \times \vec{B} = \begin{vmatrix} \hat{i} & \hat{j} & \hat{k} \\ A_x & A_y & A_z \\ B_x & B_y & B_z \end{vmatrix}$

➢ If $\vec{A}+\vec{B}+\vec{C} = \vec{0}$

then $\vec{A} \times \vec{B} = \vec{B} \times \vec{C} = \vec{C} \times \vec{A}$

- $\sin\theta = \dfrac{|\vec{A}\times\vec{B}|}{|\vec{A}|\,|\vec{B}|}$
- $\cos\theta = \dfrac{\vec{A}\cdot\vec{B}}{|\vec{A}|\,|\vec{B}|}$
- $\tan\theta = \dfrac{\vec{A}\times\vec{B}}{\vec{A}\cdot\vec{B}}$

➢ **For motion along *X*-axis,**

$$v_x = u_x + a_x t \text{ and } x = x_0 + u_x t + \frac{1}{2}a_x t^2$$

➢ **For motion along *Y*-axis,**

$$v_y = u_y + a_y t \text{ and } y = y_0 + u_y t + \frac{1}{2}a_y t^2$$

➢ **Velocity of projective at an instant of its flight is**

$$v = \sqrt{{v_x}^2 + {v_y}^2}$$

and $\tan\gamma = \dfrac{v_y}{v_x}$

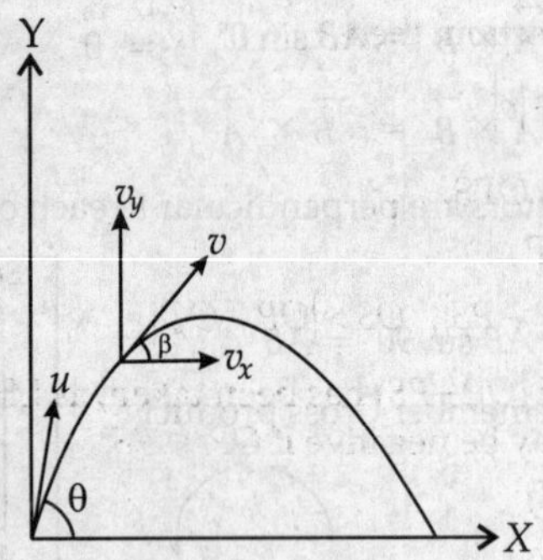

u = initial speed

θ = angle of projection

➢ **Angular projection of projectile :**

(i) Time of flight, $T = \dfrac{2u\sin\theta}{g}$

(ii) Maximum height, $h = \dfrac{u^2\sin^2\theta}{2g}$

(iii) Horizontal range, $R = \dfrac{u^2\sin 2\theta}{g}$

(iv) Maximum horizontal range $R_{max} = \dfrac{u^2}{g}$ for θ = 45°

(v) Range is same for for angles θ and (90° – θ) if *u* & *g* remains unchanged

➢ **Circular Motion**

- $\omega = \theta/t$
- $\omega = 2\pi\nu = \dfrac{2\pi}{t}$
- $a_c = \omega^2 r = \omega v = v^2/r$
- $a_T = r\alpha$

where, a_c = centripetal acceleration

a_T = tangential acceleration

ω = angular velocity

ν = frequency

T = Time period

Mnemonics

Concept: Cross and dot product of two vectors.

Mnemonics: A and **B c**rossed **S**ikkim and **d**rove to **C**alcutta.

Interpretation:

A - $\vec{A}$

B - $\vec{B}$

c - Cross product

s - sin θ

d - dot product

c - cos θ

$\vec{A}\times\vec{B}$ = AB sin θ

$\vec{A}.\vec{B}$ = AB cos θ

NCERT CORNER

Q. 1. State, for each of the following physical quantities, if it is a scalar or a vector:

Volume, mass, speed, acceleration, density, number of moles, velocity, angular frequency, displacement, angular velocity. **[NCERT Ex., Q. 3.1, Page 46]**

Ans.

Scalars	Vectors
volume	acceleration
mass	velocity
speed	displacement
density	angular velocity
number of moles	angular frequency

Q. 2. Pick out the two scalar quantities in the following list:
Force, angular momentum, work, current, linear momentum, electric field, average velocity, magnetic moment, relative velocity. [NCERT Ex., Q. 3.2, Page 46]

Ans. Work, Current.

Q. 3. Pick out the only vector quantity in the following list:
Temperature, pressure, impulse, time, power, total path length, energy, gravitational potential, coefficient of friction, charge.

Ans. Impulse, as Impulse = Force × time

Q. 4. State with reasons, whether the following algebraic operations with scalar and vector physical quantities are meaningful:
(a) adding any two scalars, (b) adding a scalar to a vector of the same dimensions, (c) multiplying any vector by any scalar, (d) multiplying any two scalars, (e) adding any two vectors, (f) adding a component of a vector to the same vector. [NCERT Ex., Q. 3.4, Page 46]

Ans. **(a)** No, adding any two scalars is not meaningful, but the scalars of same dimensions, (i.e., of same nature) can be added.

(b) No, adding a scalar to a vector of the same dimension is not meaningful as a scalar cannot be added to a vector.

(c) Yes, multiplying any vector by any scalar is meaningful in algebraic operation. It is because when any vector is multiplied by any scalar, then we get a vector having magnitude equal to scalar number of times the magnitude of the given vector. For example, when acceleration a is multiplied by mass m, we get force $F = ma$ which is a meaningful operation.

(d) Yes, it is product of two scalar gives a meaningful result. For example, when power P is multiplied by time t, then we get work done (W), i.e., $W = Pt$, which is a useful algebraic operation.

(e) No, as the two vectors of same dimensions (i.e., of the same nature) can only be added. So addition of any two vectors of same dimension is a meaningful algebraic operation.

(f) Addition of a component of a vector to the same vector can be done by the law of vector addition. So algebraic operation is a meaningful operation.

Q. 5. Read each statement below carefully and state with reasons, if it is true or false:
(a) The magnitude of a vector is always a scalar.
(b) Each component of a vector is always a scalar.
(c) The total path length is always equal to be magnitude of the displacement vector of a particle.
(d) The average speed of a particle (defined as total path length divided by the time taken to cover the path) is either greater or equal to the magnitude of average velocity of the particle over the same interval of time.
(e) Three vectors not lying in a plane can never add up to give a null vector. [NCERT Ex., Q. 3.5, Page 46]

Ans. **(a)** True, magnitude is pure number.

(b) False, each component is vector.

(c) True, only if particle moves along a straight line and in same direction otherwise false.

(d) True, because-
Total path length ≥ Magnitude of displacement vector

(e) True, because these three vectors cannot represent three sides of triangle which taken in same order.

Q. 6. Establish the following vector inequalities geometrically or otherwise:
(a) $|\vec{a}+\vec{b}| \le |\vec{a}|+|\vec{b}|$
(b) $|\vec{a}+\vec{b}| \ge ||\vec{a}|+|\vec{b}||$
(c) $|\vec{a}-\vec{b}| \le |\vec{a}|+|\vec{b}|$
(d) $|\vec{a}-\vec{b}| \ge ||\vec{a}|-|\vec{b}||$
When does the equality sign above apply? [NCERT Ex., Q. 3.6, Page 46]

Ans. **(a)** As-

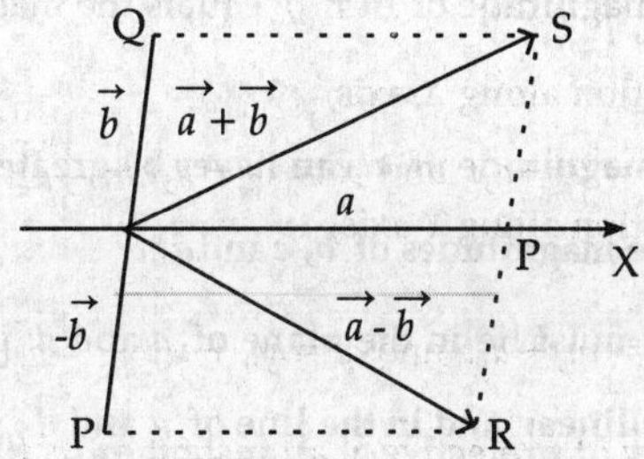

Length of one side of triangle is always less than sum of lengths of other two sides.

So, $|\vec{a}+\vec{b}| < |\vec{a}|+|\vec{b}|$ (I)

If the two vectors are acting along same straight line and in same direction, then

$|\vec{a}+\vec{b}| = |\vec{a}|+|\vec{b}|$ (II)

(b) From Δ OPS,

$OS+PS>OP$

$\Rightarrow OS > |OP-PS|,\ OS > |OP-OQ|$ **(III)**

Modulus of $(OP-PS)$ has been taken, as LHS is positive but RHS may be negative if $OP < PS$.

From eq.(III)

$|\vec{a}+\vec{b}| > ||\vec{a}|-|\vec{b}||$ (IV)

If $\vec{a}$ and $\vec{b}$ are acting along straight line but in opposite direction,

$|\vec{a}+\vec{b}| = ||\vec{a}|-|\vec{b}||$ (V)

from eq (IV) &(V)

$|\vec{a}+\vec{b}| \ge ||\vec{a}|-|\vec{b}||$

(c) From ΔORP, $OR<OP+PR$

So, $|\vec{a}-\vec{b}| < ||\vec{a}|+|\vec{b}||$ (VI)

Now, two vectors are acting along straight line in opposite direction-

$$|\vec{a}-\vec{b}| = ||\vec{a}|+|\vec{b}|| \quad \text{(VII)}$$

from eq. (VI) & (VII)

$$|\vec{a}-\vec{b}| \le |\vec{a}|+|\vec{b}|$$

(d) From ΔOPR, $OR > |OP - PR|$

$|\overline{OP} - \overline{PR}|$ has been taken, because LHS = positive, RHS may be negative if $OP<PR$,

$$\therefore \quad |\vec{a}-\vec{b}| > ||\vec{a}|-|\vec{b}||$$

Q. 7. Given $\vec{a}+\vec{b}+\vec{c}-\vec{d} = 0$, which of the following statements are correct:

(a) $(\vec{a},\vec{b},\vec{c})$ and $\vec{d}$ must each be a null vector,

(b) The magnitude of $(\vec{a}+\vec{c})$ equals the magnitude of $(\vec{b}+\vec{d})$,

(c) The magnitude of $\vec{a}$ can never be greater than the sum of the magnitudes of $\vec{b}, \vec{c}$ and $\vec{d}$,

(d) $\vec{b}+\vec{c}$ must lie in the plane of $\vec{a}$ and $\vec{d}$ if $\vec{a}$ and $\vec{d}$ are not collinear, and in the line of $\vec{a}$ and $\vec{d}$, if they are collinear? [NCERT Ex., Q. 3.7, Page 47]

Ans. (a) Incorrect

In order to make, $\vec{a}+\vec{b}+\vec{c}+\vec{d}=\vec{0}$ it is not necessary to have all the four given vectors to be null vectors. There are many other combinations which can give the sum zero.

(b) Correct

$$\vec{a}+\vec{b}+\vec{c}+\vec{d}=\vec{0}$$

$$\vec{a}+\vec{c}=-(\vec{b}+\vec{d})$$

Taking modulus on both the sides, we get:

$$|\vec{a}+\vec{c}| = |-(\vec{b}+\vec{d})| = |\vec{b}+\vec{d}|$$

Hence, the magnitude of $(\vec{a}+\vec{c})$ is the same as the magnitude of $(\vec{b}+\vec{d})$

(c) Correct

$$\vec{a}+\vec{b}+\vec{c}+\vec{d}=\vec{0}$$

$$\vec{a}=-(\vec{b}+\vec{c}+\vec{d})$$

Taking modulus both sides, we get the magnitude of $\vec{a}$ to be equal to the magnitude of $(\vec{b}+\vec{c}+\vec{d})$:

$$|\vec{a}| = |(\vec{b}+\vec{c}+\vec{d})|$$

$$|\vec{a}| \le |\vec{b}|+|\vec{c}|+|\vec{d}| \quad \text{...(i)}$$

Now, $(\vec{b}+\vec{c}+\vec{d})$ is the sum of vectors $\vec{b}$, $\vec{c}$ and $\vec{d}$. Therefore, the magnitude of $(\vec{b}+\vec{c}+\vec{d})$ is less than, or equal to the sum of the magnitudes of $\vec{b}$, $\vec{c}$ and $\vec{d}$. Hence, the magnitude of $\vec{a}$ can never be greater than the sum of the magnitudes of $\vec{b}$, $\vec{c}$ and $\vec{d}$. Equation (*i*) shows that the magnitude of $\vec{a}$ is equal to or less than the sum of the magnitudes of $\vec{b}$, $\vec{c}$ and $\vec{d}$.

(d) Correct

For, $\vec{a}+\vec{b}+\vec{c}+\vec{d}=0$

$$\vec{a}+(\vec{b}+\vec{c})+\vec{d}=0$$

The resultant sum of the three vectors $\vec{a}$, $(\vec{b}+\vec{c})$, and $\vec{d}$ can be zero only if $(\vec{b}+\vec{c})$ lie in the same plane as $\vec{a}$ and $\vec{d}$.

If $\vec{a}$ and $\vec{d}$ are collinear, then it implies that the vector $(\vec{b}+\vec{c})$ is in the line of $\vec{a}$ and $\vec{d}$. This implication holds true in this scenario and the vector sum of all the vectors will be zero.

Q. 8. Three girls skating on a circular ice ground of radius 200 m start from a point P on the edge of the ground and reach a point Q diametrically opposite to P following different paths as shown in Figure. (i) What is the magnitude of the displacement vector for each? (ii) For which girl is this equal to the actual length of path skate ?

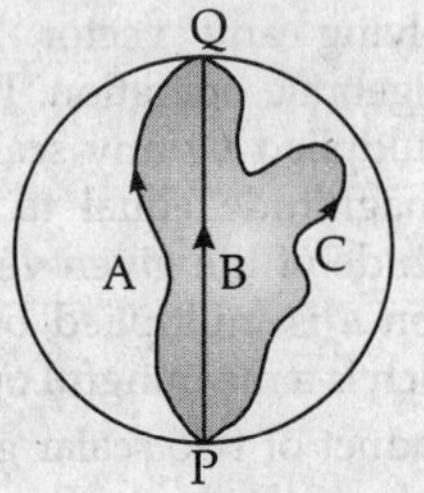

[NCERT Ex., Q. 3.8, Page 47]

Ans. (i) PQ = diameter
= displacement for each girl
= $2r = 2 \times 200 = 400$ m

Since, displacement vector does not depend upon the actual path length and it is the shortest distance between initial and final position, so in the case of each girl the displacement is 400 m.

(ii) For girl B, the displacement is equal to the actual length of path skate.

Q. 9. A cyclist starts from the centre O of a circular park of radius 1 km, reaches the edge P of the park, then cycles along the circumference and returns to the centre along QO as shown. If the round trip takes 10 min, what is the (a) net displacement, (b) average velocity and (c) average speed of the cyclist ?

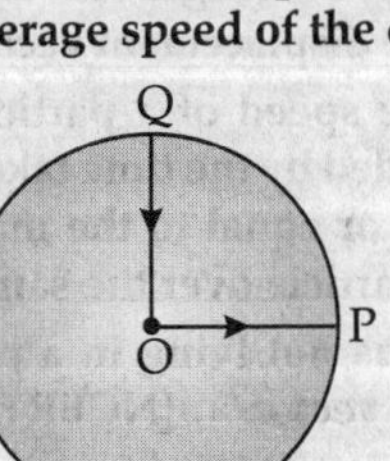

[NCERT Ex., Q. 3.9, Page 47]

Ans. Given, radius of circular park = 1 km

(a) As cyclist returns to its initial state, therefore the net displacement of the cyclist is zero.

(b) Average velocity $= \dfrac{\text{Total displacement}}{\text{Total time taken}}$

$$= \frac{0}{\text{Total time taken}}$$

$$= 0$$

(c) Total distance travelled by the cyclist

$$= OP + \text{arc } PQ + QO$$

$$= r + \left(\frac{1}{4} \times 2\pi r\right) + r$$

$$= 1 + \left(\frac{1}{2} \times \frac{22}{7} \times 1\right) + 1$$

$$= 2 + \frac{11}{7}$$

$$= \frac{25}{7} \text{ km}$$

Total time taken = 10 min

$$= \frac{10}{60} \text{ h} = \frac{1}{6} \text{ h}$$

$\therefore$ Average speed of the cyclist

$$= \frac{\text{Total distance travelled}}{\text{Total time taken}}$$

$$= \frac{25/7}{1/6} = \frac{150}{7}$$

$$= 21.43 \text{ km/h}$$

Q. 10. On an open ground, a motorist follows a track that turns to his left by an angle of 60° after every 500 m. Starting from a given turn, specify the displacement of the motorist at the third, sixth and eighth turn. Compare the magnitude of the displacement with the total path length covered by the motorist in each case. [NCERT Ex., Q. 3.10, Page 47]

Ans. The path followed by the motorist is a regular hexagon with side 500 m, as shown in the given figure

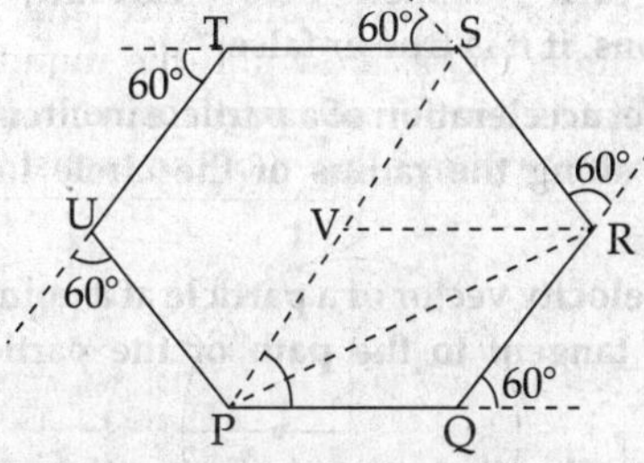

Let the motorist start from point P.

The motorist takes the third turn at S.

$\therefore$ Magnitude of displacement = PS = PV + VS = 500 + 500 = 1000 m

Total path length = PQ + QR + RS = 500 + 500 + 500 = 1500 m

The motorist takes the sixth turn at point P, which is the starting point.

$\therefore$ Magnitude of displacement = 0

Total path length = PQ + QR + RS + ST + TU + UP

= 500 + 500 + 500 + 500 + 500 + 500 = 3000 m

The motorist takes the eight turn at point R

$\therefore$ Magnitude of displacement = PR

$$= \sqrt{PQ^2 + QR^2 + 2(PQ).(QR)\cos 60^\circ}$$

$$= \sqrt{500^2 + 500^2 + (2 \times 500 \times 500 \times \cos 60^\circ)}$$

$$= \sqrt{250000 + 250000 + \left(500000 \times \frac{1}{2}\right)}$$

$$= 866.03 \text{ m}$$

Total path length

= Circumference of the hexagon + PQ + QR

= 6 × 500 + 500 + 500 = 4000 m

The magnitude of displacement and the total path length corresponding to the required turns is shown in the given table

Turn	Magnitude of displacement (m)	Total path length (m)
Third	1000	1500
Sixth	0	3000
Eighth	866.03	4000

Q. 11. A passenger arriving in a new town wishes to go from the station to a hotel located 10 km away on a straight road from the station. A dishonest cabman takes him along a circuitous path 23 km long and reaches the hotel in 28 min. What is

(a) the average speed of the taxi?

(b) the magnitude of average velocity? Are the two equal? [NCERT Ex., Q. 3.11, Page 47]

Ans. (a) Total distance travelled = 23 km

Total time taken = 28 min $= \dfrac{28}{60}$ h

$\therefore$ Average speed of the taxi $= \dfrac{\text{Total distance travelled}}{\text{Total time taken}}$

$$\Rightarrow \frac{23}{\left(\frac{28}{60}\right)} = 49.29 \text{ km/h}$$

(b) Distance between the hotel and the station = 10 km = Displacement of the car

$$\therefore \text{Average velocity} = \frac{10}{\left(\frac{28}{60}\right)} = 21.43 \text{ km/h}$$

Therefore, the two physical quantities (average speed and average velocity) are not equal.

Q. 12. The ceiling of a long hall is 25 m high. What is the maximum horizontal distance that a ball thrown with a speed of 40 ms^{-1} can go without hitting the ceiling of the hall ? [NCERT Ex., Q. 3.12, Page 47]

Ans. **Step 1:** Using $H = \frac{u^2 \sin^2 \theta}{2g}$

when $H = 25\ m, u = 40$ m/s

and $g = 9.8$ m/s^2

$$25 = \frac{40^2 \sin^2 \theta}{2 \times 9.8}$$

i.e., $\sin^2 \theta = \frac{490}{40^2}$

$$\sin \theta = \frac{\sqrt{490}}{40} = 0.5534$$

i.e., $\theta = 33.6°$

Step 2: $R = \frac{u^2 \sin 2\theta}{g}$

$$R = \frac{40^2 \sin 2(33.6)}{9.8} \text{ m}$$

$$= \frac{40^2 \sin 67.2}{9.8} \text{ m}$$

$$= \frac{40^2 \times 0.9219}{9.8} \text{ m}$$

$$= 150.514 \text{ m}$$

Q. 13. A cricketer can throw a ball to a maximum horizontal distance of 100 m. How much high above the ground can the cricketer throw the same ball ?

[NCERT Ex., Q. 3.13, Page 47]

Ans. From the formula the horizontal range is given by

$$R = \frac{u^2 \sin 2\theta}{g} \quad ...(i)$$

For $R = R_{max}$, $\theta = 45°$, i.e., $\sin 2\theta = \sin 90° = 1$

Putting the given value is eq. (i), we

$$\therefore \quad R_{max} = \frac{u^2}{g}$$

$$\Rightarrow \quad 100 = \frac{u^2}{g} \quad (\because R_{max} = 100 \text{ given}) \quad ...(ii)$$

Suppose H = height upto which the ball goes when the cricketer throws it with velocity u. Since, the final velocity of the ball, $v = 0$.

$\therefore$ Applying the relation, $v^2 - u^2 = 2as$,

($\because$ here, $v = 0, a = -g, s = H$)

or $H = \frac{u^2}{2g}$

$$H = \frac{1}{2}\left(\frac{u^2}{g}\right)$$

$$= \frac{1}{2} \times (100) \quad \text{[by using (ii)]}$$

$$H = 50 \text{ m.}$$

Q. 14. A stone tied to the end of a string 80 cm long is whirled in a horizontal circle with a constant speed. If the stone makes 14 revolutions in 25 s, what is the magnitude and direction of acceleration of the stone ?

[NCERT Ex., Q. 3.14, Page 48]

Ans. Given, Radius of the horizontal circle, $r = 80$ cm $= 0.80$ m, frequency $= f = \frac{14}{25}$ rps

Angular speed of revolution of the stone is given by

$$\omega = 2\pi f$$

$$\Rightarrow \quad \omega = 2 \times \frac{22}{7} \times \left(\frac{14}{25}\right)$$

$$\Rightarrow \quad \omega = \frac{88}{25} \text{ rad/sec.}$$

$\therefore$ Magnitude of acceleration produced in the stone will be equal to the magnitude of centripetal acceleration.

$$= r\omega^2$$

$$= 0.80 \times \left(\frac{88}{25}\right)^2$$

$$= 0.80 \times \frac{88}{25} \times \frac{88}{25}$$

$$= 9.90 \text{ ms}^{-2}$$

We know that, the direction of the acceleration is towards the centre of the circle along its radius.

Q. 15. An aircraft executes a horizontal loop of radius 1.00 km with a steady speed of 900 km/h. Compare its centripetal acceleration with the acceleration due to gravity. **[NCERT Ex., Q. 3.15, Page 48]**

Ans. Given: $r = 1 \text{ km} = 1000 \text{ m};$

$$v = 900 \text{ kmh}^{-1}$$

$$= 900 \times \frac{1000}{3600} \text{ ms}^{-1}$$

$$= 250 \text{ ms}^{-1}$$

The centripetal acceleration of the aircraft is

$$a = \frac{v^2}{r} = \frac{(250)^2}{1000}$$

$$= \frac{62500}{1000} = 62.5 \text{ ms}^{-2}$$

Acceleration due to gravity,

$$g = 9.8 \text{ ms}^{-2}$$

$$\therefore \quad \frac{\text{Centripetal acceleration}}{\text{Acceleration due to gravity}} = \frac{a}{g}$$

$$= \frac{62.5}{9.8}$$

or $a = 6.38\ g$

Q. 16. Read each statement below carefully and state, with reasons, if it is true or false:

(a) The net acceleration of a particle in circular motion is always along the radius of the circle towards the centre.

(b) The velocity vector of a particle at a point is always along the tangent to the path of the particle at that point.

(c) The acceleration vector of a particle in uniform circular motion over one cycle is a null vector.

[NCERT Ex., Q. 3.16, Page 48]

Ans. (a) False—The net acceleration of a particle in circular motion is towards the centre only if its speed is constant.

(b) True—A particle released at any point of its path will always move along the tangent to the path at the point.

(c) True—For any two diametrically opposite points on the circumference, the acceleration vectors are equal and opposite. Hence, the acceleration vector average over one completely cycle is null vector.

Q. 17. The position vector of a particle is given by

$$\vec{r} = 3.0t\hat{i} - 2.0t^2\hat{j} + 4.0\hat{k}\text{ m}$$

where t is in seconds and the coefficients have the proper units for $\vec{r}$ to be in metres.

(a) Find the $\vec{v}$ and $\vec{a}$ of the particle ?

(b) What is the magnitude and direction of velocity of the particle at $t = 2.0$ s ? [NCERT Ex., Q. 3.17, Page 48]

Ans. The position vector ($\vec{r}$) of the particle is

$$\vec{r} = 3.0t\hat{i} - 2.0t^2\hat{j} + 4.0\hat{k}\text{ m} \quad \text{...(i)}$$

(a) velocity $\vec{v}$ (t) of the particle is given by

$$\vec{v}(t) = \frac{d\vec{r}}{dt} = \frac{d}{dt}(\vec{r})$$

$$= \frac{d}{dt}(3.0t\hat{i} - 2.0t^2\hat{j} + 4.0\hat{k})$$

$$\vec{v}(t) = 3i - 4t\hat{j} + 0 \quad \text{....(ii)}$$

Also, acceleration $\vec{a}$ (t) of the participle is given by

$$\vec{a}(t) = \frac{d\vec{v}(t)}{dt} = \frac{d}{dt}\vec{v}(t)$$

$$= \frac{d}{dt}\left(3\hat{i} - 4t\hat{j}\right) \text{ [by using (ii)]}$$

$$= 0 - 4\hat{j}$$

$$\vec{a}(t) = -4\hat{j}\text{ ms}^2 \quad \text{....(iii)}$$

(b) At time t, the velocity of the particle is given by using to equation (ii).

$$\vec{v}(t) = 3.0\hat{i} - 4t\hat{j} \quad \text{[by using (ii)]}$$

∴ At $t = 2$s,

$$v = 3.0\hat{i} - 4 \times 2\hat{j}$$

$$= 3.0\hat{i} - 8.0\hat{j}$$

∴ Its magnitude is

$$v = \sqrt{3^2 + (-8)^2}$$

$$= \sqrt{9 + 64}$$

$$= \sqrt{73} = 8.544\text{ ms}^{-1}$$

and, direction of v is given by

$$\therefore \quad \theta = \tan^{-1}\left(\frac{v_y}{v_x}\right)$$

$$= \tan^{-1}\left(\frac{-8}{3}\right)$$

$= -70°$ with x-axis

Q. 18. A particle starts from the origin at $t = 0$ s with a velocity of 10.0 $\hat{j}$ and moves in the x-y plane with a constant acceleration of $(8.0\hat{i} + 2.0\hat{j})$ ms^{-2}

(a) At what time is the x-coordinate of the particle 16 m? What is the y-coordinate of the particle at that time?

(b) What is the speed of the particle at the time?

[NCERT Ex., Q. 3.18, Page 48]

Ans. (a) Velocity of the particle, $\vec{u} = 10.0\hat{j}$ *m/s*

Acceleration of the particle $\vec{a} = (8.0\hat{i} + 2.0\hat{j})$

Also,

But, $\vec{a} = \frac{d\vec{v}}{dt} = 8.0\hat{i} + 2.0\hat{j}$

$$d\vec{v} = (8.0\hat{i} + 2.0\hat{j})dt$$

Integrating both sides:

$$\vec{v} = 8.0\hat{i}\,t + 2.0\hat{j}t + \vec{u}$$

Where,

$\vec{u}$ = Velocity vector of the particle at $t = 0$

$\vec{v}$ = Velocity vector of the particle at time t

Again, $\vec{v} = \frac{d\vec{r}}{dt}$

$$d\vec{r} = \vec{v}\,dt = (8.0\hat{i}\,t + 2.0\hat{j}\,t + \vec{u})dt$$

Integrating

$$\vec{r} = \vec{u}t + \frac{1}{2}8.0t^2\hat{i} + \frac{1}{2}2.0t^2\hat{j}$$

$$= \vec{u}t + 4.0t^2\hat{i} + t^2\hat{j}$$

$$= (10.0\hat{j})t + 4.0t^2\hat{i} + t^2\hat{j}$$

$$x\hat{i} + y\hat{j} = 4.0t^2\hat{i} + (10t + t^2)\hat{j}$$

Since, the motion of the particle is confined to the x-y plane, on equating the coefficients of $\hat{i}$ and $\hat{j}$, we get:

$x = 4t^2$

or, $t = \left(\frac{x}{4}\right)^{1/2}$

And $y = 10t + t^2$

When $x = 16m$:

$$t = \left(\frac{16}{4}\right)^{\frac{1}{2}} = 2s$$

$\therefore y = 10 \times 2 + (2)^2 = 24$m

(b) Velocity of the particle is given by:

$$\vec{v} = 8.0t\hat{i} + 2.0t\hat{j} + \vec{u}$$

at $t = 2$s

$$\vec{v} = 8.0 \times 2\hat{i} + 2.0 \times 2\hat{j} + 10\hat{j}$$

$$= 16\hat{i} + 14\hat{j}$$

∴ Speed of the particle:

$$|\vec{v}| = \sqrt{(16)^2 + (14)^2}$$

$$= \sqrt{256 + 196} = \sqrt{452}$$

$$= 21.26\ m/s$$

Q. 19. (i) $\hat{i}$ and $\hat{j}$ are unit vector along *X*-and *Y*-axis respectively. What is the magnitude and direction of the vectors $\hat{i} + \hat{j}$ and $\hat{i} - \hat{j}$?

(ii) What are the components of a vector $A = 2\hat{i} + 3\hat{j}$ along the directions of $\hat{i} + \hat{j}$ and $\hat{i} - \hat{j}$? You may use graphical method. [NCERT Ex., Q. 3.19, Page 48]

Ans. (i) Magnitudes of $(\hat{i} + \hat{j})$ and $(\hat{i} - \hat{j})$ vectors: $\hat{i}$ and $\hat{j}$ are the unit vectors along X-and Y-axis respectively.

$$|\hat{i}| = |\hat{j}| = 1$$

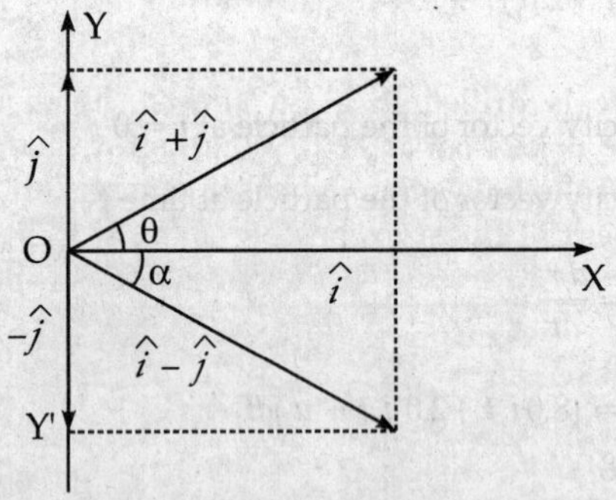

The magnitude of vector $\hat{i} + \hat{j}$ is given by

$$|\hat{i} + \hat{j}| = \sqrt{1^2 + 1^2 + 2 \times 1 \times 1 \times \cos 90°}$$

$$= \sqrt{2 + 0} = \sqrt{2}$$

$$= 1.414 \text{ units.}$$

The magnitude of vector $\hat{i} - \hat{j}$ is given by

$$|\hat{i} - \hat{j}| = \sqrt{1^2 + 1^2 - 2 \times 1 \times 1 \times \cos 90°}$$

$$= \sqrt{2 - 0} = \sqrt{2}$$

$$= 1.414 \text{ units.}$$

Directions of $\hat{i} + \hat{j}$ and $\hat{i} - \hat{j}$:

Let θ be the angle made by $\hat{i} + \hat{j}$ with $\hat{i}$, i.e., with X-axis.

By definition of scalar product of two vectors

$$(\hat{i} + \hat{j}).\hat{i} = |\hat{i} + \hat{j}|.|\hat{i}| \cos\theta$$

or $\hat{i}.\hat{i} + \hat{i}.\hat{j} = \sqrt{2} \times 1 \times \cos\theta$

or $1 + 0 = \sqrt{2}\cos\theta$

$(\because \hat{i}.\hat{i} = 1 \text{ and } \hat{i}.\hat{j} = 0)$

or $\cos\theta = \dfrac{1}{\sqrt{2}} = \cos 45°$

$$\theta = 45°$$

Also let α be the angle made by $\hat{i} - \hat{j}$ with $\hat{i}$, *i.e.*, with X-axis

Then $(\hat{i} - \hat{j}).\hat{i} = |\hat{i} - \hat{j}|.|\hat{i}| \cos\alpha$

or $\hat{i}.\hat{i} - \hat{i}.\hat{j} = \sqrt{2} \times 1 \times \cos\alpha$

or $1 - 0 = \sqrt{2}\cos\alpha$

or $\cos\alpha = \dfrac{1}{\sqrt{2}} = \cos 45°$

$$\alpha = 45°$$

As $-\hat{j}$, is –ve, so $\hat{i} - \hat{j}$ makes –45° with $-\hat{j}$.

Thus, $(\hat{i} + \hat{j})$ and $(\hat{i} - \hat{j})$ act at 45° and –45° with X-axis respectively.

(ii) (a) Let us now determine the component of $\vec{A} = 2\hat{i} + 3\hat{j}$ in the direction of $(\hat{i} + \hat{j})$

Let $\vec{B} = \hat{i} + \hat{j}$

$\therefore$ $\vec{A}.\vec{B} = AB\cos\beta$

$$= (A\cos\beta)B$$

or $A\cos\gamma = \dfrac{\vec{A}\cdot\vec{B}}{B}$

Magnitude of the component of $\vec{A}$ in the direction of $\vec{B}$, i.e., $(\hat{i} + \hat{j})$ is A cos γ

$$= \frac{\vec{A}\cdot\vec{B}}{B} = \frac{(2\hat{i} + 3\hat{j}).(\hat{i} + \hat{j})}{|\hat{i} + \hat{j}|}$$

$$= \frac{(2\hat{i}\cdot\hat{i} + 3\hat{j}\cdot\hat{j})}{\sqrt{2}}$$

$(\because \hat{j}\cdot\hat{i} = \hat{i}\cdot\hat{j} = 0)$

$$= \frac{2 + 3}{\sqrt{2}} = \frac{5}{\sqrt{2}}$$

If $\hat{n}_1$ = unit vector along $(\hat{i} + \hat{j})$, then

$$\hat{n}_1 = \frac{(\hat{i} + \hat{j})}{|\hat{i} + \hat{j}|} = \frac{(\hat{i} + \hat{j})}{\sqrt{2}}$$

$\therefore$ Component of A along $(\hat{i} + \hat{j})$ = Magnitude of the component of A along $\hat{i} + \hat{j}$ i.e., $\hat{n}_1$

$$= \frac{5}{\sqrt{2}} \cdot \frac{(\hat{i} + \hat{j})}{\sqrt{2}} = \frac{5}{2}(\hat{i} + \hat{j})$$

(b) Let us now determine the component of $\vec{A}$ along $\hat{i} - \hat{j}$.

Let $\hat{n}_2$ = unit vector acting along $\hat{i} - \hat{j}$

$$\hat{i}-\hat{j} = |\hat{i}-\hat{j}|\,\hat{n}_2 = \sqrt{2}\hat{n}_2$$

$$\therefore \quad \hat{n}_2 = \frac{(\hat{i}+\hat{j})}{\sqrt{2}}$$

$\therefore$ Magnitude of the component of $\vec{A}$ along $(\hat{i}-\hat{j})$

$$= \vec{A}\cdot\hat{n}_2 = (2\hat{i}+3\hat{j})\cdot\frac{\hat{i}-\hat{j}}{\sqrt{2}}$$

$$= \frac{2-3}{\sqrt{2}} = -\frac{1}{\sqrt{2}}$$

$\therefore$ Component of $\vec{A}$ along $(\hat{i}-\hat{j})$

$$= \left(\vec{A}\cdot\hat{n}_2\right)\hat{n}_2$$

$$= \left(-\frac{1}{\sqrt{2}}\right)\left(\frac{\hat{i}-\hat{j}}{\sqrt{2}}\right)$$

$$= \frac{-1}{2}(\hat{i}-\hat{j})$$

Q. 20. For any arbitrary motion in space, which of the following relations are true:

(a) $\vec{v}_{average} = \left(\frac{1}{2}\right)(\vec{v}(t_1)+\vec{v}(t_2))$

(b) $\vec{v}_{average} = \frac{[\vec{r}(t_2)-\vec{r}(t_1)]}{(t_2-t_1)}$

(c) $\vec{v}(t) = \vec{v}(0)+\vec{a}t$

(d) $\vec{r}(t) = \vec{r}(0)+\vec{v}(0)t+\left(\frac{1}{2}\right)\vec{a}t^2$

(e) $\vec{a}_{average} = \frac{[(t_2)-\vec{v}(t_1)]}{(t_2-t_1)}$

(The 'average' stands for average of the quantity over the time interval t_1 to t_2)

[NCERT Ex., Q. 3.20, Page 48]

Ans. (a) False.

It is given that the motion of the particle is arbitrary. Therefore, the average velocity of the particle cannot be given by this equation.

(b) True.

The arbitrary motion of the particle can be represented by this equation.

(c) False.

The motion of the particle is arbitrary. The acceleration of the particle may also be non-uniform. Hence, this equation cannot represent the motion of the particle in space.

(d) False.

The motion of the particle is arbitrary; acceleration of the particle may also be non-uniform. Hence, this equation cannot represent the motion of particle in space.

(e) True.

The arbitrary motion of the particle can be represented by this equation.

Q. 21. Read each statement below carefully and state, with reasons and examples, if it is true or false:

A scalar quantity is one that

(a) is conserved in a process.

(b) can never take negative values.

(c) must be dimensionless.

(d) does not vary from one point to another in space.

(e) has the same value for observes with different orientations of the axes.

[NCERT Ex., Q. 3.21, Page 48]

Ans. (a) False, because energy is not conserved during inelastic collision.

(b) False, because temperature and electrical potential energy can be negative.

(c) False, scalar quantity like mass density are not dimensionless.

(d) False, because gravitational potential energy vary from point to point.

(e) True, as the R values of scalar does not change with orientation of axes.

Q. 22. An aircraft is flying at a height of 3400 m above the ground. If the angle subtended at a ground observation point by the aircraft positions 10.0 s apart is 30°, what is the speed of the aircraft? [NCERT Ex., Q. 3.22, Page 48]

Ans. The positions of the observer and the aircraft are shown in the figure.

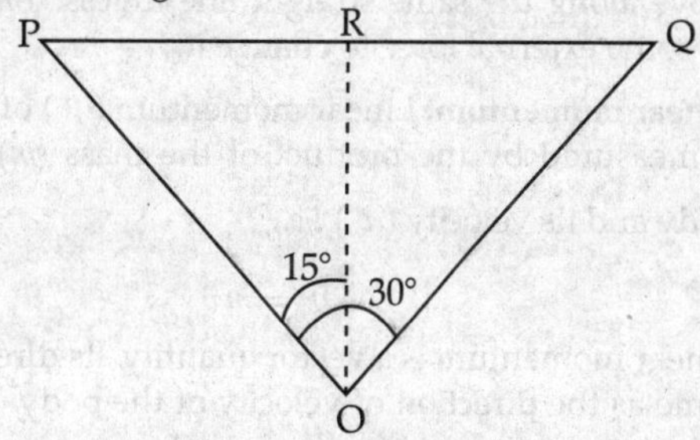

Height of the aircraft from ground, $OR = 3400$ m

Angle subtended between the positions, $\angle POQ = 30°$

Time = 10 s

In ΔPRO:

$$\tan 15° = \frac{PR}{OR}$$

$PR = OR \tan 15° = 3400 \times \tan 15°$

ΔPRO is similar to ΔRQO.

$\therefore PR = RQ$

$PQ = PR + RQ$

$= 2PR = 2 \times 3400 \tan 15°$

$= 6800 \times 0.268 = 1822.4$ m

$\therefore$ Speed of the aircraft $= \frac{1822.4}{10} = 182.24\ m/s$

LAWS OF MOTION

CHAPTER 4

Newton's Law of Motion

Newton's I law: A body continues to be in its state of rest or of uniform motion along a straight line, unless it is acted upon by some non-zero external force to change the state. This law defines forces and is also called law of inertia.

Scan to know more about this topic

Inertia and law of conservation of momentum

- **Inertia** of a body is of three types as follows:

(i) **Inertia of rest** of a body is inability to change by itself, its state on its own.

(ii) **Inertia of motion** of a body is the inability to change by itself its state of uniform motion i.e., body in uniform motion can neither accelerate nor retard on its own and comes to rest.

(iii) **Inertia of direction** of a body is inability to change by itself its direction of motion, *i.e.*, body continues to move along the same straight line unless compelled by some external force to change it.

- **Linear momentum:** Linear momentum ($\vec{p}$) of a body is measured by the product of the mass (m) of the body and its velocity ($\vec{v}$) *i.e.*,

$$\vec{p} = m\vec{v}$$

Linear momentum is a vector quantity. Its direction is same as the direction of velocity of the body. The S.I. unit of linear momentum is kg ms^{-1}.

- **Newton's II law: The rate of change of linear momentum ($\vec{p} = m\vec{v}$) of a body is directly proportional to the external force applied on the body and this change takes place always in the direction of the applied force,** *i.e.*,

$$\vec{F} \propto \frac{d\vec{p}}{dt}$$

or

$$\vec{F} = k\frac{d\vec{p}}{dt} = k\frac{d}{dt}(m\vec{v})$$

$$= km\left(\frac{d\vec{v}}{dt}\right) = km\vec{a}$$

where $\frac{d\vec{v}}{dt} = \vec{a}$, which is called acceleration of the

Force can be defined in such a way that $k = 1$, then Newton's second law is written as

$$\vec{F} = m\frac{d\vec{v}}{dt} = m\vec{a}$$

- **Newton's III law:** To every action, there is always an equal and opposite reaction. The action and reaction act on different bodies, so they never cancel each other.

$$\vec{F}_{AB} = -\vec{F}_{BA}$$

$\vec{F}_{AB}$ = Force exerted on A by B

$\vec{F}_{BA}$ = Force exerted on B by A

(i) **Principle of conservation of linear momentum:** From this principle, in an isolated system, the vector sum of the linear momentum of all the bodies of the system is conserved and is unaffected due to their mutual action and reaction. The total linear momentum of all the bodies in the system is given by

$$\vec{p} = m_1\vec{v}_1 + m_2\vec{v}_2 + ... + m_n\vec{v}_n = M\vec{v}_{c.m} = \text{constant}$$

where, M is the total mass of the system and $\vec{v}_{c.m}$ is the velocity of the centre of mass of the system.

(ii) **Rocket propulsion:** The propulsion of a rocket is based on the principle of conservation of linear momentum of Newton's third law of motion.

Scan to know more about this topic

The Rocket Equation

Suppose,

M_0 = Initial mass of rocket,

$\frac{\Delta M}{\Delta t}$ = Rate of ejection of fuel,

M = Mass of rocket at any instant,

$\vec{v}$ = Relative velocity of ejected gases w.r.t. rocket.

Then, thrust on the rocket in the absence of gravity

$$= \frac{\Delta M}{\Delta t} \times \vec{v}$$

Acceleration of the rocket in the absence of gravity

$$= \frac{\Delta M}{\Delta t} \times \frac{\vec{v}}{M}$$

Thrust on the rocket in the presence of gravity,

$$\vec{F} = \frac{\Delta M}{\Delta t} \times \vec{v} - M\vec{g}$$

Acceleration of the rocket in the presence of gravity,

$$\vec{a} = \frac{\Delta M}{\Delta t} \times \frac{\vec{v}}{M} - \vec{g}$$

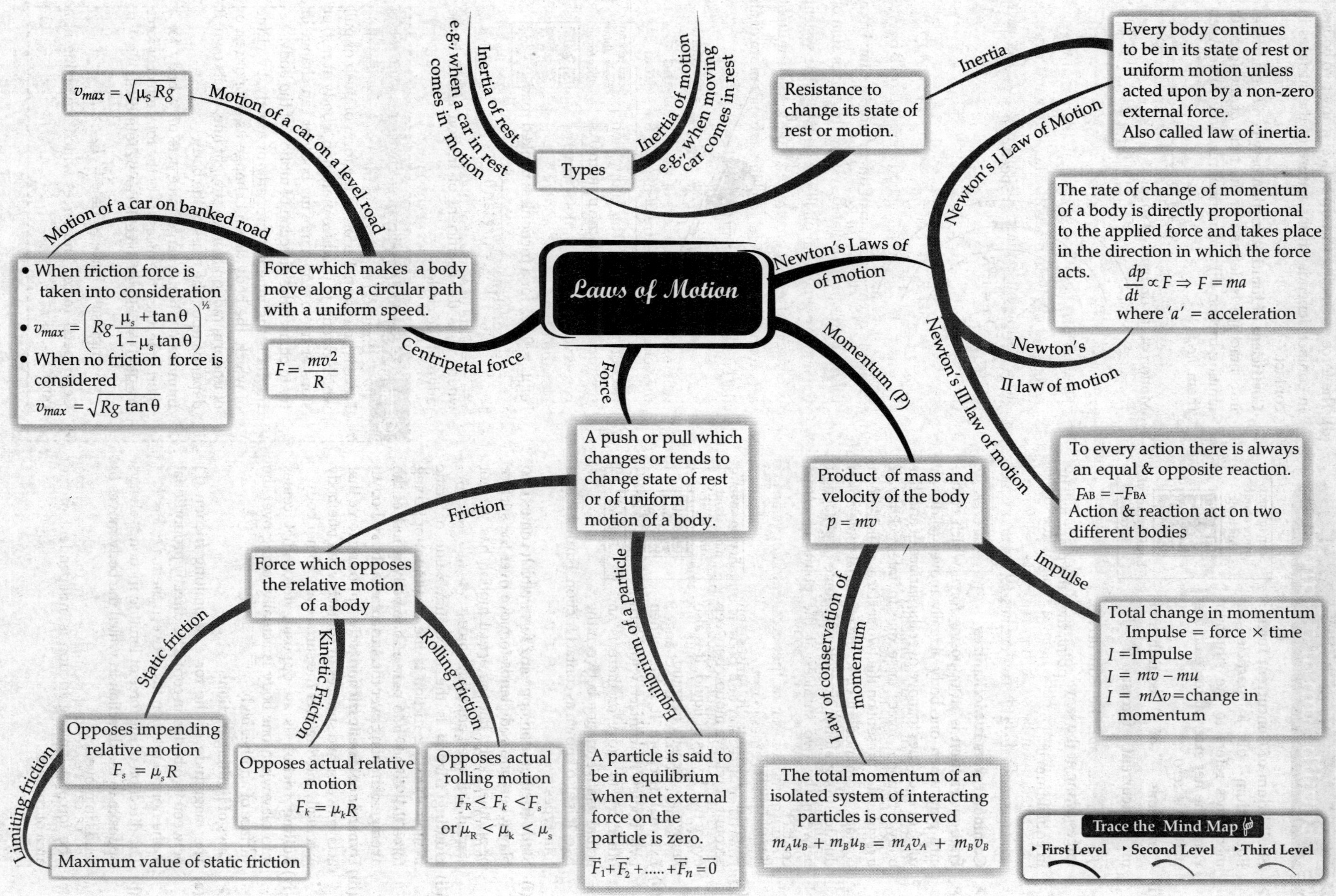
Laws of Motion
Newton's Laws of motion
Newton's I Law of Motion
Every body continues to be in its state of rest or uniform motion unless acted upon by a non-zero external force. Also called law of inertia.
Inertia
Resistance to change its state of rest or motion.
Types
Inertia of rest
e.g., when a car in rest comes in motion
Inertia of motion
e.g., when moving car comes in rest
Newton's II law of motion
The rate of change of momentum of a body is directly proportional to the applied force and takes place in the direction in which the force acts. $\frac{dp}{dt} \propto F \Rightarrow F = ma$
where 'a' = acceleration
Newton's III law of motion
To every action there is always an equal & opposite reaction.
$F_{AB} = -F_{BA}$
Action & reaction act on two different bodies
Momentum (P)
Product of mass and velocity of the body
$p = mv$
Impulse
Total change in momentum
Impulse = force × time
I = Impulse
$I = mv - mu$
$I = m\Delta v$ = change in momentum
Law of conservation of momentum
The total momentum of an isolated system of interacting particles is conserved
$m_A u_B + m_B u_B = m_A v_A + m_B v_B$
Force
A push or pull which changes or tends to change state of rest or of uniform motion of a body.
Equilibrium of a particle
A particle is said to be in equilibrium when net external force on the particle is zero.
$\overline{F_1} + \overline{F_2} + ... + \overline{F_n} = \overline{0}$
Friction
Force which opposes the relative motion of a body
Static friction
Opposes impending relative motion
$F_s = \mu_s R$
Limiting friction
Maximum value of static friction
Kinetic Friction
Opposes actual relative motion
$F_k = \mu_k R$
Rolling friction
Opposes actual rolling motion
$F_R < F_k < F_s$
or $\mu_R < \mu_k < \mu_s$
Centripetal force
Force which makes a body move along a circular path with a uniform speed.
$F = \frac{mv^2}{R}$
Motion of a car on a level road
$v_{max} = \sqrt{\mu_s Rg}$
Motion of a car on banked road
• When friction force is taken into consideration
• $v_{max} = \left(Rg \frac{\mu_s + \tan\theta}{1 - \mu_s \tan\theta}\right)^{1/2}$
• When no friction force is considered
$v_{max} = \sqrt{Rg \tan\theta}$
Trace the Mind Map
First Level
Second Level
Third Level

Equilibrium of a Particle

- **Equilibrium of Concurrent forces:** Equilibrium of a particle in mechanics refers to the situation when the net external force on the particle is zero.

Scan to know more about this topic

Equilibrium of Forces

(i) Conditions of equilibrium of concurrent forces: If $\vec{F_1}$, $\vec{F_2}$, $\vec{F_3}$ ...... are the concurrent forces acting at the same point, then the point will be in equilibrium if

$$\vec{F_1} + \vec{F_2} + \vec{F_3} + ... = \vec{0}$$

- **Common Forces in Mechanizes**
- **Friction: Friction** is an opposing force which comes into play when one body actually moves (slides or rolls) or even tries to move over the surface of another body. Frictional forces arise due to interlocking of irregularities present on the two surfaces which are in contact. From modern view, the frictional force arises due to strong atomic or molecular force of attraction between the two surfaces at the points of actual contact.

It is of two types:

(a) Internal friction: It arises on account of relative motion between every two layers of liquid. It is also known as viscosity of liquid.

Scan to know more about this topic

Friction

(b) External friction: It arises when two bodies in contact with each other try to move or there is an actual relative motion between the two. It is also known as contact friction. Further it is of four types:

(i) **Static friction** is an opposing force which comes into play when one body tends to move over the surface of another body, but the actual motion has yet not started. It is a self-adjusting force.

(ii) **Limiting friction** is the maximum value of static friction. Limiting friction is the maximum opposing force that comes into play of one body is just at the average of moving over the surface of another body.

(iii) **Dynamic or kinetic friction** is the opposing force that acts between two surfaces in contact when one body is actually moving over the surface of another body.

(iv) **Rolling friction** is an opposing force that comes into play when one body is actually rolling over the surface of another body.

- **Laws of limiting friction:**

(a) The magnitude of the force of limiting friction (F) between two bodies in contact is directly proportional to the normal reaction (R) between them, *i.e.,* $F \propto R$.

(b) The direction of the force of limiting friction is always opposite to the direction in which the body moves or tends to move.

(c) The force of limiting friction is independent of the area of contact.

(d) The force of limiting friction between any two bodies in contact depends on the nature of the surfaces in contact.

- **Coefficient of limiting friction** between two surfaces in contact (μ) is defined as the ratio of the force of limiting friction (F) and normal reaction (R) between them, *i.e.,*

$$\mu = F/R$$

- **Motion of car on banked road:**

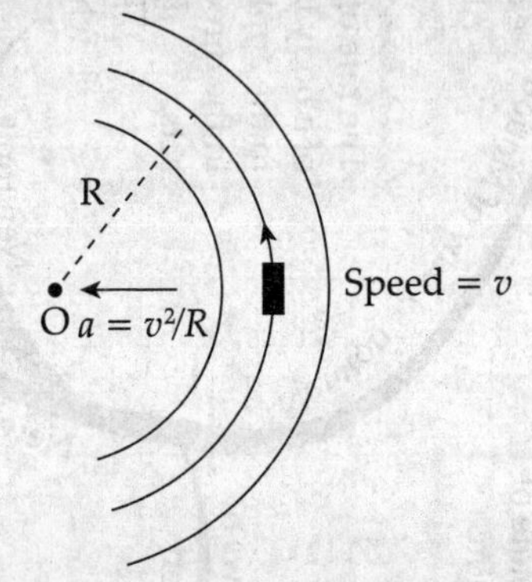

$$V_{max} = \sqrt{\mu_s Rg}$$

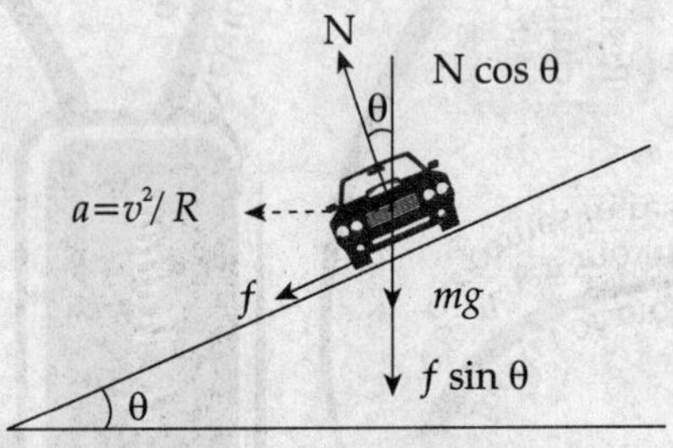

$$V_{max} = \left[\frac{rg(\mu_s + \tan\theta)}{1 - \mu_s \tan\theta}\right]$$

For $\mu_s = 0$ i.e., for a frictionless banked road

$$V_{max} = \sqrt{rg\tan\theta}$$

where, μ_s is the coefficient of friction and R is the radius of the circle.

Key Words

- **Force** is an external effort in the form of push or pull which can try to produce motion in a body at rest, or stops or try to stop a moving body or can change or try to change the direction of motion of the body.
- **Inertia** is the inherent property of a body, by virtue of which, the body doesn't change its state of rest or of uniform motion along a straight line, on its own. It depends upon the mass of the body.
- **Impulse :** When a large force acts on a body for a short time, then the measure of the total effect of force is called impulse of force. It can be found out

$$\text{Impulse} = \text{Force} \times \text{Time} = \vec{F}_{av} \times \Delta t$$

- **Centripetal force:** The forces which are acting at a point.

- **Contact force arises due to contact with some other object:** solid or fluid.
- **Non-contact** force are forces experienced by an object without actual contact. e.g., force of gravity of earth.
- **Centripetal force** is the force required to move a body uniformly in a circle. This force acts along the radius and towards the centre of the circle.
- **Angle of friction** is the angle in which the direction of resultant of the force of friction and normal reaction makes with the direction of normal reaction. It is represented by θ.

$$\tan\theta = \mu$$

- **Angle of repose** is the maximum angle of inclination of a plane with the horizontal, at which the body placed on the plane is just in limiting equilibrium.
- **Centrifugal force** is a force that arises when a body is moving actually along a circular path, by virtue of tendency of the body to regain its natural straight line path.

Key Formulae

- $\vec{R} = \vec{A} + \vec{B}$
- **Linear Momentum :** $\vec{p} = m\vec{v}$
- Force $= \dfrac{d\vec{p}}{dt} = m\,\vec{a}$
- **Impulse = Force × time**

$$\vec{I} = \vec{F} \times t = m(\vec{v} - \vec{u})$$

- **Principle of Conservation of Linear Momentum**

$$m_1\vec{v}_1 + m_2\vec{v}_2 + ... + m_n\vec{v}_n = \text{Constant}$$

- **Recoil velocity of gun** $(\vec{v}_2) = \dfrac{-m_1\vec{v}_1}{m_2}$

m_2 = Mass of gun

m_1 = Mass of bullet

v_1 = Velocity of bullet

- **Angle of friction,** $\tan\theta = \mu$.
- **Angle of repose,** $\mu = \dfrac{F}{R} = \tan\theta$.
- **Centripetal force** $= \dfrac{mv^2}{r} = mr\omega^2$.

$$= mr(2\pi\nu)^2.$$

- $\tan\theta = v^2/rg$.
- $\tan\theta = \dfrac{h}{\sqrt{b^2 - h^2}} = v^2/rg$.

h = **height between outer edge and inner edge**

- b = **breadth of road**
- Maximum speed of car on circular banked road

$$= v_{max} = \left[\frac{rg(\mu_s + \tan\theta)}{(1 - \mu_s \tan\theta)}\right]^{1/2}$$

Key Formulae

- **At any position of angular displacement θ along a vertical circle**

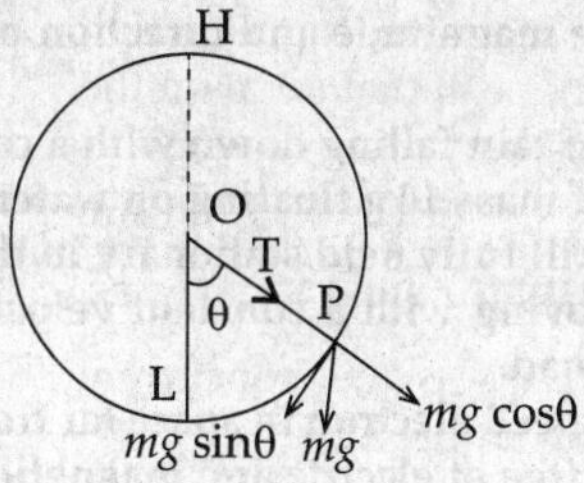

$$T = \frac{mv^2}{r} + mg\cos\theta.$$

- **At lowest point of vertical circle,**

$$\theta = 0°;\ T_L = \frac{mv_L^2}{r} + mg.$$

- **At highest point of vertical circle,**

$$\theta = 180°$$

$$T_H = \frac{mv_H^2}{r} - mg.$$

- **Minimum velocity at highest point, at H**

$$v_H = \sqrt{gr}$$

- **Minimum velocity at lowest point, at L**

$$v_L = \sqrt{5gr}$$

- **When,** $\theta = 90°$

$$v = \sqrt{3gr}$$

- **Height through which a body should fall for looping the vertical loop**

$$h = 5r/2.$$

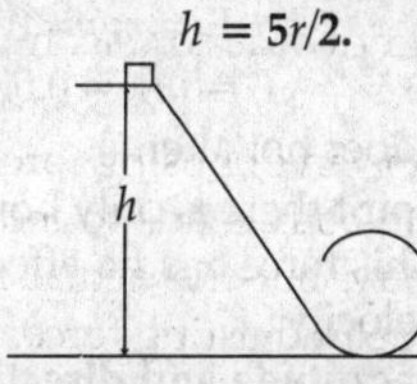

Mnemonics

Newton's Laws of Motion: Newton, Newton don't kick cow She may move ahead little bit now Newton hears her MAAA sound Cow gives Newton a kick rebound

Interpretation: 1st two lines of the rhyme depicts the 1st law of motion

Newton's 1st law: A body continues its state of rest or state of motion unless it is acted upon by an unbalanced force.

3rd line depicts the 2nd law of motion

Newton's 2nd law: F = ma

Last line depicts the 3rd law of motion

Newton's 3rd law: Every action has its equal and opposite reaction.

NCERT CORNER

Q. 1. Give the magnitude and direction of the net force acting on
(a) a drop of rain falling down with a constant speed.
(b) a cork of mass 10 g floating on water.
(c) a kite skill fully held stationary in the sky.
(d) a car moving with a constant velocity of 30 km/h on a rough road.
(e) a high-speed electron in space far from all material objects, and free of electric and magnetic fields.
[For Simplicity in numerical calculations, take $g = 10$ ms^{-2}] [NCERT Ex., Q. 4.1, Page 68]

Ans. (a) Acceleration, $a = 0$, net force $F = ma = 0$

(b) Net force, $F = 0$, as its weight is being balanced by the upthrust.

(c) From Newton's I law, as kite is stationary,
So, net force, $F = 0$.

(d) As, velocity v constant
$\therefore$ acceleration, $a = 0$.
$F = ma = 0$.

(e) Net force, $F = 0$ because there is no fields.

Q. 2. A pebble of mass 0.05 kg is thrown vertically upwards. Give the direction and magnitude of the new force on the pebble:
(a) during its upward motion.
(b) during its downward motion.
(c) at the highest point where it is momentarily at rest. Do your answer alter if the pebble was thrown at an angle of 45° with horizontal direction Ignore air resistance ? [NCERT Ex., Q. 4.2, Page 68]

Ans. (a) Force $F = mg = 0.05 \times 9.8 = 0.49 \text{ N} \downarrow$

(b) In this situation also
$F = mg = 0.05 \times 9.8 = 0.49 \text{ N} \downarrow$

(c) Again, $F = mg = 0.05 \times 9.8 = 0.49 \text{ N} \downarrow$

No, the answer does not alter.
At the highest point there is only horizontal component of velocity and this force has no effect on the horizontal component of velocity.

Q. 3. Give the magnitude and direction of the net force acting on a stone of mass 0.1 kg.
(a) just after it is dropped from the window of a stationary train.
(b) just after it is dropped from the window of a train running at a constant velocity of 36 km/h.
(c) just after it is dropped from the window of a train accelerating with ms^{-2}.
(d) lying on the floor of a train which is accelerating with 1 ms^{-2} the stone being at rest relative to the train. Neglect air resistance throughout. [NCERT Ex., Q. 4.3, Page 68]

Ans. (a) Net force, $F = mg$.
$= 0.1 \times 10 = 1.0 \text{ N}$
Direction–vertically downwards.

(b) Speed of train is constant, so acceleration = 0.
No force acts on stone because of this motion.
$\therefore$ Force on stone is same i.e., 1.0 N.

(c) As, acceleration = 1 m/s^2
$\therefore F_1 = ma = 0.1 \times 1 = 0.1 \text{ N}$, horizontal
Net force on stone –
$F = mg = 0.1 \times 10$ (F_1 is not considered as it stops acting as stone is released)
$= 1 \text{ N}$
It is vertically downwards.

(d) Stone is lying on the floor of train.
So, acceleration is same for stone and train.
$\therefore F = ma = 0.1 \times 1 = 0.1 \text{ N}$
along the direction of motion of the train.

Q. 4. One end of a string of length l is connected to particle of mass m and the other to a small peg on smooth horizontal table. If the particle moves in a circle with speed v, the net force on the particle (directed towards the centre) is: (T is the tension in the string)

(i) $T = \dfrac{mv^2}{l}$ **(ii) $T - \dfrac{mv^2}{l}$**

(iii) $T + \dfrac{mv^2}{l}$ **(iv) 0**

[NCERT Ex., Q. 4.4, Page 69]

Ans. (i) The net force on the particle is T because tension T provides the necessary centripetal force, i.e.,

$$T = \frac{mv^2}{l}$$

Q. 5. A constant retarding force of 50 N is applied to a body of mass 20 kg moving initially with a speed of 15 ms^{-1}. How long does the body take to stop ? [NCERT Ex., Q. 4.5, Page 69]

Ans. Force $F = ma$

$$a = \frac{F}{m} = -\frac{50}{20}$$
$$= -2.5 \text{ ms}^{-2}$$

Using, $v = u + at$
When, $u = 15 \text{ ms}^{-1}, v = 0$
We get, $0 = 15 - 2.5 \times t$

$$t = \frac{15}{2.5}$$

or $t = 6$ s.

Q. 6. A constant force acting on a body of mass 3 kg changes its speed from 2 ms^{-1} to 3.5 ms^{-1} in 25 s. The direction of motion of the body remains unchanged. What is the magnitude and direction of the force ? [NCERT Ex., Q. 4.6, Page 69]

Ans. **Step 1.** Using $v = u + at$
When $v = 3.5 \text{ ms}^{-1}, u = 2\text{ms}^{-1}, t = 25$ s
We get, $3.5 = 2 + a \times 25$

$$a = \frac{3.5-2}{25}$$
$$= 0.06 \text{ ms}^{-2}$$

Step 2. Force $= m \times a = 3 \times 0.06$
$= 0.18$ N acting in the direction of motion of the body.

Q. 7. A body of mass 5 kg is acted upon by two perpendicular forces, 6 N and 8 N. Give the magnitude and directon of the accleration of the body. [NCERT Ex., Q. 4.7, Page 69]

Ans.

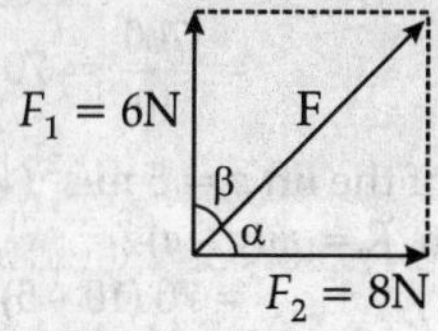

Given situation is shown in figure

$$m = 5 \text{ kg}$$

$$F = \sqrt{F_1^2 + F_2^2} = \sqrt{6^2 + 8^2} = 10 \text{ N}$$

∴ Acceleration of body,

$$a = \frac{F}{m} = \frac{10}{5} = 2\text{m/s}^2$$

direction of acceleration

$$\tan\alpha = \frac{F_1}{F_2} = \frac{6}{8} = \frac{3}{4}$$

$\therefore \alpha = \tan^{-1}\left(\frac{3}{4}\right)$ with respect to 8 N of force.

$$\tan\beta = \frac{F_2}{F_1} = \frac{8}{6} = \frac{4}{3}$$

$\therefore \beta = \tan^{-1}\left(\frac{4}{3}\right)$ with respect to 6 N of force.

Q. 8. The driver of a three wheeler moving with a speed of 36 km/h sees a child standing in the middle of the road and brings his vehicle to rest in 4 s, just in time to save the child. What is the average retarding force on the vehicle ? The mass of the three wheeler is 400 kg and the mass of the driver is 65 kg. [NCERT Ex., Q. 4.8, Page 69]

Ans. Using, $v = u + at$

When, $u = 36 \text{ kmh}^{-1}$

$$= \frac{36 \times 1000}{3600} \text{ m/s} = 10 \text{ ms}^{-1}$$

$$v = 0, t = 4 \text{ s}$$

We get, $0 = 10 + a \times 4$

or $a = -2.5 \text{ ms}^{-2}$

Total mass of the driver and the three wheeler,

$$M = 65 + 400 = 465 \text{ kg}$$

Retarding force $F = 465 \times 2.5 \text{ N} = 1162.5 \text{ N}$

Q. 9. A rocket with a lift-off mass 20,000 kg is blasted upwards with as initial acceleration of 5 ms^{-2}, Calculate the initial the thrust (force) of the blast. [NCERT Ex., Q. 4.9, Page 69]

Ans. Here, total acceleration

$$a' = (g + a)$$

or $a' = (9.8 + 5) = 14.8 \text{ ms}^{-2}$

∴ Thrust of blast of rocket

$$= m \times a' = 20000 \times 14.8$$

$$= 2.96 \times 10^5 \text{ N}$$

Q. 10. A body of mass 0.40 kg moving initially with a constant speed of 10 ms^{-1} to the north is subject to a constant force of 8.0 N directed towards the south for 30 s. Take the instant the force is applied to be $t = 0$, the position of the body at that time to be $x = 0$ and predict its position at t = –5 s, 25 s, 100 s. [NCERT Ex., Q. 4.10, Page 69]

Ans. Mass of the body, $m = 0.40$ kg

Initial speed of the body, $u = 10$ m/s due north

Force acting on the body, $F = -8.0$ N

Acceleration produced in the body,

$$a = \frac{F}{m} = \frac{-8.0}{0.40} = -20\text{m/s}^2$$

At $t = -5$ s

Acceleration, $a' = 0$ and $u = 10$ m/s

$$s = ut + \frac{1}{2}a't^2$$

$$= 10 \times (-5) = -50 \text{ m}$$

At $t = 25$ s

Acceleration, $a'' = -20$ m/s^2 and $u = 10$ m/s

$$s' = ut' + \frac{1}{2}a''t^2$$

$$= 10 \times 25 + \frac{1}{2} \times (-20) \times (25)^2$$

$$= 250 + 6250 = -6000m$$

At $t = 100$ s

For $0 \le t \le 30s$

$$a = -20 \text{ m/s}^2$$

$$u = 10 \text{ m/s}$$

$$s_1 = ut + \frac{1}{2}a''t^2$$

$$= 10 \times 30 + \frac{1}{2} \times (-20) \times (30)^2$$

$$= 300 - 9000 = -8700\text{m}$$

For $30 \text{ s} < t \le 100s$

As per the first equation of motion, for $t = 30$ s, final velocity is given as: $v = u + at$

$$= 10 + (-20) \times 30 = -590 \text{ m/s}$$

Velocity of the body after 30 s = –590 m/s

For motion between 30 s to 100 s, i.e., in 70 s:

$$s_2 = vt + \frac{1}{2}a''t^2$$

$$= -590 \times 70 = -41300 \text{ m}$$

∴ Total distance, $s'' = s_1 + s_2$

$$= -87000 - 41300 = -50000 \text{ m}$$

Q. 11. A truck starts from rest and accelerates uniformly at 2.0 ms^{-2}. At $t = 10$ s, a stone is dropped by a person standing on the top of the truck (6 m high from the ground). What are the (a) velocity, and (b) acceleration of the stone at t = 11 s? (Neglect air resistance.) [NCERT Ex., Q. 4.11, Page 68]

Ans. (a) Initial velocity of the truck, $u = 0$

Acceleration, $a = 2$ *m/s^2*

Time $t = 10$ s

As per the first equation of motion, final velocity is given as:

$$v = u + at$$

$$= 0 + 2 \times 10 = 20 \text{ m/s}$$

The final velocity of the truck and hence, of the stone is 20 m/s.

At $t = 11$ s, the horizontal component (v_x) of velocity, in the absence of air resistance, remains unchanged, i.e.,

$v_x = 20$ *m / s*

The vertical component (v_y) of velocity of the stone is given by the first equation of motion as:

$$v_y = u + a_y \Delta t$$

Where, $\Delta t = 11 - 10 = 1$ s and $a = g = 10 \text{ m/s}^2$

$\therefore v_y = 0 + 10 \times 1 = 10$ m/s

The resultant velocity (v) of the stone is given as:

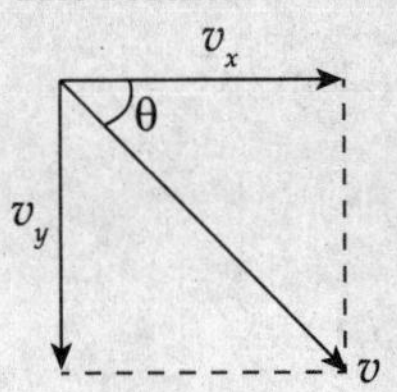

$$v = \sqrt{v_x^2 + v_y^2}$$
$$= \sqrt{20^2 + 10^2} = \sqrt{400 + 100}$$
$$= \sqrt{500} = 22.36 \text{ m/s}$$

(b) Let θ be the angle made by the resultant velocity with the horizontal component of velocity, v_x

$$\therefore \quad \tan\theta = \left(\frac{v_y}{v_x}\right)$$
$$\theta = \tan^{-1}\left(\frac{10}{20}\right)$$
$$= \tan^{-1}(0.5)$$
$$= 26.57°$$

When the stone is dropped from the truck, the horizontal force acting on it becomes zero. However, the stone continues to move under the influence of gravity. Hence, the acceleration of the stone is $10\,m/s^2$ and it acts vertically downward.

Q. 12. A bob of mass 0.1 kg hung from the ceiling of a room by a string 2 m long is set into oscillation. The speed of the bob at its mean position is 1 ms^{-1}. What is the trajectory of the bob if the string is cut when the bob is:

(a) at one of its extreme position.

(b) at its mean position. [NCERT Ex., Q. 4.12, Page 69]

Ans. (a) We know that at each extreme position, the instantaneous velocity of the bob is zero. If the string is cut at the extreme position, it is under the action of 'g' only, hence, the bob will fall vertically downwards.

(b) When the bob is at the mean position, it is affected by gravity. At mean position of the bob is having velocity of 1 ms^{-1} along the tangent to the arc which is in the horizontal direction. If the string is cut at the mean position, the bob will behave as a horizontal projectile. Hence, it will follow a parabolic path.

Q. 13. A man of mass 70 kg stands on a weighing scale in a lift which is moving:

(a) upward with uniform speed of 10 ms^{-2} ?

(b) downward with a uniform acceleration of 5 ms^{-2} ?

(c) upward with uniform acceleration of 5 ms^{-2}. What would be the readings on the scale in each case ?

(d) What would be the reading if the lift mechanism failed and it came down freely under gravity ?

[NCERT Ex., Q. 4.13, Page 69]

Ans. Given, mass of man (m) = 70 kg

In each case the weighing scale will read the reaction R, i.e. the apparent weight.

(a) As lift is moving upward with a uniform speed, therefore its acceleration $a = 0$

$\therefore$ Normal reaction $w = R = mg$
$= 70 \times 10$ N
$= 700$ N

w acts vertically downward and R acts vertically upwards.

$\therefore$ Reading on weighing scale

$$= \frac{700}{10} = 70 \text{ kg}$$

(b) Acceleration of the lift $a = 5$ m/s^2 (↓)

$\therefore$ Normal reaction, $R = m(g - a)$
$= 70\,(10 - 5)$ N
$= 70 \times 5$ N $= 350$ N

$\therefore$ Reading on weighing scale

$$= \frac{350 \text{ N}}{10\,\text{m/s}^2}$$
$$= 35 \text{ kg.}$$

(c) Acceleration of the lift $a = 5$ m/s^2 (↑)

$\therefore$ Normal reaction $R = m(g + a)$
$= 70\,(10 + 5)$
$= 1050$ N

$\therefore$ Reading on weighing scale

$$= \frac{1050}{10 \text{ m/s}^2} = 105 \text{ kg.}$$

(d) Acceleration of the lift when it is falling freely under gravity

$$a = g\,(\downarrow)$$

$\therefore$ Normal reaction $R = m(g - a)$
$= m(g - g) = 0$

$\therefore$ Reading on weighing scale = 0

This is the state of weightlessness.

Q. 14. Figure below shows the position-time graph of a particle of mass 4 kg. What is the

(a) force on the particle for $t < 0$, $t > 4$ s, $0 < t < 4$ s?

(b) impulse at $t = 0$ and $t = 4$ s ? (Consider one dimensional motion only.)

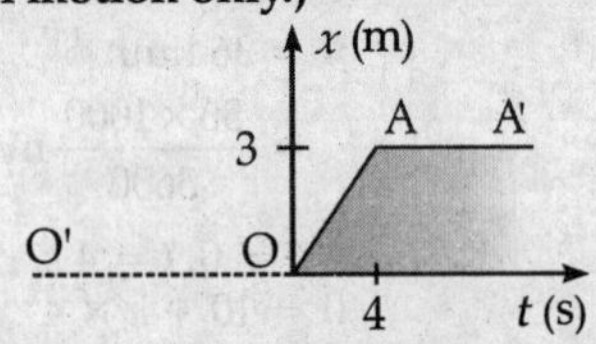

[NCERT Ex., Q. 4.14, Page 69]

Ans. Mass of particle = m = 4 kg

(a) (1) For $t < 0$, the position-time graph is O'O which means displacement of the particles is zero, i.e., the particle is at rest. Therefore, force on the particle must be zero, i.e.,

$$F = 0$$

(2) For $t > 4$ s, the position-time graph AA' is parallel to time axis. Therefore the particle remains at a distance of 3 m from the origin, and, it is at rest. Hence, no force is acting on the particle for this interval, i.e., $F = 0$.

(3) For $0 < t < 4$ s, the particle is changing its position continuously. The position-time graph (OA) during this interval represents uniform motion of the particle, i.e., it moves with a constant speed and thus its acceleration is zero. Therefore

$$F = ma$$
$$= 0 \text{ during this interval}$$

(b) Impulse at $t = 0$

We know that,

Impulse= change in momentum
$= mv - mu$
$= m(v - u)$ ...(i)

Hence, $u = 0$ as the particle is at rest before $t = 0$.

After $t = 0$, the particle has a constant velocity v where v = slope of line OA = velocity from point O to point A

$$= \frac{3\text{ m}}{4\text{ s}} = 0.75\text{ ms}^{-1} \quad ...(ii)$$

From equation (i) and (ii), we get

$$\text{impulse} = 4\,(0.75 - 0)$$

$$= 4 \times \frac{3}{4} = 3\text{ kg ms}^{-1}$$

Impulse at $t = 4$ s

Before $t = 4$ s, the particle has a constant velocity

$$u = \frac{3}{4}\text{ ms}^{-1}$$

After $t = 4$ s, the particle is at rest, i.e., $v = 0$

∴ By definition of impulse, we get

$$\text{Impulse} = mv - mu$$

$$= m\,(v - u)$$

$$= 4\,(0 - \frac{3}{4})$$

$$= -3\text{ kg ms}^{-1}.$$

Q. 15. Two bodies A and B of masses 10 kg and 20 kg respectively kept on a smooth, horizontal surface are tied to the ends of a light string. A horizontal force F = 600 N is applied to (i) A, (ii) B along the direction of string. What is the tension in the string in each case? [NCERT Ex., Q. 4.15, Page 69]

Ans. Given: $F = 600$ N

Suppose $m_1 = 10$ kg

and $m_2 = 20$ kg

be the masses lying on a frictionless horizontal table.

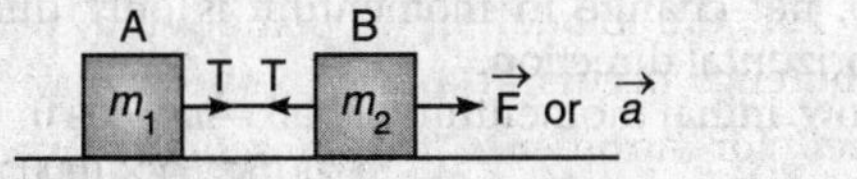

Suppose T be the tension in the string and 'a' be the acceleration of the system, in the direction of force applied.

(i) **If the force is applied on lighter mass i.e. A,**

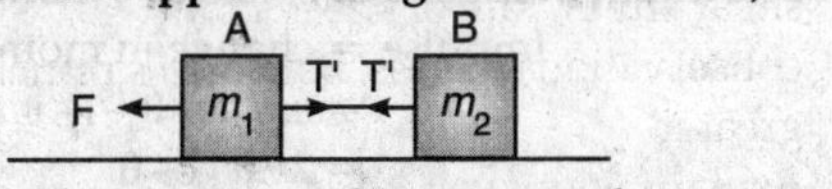

Suppose T be the tension in the string in this case

Then, equations of motion of A and B are

$$F - T' = m_1 a \quad ...(iii)$$

and $$T' = m_2 a \quad ...(iv)$$

Equation (iii) and (iv) gives

$$\frac{F - T}{T} = \frac{m_1 a}{m_2 a}$$

or $$\frac{F}{T} - 1 = \frac{m_1}{m_2} = \frac{10}{20} = \frac{1}{2}$$

or $$\frac{F}{T} = 1 + \frac{1}{2} = \frac{3}{2}$$

or $$T' = \frac{2}{3}F = \frac{2}{3} \times 600$$

$$= 400\text{ N}$$

(ii) **If force is applied on the heavier mass i.e., B**

Then, equations of motion of A and B are

$$m_1 a = T \quad ..(i)$$

$$m_2 a = F - T \quad ...(ii)$$

Dividing equation (ii) by equation (i), we get

$$\frac{m_2}{m_1} = \frac{F - T}{T} = \frac{F}{T} - 1$$

or $$\frac{20}{10} = \frac{F}{T} - 1$$

or $$\frac{F}{T'} = 2 + 1 = 3$$

or $$T = \frac{F}{3} = \frac{600}{3}$$

$$= 200\text{ N}$$

Q. 16. Two masses 8 kg and 12 kg are connected at the two ends of a light inextensible string that goes over a frictionless pulley. Find the acceleration of the masses and the tension in the string when the masses are released. [NCERT Ex., Q. 4.16, Page 70]

Ans. Suppose m_1 and m_2 be the masses suspended at the ends of a light inextensible string passing over the pulley.

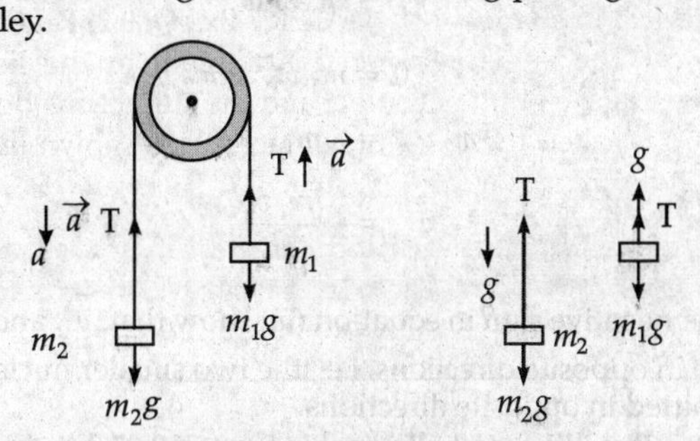

∴ $m_1 = 8$ kg, $m_2 = 12$ kg

Suppose, T = tension in the string

a = common acceleration with which m_1 moves upward and m_2 moves downward

The equations of motion of m_1 and m_2 are given by

$$T - m_1 g = m_1 a \quad ...(i)$$

and $$m_2 g - T = m_2 a \quad ...(ii)$$

Adding equations (i) and (ii),

$$(m_2 - m_1)\,g = (m_1 + m_2)\,a$$

$$a = \frac{(m_2 - m_1)g}{m_1 + m_2} \quad ...(iii)$$

∴ From equations (i) and (iii),

$$T = m_1 g + m_1 \frac{(m_2 - m_1)g}{m_1 + m_2}$$

or $$T = \frac{m_1 g}{m_1 + m_2}(m_1 + m_2 + m_2 - m_1)$$

or $$T = \frac{2m_1 m_2}{m_1 + m_2}\,g \quad ...(iv)$$

Putting $m_1 = 8$ kg and $m_2 = 12$ kg and $g = 10\text{ ms}^{-2}$, in equation (iii) and (iv), we get

$$a = \frac{(12 - 8)}{(8 + 12)} \times 10$$

or $$= \frac{4}{20} \times 10 = 2\text{ms}^{-2}$$

From eq. (i) $$T = m_1 a + m_1 g$$

$$= 8 \times 2 + 8 \times 10 = 96\text{ N}$$

Q. 17. A nucleus is at rest in the laboratory frame of reference. Show that if it disintegrates into two smaller nuclei, the products must be emitted in opposite directions. [NCERT Ex., Q. 4.17, Page 70]

Ans. Suppose m = mass of the nucleus at rest

u = its initial velocity = 0 as it is at rest

Also suppose m_1, m_2 be the masses of the two smaller nuclei also called product nuclei and $\vec{v}_1$, $\vec{v}_2$ be their respective velocities.

When $\vec{p}_i$ and $\vec{p}_f$ be the initial and final momentum of the nucleus and the two nuclei respectively, then

$$\vec{p}_i = m\vec{u} = 0 \quad ...(i)$$

and
$$\vec{p}_f = m_1\vec{v}_1 + m_2\vec{v}_2 \quad ...(ii)$$

Now according to the law of conservation of linear momentum, we know that

$$\vec{p}_i = \vec{p}_f$$

$$\Rightarrow \quad 0 = m_1\vec{v}_1 + m_2\vec{v}_2$$

$$\Rightarrow \quad m_2\vec{v}_2 = -m_1\vec{v}_1$$

$$\Rightarrow \quad \vec{v}_2 = -\frac{m_1\vec{v}_1}{m_2} \quad ...(iii)$$

The negative sign in equation (iii) show that $\vec{v}_1$ and $\vec{v}_2$ are in opposite directions, i.e., the two smaller nuclei are emitted in opposite directions.

Q. 18. Two billiard balls each of mass 0.05 kg moving in opposite directions with speed 6 ms^{-1} collide and rebound with the same speed. What is the impulse imparted to each ball due to the other ? [NCERT Ex., Q. 4.18, Page 70]

Ans. Given: Mass of each ball, m = 0.05 kg

Speed of each ball, v = 6 ms^{-1}

∴ Initial momentum of each ball

$$= m\vec{v}$$
$$= (0.05)\,(6)\text{ kg ms}^{-1}$$
$$= 0.30\text{ kg ms}^{-1}$$

As after collision, the direction of velocity of each ball is reversed on rebounding.

∴ Final momentum of each ball will be

$$\vec{p}_f = m(-\vec{v})$$
$$= 0.05\,(-6)$$
$$= -0.30\text{ kg ms}^{-1}$$

∴ Impulse imparted to each ball

$$= \vec{p}_f - \vec{p}_i$$

change in momentum of each ball

$$= -0.30 - (0.30)$$
$$= -0.60\text{ kg ms}^{-1}$$

or magnitude of impulse imparted by one ball due to collision with the other – 0.6 kg ms^{-1}. The two impulses are opposite in directions.

Q. 19. A shell of mass 0.02 kg is fired by a gun of mass 100 kg. If the muzzle speed of the shell is 80 ms^{-1}, what is the recoil speed of the gun? [NCERT Ex., Q. 4.19, Page 70]

Ans. Given: mass of gun, m_g = 100 kg, mass of shell m_b = 0.02 kg, velocity of shell, v_b = 80 ms^{-1}

Total initial momentum = 0

(∵ the gun and shell have no initial velocity as they are initially at rest)

Total final momentum = momentum of bullet + momentum of gun

$$= m_bv_b + m_gv_g$$

Applying law of conservation of momentum,

$$0 = m_bv_b + m_gv_g$$

i.e.,
$$m_bv_b = -m_gv_g$$

i.e.,
$$0.02 \times 80 = -100 \times v_g$$

or
$$v_g = -\frac{0.02 \times 80}{100}$$
$$= -0.016\text{ ms}^{-1}$$

Hence, recoil speed of the gun is

$$= 0.016\text{ ms}^{-1}.$$

Q. 20. A batsman deflects a ball by an angle of 45° without changing its initial speed, which is equal to 54 kmh^{-1}. What is the impulse imparted to the ball ? Mass of the ball is 0.15 kg. [NCERT Ex., Q. 4.20, Page 70]

Ans. The ball struck by the bat is deflected back such that total angle is 45°.

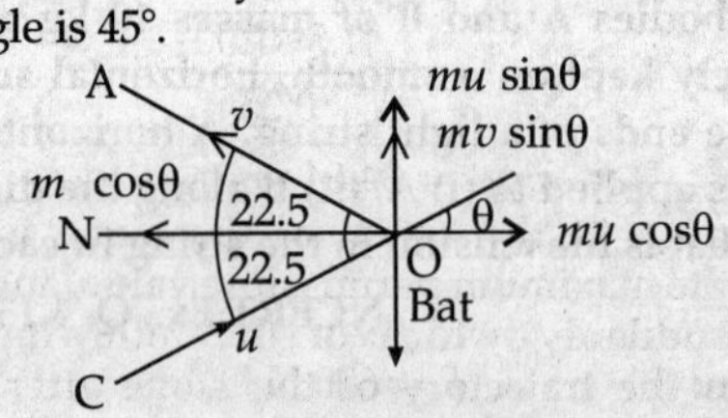

Change in momentum in vertical direction,

$$= mv\sin\theta - mu\sin\theta$$

= 0(since, $v = u$ & θ is same)

So, net change in momentum is only due to that in horizontal direction.

Now, initial momentum of ball = $mu\cos\theta$

$$= \frac{0.15 \times 54 \times 1000 \times \cos 22.5}{3600}$$

= 0.15 × 15 × 0.9239 along NO

Final momentum of ball = $mu\cos\theta$ along ON

Impulse = change in momentum

$$= mu\cos\theta - (-mu\cos\theta)$$
$$= 2mu\cos\theta$$
$$= 2 \times 0.15 \times 15 \times 0.9239$$

i.e., Impulse = 4.16 kg ms^{-1}

Q. 21. A stone of mass 0.25 kg tied to the end of a string is whirled round in a circle of radius 1.5 m with speed 40 rev./min in a horizontal plane. What is the tension in the string ? What is the maximum speed with which the stone can be whirled around if the string can withstand a maximum tension of 200 N ? [NCERT Ex., Q. 4.21, Page 70]

Ans. Frequency of revolution of stone is given by

$$f = 40\text{ rev/min} = \frac{40}{60}\text{ rev/s}$$

Mass of stone, m = 0.25 kg

Radius of circle, r = 1.5 m

By formula angular speed of the stone,

$$\omega = 2\pi f$$

or
$$\omega = 2\pi \times \frac{40}{60}$$
$$= \frac{4\pi}{3}\text{ rad s}^{-1}$$

T = tension in the string = ?

T_{max} = maximum tension in the string = 200 N

i.e., $$T = \frac{mv^2}{r} = mr\omega^2$$

or $$T = 0.25 \times 1.5 \times \left(\frac{4\pi}{3}\right)^2 \text{ N}$$

or $$T = 0.25 \times 1.5 \times \frac{16}{9} \times 9.87$$

$$(\because \pi^2 = 9.87)$$

or $$T = 6.58 \text{ N} \approx 6.6 \text{ N}$$

As the string can withstand a maximum tension of 200 N,

$\therefore$ $$T_{max} = \frac{mv^2_{max}}{r}$$

or $$v_{max} = \sqrt{\frac{rT_{max}}{m}}$$

$$= \sqrt{\frac{1.5 \times 200}{0.25}}$$

or $$v_{max} = 34.64 \text{ ms}^{-1}.$$

Q. 22. If in Q. 21 the speed of the stone is increased beyond the maximum permissible value, and the string breaks suddenly, which of the following correctly describes the trajectory of the stone after the string breaks ?

(a) The stone jerks radially outwards.

(b) The stone flies off tangentially from the instant the string breaks.

(c) The stone flies off at the angle with the tangent whose magnitude depends on the speed of particle.

[NCERT Ex., Q. 4.22, Page 70]

Ans. **(b)** Correctly describes the trajectory of the stone after the string breaks, i.e., the stone flies off tangentially from the instant the string breaks.

The velocity always acts tangentially to the circle at each point in the circular motion. At the time, the string breaks, the particle continues to move in the tangential direction according to Newton's first law of motion.

Q. 23. Explain why:

(a) a horse cannot pull a cart and run in empty space,

(b) passengers are thrown forward from their seats when a speeding bus stops suddenly,

(c) it is easier to pull a lawn mover than to push it,

(d) a cricketer moves his hands backwards when holding a catch. **[NCERT Ex., Q. 4.23, Page 70]**

Ans. **(a)** While trying to pull a cart, a horse pushes the ground backwards with a certain force at an angle. The ground offers an equal reaction in opposite direction; on the feet of the horse. The forward component of this reaction is responsible for the motion of cart.

In empty space, there is no reaction and hence horse cannot pull the cart and run.

(b) This is due to inertia of motion possessed by the passenger in a speeding bus. The lower portion of the body of passenger (which is in contact with the bus) comes to rest. But due to inertia of motion, the upper portion of the body tends to keep on moving. As a result, the passenger thrown forward.

(c) Consider the free body diagram in the two cases, the lawn mover is represented by the point O.

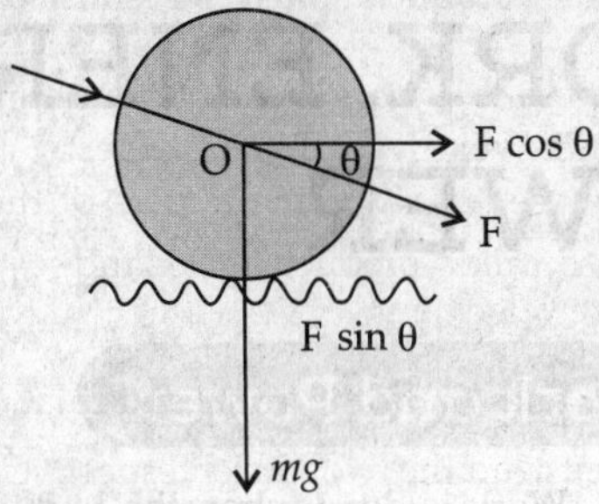

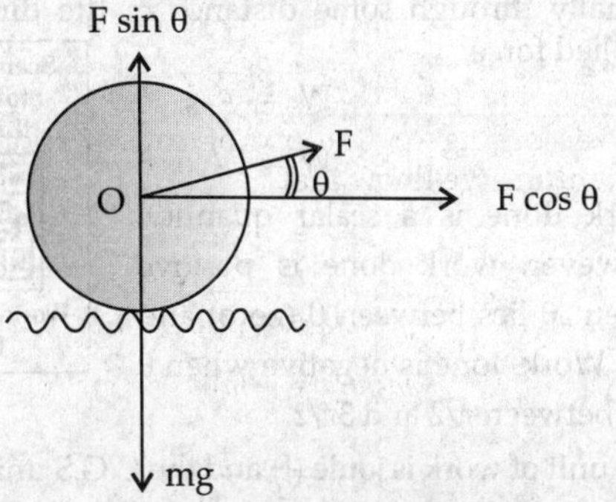

The forces acting on the lawn mover are (i) applied force F, (ii) weight of the mover W downward, (iii) force of friction acting opposite to the direction of motion, (iv) reaction of ground on the mover (R).

In case of pushing the mover, the horizontal component of push F$\cos\theta$ in forward direction and vertical component F$\sin\theta$ in downward direction. The total downward force $= W + F\sin\theta$.

Therefore, the reaction

$$R = W + F\sin\theta$$

(Newton's third law of motion) and force of friction,

$$f = \mu R$$
$$= \mu(W + F\sin\theta) \quad (\because W = mg)$$

where, μ = coefficient of friction.

When P be the net forward force, then

$$P = F\cos\theta - f$$
$$= F\cos\theta - \mu(mg + F\sin\theta)$$

...(i)

In case of pull, the forward component of pull

$$= F\cos\theta$$

and vertical component $= F\sin\theta$

where R′ be the normal reaction in the case, then

$$F' = W - F\sin\theta$$
$$= mg - F\sin\theta$$

$\therefore$ if f' be the force of friction in this case, then net force

$$P' = F\cos\theta - f' = F\cos\theta - \mu R'$$
$$= F\cos\theta - \mu(mg - F\sin\theta) \quad ...(ii)$$

From equation (i) and (ii), we see that $P' > P$. Therefore, it is easier to pull than to push the lawn mover.

(d) While holding a catch, the impulse received by the hands, $F \times t$ = change in momentum of the ball is constant. By moving his hands backwards, the cricketer increases the time of impact (t) to complete the catch. Since, t increases, F decreases and as a reaction, the ball hurts hands lesser.

□□

CHAPTER 5

WORK, ENERGY AND POWER

Work and Power

➢ **Work:** Work is done when the body is displaced actually through some distance in the direction of applied force.

$$W = \vec{F} \cdot \vec{s}$$

$$W = Fs\cos\theta$$

Scan to know more about this topic

Work done by a force

- Work done is a scalar quantity. However, work done is positive when θ lies between 0 (zero) and π/2. Work done is negative when θ lies between π/2 and 3π/2.
- S. I. unit of work is joule (J) and the C.G.S unit of work is erg, where 1 joule = 10^7 erg.
- Work done by a body does not depend on the time taken to complete the work.

➢ **Internal work or zero work:** The work in which muscles are strained, but work done is not useful, is called internal work. For example, when a person carrying load keeps on standing at the same place, work done is zero, but he gets tired on account of internal work.

Dimensions: $[ML^2T^{-2}]$

Power: Power of a body is defined as the time rate of doing work by the body. Thus, in power, time taken by the body to complete the work is significant.

$$\text{Power} = \frac{\text{Work done}}{\text{Time taken}}$$

$$P = \vec{F} \cdot \vec{v} = Fv\cos\theta$$

- Here, θ is the angle between force $\vec{F}$ and velocity $\vec{v}$ of the body.
- **Unit:** 1 W = 1 Js^{-1}
- **Dimensions:** $[ML^2T^{-3}]$
- Power is a scalar quantity.

Energy

➢ **Energy:** Energy of a body is defined as the capacity of the body to do the work. Energy is a scalar quantity. It has the same units and dimensions as those of work. Some practical units of energy and their relation with S.I. unit of energy (joule) are:

(i) 1 calorie = 4.2 J

(ii) 1 kiloWatt hour (kWh) = 3.6 × 10^6 J

(iii) 1 electron volt (1 eV) = 1.6 × 10^{-19} J

➢ **Work-Energy Theorem:** According to this principle, work done by net force in displacing a body is equal to change in kinetic energy of the body and *i.e.,*

$$W = K_f - K_i$$

K_f = final *K.E.*

K_i = initial *K.E.*

➢ **Collisions:** When a body strikes against another body such that there is exchange of energy and linear momentum then the two are said to collide. Collisions are of two types:

Scan to know more about this topic

Work energy theorem

(i) **Perfectly elastic collision** is that in which there is no change in kinetic energy of the system, i.e.,

Total *K.E.* before collision = Total *K.E.* after collision.

e.g., collisions between atomic and subatomic particles are perfectly elastic collisions.

(ii) **Perfectly inelastic collision** is that in which *K.E.* is not conserved. Here, the bodies stick together after impact. Linear momentum is conserved in every collision elastic as well as inelastic, further total energy is also conserved in all such collisions. Kinetic energy alone is not conserved in inelastic collisions.

Key Words

➢ **Conservative force** is a force if work done by or against the force in moving a body depends only on the initial & final positions of the body and not on the nature of path followed between initial and final positions, *e.g.,* gravitational force, electrostatic force between two electric charges, all central forces, etc.

➢ **Non-conservative force** is a force if work done by or against the force in moving a body from one position to another depends on the path followed between these two positions. *e.g.,* frictional forces, elastic forces, etc.

➢ **Kinetic Energy** is the energy possessed by the body by virtue of its motion. It is always positive.

➢ **Potential Energy** is the energy possessed by the body by virtue of its position. It can be both negative as well as positive.

➢ **Gravitational Potential Energy** is the energy possessed by the body by virtue of its position with respect to center of Earth or other body.

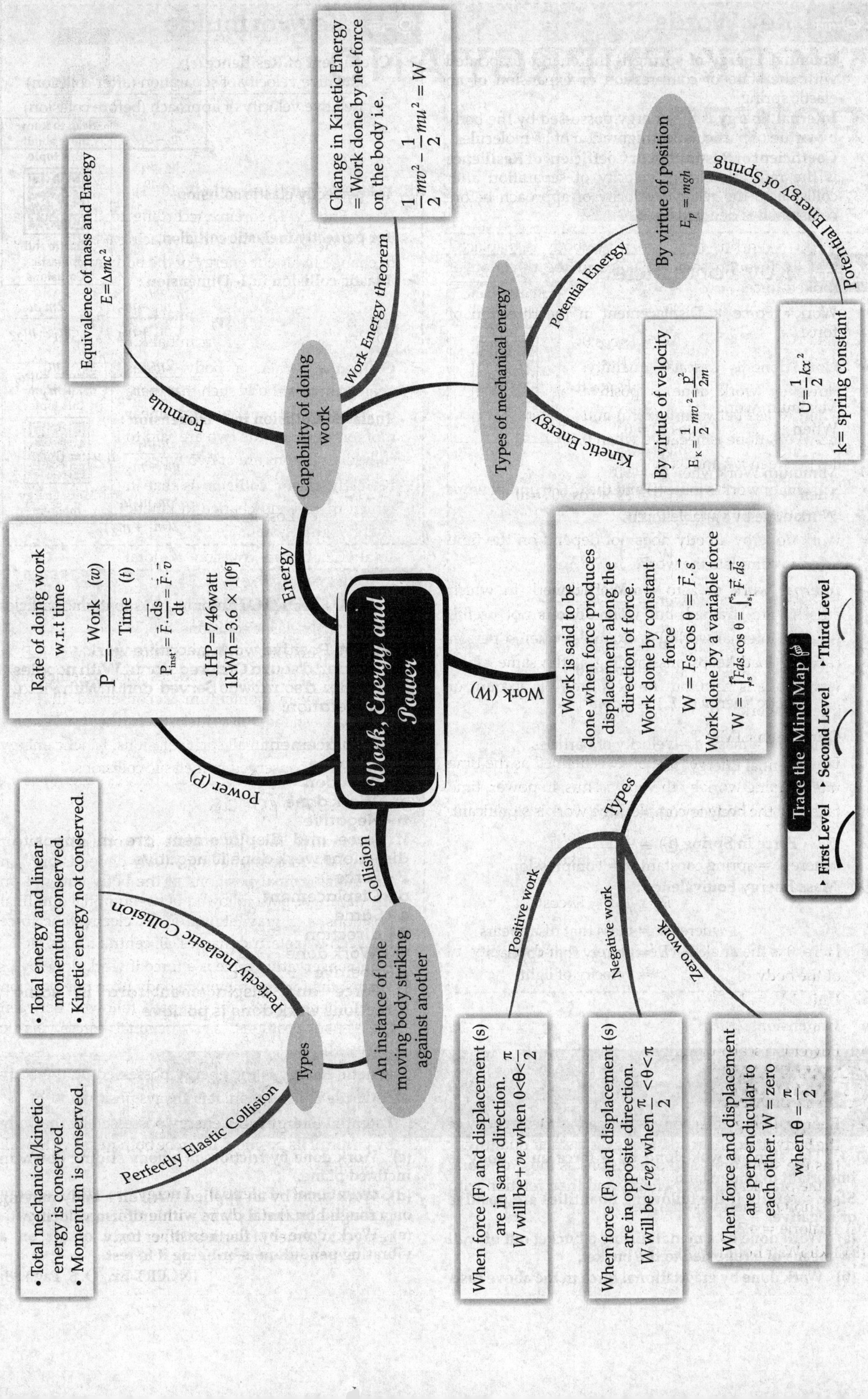
Work, Energy and Power
Energy
Capability of doing work
Formula
Equivalence of mass and Energy $E=\Delta mc^2$
Work Energy theorem
Change in Kinetic Energy = Work done by net force on the body i.e.
$\frac{1}{2}mv^2 - \frac{1}{2}mu^2 = W$
Types of mechanical energy
Potential Energy
By virtue of position $E_p = mgh$
Potential Energy of Spring
$U = \frac{1}{2}kx^2$
k= spring constant
Kinetic Energy
By virtue of velocity $E_K = \frac{1}{2}mv^2 = \frac{p^2}{2m}$
Work (W)
Work is said to be done when force produces displacement along the direction of force.
Work done by constant force
$W = Fs\cos\theta = \vec{F}\cdot\vec{s}$
Work done by a variable force
$W = \int_{s}^{} Fds.\cos\theta = \int_{s_1}^{s_2} \vec{F}\cdot d\vec{s}$
Types
Positive work
When force (F) and displacement (s) are in same direction. W will be +ve when $0<\theta<\frac{\pi}{2}$
Negative work
When force (F) and displacement (s) are in opposite direction. W will be (-ve) when $\frac{\pi}{2}<\theta<\pi$
Zero work
When force and displacement are perpendicular to each other. W = zero when $\theta = \frac{\pi}{2}$
Power (P)
Rate of doing work w.r.t time
$P = \frac{\text{Work } (w)}{\text{Time } (t)}$
$P_{inst} = \vec{F}\cdot\frac{d\vec{s}}{dt} = \vec{F}\cdot\vec{v}$
1HP = 746watt
1kWh = 3.6×10^6 J
Collision
An instance of one moving body striking against another
Types
Perfectly Inelastic Collision
• Total energy and linear momentum conserved.
• Kinetic energy not conserved.
Perfectly Elastic Collision
• Total mechanical/kinetic energy is conserved.
• Momentum is conserved.
Trace the Mind Map
First Level
Second Level
Third Level

Key Words

- **Potential Energy of spring** is the energy associated with the state of compression or expansion of an elastic spring.
- **Internal Energy** is the energy possessed by the body by virtue of particular configuration of its molecules.
- **Coefficient of Restitution or Coefficient of Resilience** is the ratio of relative velocity of separation after collision to the relative velocity of approach before collision. It is denoted by '*e*'.

Key Formulae

- Work= Force × Displacement in the direction of force
- $$W = \vec{F}.\vec{s}$$ $$= Fs \cos \theta$$
- Maximum work
  When $\cos \theta = 0°$
  $W = Fs$
- Minimum Work when $\theta° = 90°$
  Then $W = Fs \times \cos 90° = 0$
- Work done by variable force :
  $$W = \int_{x_A}^{x_B} \vec{F}.d\vec{x}$$
- $$\text{Power} = \frac{\text{Work done}}{\text{Time Taken}}$$
- $$P = \vec{F} \cdot \vec{v}$$
- $$P = Fv \cos \theta.$$
- $$\text{Kinetic Energy } (K.E.) = \frac{1}{2} mv^2,$$
  where, m = mass, v = velocity of particles
- Potential Energy ($P.E.$)
  $= mgh$
  $$\text{Velocity } (v) = \sqrt{2gh}$$
- **Force in Spring (*F*)** $= -kx$,
  where, k = spring constant, x = compression.
- **Mass Energy Equivalence :**
  $$E = mc^2$$
  where, m = mass that disappears
  E = energy that appears
  c = velocity of light

Key Formulae

- **Coefficient of Resilience** (*e*)
  $$= \frac{\text{Relative velocity of separation (after collision)}}{\text{Relative velocity of approach (before collision)}}$$
  $$e = \frac{v_2 - v_1}{u_2 - u_1}$$
  for perfectly elastic collision,
  $$e = 1$$
  for perfectly inelastic collision,
  $$e = 0$$

Scan to know more about this topic

Elastic and Inelastic Collisions

- **Elastic collision in 1- Dimension :**
  $$v_1 = \left(\frac{m_1 - m_2}{m_1 + m_2}\right)u_1 + \frac{2m_2u_2}{m_1 + m_2}$$
  $$v_2 = \frac{2m_1u_1}{m_1 + m_2} + \left(\frac{m_2 - m_1}{m_1 + m_2}\right)u_2$$
- **Inelastic Collision in 1–Dimension :**
  $$v = \frac{m_1u_1}{m_1 + m_2} \quad if\ u_2 = 0$$
  $$\text{Loss in } K.E. = \frac{m_1m_2u_1^2}{2(m_1 + m_2)}$$

Mnemonics

Concept: Positive work, negative work
Fernandez **d**'souza **O**rdered **d**onut **W**ith **n**oodles
Fernandez **d**'souza was **S**erved **d**onut **W**ith **P**izza.
Interpretation:
F - Force
d - Displacement
o - opposite
d - direction
w - Work done
n - Negative
If Force and displacement are in opposite directions work done is negative.
F - Force
d - Displacement
s - Same
d - direction
w - Work done
p - positive
If Force and displacement are in same directions work done is positive

NCERT CORNER

Q. 1. The sign of wok done by a force an a body is important to understand.
State carefully if the following quantities are positive or negative.
(a) Work done by a man in lifting a bucket out of well by means of a rope tied to the bucket.
(b) Work done by gravitational force in the above case.
(c) Work done by friction on a body sliding down an inclined plane.
(d) Work done by an applied force on a body moving on a rough horizontal plane with uniform velocity.
(e) Work done by the resistive force of air on a vibrating pendulum is bringing it to rest.
[NCERT Ex., Q. 5, Page 88]

As, $W = Fs\cos\theta$

(a) $\theta = 0°$, work is positive.

(b) $\theta = 180°$, work is negative.

(c) As force of friction act opposite to direction of motion, work is negative.

(d) As applied force acts in the direction of motion, work is positive.

(e) The resistive force of air acts opposite to direction of the motion, hence work is negative.

Q. 2. A body of mass 2kg initially at rest moves under the action of an applied horizontal force of 7 N on a table with coefficient of kinetic friction = 0.1. Compute the

(a) Work done by the applied force in 10 s,

(b) Work done by friction in 10 s,

(c) Work done by the net force on the body in 10 s,

and interpret your results. [NCERT Ex., Q. 5.2, Page 88]

Given: $m = 2$ kg, $u = 0$, F = 7N, $\mu = 0.1$, $t = 10$s

$$\text{Acceleration} = a_1 = \frac{F}{m} = \frac{7}{2} = 3.5\,\text{ms}^{-2}$$

$$\text{Frictional force} = f = \mu R = \mu mg = 0.1 \times 2 \times 9.8 = 1.96\text{ N.}$$

Retardation-

$$a_2 = \frac{-f}{m} = \frac{-1.96}{2} = -0.98\text{ ms}^{-2}$$

Net acceleration, $a = a_1 + a_2 = 3.5 - 0.98 = 2.52\text{ ms}^{-2}$

Distance, in 10 seconds

$$s = ut + \frac{1}{2}at^2$$

$$= 0 + \frac{1}{2} \times 2.52 \times (10)^2$$

$$= 126\text{m}$$

(a) Work done (applied force) = F.s = 7 × 126 = 882 J.

(b) Work done (frictional force) = $-f.s$
$= -1.96 \times 126$
$= -247$ J

(c) Work done (net force) = Net force × s

Net force, F = 7 – 1.96 = 5.04

Work done = 5.04 × 126 = 635 J.

(d) Velocity at the end of 10 second.

$v = u + at = 0 + 2.52 \times 10 = 25.2$ m/s.

Initial $KE = 0$

$$\text{Final } KE = \frac{1}{2}mv^2 = \frac{1}{2} \times 2 \times (25.2)^2 = 635\text{J}$$

Change in $K.E. = 635 - 0 = 635$J.

∴ $K.E.$'s change is equal to work done by net force.

Q. 3. Given in figures are examples of some potential energy functions in one dimension. The total energy of the particle is indicated by a cross on the In each case, specify the regions, if any, in which the particle cannot be found for the given energy. Also, indicate the minimum total energy the particle must have in each case. Th ık of simple physical contexts for which these potential energy shapes are relevant.

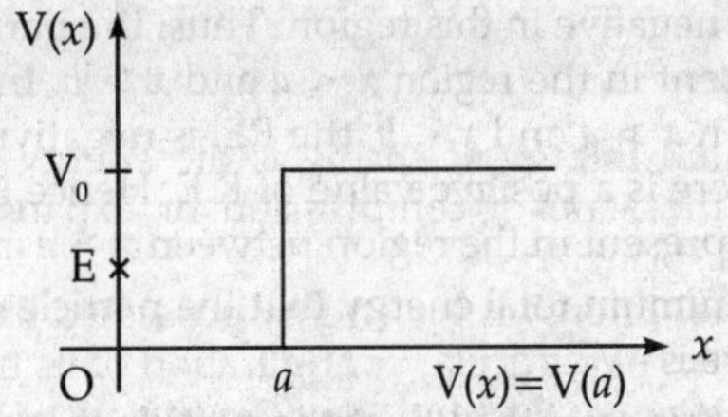

(i)

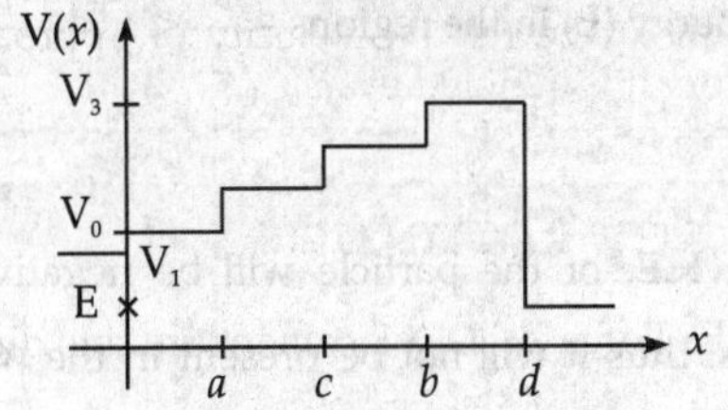

(ii)

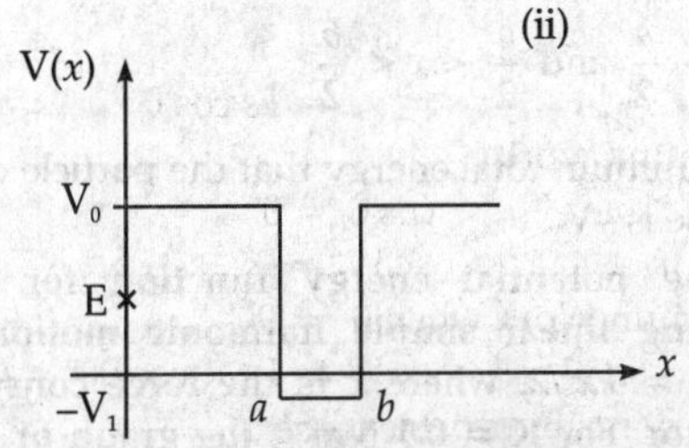

(iii)

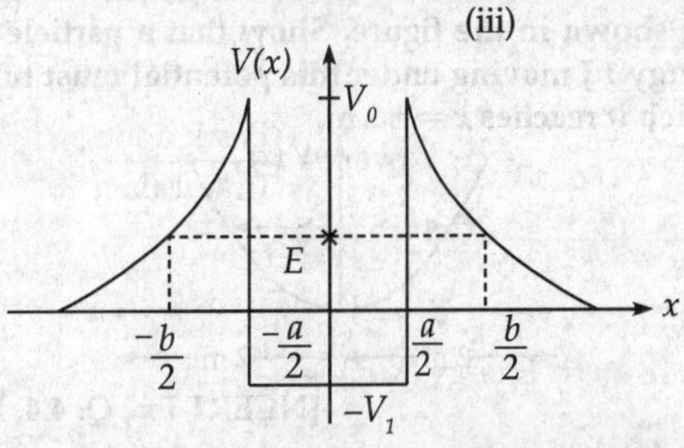

(iv)

[NCERT Ex., Q. 5.3, Page 88]

Ans. It is clear that the total energy of the body is given by

$$E = K.E. + P.E.$$

or

$$K.E. = E - P.E. = \frac{1}{2}mv^2$$

Hence, K.E. of the body can never be negative. Thus, P.E. cannot be greater than E.

(i) In the region between $x = 0$ and $x = a$, P.E. is zero, so K.E. is positive. In the region $x > a$, the P.E. (V_0) has a value greater than E. So, K.E. will be negative in the region. Hence, the particle can't be present in the region $x > a$.

The minimum total energy that the particle can have in this case is zero.

(ii) Here, in all the regions, i.e., $-\infty < x < a$, $a < x < b$, $b < x < c$, $c < x < d$ and $d < x < \infty$, the P.E. is greater than the total energy. Hence, the particle cannot be present in the region $-\infty < x < \infty$.

The minimum total energy that the particle can have in this case is V_1.

(iii) In region $x < a$ and $x > b$, the P.E. is V_0 which is greater than the total energy of the particle. So, K.E.

will be negative in this region. Thus, the particle cannot be present in the region $x < a$ and $x > b$. In the region between $x > a$ and $x < b$, the P.E. is negative this clears that there is a positive value of K.E. Hence, the particle can be present in the region between $x > a$ and $x < b$.

The minimum total energy that the particle can have in this case is $-V_1$.

(iv) In this case, the P.E. of the particle is more than the total energy (E) in the regions $-\frac{b}{2} < x < -\frac{a}{2}$ and $\frac{a}{2} < x < \frac{b}{2}$.

Hence, K.E. of the particle will be negative in these regions, thus it will not be present in the regions $-\frac{b}{2} < x < -\frac{a}{2}$ and $\frac{a}{2} < x < \frac{b}{2}$.

The minimum total energy that the particle can have in this case is $-V_1$.

Q. 4. The potential energy function for a particle executing linear simple harmonic motion is given by $V_{(x)} = kx^2/2$, where k is the force constant of the oscillator. For K = 0.5 Nm^{-1}, the graph of $V_{(x)}$ versus x is shown in the figure. Show that a particle of total energy 1 J moving under this potential must turn back' which it reaches $x = \pm 2$ m.

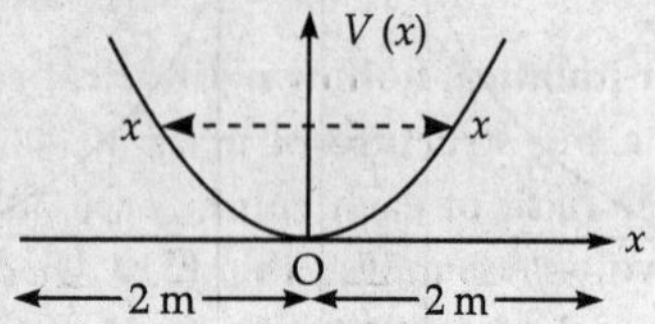

[NCERT Ex., Q. 4.4, Page 89]

Ans. Total energy,

$$E = K.E. + P.E.$$

$$= \frac{1}{2}mv^2 + \frac{1}{2}kx^2$$

where, m = mass of particle

k = force constant = 0.5 Nm^{-1}

x = displacement, v = velocity of particle

or $$1 = \frac{1}{2}mv^2 + \frac{1}{2} \times \frac{1}{2}x^2$$

or $$x^2 + 2mv^2 = 4$$

Then particle turns back at x when $v = 0$

$\therefore$ $$x^2 + 2m(0)^2 = 4$$

or $$x = \pm 2 \text{ m}.$$

Q. 5. Answer the following:

(a) The casing of a rocket in flight burns up due to friction. At whose expense is the heat energy required for burning obtained? The rocket or the atmosphere?

(b) Comets move around the sun in highly elliptical orbits. The gravitational force on the comet due to the sun is not normal to the comet's velocity in general. Yet the work done by the gravitational force over every complete orbit of the comet is zero. Why?

(c) An artificial satellite orbiting the Earth in very thin atmosphere loses its energy gradually due to dissipation against atmospheric resistance, however small. Why then does its speed increase progressively as it comes closer and closer to the Earth?

(d) In Figure (i) the man walks 2 m carrying a mass of 15 kg on his hands. In Figure (ii), he walks the same distance pulling the rope behind him. The rope goes over a pulley, and a mass of 15 kg hangs at its other end. In which case is the work done greater?

(i) (ii)

[NCERT Ex., Q. 5.5, Page 89]

Ans. (a) Rocket

The burning of the casing of a rocket in flight (due to friction) results in the reduction of the mass of the rocket.

According to the conservation of energy:

Total energy = Potential energy + Kinetic energy = $mgs + (1/2)\, mv^2$

The reduction in the rocket's mass causes a drop in the total energy. Therefore, the heat energy required for the burning is obtained from the rocket.

(b) Gravitational force is a conservative force. Since the work done by a conservative force over a closed path is zero, the work done by the gravitational force over every complete orbit of a comet is zero.

(c) When an artificial satellite, orbiting around Earth, moves closer to Earth, its potential energy decreases because of the reduction in the height. Since, the total energy of the system remains constant, the reduction in P.E. results in an increase in K.E. Hence, the velocity of the satellite increases. However, due to atmospheric friction, the total energy of the satellite decreases by a small amount.

(d) Work done in figure (i)

Mass, m = 15 kg

Displacement, $s = 2\ m$

Work done, $W = Fs \cos\theta$

Where, θ = Angle between force and displacement

So, Work done = $mgs \cos\theta = 15 \times 2 \times 9.8 \cos 90°$

$= 0$

Work done in figure (ii)

Mass, $m = 15\ kg$

Displacement, $s = 2\ m$

Here, the direction of the force applied on the rope and the direction of the displacement of the rope are same.

Therefore, the angle between them, $\theta = 0°$

Since, $\cos 0° = 1$

Work done, $W = Fs \cos\theta = mgs$

$= 15 \times 9.8 \times 2 = 294$ J

Hence, more work is done in the figure (ii).

Q. 6. Underline the correct alternative:

(a) When a conservative force does positive work on a body, the potential energy of the body increases/ decreases/remains unaltered.

(b) Work done by a body against friction always results in a loss of its kinetic/potential energy.

(c) The rate of change of total momentum of a many-particle system is proportional to the external force/sum of the internal forces on the system.

(d) In an inelastic collision of two bodies, the quantities which do not change after the collision are the total kinetic energy/total linear momentum/total energy of the system of two bodies.

[NCERT Ex., Q. 5.6, Page 89]

Ans. (a) Decreases

A conservative force does a positive work on a body when it displaces the body in the direction of force. As a result, the body advances toward the center of force. It decreases the separation between the two, thereby decreasing the potential energy of the body.

(b) Kinetic energy

The work done against the direction of friction reduces the velocity of a body. Hence, there is a loss of kinetic energy of the body.

(c) External force

Internal forces, irrespective of their direction, cannot produce any change in the total momentum of a body. Hence, the total momentum of a many- particle system is proportional to the external forces acting on the system.

(d) Total linear momentum

The total linear momentum always remains conserved whether it is an elastic collision or an inelastic collision.

Q. 7. State if each of the following statements is true or false. Give reasons for your answer.

(a) In an elastic collision of two bodies, the momentum and energy of each body is conserved.

(b) Total energy of a system is always conserved, no matter what internal and external forces on the body are present.

(c) Work done in the motion of a body over a closed loop is zero for every force in nature.

(d) In an inelastic collision, the final kinetic energy is always less than the initial kinetic energy of the system. [NCERT Ex., Q. 5.7, Page 89]

Ans. (a) False, it is total momentum and total energy which are conserved.

(b) False, force on the system can change total energy of the system.

(c) False, in the case of non-conservative forces like friction, the work done in a closed loop is not zero.

(d) True, there is at least some loss of kinetic energy in an inelastic collision.

Q. 8. Answer carefully, with reasons:

(a) In an elastic collision of two billiard balls, is the total kinetic energy conserved during the short time of collision of the balls (i.e., when they are in contact) ?

(b) Is the total linear momentum conserved during the short time of an elastic collision of two balls?

(c) What are the answers to (a) and (b) for an inelastic collision ?

(d) If the potential energy of two billiard balls depends only on the separation distance between their centres, is the collision elastic or inelastic ?

[NCERT Ex., Q. 5.8, Page 89]

Ans. (a) No, the total kinetic energy is not conserved during the given elastic collision due to a part of the kinetic energy is used in deforming the balls in that short interval for which they are in contact during collision and gets converted into potential energy. In an elastic collision, the K.E. before and after collision is same.

(b) Yes, the total linear momentum is conserved during the short time of an elastic collision of two balls.

(c) In an inelastic collision, total K.E. is not conserved during collision and even after collision. The total linear momentum is however conserved after collision.

(d) The collision is elastic because involved forces are conservative.

Q. 9. A body is initially at rest. It undergoes one -dimensional motion with constant acceleration. The power delivered to it in time t is proportional to:

(i) $t^{1/2}$, (ii) t, (iii) $t^{3/2}$, (iv) t^2 [NCERT Ex., Q. 5.9, Page 90]

Ans. (ii) Suppose, m = mass of the body

Given:

a = acceleration produced in the body

v = velocity of the body

P = Power delivered to the body in a time t

$$a=\frac{dv}{dt}=\frac{F}{m}$$

$$v=at=\frac{F}{m}t$$

$$P=Fv=F\times\frac{F}{m}t$$

$$=\frac{F^2}{m^2}\times mt=\left(\frac{F}{m}\right)^2 m\times t$$

or $$P=a^2 mt$$

Since, a and m are constants, therefore

P = constant × t

or $P \propto t$

Q. 10. A body is moving uni-directionally under the influence of a source of constant power. Its displacement in time t is proportional to:

(i) $t^{1/2}$, (ii) t, (iii) $t^{3/2}$, (iv) t^2

[NCERT Ex., Q. 5.10, Page 90]

Ans. (iii) Suppose constant power acts on the body of the mass m for a time t to give it a velocity v

$K.E$ = work done = power × time

or $$\frac{1}{2}mv^2=Pt$$

or $$v=\sqrt{\frac{2Pt}{m}} \quad ...(i)$$

$$v=\frac{dx}{dt} \text{ or } dx=vdt$$

$$x = \int dx = \int v dt = \sqrt{\frac{2P}{m}} \int t^{1/2} dt$$

$$= \sqrt{\frac{2P}{m}} \left(\frac{t^{1/2+1}}{\frac{1}{2}+1} \right)$$

$$= \sqrt{\frac{2P}{m}} \frac{t^{3/2}}{3/2} = \frac{2}{3} \sqrt{\frac{2P}{m}} t^{3/2}$$

Here, P = constant and m is also constant for a body, so x = constant $\times\, t^{3/2}$ or x is directly proportional to $t^{3/2}$.

Q. 11. A body constrained to move along Z-axis of a co-ordinate system is subjected to a constant force $\vec{F} = (-\hat{i} + 2\hat{j} + 3\hat{k})$ N. What is the work done by this force, in moving the body over a distance of 4 m along the Z-axis ? [NCERT Ex., Q. 5.11, Page 90]

Here,

$\vec{F} = -\hat{i} + 2\hat{j} + 3\hat{k}$

$\vec{s} = 4\hat{k}$

($\because \vec{s}$ = 4 m distance is along Z-axis).

W =?

$W = \vec{F}.\vec{s}$

$$W = \left(-\hat{i} + 2\hat{j} + 3\hat{k}\right)\left(4\hat{k}\right)$$

$$= 12\hat{k}\cdot\hat{k} = 12\text{J} \qquad \left(\because \hat{k}.\hat{k} = 1\right)$$

Q. 12. An electron and a proton are detected in a cosmic ray experiment, the first with kinetic energy 10 *keV*, and the second with 100 *keV*. Which is faster, the electron or the proton? Obtain the ratio of their speeds. (electron mass = 9.11 × 10^{-31}, proton mass = 1.67 × 10^{-27}, 1eV = 1.60 × 10^{-19} J). [NCERT Ex., Q. 5.12, Page 90]

Ans. Mass of the electron, $m_e = 9.11 \times 10^{-31}\ kg$

Mass of the proton, $m_p = 1.67 \times 10^{-27}\ kg$

Kinetic energy of the electron, $E_{Ke} = 10\ keV = 10^4\ eV$

$= 10^4 \times 1.60 \times 10^{-19}$

$= 1.60 \times 10^{-15}\ J$

Kinetic energy of the proton, $E_{Kp} = 100\ ke$ V $= 10^5\ eV = 1.60 \times 10^{-14}$ J

For the velocity of an electron V_e, its kinetic energy is given by the relation:

$E_{Ke} = (1/2)\, mv^2_e$

$\therefore \quad V_e = (2E_{Ke}/m)^{1/2}$

$= (2 \times 1.60 \times 10^{-15} / 9.11 \times 10^{-31})^{1/2} = 5.93 \times 10^7\ m/s$

For the velocity of a proton V_p, its kinetic energy is given by the relation:

$E_{kp} = (1/2)\, mv^2_p$

$v_p = (2 \times 1.6 \times 10^{-14} / 1.67 \times 10^{-27})^{1/2}$

$= 4.38 \times 10^6\ m/s$

Hence, the electron is moving faster than the proton.

The ratio of their speeds $\frac{V_e}{V_p} = 5.93 \times 10^7 / 4.38 \times 10^6 = 13.54 : 1$

Electron is faster; Ratio of speeds is 13.54: 1

Q.13. A rain drop of radius 2 mm falls from a height of 500 m above the ground. It falls with decreasing acceleration (due to viscous resistance of the air) until at half its original height. It attains its maximum (terminal) speed, and moves with uniform speed thereafter. What is the work done by the gravitational force on the drop in the first and second half of its journey ? What is the work done by the resistive force in the entire journey if its speed on reaching the ground is 10 ms^{-1} ? [NCERT Ex., Q. 5.13, Page 90]

Ans. Given, r = 2 mm = 2 × 10^{-3} m

Using formula,

$P.E. = mgh$

where, $m = \frac{4}{3}\pi r^3 \rho$

$m = \frac{4}{3} \times \frac{22}{7} \times (2 \times 10^{-3})^3 \times 10^3$

$= \frac{32 \times 22}{21} \times 10^{-6}$ kg

and distance moved,

$h = \frac{d}{2} = 250$ m

$\therefore$ Work done during each half = $P.E.$

$= \frac{32 \times 22 \times 10^{-6}}{21} \times 9.8 \times 250$

= 0.082 J.

$K.E.$ on reaching the ground $= \frac{1}{2} mv^2$

$= \frac{1}{2} \times \left(\frac{32 \times 22}{21}\right) \times 10^{-6} \times (10)^2 = 0.00168$

Work done by resistive force

= $K.E.$ – work done by gravitational force

= 0.00168 – 2 × 0.082

= – 0.163 J

Q.14. A molecule in a gas container hits a horizontal wall with speed 200 ms^{-1} and angle 30° with the normal and rebounds with the same speed. Is momentum conserved in the collision? Is the collision elastic or inelastic? [NCERT Ex., Q. 5.14, Page 90]

Ans. Since, the wall is too heavy, the recoiling molecule produces no velocity in the wall.

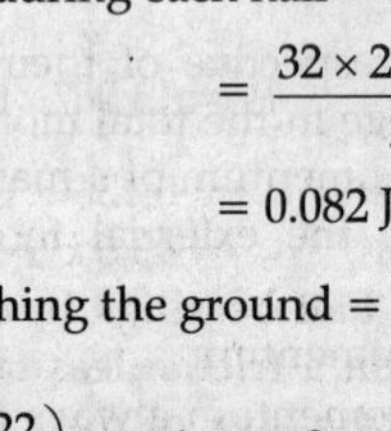

When m is mass of the gas molecule and M is mass of wall, the total $K.E.$ after collision,

$E_2 = \frac{1}{2} m\, (200)^2 + \frac{1}{2} M\, (0)^2$

or $E_2 = 2 \times 10^4\ mJ$

which is equal to the K.E. of the molecule before collision.

$[E_1 = \frac{1}{2} m(200)^2 = 2 \times 10^4 mJ]$

Hence, the collision is elastic.

Q. 15. A pump on the ground floor of a building can pump up water to fill a tank of volume 30 m³ in 15 min. If the tank is 40 m above the ground, and the efficiency of the pump is 30%, how much electric power is consumed by the pump? [NCERT Ex., Q. 5.15, Page 90]

Ans. Volume of the tank, $V = 30\ m^3$

Time of operation, $t = 15\ min = 15 \times 60 = 900\ s$

Height of the tank, $h = 40\ m$

Efficiency of the pump, $\eta = 30\ \%$

Density of water, $\rho = 10^3\ kg/m^3$

Mass of water, $m = \rho V = 30 \times 10^3\ kg$

Output power can be obtained as:

$P_0 =$ Work done / Time $= mgh/t$

$= 30 \times 10^3 \times 9.8 \times 40 / 900 = 13.067 \times 10^3\ W$

For input power P_i, and efficiency η, is given by the relation:

$$\eta = P_o/P_i = \frac{30}{100}$$

$$P_i = 13.067 \times 10^3 \times \frac{100}{30}$$

$$= 0.436 \times 10^5 W$$

$$= 43.6\ kW$$

Q. 16. Two identical ball bearings in contact with each other and resting on a frictionless table are hit head-on by another ball bearing of the same mass moving initially with a speed v. If the collision is elastic, which of the following is a possible result after collision ?

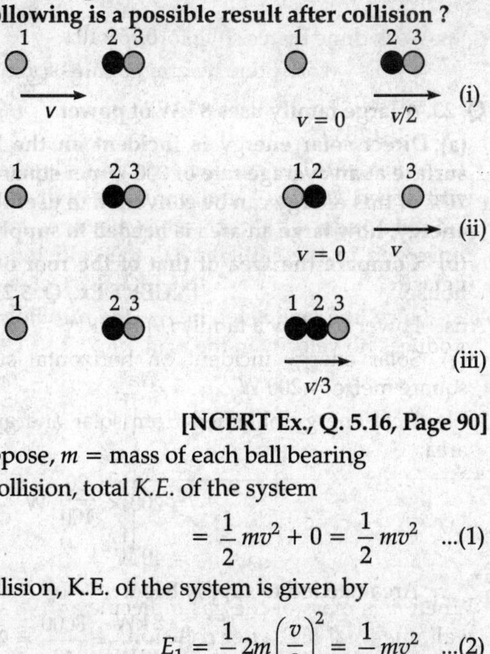

[NCERT Ex., Q. 5.16, Page 90]

Ans. Suppose, m = mass of each ball bearing

Before collision, total *K.E.* of the system

$$= \frac{1}{2}mv^2 + 0 = \frac{1}{2}mv^2 \quad ...(1)$$

After collision, K.E. of the system is given by

case (i) $$E_1 = \frac{1}{2}2m\left(\frac{v}{2}\right)^2 = \frac{1}{4}mv^2 \quad ...(2)$$

case (ii) $$E_2 = \frac{1}{2}mv^2 \quad ...(3)$$

case (iii) $$E_3 = \frac{1}{2}(3m)\left(\frac{v}{3}\right)^2 = \frac{1}{6}mv^2 \quad ..(4)$$

Hence, from above equations, we see that the K.E. is conserved only in case (ii), so, case (ii) is the only possible result after collision.

Q. 17. The bob A of a pendulum released from 30° to the vertical hits another bob B of the same mass at rest on a table as shown in figure given below. How high does the bob A rise after the collision ? Neglect the size of the bobs and assume the collision to be elastic.

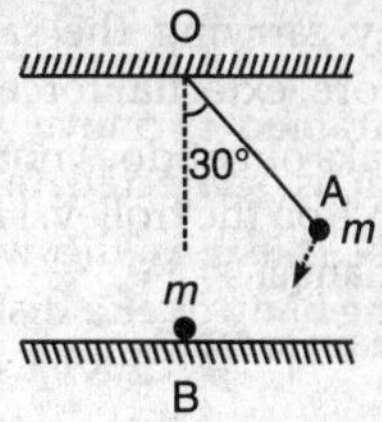

[NCERT Ex., Q. 5.17, Page 91]

It is quite clear that in perfectly elastic head on collision, when two equal masses collide with each other, then they exchange their speeds.

In the present case, bob A is moving with certain speed and bob B is at rest. So after collision, bob A comes to rest and the bob B starts moving with the speed of the bob A. The bob A transfers whole of its momentum to bob B and so, bob A, will not rise at all after the collision.

Note: The bob shall not rise because when two bodies of same mass undergo an elastic collision, there velocities are interchanged and ball A rests and ball B moves.

Q.18. The bob of a pendulum is released from a horizontal position A as shown in figure. If the length of the pendulum is 1·5 m, what is the speed with which the bob arrives at the lower most point B, given that it dissipates 5% of its initial energy against air resistance. [NCERT Ex., Q. 5.18, Page 91]

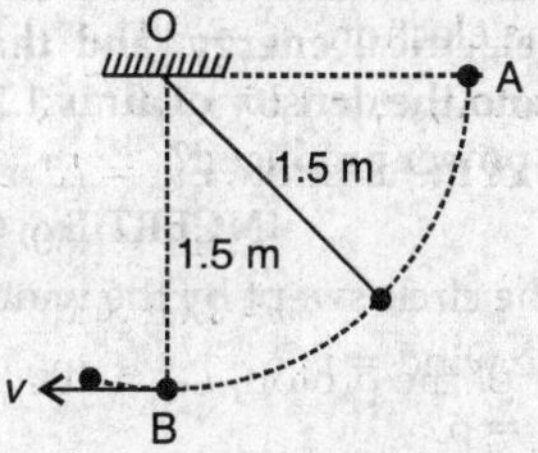

Ans. Given: $h = 1{\cdot}5$ m, v = ?, Energy dissipated = 5%.

Taking B as the lowest position of the bob, its potential energy at B is zero. At the horizontal position A, total potential energy of the bob is mgh. In going from A to B, P.E. of the bob is converted into *K.E.*

Energy converted = 95% (mgh)

When v is velocity acquired at B, then

$$K.E. = \frac{95}{100}mgh$$

or $$\frac{1}{2}mv^2 = \frac{95}{100}mgh$$

$$v = \sqrt{\frac{95}{100} \times 2gh}$$

or $$v = \sqrt{\frac{19}{20} \times 2 \times 9.8 \times 1.5}$$

or $v = 5.285 \text{ ms}^{-1}$

$\approx 5.3 \text{ ms}^{-1}$

Q. 19. A trolley of 300 kg carrying a sand bag of 25 kg is moving uniformly with a speed of 27 km/h on a frictionless track. After a while, sand starts leaking out of a hole on the trolleys floor at the rate of 0.05 kgs^{-1}. What is the speed o the trolley after the entire sand bag is empty? [NCERT Ex., Q. 5.19, Page 91]

Ans. As the trolley carrying the sand bag is moving uniformly, therefore, external force on system= zero.

When the sand leaks out, it does not lead to application of any external force on the trolley. Hence, the speed the trolley shall not change.

So, speed will remain same.

Speed = 27 km/h.

Q. 20. A body of mass 0.5kg travels in a straight line with velocity $v = a\, x^{\frac{3}{2}}$ where $a = 5\text{m}^{-1/2}\text{s}^{-1}$. What is the work done by the net force during its displacement from $x = 0$ to $x = 2$ m? [NCERT Ex., Q. 5.20, Page 91]

Ans. $v = ax^{3/2}$

At $x = 0, v(0) = 0$

At $x = 2, v(2) = a \times 2^{3/2} = 5 \times 2^{3/2}$

Now, Work done $= KE_f - KE_i$

or, Work done $= \frac{1}{2} m\,[v(2)]^2 - \frac{1}{2} m[v(0)]^2$

or, Work done $= \frac{1}{2} m[v(2)]^2$

or, Work done $= \frac{1}{2} \times 0.5 \times [5 \times 2^{3/2}]^2$

$\therefore$ Work done = 50 J

Q. 21. The blades of a windmill sweep out a circle of area (a) If the wind flows at a velocity v perpendicular to the circle, what is the mass of the air passing through it in time ?(b) What is the kinetic energy of the air? (c) Assume that the windmill converts 25% of the wind's energy into electrical energy, and that $A = 30 \text{ m}^3$, $v = 36$ km/h and the density of air is 1.2 kg m^3. What is the electrical power produced?

[NCERT Ex., Q. 5.21, Page 91]

Ans. Area of the circle swept by the windmill $=A$

Velocity of the wind $= v$

Density of air $= \rho$

(a) Volume of the wind flowing through the windmill per sec $=Av$

Mass of the wind flowing through the windmill per sec $= \rho Av$

Mass m, of the wind flowing through the windmill in time $t = \rho Avt$

(b) Kinetic energy of air $= (1/2)mv^2$

$= (1/2)(\rho Avt)v^2 = (1/2)\rho Av^3t$

(c) Area of the circle swept by the windmill $=A= 30\ m^2$

Velocity of the wind $=v= 36\ km/h$

Density of air, $\rho = 1.2\ kg\ m^{-3}$

Electric energy produced = 25% of the wind energy

$= (25/100) \times$Kinetic energy of air

$= (1/8)\rho Av^3t$

Electrical power = Electrical energy / Time

$= (1/8)\rho Av^3t/t$

$= (1/8)\rho Av^3$

$= (1/8) \times 1.2 \times 30 \times (10)^3$

$= 4.5$ kW

Q. 22. A person trying to loose weight (dieter) lifts a 10 kg mass 0.5 m 1000 times. Assuming that the potential energy lost each time she lowers the mass is dissipated.
(a) How much work does she do against the gravitational force ?
(b) Fat supplies 3.8 × 10^7 J of energy per kilogram, which is converted to mechanical energy with a 20 % efficiency rate. How much fat will the dieter use up ?

[NCERT Ex., Q. 5.22, Page 91]

Ans. Mass m= 10 kg

Height h = 0.5

Number of times the mass lifted (n) = 1000

(a) Work done against gravitational force

$= n \times mgh$

$= 1000 \times 10 \times 9.8 \times 0.5$

$= 49000$ J.

(b) Energy supplied by fat per kilogram

$= 3.8 \times 10^7$ J

Mechanical energy supplied by fat per kilogram

= 20% of total energy supplied by fat

$= \frac{20}{100} \times 3.8 \times 10^7$

$= 0.76 \times 10^7$ J/kg

Fat used up by the dieter

$= \frac{1}{0.76 \times 10^7} \times 49000$

$= 6.45 \times 10^{-3}$ kg.

Q. 23. A large family uses 8 kW of power.
(a) Direct solar energy is incident on the horizontal surface at an average rate of 200 W per square metre. If 20% of this energy can be converted to useful electrical energy, how large an area is needed to supply 8 kW ?
(b) Compare the area of that of the roof of a typical house. [NCERT Ex., Q. 5.23, Page 91]

Ans. Power used by a family (P) = 8 kW

(a) Solar energy incident on horizontal surface per square metre = 200 W

Electrical energy obtained from solar energy per unit area

$= 200 \times \frac{20}{100}$ W

$= 40$ W

$\therefore$ Area needed to supply 8 kW.

$= \frac{8\text{kW}}{40\text{W}} = \frac{8000}{40} = 200 \text{ m}^2.$

(b) This area is comparable to the roof of a large house of 14 m × 14 m = 196 m^2

□□

SYSTEM OF PARTICLES AND ROTATIONAL MOTION

CHAPTER 6

Kind of Motion of Rigid body

➤ **Kinds of Motion of Rigid Body**

(i) Pure Translational Motion: All the particles of body are moving together with same velocity at particular instant of time. e.g., A car moving is a straight line.

(ii) Pure Rotational Motion: A rigid body rotates about a fixed axis. Every particle of the body moves in a circle which lies in a plane perpendicular to axis and has its centre on the axis. e.g., A potter's wheel.

(iii) Combination of Translational and Rotational Motion: The motion of rigid body, which is not pivoted or fixed in some way is either pure translation motion or a combination of translation and rotation. eg., A vehicle's wheel.

Centre of Mass

➤ **Center of Mass of a two particle system:** Position vector of centre of mass of a two particle system is such that the product of total mass of the system and position vector of centre of mass is equal to sum of the products of masses of two particles and their respective position vectors.

Scan to know more about this topic

Examples: Centre of mass

➤ **Momentum Conservation:** Total linear momentum of a system of particles is equal to the product of the total mass of the system and the velocity of its centre of mass.

$$\vec{p} = M\vec{v} = m_1\vec{v}_1 + m_2\vec{v}_2 + ... + m_n\vec{v}_n$$

Differentiating it,

$$\frac{d\vec{p}}{dt} = M\frac{d\vec{v}}{dt} = M\vec{a} = \vec{F}_{ext}.$$

This is Newton's II law.

For isolated system, $\vec{F}_{ext} = \vec{0}$.

$$\therefore \quad \frac{d\vec{p}}{dt} = F_{ext} = 0 \text{ or } \vec{p} = \text{constant}$$

$$\therefore \quad M\vec{v} = \text{Constant.}$$

➤ **Moment of Force or Torque:** Torque due to a force is moment of force and measures the turning effect to the force about the axis of rotation. The general expression for torque is

$$\vec{\tau} = \vec{r} \times \vec{F}$$

➤ **Angular Momentum and its Conservation: Angular momentum** of a particle about a given axis is the moment of linear momentum of the particle about the axis. It is equal to the product of linear momentum of the particle and the perpendicular distance of the line of action of linear momentum from the axis of rotation. It is the product of linear momentum and the perpendicular distance of its line of action from the axis of rotation.

Scan to know more about this topic

Conservation of angular momentum

$$\vec{L} = \vec{r} \times \vec{p} = rp \sin \phi$$
$$= \vec{d} \times \vec{p}$$

where, $d = r\sin \phi$ = perpendicular distance of line of action of $\vec{p}$ from the axis. Angular momentum is a vector quantity, whose direction is given by **right handed screw rule.**

- $\vec{L} \perp \vec{d}$ **and** $\vec{L} \perp \vec{p}$
- **Rate of change of angular momentum is torque**, i.e., $\vec{\tau} = d\vec{L}/dt$.

As $\quad \vec{\tau} = \dfrac{d\vec{L}}{dt} = \vec{\tau}_{ext}.$

for isolated system $\vec{\tau}_{ext} = \vec{0}$.

$$\therefore \quad \vec{\tau}_{ext} = \frac{d\vec{L}}{dt} = \vec{0}.$$

So, $\quad \vec{L}$ = constant.

➤ **Equilibrium of Rigid Bodies:**

1st Condition: A rigid body is said to be in translational equilibrium, if it remains at rest or moving with a constant velocity in a particular direction. For this, the net external force or the vector sum of all external forces acting on the body must be zero *i.e.*,

$$\Sigma\vec{\tau}_i = \vec{0}.$$

Translational Static Equilibrium is of 3 types:

(i) Stable Equilibrium

(ii) Unstable Equilibrium

(iii) Neutral Equilibrium

2nd Condition: A rigid body is said to be in rotational equilibrium, if the body does not rotate or rotates with constant angular velocity. For this, the net external torque or the vector sum of all the torques acting on the body must be zero i.e.,

$$\Sigma\vec{\tau}_i = \vec{0}.$$

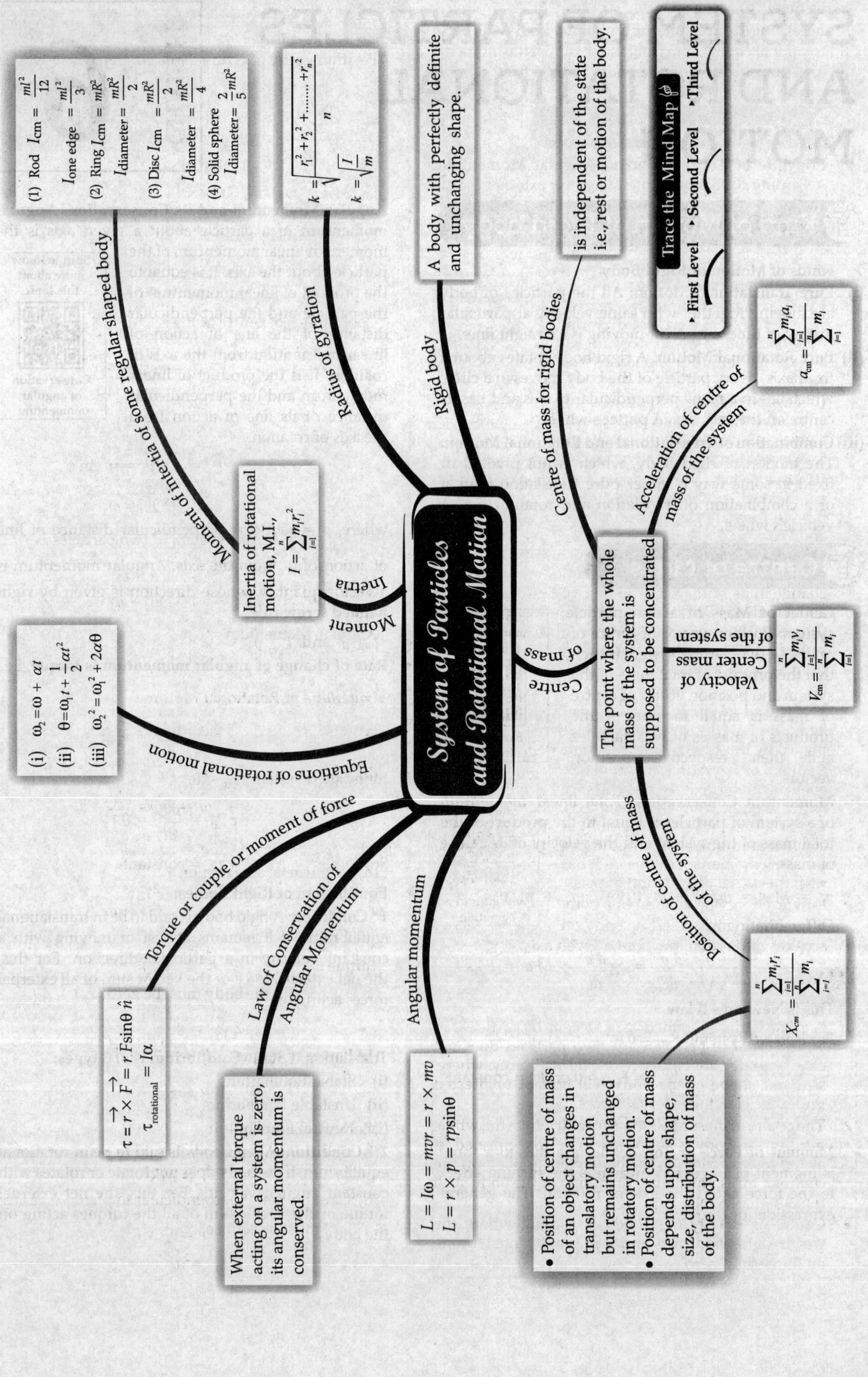
Trace the Mind Map
First Level
Second Level
Third Level
System of Particles and Rotational Motion
Rigid body
A body with perfectly definite and unchanging shape.
Centre of mass for rigid bodies
is independent of the state i.e., rest or motion of the body.
Radius of gyration
$k = \sqrt{\frac{r_1^2 + r_2^2 + ... + r_n^2}{n}}$
$k = \sqrt{\frac{I}{m}}$
Moment of inertia of some regular shaped body
(1) Rod $I_{cm} = \frac{ml^2}{12}$
$I_{one\ edge} = \frac{ml^2}{3}$
(2) Ring $I_{cm} = mR^2$
$I_{diameter} = \frac{mR^2}{2}$
(3) Disc $I_{cm} = \frac{mR^2}{2}$
$I_{diameter} = \frac{mR^2}{4}$
(4) Solid sphere $I_{diameter} = \frac{2}{5}mR^2$
Moment Inertia
Inertia of rotational motion, M.I., $I = \sum_{i=1}^{n} m_i r_i^2$
Equations of rotational motion
(i) $\omega_2 = \omega + \alpha t$
(ii) $\theta = \omega_1 t + \frac{1}{2}\alpha t^2$
(iii) $\omega_2^2 = \omega_1^2 + 2\alpha\theta$
Torque or couple or moment of force
$\vec{\tau} = r \times \vec{F} = r.F\sin\theta\,\hat{n}$
$\tau_{rotational} = I\alpha$
Law of Conservation of Angular Momentum
When external torque acting on a system is zero, its angular momentum is conserved.
Angular momentum
$L = I\omega = mvr = r \times mv$
$L = r \times p = rp\sin\theta$
Centre of mass
The point where the whole mass of the system is supposed to be concentrated
Velocity of Center mass of the system
$V_{cm} = \frac{\sum_{i=1}^{n} m_i v_i}{\sum_{i=1}^{n} m_i}$
Acceleration of centre of mass of the system
$a_{cm} = \frac{\sum_{i=1}^{n} m_i a_i}{\sum_{i=1}^{n} m_i}$
Position of centre of mass of the system
$X_{cm} = \frac{\sum_{i=1}^{n} m_i r_i}{\sum_{i=1}^{n} m_i}$
• Position of centre of mass of an object changes in translatory motion but remains unchanged in rotatory motion.
• Position of centre of mass depends upon shape, size, distribution of mass of the body.

- **Principle of Moments**

  According to principle of moments, body will be in rotational equilibrium if algebraic sum of the moments of all forces acting on the body, about a fixed point is zero.

Moment of Inertia

- **Principle of Conservation of Angular Momentum:** According to this principle, when no external torque acts on a system of particles, then the total angular momentum of system always remains a constant. i.e.,

  $$\vec{L} = \vec{L_1} + \vec{L_2} + \vec{L_3} + ... + \vec{L_n} = \text{constant.}$$

- **Laws of Rotational Motion**

  I Law: A body continues to be in a state of rest or in a state of uniform rotation about a given axis unless an external torque is applied on the body.

  II Law: The rate of change of angular momentum of a body about a given axis is directly proportional to external torque applied on the body.

  III Law: When a rigid body A exerts a torque on another rigid body B in contact with it, then the body B would exert an equal and opposite torque on the body A.

Scan to know more about this topic

Moment of inertia

- **Moment of inertia** of a body about a given axis is the property by virtue of which, the body opposes any change in its state of rest or state of uniform rotation about that axis. For a single particle, moment of inertia (I) is equal to product of mass (m) of the particle and square of perpendicular distance (r) of the particle from the axis of rotation.,

  i.e., $I = mr^2$.

  Moment of inertia is a scalar quantity, whose unit is kgm^2. It plays the same role in rotational motion as is played by the mass in linear motion.

- **Radius of gyration** of a body about a given axis is the distance (K) of a point from the given axis, where if whole mass of the body is concentrated, the body would have the same moment of inertia, as it has with the actual distribution of mass.

Scan to know more about this topic

Radius of gyration

- Kinetic energy of rotation of a body is the energy possessed by body on account of its rotation about a given axis.

Key Words

- **A rigid body** is defined as a system of particles, in which distance between any two particles does not change under the influence of external forces, where, size and shape of the body will remain unaffected under the effect of external forces.
- **The centre of mass** of a body is a point where the whole mass of the body is supposed to be concentrated. If all the forces acting on the body were applied on the centre of mass, the nature of motion of the body shall remain unaffected.
- **Centre of gravity** of a body is a point where the weight of the body acts and total gravitational torque on the body is zero.

Key Formulae

- **Position vector of centre of mass of n particles system**

  $$\vec{r} = \frac{\sum_{i=1}^{n} m_i \vec{r_i}}{M}$$, where, M is the total mass to the system

  i.e., $M = \sum_{i=1}^{n} m_i$

- **For two particle system**

  $$\vec{r} = \frac{m_1 \vec{r_1} + m_2 \vec{r_2}}{m_1 + m_2}$$

- **Coordinates of centre of mass**

  $$x = \frac{m_1 x_1 + m_2 x_2}{m_1 + m_2}$$

  $$y = \frac{m_1 y_1 + m_2 y_2}{m_1 + m_2}$$

  $$z = \frac{m_1 z_1 + m_2 z_2}{m_1 + m_2}$$

- **Velocity of C.M. of a system of two particles is**

  $$\vec{v}_{CM} = \frac{m_1 \vec{v_1} + m_2 \vec{v_2}}{m_1 + m_2}$$

- **Angular Momentum**

  $$\vec{L} = \vec{r} \times m\vec{v}$$

- **Equations of Rotational Motion :**

  (a) $\theta = \omega_1 t + \frac{1}{2}\alpha t^2$

  (b) $v = r\omega$

  $\omega = 2\pi\nu = \frac{2\pi}{T}$

  (c) $a = r\alpha$

  (d) Centripetal acceleration

  $= \frac{v^2}{r} = r\omega^2$

- **Torque :** $\vec{\tau} = \vec{r} \times \vec{F}$

  (i) Work done by torque

  $dW = \tau(d\theta)$

  (ii) Power of torque $P = \frac{dW}{dt} = \tau\left(\frac{d\theta}{dt}\right)$

  $P = \tau\omega$

- **Moment of Inertia—**

  (i) Circular ring : (perpendicular to plane, at centre)

  $I = MR^2$

  (ii) Circular disc : (perpendicular to plane, at centre)

  $I = \frac{1}{2}MR^2$

Key Formulae

(iii) Angular disc (or ring) —

(R = outer radius, r = inner radius) $I = \frac{1}{2}(R^2 + r^2)$

(iv) Thin rod: (axis perpendicular to its length at mid point) $I = \frac{Ml^2}{12}$, Where l is the length of the rod.

(v) Soild cylinder: (along axis of cylinder)

$$I = \frac{1}{2}MR^2$$

(vi) Hollow cylinder: $I = MR^2$
about its long axis of symmetry.

(vii) Solid sphere: (about its diameter.)

$$I = \frac{2}{5}MR^2$$

(viii)Hollow sphere (or thin spherical shell) : (about its diameter) $I = \frac{2}{3}MR^2$

(ix) Solid cylinder (or ring): (about central axis)

$$I = \frac{1}{2}MR^2$$

Mnemonics

NConcept: Position of centre of mass of different objects.

Mnemonics: R S Das in a **C**inema hall met Chiranjeet **m**all **a**rea and **R**am **C**handran behind **C**entral **d**oor.

Interpretation:

R - Ring
S - Sphere
D - Disc
C - Centre
} Ring, sphere, disc have centres of mass at their respective centre.

C - Cylinder
m - mid-point
a - Axis
} Cylinders have centres of mass at the mid-point on the respective axis.

R - Rectangular lamina
c - cube
c - cross-point
d - diagonal
} Rectangular lamina, cube have centres of mass at the cross point of

NCERT CORNER

Q. 1. Give the location of the centre of mass of a (i) sphere, (ii) cylinder, (iii) ring, and (iv) cube each of uniform mass density. Does the centre of mass of a body necessarily lie inside the body?

[NCERT Ex., Q. 6.1, Page 125]

Ans. In all four cases (i),(ii),(iii),(iv), centre of mass is situated at their respective geometrical centres.

No, it is not necessary that centre of mass of a body lie inside it because in some cases e.g., ring, hollow sphere, a hollow cylinder, etc. centre of mass lies outside.

Q.2. In the HCl molecule, the separation between the nuclei of the two atoms is about 1·27 Å (1 Å = 10^{-10} m). Find the approximate location of the C.M. of the molecule, given that a chlorine atom is about 35·5 times as massive as a hydrogen atom and nearly all the mass of an atom is concentrated in its nucleus.

[NCERT Ex., Q. 6.2, Page 125]

Ans. Let us choose the nucleus of the hydrogen atom as the origin for measuring distance.

Mass of hydrogen atom,

$$m_1 = 1 \text{ unit (say)}$$

Mass of chlorine atom,

$$m_2 = 35{\cdot}5 \text{ unit (say)}$$

Now, $x_1 = 0$

and $x_2 = 1{\cdot}27$ Å $= 1{\cdot}27 \times 10^{-10}$ m

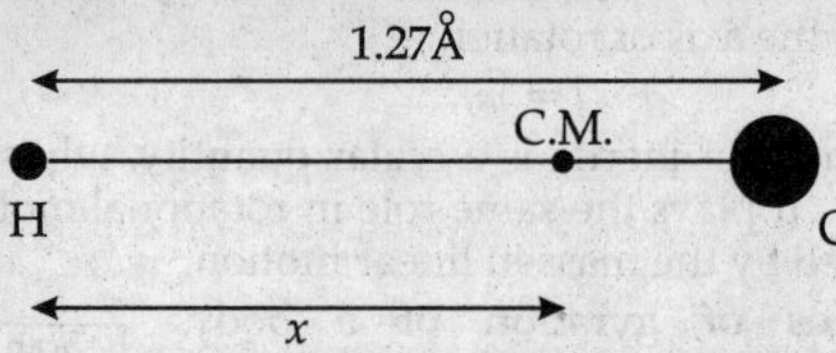

Distance of C.M. of HCl molecule from the origin is given by

$$x = \frac{m_1x_1 + m_2x_2}{m_1 + m_2}$$

$$= \frac{(1 \times 0) + (35.5 \times 1.27 \times 10^{-10})}{(1 + 35.5)}$$

$$= 1{\cdot}235 \times 10^{-10} \text{ m}$$

$$x = 1{\cdot}235 \text{ Å}$$

Q.3. A child sits stationary at one end of a long trolley moving uniformly with a speed v on a smooth horizontal floor. If the child gets up and runs about on the trolley in any manner, what is the speed of C.M. (Centre of Mass) of the (trolley + child) system ?

[NCERT Ex., Q. 6.3, Page 125]

Ans. Trolley and the child make the system, speed of the C.M. of this system remains same irrespective of the movement of the child inside the trolley in any manner because C.M. is affected by external forces and not by the internal forces.

Q.4. Show that the area of the triangle contained between the vectors $\vec{a}$ and $\vec{b}$ is one-half of the magnitude of $\vec{a}\times\vec{b}$. [NCERT Ex., Q. 6.4, Page 125]

Ans. Let $\vec{a}$ be represented by $\vec{OP}$ and $\vec{b}$ be represented by $\vec{OQ}$. Let $\angle POQ = \theta$

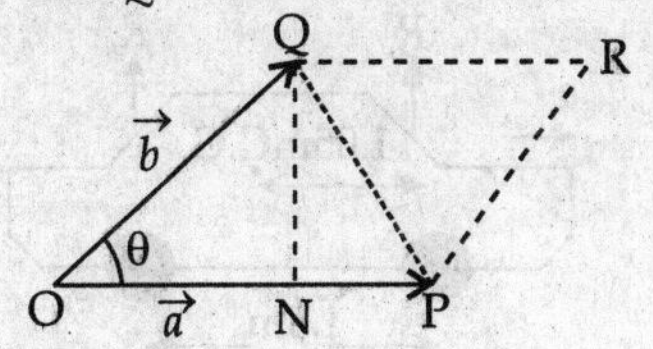

Completed the parallelogram OPRQ. Joined PQ. QN drawn perpendicular on OP.

In ΔQNO, $\sin\theta = \dfrac{QN}{OQ} = \dfrac{QN}{b}$

$$QN = b\sin\theta$$

Now, by definition,

$$|\vec{a}\times\vec{b}| = ab\sin\theta$$
$$= (OP)(QN)$$
$$= \frac{2(OP)(QN)}{2}$$
$$= 2\times \text{area of } \Delta OPQ$$

$\therefore$ Area of $\Delta OPQ = \dfrac{1}{2}|\vec{a}\times\vec{b}|$ **Proved.**

Q. 5. Show that $\vec{a}.(\vec{b}\times\vec{c})$ is equal in magnitude to the volume of the parallelepiped formed on the three vectors, $\vec{a}, \vec{b}$ and $\vec{c}$. [NCERT Ex., Q. 6.5, Page 125]

Ans. A parallelepiped with origin O and sides *a*, *b*, and *c* is shown in the following figure.

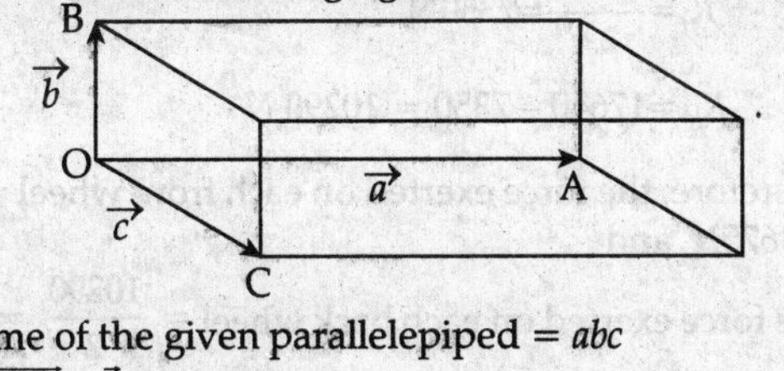

Volume of the given parallelepiped = abc

$\overline{OA} = \vec{a}$

$\overline{OB} = \vec{b}$

$\overline{OC} = \vec{c}$

Let $\hat{n}$ be a unit vector perpendicular to both *b* and *c*. Hence, $\hat{n}$ and $\vec{a}$ have the same direction.

$\therefore\ \vec{b}\times\vec{c} = bc\sin\theta\,\hat{n}$

$= bc\sin 90^\circ n = bc\hat{n}$

$\vec{a}.(\vec{b}\times\vec{c}) = \vec{a}.(bc\hat{n})$

$= abc\cos\theta$ $\quad\because(|\hat{n}| = 1)$

$= abc\cos 0^\circ$

$= abc$

= Volume of the parallelepiped

Q. 6. Find the components along the *x*, *y*, *z* axes of the angular momentum of a particle, whose position vector is $\vec{r}$ with components *x*, *y*, *z* and momentum is $\vec{p}$ with components p_x, p_y, p_z. Show that if the particle moves only in the *x-y* plane the angular momentum has only a *z*-component. [NCERT Ex., Q. 6.6, Page 125]

Ans. Angular momentum l of a particle-

$\vec{l} = \vec{r}\times\vec{p}$ $\quad\left[\begin{array}{l}\vec{r} = \text{position vector}\\ \vec{p} = \text{momentum}\end{array}\right]$

$$\vec{r} = \left[x\hat{i} + y\hat{j} + z\hat{k}\right]$$

Where *x*, *y*, *z* are components of $\vec{r}$ and

$$\vec{p} = \left[p_x\hat{i} + p_y\hat{j} + p_z\hat{k}\right]$$

$$\therefore\ \vec{l} = \vec{r}\times\vec{p}$$
$$= \left[x\hat{i} + y\hat{j} + z\hat{k}\right]\times\left[p_x\hat{i} + p_y\hat{j} + p_z\hat{k}\right]$$

$$\left(l_x\hat{i} + l_y\hat{j} + l_z\hat{k}\right) = \begin{vmatrix}\hat{i} & \hat{j} & \hat{k}\\ x & y & z\\ p_x & p_y & p_z\end{vmatrix}$$

$$= \left(yp_z - zp_y\right)\hat{i} + \left(zp_x - xp_z\right)\hat{j} + \left(xp_y - yp_x\right)\hat{k}$$

We conclude that:

$l_x = yp_z - zp_y,\ l_y = zp_x - xp_z,\ l_z = xp_y - yp_x$

If given particle moves only in *x-y* plane,

Then $z=0$, $p_z=0$,

hence, $l_x=0$, $l_y=0$ $l_z = \left(xp_y - yp_x\right)\hat{k}$

(which is only z-component of *l*)

Therefore, particle moves only in *x-y* plane, the angular momentum has only *z*-component.

Q.7. Two particles, each of mass *m* and speed *v*, travel in opposite directions along parallel lines separated by a distance *d*. Show that the angular momentum vector of the two particle system is the same whatever be the point about which the angular momentum is taken. [NCERT Ex., Q. 6.7, Page 125]

Ans. Angular momentum vector of the two particles system about any point A on x_1y_1 is

$$\vec{L}_A = \vec{d}\times(m\vec{v})$$

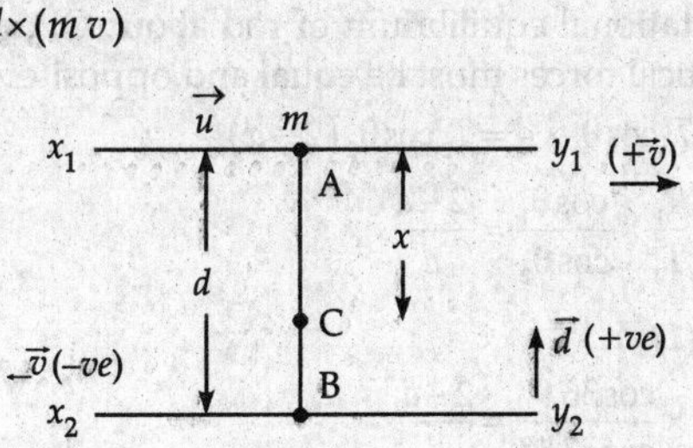

Similarly, angular momentum vector of the two particle system about any point B on x_2y_2 is

$$\vec{L}_B = \vec{d}\times(m\vec{v})$$

Let us consider any other point C on AB, where $AC = x$.

$\therefore$ Angular momentum vector of the two particle system about C at a distance *x* from B is

$$\vec{L}_C = \vec{x}\times m\vec{v} - (\vec{d} - \vec{x})\times(-m\vec{v}) = \vec{d}\times(m\vec{v})$$

So, $\vec{L}_A = \vec{L}_B = \vec{L}_C$ **Proved**

Q.8. A non-uniform bar of weight W is suspended at rest by two strings of negligible weight as shown in Fig. The angles made by the strings with the vertical are 36.9° and 53.1° respectively. The bar is 2 m long. Calculate the distance d of the centre of gravity of the bar from its left end.

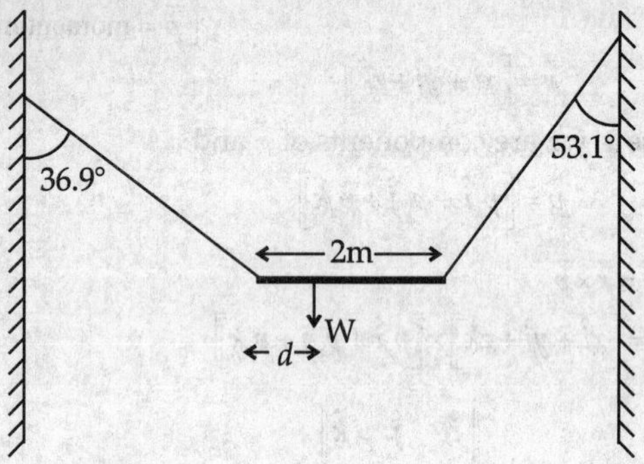

[NCERT Ex., Q. 6.8, Page 125]

Ans. Given: $\theta_1 = 36.9°$, $\theta_2 = 53.1°$

Let T_1& T_2 be tensions in two strings. For equilibrium condition,

$$T_1 \sin\theta_1 = T_2 \sin\theta_2$$

$$\frac{T_1}{T_2} = \frac{\sin\theta_2}{\sin\theta_1} = \frac{\sin 53.1°}{\sin 36.9°}$$

$$\frac{T_1}{T_2} = \frac{0.7407}{0.5477} = 1.3523 \quad (1)$$

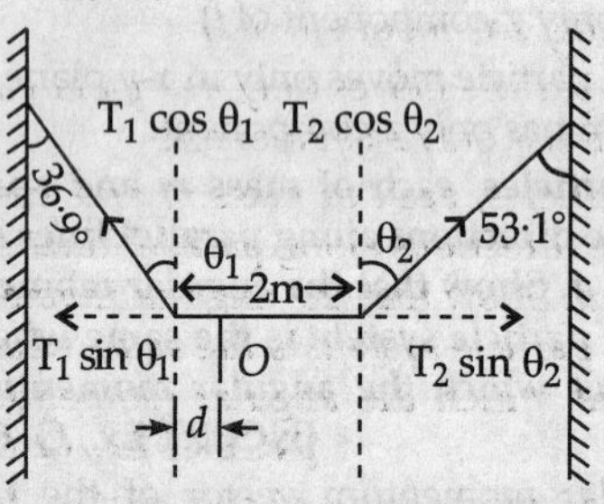

Let O be the position of centre of gravity of rod from left & at distance d.

For rotational equilibrium of rod about O, the moment of vertical forces must be equal and opposite:

$$T_1 \cos\theta_1 \times d = T_2 \cos\theta_2 (2-d)$$

or $$\frac{T_1}{T_2} \times \frac{\cos\theta_1}{\cos\theta_2} = \frac{2-d}{d}$$

From (1)

$$1.3317 \times \frac{\cos 36.9°}{\cos 53.1°} = \frac{2-d}{d}$$

$$1.3317 \times \frac{0.7996}{0.6004} = \frac{2}{d} - 1$$

$$\frac{2}{d} = \frac{1.3317 \times 0.7996}{0.6004} + 1$$

$$d = 0.7211\text{m}$$

Q. 9. A car weighs 1800 kg. The distance between its front and back axles is 1.8 m. Its centre of gravity is 1.05 m behind the front axle. Determine the force exerted by the level ground on each front wheel and each back wheel. **[NCERT Ex., Q. 6.9, Page 125]**

Ans. Mass of the car, m = 1800 kg

Distance between the front and back axles, d= 1.8 m

Distance between the C.G. (centre of gravity) and the back axle = 1.05 m

The various forces acting on the car are shown in the following figure.

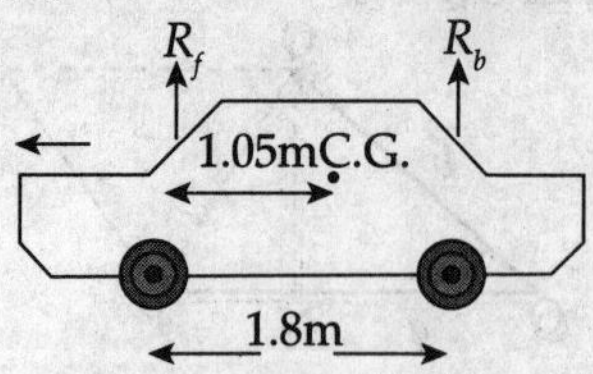

R_f *and* R_b are the forces exerted by the level ground on the front and back wheels respectively.

At translational equilibrium:

$$R_f + R_b = mg$$
$$= 1800 \times 9.8$$
$$= 17640 \text{ N} \quad \ldots(i)$$

For rotational equilibrium, on taking the torque about the C.G., we have:

$$R_f (1.05) = R_b (1.8\text{-}1.05)$$

$$R_f \times (1.05) = R_b \times 0.75$$

$$\frac{R_f}{R_b} = \frac{0.75}{1.05} = \frac{5}{7}$$

$$\frac{R_b}{R_f} = \frac{7}{5}$$

$$R_b = 1.4R_f \quad \ldots(ii)$$

Solving equations *(i)* and *(ii)*, we get

$$1.4R_f + R_f = 17640$$

$$R_f = \frac{17640}{2.4} = 7350\text{N}$$

$$\therefore \quad R_b = 17640 - 7350 = 10290\ N$$

Therefore, the force exerted on each front wheel = $\frac{7350}{2}$ = 3675*N*, and

The force exerted on each back wheel = $\frac{10290}{2}$ = 5145N

Q.10. Torques of equal magnitude are applied to a hollow cylinder and a solid sphere, both having the same mass and radius. The cylinder is free to rotate about its standard axis of symmetry, and the sphere is free to rotate about an axis passing through its centre. Which of the two will acquire a greater angular speed after a given time ?

[NCERT Ex., Q. 6.10, Page 126]

Ans. Moment of inertia of the cylinder

$$I_1 = MR^2$$

and Moment of inertia of the sphere

$$I_2 = \frac{2}{5}MR^2$$

Angular acceleration of cylinder

$$\gamma_1 = \frac{\tau}{I_1} = \frac{\tau}{MR^2}$$

Angular acceleration of sphere

$$\gamma_2 = \frac{\tau}{I_2} = \frac{\tau}{\frac{2}{5}MR^2}$$

$$= 2{\cdot}5\,\frac{\tau}{MR^2}$$

$$= 2{\cdot}5\,\gamma_1$$

From $\omega = \omega_0 + \alpha t$, we find that for given ω_0 and t, $\omega_2 > \omega_1$ i.e., angular speed of solid sphere will be greater than angular speed of hollow cylinder.

Q.11. A solid cylinder of mass 20 kg rotates about its axis with angular speed 100 rad s^{-1}. The radius of the cylinder is 0.25m. What is the kinetic energy associated with the rotation of the cylinder ? What is the magnitude of angular momentum of the cylinder about its axis ? [NCERT Ex., Q. 6.11, Page 126]

Ans. As $(K.E.)_{rot} = \frac{1}{2}I\omega^2$

Here, $I = \frac{1}{2}MR^2 = \frac{20}{2} \times (0{\cdot}25)^2$

$= 0{\cdot}625$ kg-m^2

$\omega = 100$ rad s^{-1},

we get $(K.E.)_{rot} = \frac{1}{2} \times 0{\cdot}625 \times (100)^2$

$= 3125$ J

Angular momentum,

$L = I\omega$

$= 0{\cdot}625 \times 100$

$= 62{\cdot}5$ kgm^{2}s^{-1}.

Q.12. (a) A child stands at the centre of a turntable with his two arms outstretched. The turntable is set rotating with an angular speed of 40 rev/min. How much is the angular speed of the child if he folds his hands back and thereby reduces his moment of inertia to 2/5 times the initial value? Assume that the turntable rotates without friction.

(b) Show that the child's new kinetic energy of rotation is more than the initial kinetic energy of rotation. How do you account for this increase in kinetic energy? [NCERT Ex., Q. 6.12, Page 126]

Ans. Given: $\omega_1 = 40$ rev/min., $I_2 = \frac{2}{5}I_1$

(a) As no external torque is acting on system

So, L=constant= $I\omega$

$I_1\omega_1 = I_2\omega_2$

or $\omega_2 = \frac{I_1}{I_2}\omega_1 = \frac{5}{2} \times 40 = 100\,\text{rpm}$

(b) $$\frac{K.E_f}{K.E_i} = \frac{\frac{1}{2}I_2\omega_2^2}{\frac{1}{2}I_1\omega_1^2} = \left(\frac{I_2}{I_1}\right)\left(\frac{\omega_2}{\omega_1}\right)^2$$

$$= \frac{2}{5} \times \left(\frac{100}{40}\right)^2$$

$= 2.5$

Therefore, $K.E_{final} = 2.5K.E_{initial}$

This increase in K.E. is because of fact that child spends his internal energy in folding his hands which is converting into its kinetic energy.

Q.13. A rope of negligible mass is wound round a hollow cylinder of mass 3 kg and radius 40 cm. What is the angular acceleration of the cylinder if the rope is pulled with a force of 30 N ? What is the linear acceleration of the rope ? Assume that there is no slipping. [NCERT Ex., Q. 6.13, Page 126]

Ans. Here, $M = 3$ kg,

$R = 40$ cm $= 0{\cdot}4$ m.

Moment of inertia of the hollow cylinder about its axis

$I = MR^2$

$= 3 \times (0{\cdot}4)^2$ kgm^2

$= 0{\cdot}48$ kg-m^2

When force of 30 N is applied over the rope wound on the cylinder, the torque will act on the cylinder. It is given by

$\tau = FR = 30 \times 0{\cdot}4 = 12$ Nm.

If γ is angular acceleration produced, then,

$\tau = I\gamma$

or $\gamma = \frac{\tau}{I} = \frac{12}{0.48} = 25$ rad s^{-2}.

The linear acceleration of the rope

$a = R\alpha = 0{\cdot}4 \times 25 = 10$ ms^{-2}

Q.14. To maintain a rotor at a uniform angular speed of 200 rad s^{-1}, an engine needs to transmit a torque of 180 Nm. What is the power required by the engine ? Assume that the engine is 100% efficient. [NCERT Ex., Q. 6.14, Page 126]

Ans. Here, $\tau = 180$ Nm, $\omega = 200$ rads^{-1}.

As $P = \tau\omega$

$\therefore$ $P = 180 \times 200$

$= 36000$ W $= 36$ kW

Hence, the power required by the engine is 36 kW.

Q.15. From a uniform disk of radius R, a circular section of radius R/2 is cut out. The centre of the hole is at R/2, from the centre of the original disc. Locate the centre of mass of the resulting flat body. [NCERT Ex., Q. 6.15, Page 126]

Ans. Suppose mass per unit area of the disc $= m$

$\therefore$ Mass of portion removed from the disc,

$M' = \pi\,(R/2)^2 \times m$

$= \frac{\pi R^2}{4}m = \frac{M}{4}$, [M = mass of disc]

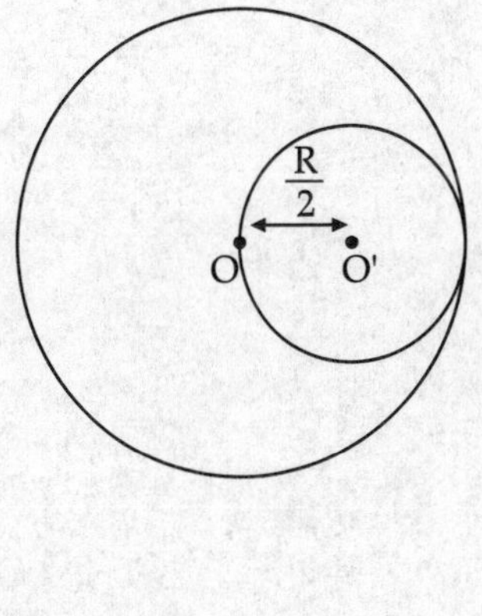

In figure, mass M is concentrated at O and mass M' is concentrated at O', where $OO' = R/2$.

After the circular disc of mass M' is removed, the remaining portion can be considered as a system of two masses M at O and $M' = \frac{M}{4}$ at O'. If x is the distance of centre of mass of the remaining part,

then, $$x = \frac{M \times 0 - M' \times R/2}{M + M'}$$

$$= \frac{\frac{-M}{4} \times \frac{R}{2}}{M - \frac{M}{4}}$$

$$= \frac{-MR}{8} \times \frac{4}{3M}$$

$$= \frac{-R}{6}$$

Negative sign shows that P is to the left of O.

Q.16. A meter stick is balanced on a knife edge at its centre. When two coins, each of mass 5 g are put one on top of the other at the 12·0 cm mark, the stick is found to be balanced at 45·0 cm. What is the mass of meter stick ? [NCERT Ex., Q. 6.16, Page 126]

Ans. Let m be the mass of the stick concentrated at C, the 50 cm mark

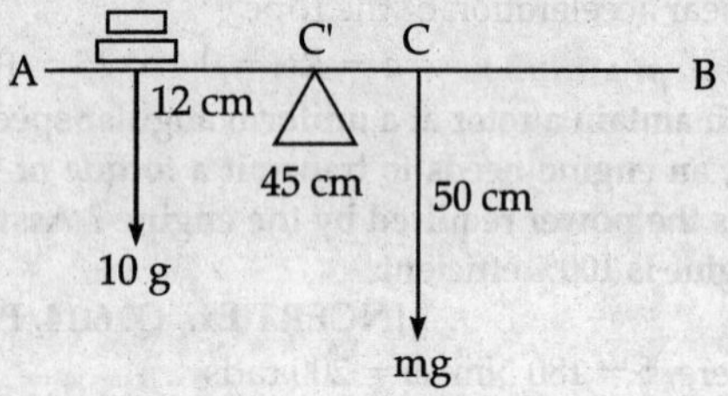

For equilibrium

$$10\,g(45 - 12) = mg(50 - 45)$$

$$10g \times 33 = mg \times 5$$

$$m = \frac{10 \times 33}{5}$$

$$= 66\,g$$

Q. 17. The oxygen molecule has a mass of 5.30 × 10⁻²⁶ kg and a moment of inertia of 1.94× 10⁻⁴⁶ *kg m²* about an axis through its centre perpendicular to the lines joining the two atoms. Suppose the mean speed of such a molecule in a gas is 500 m/s and that its kinetic energy of rotation is two thirds of its kinetic energy of translation. Find the average angular velocity of the molecule. [NCERT Ex., Q. 6.17, Page 126]

Ans. Mass of an oxygen molecule, $m = 5.30 \times 10^{-26}$ kg

Moment of inertia, $I = 1.94 \times 10^{-46}$ kg m²

Velocity of the oxygen molecule, $v = 500$ m/s

The separation between the two atoms of the oxygen molecule = $2r$

Mass of each oxygen atom = $\frac{m}{2}$

Hence, moment of inertia I, is calculated as:

$$\left(\frac{m}{2}\right)r^2 + \left(\frac{m}{2}\right)r^2 = mr^2$$

$$r = \sqrt{\frac{I}{m}}$$

$$r = \sqrt{\frac{1.94 \times 10^{-46}}{5.30 \times 10^{-26}}} = 0.60 \times 10^{-10}\,\text{m}$$

It is given that:

$$KE_{rot} = \frac{2}{3} KE_{trans}$$

$$\frac{1}{2} I\omega^2 = \frac{2}{3} \times \frac{1}{2} \times mv^2$$

$$mr^2\omega^2 = \frac{2}{3} mv^2$$

$$\omega = \sqrt{\frac{2}{3}} \frac{v}{r}$$

$$= \sqrt{\frac{2}{3}} \times \frac{500}{0.6 \times 10^{-10}}$$

$$= 6.80 \times 10^{12}\,\text{rad/s}$$

□□

GRAVITATION

CHAPTER 7

Kepler's Law

➢ **Kepler's Laws of Planetary Motion:**

(a) Kepler's I Law (Law of Orbits): Each planet revolves around the Sun in an elliptical orbit. The Sun is situated at one foci of the ellipse.

(b) Kepler's II Law (Law of Areas): The position vector of the planet from the Sun sweeps out equal area in equal interval of time. That is the areal velocity of the planet around the Sun is constant.

(c) Kepler's III Law (Law of Periods): The square of the time period of any planet about the Sun is proportional to the cube of the semi-major axis of the elliptical orbit.

$$\frac{T_1^2}{T_2^2} = \frac{r_1^3}{r_2^3}$$

Scan to know more about this topic

Kepler's law

Universal Law of Gravitation

It states that every body in universe attracts every other body with a force which is directly proportional to the product of their masses and is inversely proportional to the square of the distance between them and its direction is along line joining the two masses.

$$\mathbf{F} \propto \frac{m_1 m_2}{r^2} \quad \text{or} \quad \mathbf{F} = \frac{G m_1 m_2}{r^2}$$

Gravitational constant (G)

➢ It is defined as the force of attraction acting between two bodies each of unit mass, whose centres are placed at unit distance apart. The value of G is constant throughout the universe. It is a *scalar quantity*. The dimensional formula of $G = [M^{-1}L^3T^{-2}]$. The value of $G = 6.67 \times 10^{-11}$ Nm^2kg^{-2}.

The value of G being too small, we do not experience gravitational force in our daily life.

➢ **Gravity:** It is the force of attraction exerted by Earth towards its centre on a body lying on or near the surface of the Earth.

Gravity is the measure of weight of the body.

The weight of the body = mass (m) × acceleration due to gravity (g) = mg.

The unit of weight of the body will be the same as those of force.

Gravity is a vector quantity. It is always directed towards the centre of Earth. Gravity holds the atmosphere around the Earth.

Acceleration due to gravity (g)

➢ **Acceleration due to gravity (g):** It is defined as the acceleration set up in a body while falling freely under the effect of gravity alone.

Acceleration due to gravity is a vector quantity. It is directed towards the centre of Earth.

The unit of g is ms^{-2} and its dimensional formula is $[M^0LT^{-2}]$.

(a) The acceleration due to gravity does not depend upon (a) the mass of body, (b) shape or size of the body.

➢ **Variation of acceleration due to gravity.**

(a) Effect of altitude: $g' = g\left(1 - \frac{2h}{R}\right)$

(b) Effect of depth: $g' = g\left(1 - \frac{d}{R}\right)$, d = depth below Earth surface

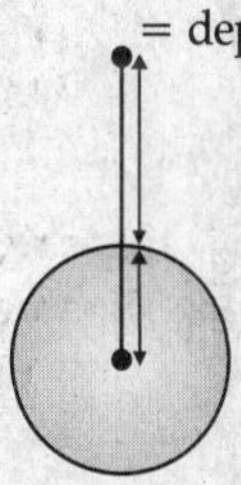

(c) Rotation of Earth: $g = g' + R\omega^2 \cos^2 \lambda$

or $g' = g - R\omega^2 \cos^2 \lambda$

where, ω is the angular velocity of rotation of Earth about its polar axis and λ is the latitude of a place.

(i) At the equator, $\lambda = 0°$,

so $g' = g - R\omega^2 \cos^2 0° = g - R\omega^2$

(ii) At the poles, $\lambda = 90°$,

so $g' = g - R\omega^2 \cos^2 90° = g$

Hence, the value of acceleration due to gravity increases from equator to pole due to rotation of Earth. It means the value of g increases with latitude.

(iii) When the Earth stops rotating about its own axis, there will be no change in the value of g on the poles, but there will be increase in the value of g by about 0.35% at the equator.

Scan to know more about this topic

Gravitational potential Escape speed

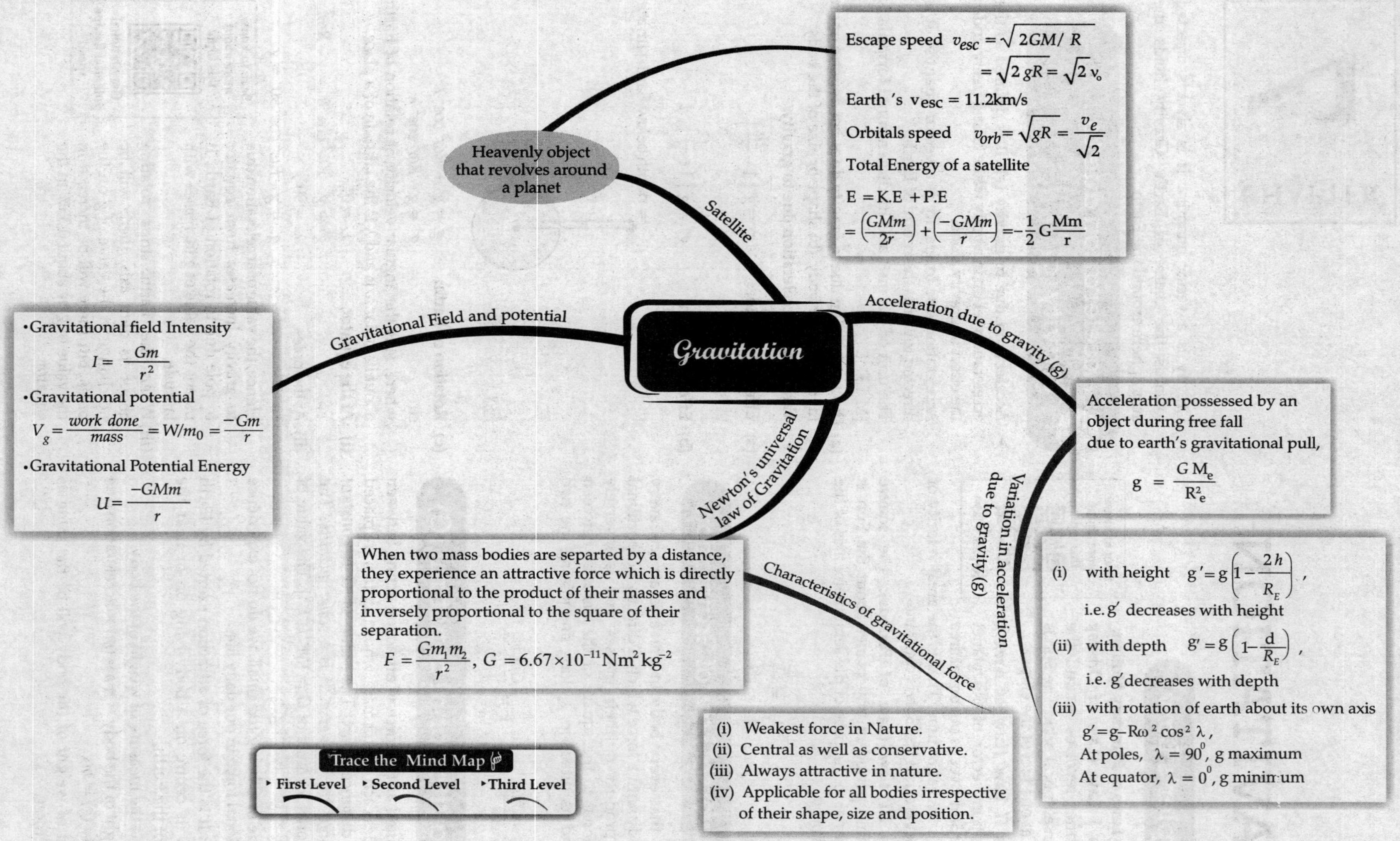
Gravitation
Satellite
Heavenly object that revolves around a planet
Escape speed $v_{esc} = \sqrt{2GM/R}$
$= \sqrt{2gR} = \sqrt{2}\,v_o$
Earth's v_{esc} = 11.2km/s
Orbitals speed $v_{orb} = \sqrt{gR} = \frac{v_e}{\sqrt{2}}$
Total Energy of a satellite
E = K.E + P.E
$= \left(\frac{GMm}{2r}\right) + \left(\frac{-GMm}{r}\right) = -\frac{1}{2}G\frac{Mm}{r}$
Acceleration due to gravity (g)
Acceleration possessed by an object during free fall due to earth's gravitational pull,
$g = \frac{GM_e}{R_e^2}$
Variation in acceleration due to gravity (g)
(i) with height $g' = g\left(1 - \frac{2h}{R_E}\right)$,
i.e. g′ decreases with height
(ii) with depth $g' = g\left(1 - \frac{d}{R_E}\right)$,
i.e. g′ decreases with depth
(iii) with rotation of earth about its own axis
$g' = g - R\omega^2\cos^2\lambda$,
At poles, $\lambda = 90^0$, g maximum
At equator, $\lambda = 0^0$, g minimum
Characteristics of gravitational force
(i) Weakest force in Nature.
(ii) Central as well as conservative.
(iii) Always attractive in nature.
(iv) Applicable for all bodies irrespective of their shape, size and position.
Newton's universal law of Gravitation
When two mass bodies are separted by a distance, they experience an attractive force which is directly proportional to the product of their masses and inversely proportional to the square of their separation.
$F = \frac{Gm_1m_2}{r^2}$, $G = 6.67\times10^{-11}\,Nm^2kg^{-2}$
Gravitational Field and potential
•Gravitational field Intensity
$I = \frac{Gm}{r^2}$
•Gravitational potential
$V_g = \frac{work\ done}{mass} = W/m_0 = \frac{-Gm}{r}$
•Gravitational Potential Energy
$U = \frac{-GMm}{r}$
Trace the Mind Map
First Level
Second Level
Third Level

(d) Shape of the Earth. Earth is not a perfect sphere. It is flattened at the poles and bulges out at the equator. The polar radius of Earth is smaller than its equatorial radius by 21 km. As $g = GM/R^2$, so $g \propto 1/R^2$.

It means the value of acceleration due to gravity increases as we go from equator to pole.

Gravitational Potential Energy

- **Gravitational potential energy (U):** The amount of work done in bringing a body from infinity to a point in gravitational field.

$$U = \frac{GMm}{r}$$

- **Escape Velocity:** The minimum velocity with which a body must be projected up in the space, so as to enable it to just overcome the gravitational pull.

$$v_e = \sqrt{\frac{2GM}{R}} = \sqrt{2gR}. \quad \text{as} \left[g = \frac{GM}{R^2}\right]$$

- **Satellite: A satellite is a body which is revolving continuously in an orbit around a comparatively much larger body.**

(i) Natural satellites: All those satellites were made by nature. ***e.g.*****, Jupiter–16 Moons. Saturn–18 Moons.**

(ii) Artificial satellites: All man-made satellites ***e.g.*****, Aryabhatta, etc.**

- Gravitational forces are **central forces** as they act along the line joining the centres of the two bodies. The gravitational forces are **conservative forces.**

Key Words

- **Areal velocity** may be defined as the area swept by the radius vector in unit time.
- **Cavendish method** determines the value of G.
- **Geodesic** is the shortest distance between two points on Earth.
- **Aphelion** is the nearest point of planet from Sun.
- **Perihelion** is the farthest point of planet from Sun.
- **Gravitational field** is the space around a material body in which its gravitational pull can be experienced.
- **Gravitational field intensity** of a body at a point in the field is defined as the force experienced by a body of unit mass placed at that point provided the presence of unit mass does not disturb the original gravitational field.
- **Gravitational potential** at a point in a gravitational field of a body is defined as the amount of work done in bringing a body of unit mass from infinity to that point without acceleration.
- **Mass** of a body is the quantity of matter possessed by body.
- **Inertial mass of a body** is equal to the magnitude of external force required to produce unit acceleration in the body.
- **Gravitational mass** of a body is defined as the magnitude of gravitational pull experienced by the body in a gravitational field of unit intensity.
- **Centre of Gravity (C.G.)** of a body placed in the gravitational field is that point where the net gravitational force of the field acts.

Key Formulae

- Kepler's Law :

$$T^2 = kr^3$$

$$\frac{T_1^2}{T_2^2} = \frac{r_1^3}{r_2^3},$$

Here, T = Time period and r = Semi major axis.

- Newton's Gravitational Law :

$$F = \frac{Gm_1m_2}{r^2}$$

- **Relation between g & G** $g = \dfrac{GM}{R^2}$
- **Gravitational Intensity :** $I = \dfrac{F}{m_0} = \dfrac{GM}{R^2} = g$
- **Graitational Potential :** $V = \dfrac{W}{m_0}$

$$V = \frac{GM}{r}$$

- **Gravitational Potential Energy :**

$$U = \frac{-GMm}{r}$$

- **Satellite :**

(a) Orbital speed : $v = R\sqrt{\dfrac{g}{R+h}} = \sqrt{\dfrac{GM}{R+h}}$

(b) Time period of revolution :

$$T = \frac{2\pi}{R}\sqrt{\frac{(R+h)^3}{g}}$$

(c) Height of satellite : $h = \left(\dfrac{T^2R^2g}{4\pi^2}\right) - R$

- **Escape speed**

$$v_e = \sqrt{\frac{2GM}{R}} = \sqrt{2gR} \Rightarrow \left[g = \frac{GM}{R^2}\right]$$

Mnemonics

Concept: Kepler's laws of planetary motion:

Mnemonics: Take **e**ssential **f**oods **e**veryday **2/3** **t**imes.

Interpretation:

e - elliptical

f - focus

1st law: Planet moves is **elliptical** orbit with sun at one of the **foci.**

e equal - 2nd law: A planet covers the **equal** area of space in **equal** interval of time.

2/3 - 2/3

t - time period

3rd law: Semi-major axis of the orbit is proportional to **(time period)$^{2/3}$**

NCERT CORNER

Q.1. Answer the following:

(a) You can shield a charge from electrical forces by putting it inside a hollow conductor. Can you shield a body from gravitational influence of nearby matter by putting it inside a hollow sphere or by some other means?

(b) An astronaut inside a small spaceship orbiting around the Earth cannot detect gravity. If the space station orbiting around the Earth has a large size can he hope to detect gravity?

(c) If you compare the gravitational force on the Earth due to the Sun to that due to the Moon, you would find that the Sun's pull is greater than Moon's pull. However, the tidal effect of the Moon's pull is greater than the tidal effect of the Sun. Why?

[NCERT Ex., Q. 7.1, Page 141]

Ans. (a) No. Electrical forces depend upon the nature of the intervening medium while the gravitational forces don't depend upon the nature of the intervening medium. So, such shielding acts are not possible in case of gravitation, i.e., gravity screens are not possible.

(b) Yes, astronaut can hope to detect gravity if the size of the spaceship is extremely large, then the magnitude of the gravity will become appreciable and hence, the gravitational effect of the spaceship may become measurable.

(c) Earth-Moon distance is very small as compared to Earth-Sun distance. Tidal effect is inversely proportional to the cube of the distance. It is not governed by inverse square law like the gravitational force (which obeys inverse square law). Hence, tidal effect of Moon is larger than that due to the Sun.

Q. 2. Choose the correct alternative

(a) Acceleration due to gravity increases/decreases with increasing altitude.

(b) Acceleration due to gravity increases/decreases with increasing depth.
(assume the Earth to be a sphere of uniform density).

(c) Acceleration due to gravity is independent of the mass of the Earth/mass of the body.

(d) The formula $-GMm\left(\frac{1}{r_2}-\frac{1}{r_1}\right)$ is more/less accurate than the formula $mg(r_2 - r_1)$ for the difference of potential energy between two points r_2 and r_1 distance away from the centre of the Earth.

[NCERT Ex., Q. 7.2, Page 142]

Ans. (a) decreases
(b) decreases
(c) independent of mass of the body
(d) more

Q. 3. Suppose there existed a planet that went around the Sun twice as fast as the earth. What would be its orbital size as compared to that of the earth?

[NCERT Ex., Q. 7.3, Page 141]

Ans. (a) Time taken by Earth to complete one revolution around the Sun,

$$T_e = 1 \text{ year}$$

Time taken by another planet to complete one revolution around the Sun, $T_p = \frac{1}{2}, T_e = \frac{1}{2}$ year

Orbital radius of the planet $= R_p$

From Kepler's Third law of planetary motion

$$\left(\frac{R_p}{R_e}\right) = \left(\frac{T_p}{T_e}\right)^2$$

$$\left(\frac{R_p}{R_e}\right) = \left(\frac{T_p}{T_e}\right)^{2/3}$$

$$(0.5)^{2/3} = 0.63\ R_e$$

Hence, the orbital radius of the planet will be 0.63 times of the Earth.

Q. 4. Io, one of the satellites of Jupiter, has an orbital period of 1.769 days and the radius of the orbit is 4.22 × 10⁸ m. Show that the mass of Jupiter is about one-thousandth that of the sun.

[NCERT Ex., Q. 7.4, Page 141]

Ans. Mass of $I_0 = m'$

Mass of Jupiter $= m$

Mass of sun, $M = 1.989 \times 10^{90}$ kg

$$\frac{Gmm'}{r^2} = m'\omega^2 r$$

or, $$Gm = \omega^2 r^3$$

or, $$m = \frac{\left(\frac{2\pi}{r}\right)^2 . r^3}{G}$$

$$= \frac{Gm^2 \times (4.22 \times 10^3)^3}{(1.769 \times 2r \times 3600)^2 \times 6.67 \times 10^{-11}} \text{ kg}$$

$$= 1.90a \times 10^{27} \text{ kg}$$

$$\frac{m}{M} = \frac{1.904 \times 10^{27}}{1.989 \times 10^{30}} \approx \frac{1}{1000}$$

Q. 5. Let us assume that our galaxy consists of 2.5 × 10¹¹ stars each of one solar mass. How long will a star at a distance of 50,000 ly from the galactic centre take to complete one revolution? Take the diameter of the Milky Way to be 10⁵ ly. [NCERT Ex., Q. 7.5, Page 141]

Ans. Mass of our galaxy Milky Way, $M = 2.5 \times 10^{11}$ solar mass

1 Solar mass = Mass of Sun $= 2.0 \times 10^{36}$ kg

Mass of our galaxy, $M = 2.5 \times 10^{11} \times 2 \times 10^{36} = 5 \times 10^{41}$ kg

Diameter of Milky Way, $d = 10^5\ ly$

Radius of Milky Way, $r = 5 \times 10^4\ ly$

$1\ ly = 9.46 \times 10^{15}$ m

$\Rightarrow r = 5 \times 10^4 \times 9.46 \times 10^{15}$

$= 4.73 \times 10^{20}$ m

Since a star revolves around the galactic centre of the Milky Way, its time period is given by the relation:

$$T = \left(\frac{4\pi^2 r^3}{GM}\right)^{1/2}$$

$$= \sqrt{\frac{4\times 3.14^2 \times 4.73^3 \times 10^{60}}{6.67\times 10^{-11}\times 5\times 10^{41}}}$$

$$= 1.12 \times 10^{16}\ \text{s}$$

$$= \frac{1.12\times 10^{16}}{365\times 24\times 60\times 60}$$

$$= 3.55 \times 10^{8}\ \text{years}$$

Q. 6. Choose the correct alternative:

(a) If the zero of potential energy is at infinity the total energy on orbiting satellite is negative of its kinetic/ potential energy.

(b) The energy required to launch an orbiting satellite out of Earth's gravitational influence is more / less than the energy required to project a stationary object at the same height (as can the satellite) out of Earth influences. [NCERT Ex., Q. 7.6, Page 142]

Ans. (a) Kinetic energy,

(b) Less.

Q. 7. Does the escape speed of body from the Earth depend upon:

(a) the mass of the body ?

(b) the location from where it is projected ?

(c) the direction of projection ?

(d) the height of location from where the body is launched ? [NCERT Ex., Q. 7.7, Page 142]

Ans. (a) No, from the formula $v_e = \sqrt{\frac{2GM}{R}}$, it is clear that escape velocity does not depend on the mass of the body.

(b) The escape velocity depends upon the value of gravitational potential at the point from where the body is projected. The gravitational potential energy of body $E = -\frac{GMm}{R}$ is slightly different at different points (the Earth is not a perfect sphere and hence R is different at different points). Because of this escape velocity depend slightly on the latitude of the place from where the body is projected.

(c) The escape velocity of a body does not depend upon its direction of projection.

(d) Since the gravitational potential energy at a point at the height h from the Earth surface is $\frac{GMm}{(R+h)}$, the escape velocity will be different for different values of h.

Q. 8. A comet orbits the Sun in a highly elliptical orbit. Does the comet have a constant:

(a) Linear speed,

(b) Angular speed,

(c) Angular momentum,

(d) Kinetic energy,

(e) Potential energy,

(f) Total energy throughout it orbit ?

Neglect mass loss of the comet when it comes very close to the Sun ? [NCERT Ex., Q. 7.8, Page 142]

Ans. (a) The linear speed ($v = \omega R$) changes because the distance, (R) of the comet from the Sun changes due to it elliptical orbit around the Sun.

(b) The angular speed of the comet also changes because it covers different angle in equal interval of time.

(c) The angular momentum of the comet is same throughout due to the conservation of angular momentum in the absence of any torque.

(d) Kinetic energy changes because linear speed is different at different points.

(e) The potential energy at different points is different because the comet is not at the same distance from the Sun (the orbit is not circular).

(f) The total energy of comet remain the same throughout the motion.

Q. 9. Which of the following symptoms is likely to afflict an astronaut in space (a) swollen feet, (b) swollen face, (c) headache, (d) orientation problem. [NCERT Ex., Q. 7.9, Page 142]

Ans. The astronaut in space will suffer from (a) swollen face, (b) headache and (c) orientation problem.

(a) We know that legs carry the weight of the body in the normal position due to gravity pull. The astronaut in space is in weightlessness state. Hence, swollen feet may not effect his working.

Due to weightlessness the astronaut may develop swollen face. As eyes, ears, nose are all embedded in face.

(b) Headache is due to mental strain. It will persist whether a person is an astronaut in space or Earth.

(c) Space also has orientation, we also have the frames of reference.

Q. 10. In the following two questions, choose the correct answer from the given ones. The gravitational intensity at the centre of a hemispherical shell of uniform mass density has the direction indicated by the arrow (see Fig).

(i) a, (ii) b, (iii) c, (iv) 0

[NCERT Ex., Q. 7.10, Page 142]

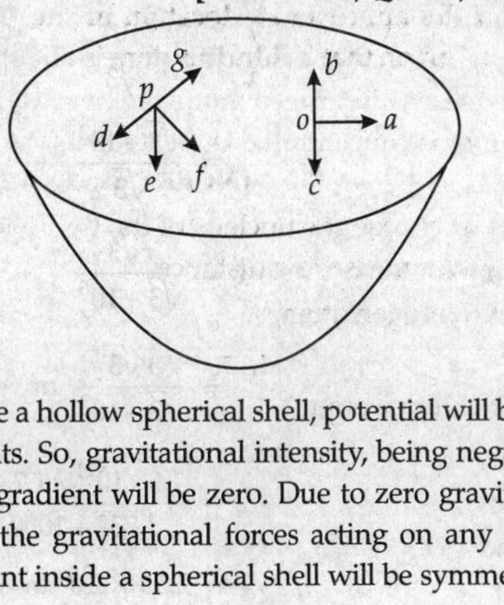

Ans. Inside a hollow spherical shell, potential will be same at all points. So, gravitational intensity, being negative of potential gradient will be zero. Due to zero gravitational intensity, the gravitational forces acting on any particle at any point inside a spherical shell will be symmetrically placed. So, if we remove the upper hemispherical shell, the net gravitational force acting on a particle at P will be downwards. Since gravitational intensity is gravitational force per unit mass, so, the direction of gravitational intensity will be along c. So, option (iii) is correct.

Q. 11. For the above problem, the direction of the gravitational intensity at any arbitrary point P is indicated by the arrow (i) *d*, (ii) *e*, (iii) *f*, (iv) *g*. [NCERT Ex., Q. 7.11, Page 142]

Ans. Using the above explanation, the direction of gravitational field intensity at P will be along e. So, option (ii) is correct.

Q. 12. A rocket is fired from the Earth towards the Sun. At what distance from the Earth's centre is the gravitational force on the rocket zero? Mass of the Sun = 2 × 10³⁰ kg, mass of the Earth = 6 × 10²⁴ kg. Neglect the effect of other planets etc. (orbital radius = 1.5 × 10¹¹ m.) [NCERT Ex., Q. 7.12, Page 142]

Ans. Here, $M_s = 2 \times 10^{30}$ kg;

$M_e = 6 \times 10^{24}$ kg;

$r = 1.5 \times 10^{11}$ m

Let x be the distance of a point from the Earth where gravitational forces on the rocket due to Sun and Earth become equal and opposite. Then distance of rocket from the Sun = $(r - x)$

If m is the mass of rocket then

$$\frac{GM_s m}{(r-x)^2} = \frac{GM_e m}{x^2}$$

or $$\frac{(r-x)^2}{x^2} = \frac{M_s}{M_e}$$

$$\frac{r-x}{x} = \sqrt{\frac{M_s}{M_e}}$$

$$= \sqrt{\frac{2\times10^{30}}{6\times10^{24}}}$$

$$= \frac{10^3}{\sqrt{3}}$$

$$\frac{r}{x} - 1 = \frac{10^3}{\sqrt{3}}$$

$$\frac{r}{x} = 1 + \frac{10^3}{\sqrt{3}}$$

$$= \frac{\sqrt{3}+10^3}{\sqrt{3}}$$

so, $$x = \frac{r\sqrt{3}}{\sqrt{3}+10^3}$$

$$= \frac{r\sqrt{3}}{\sqrt{3}+10^3} \text{ m}$$

$$= \frac{1.5\times10^{11}\times1.732}{1.732+1000} \text{ m}$$

$$= 2.55 \times 10^8 \text{ m}$$

Q. 13. How will you weigh the Sun, i.e., estimate its mass ? The mean orbital radius of the Earth around the Sun is 1·5 × 10⁸ km. [NCERT Ex., Q. 7.13, Page 142]

Ans. It is clear that Earth revolves around the Sun in an orbit of radius 1.5 × 10¹¹ m and completes a revolution around the Sun in 365 days.

$\therefore R$ = radius of orbit of Earth = 1.5×10^{11} m

T = Time period of Earth around the Sun = 365 days = 365 × 24 × 60 × 60 s.

$G = 6.67 \times 10^{11}$ Nm² kg⁻²

From the relation,

$$\frac{R^3}{T^2} = \frac{GM_s}{4\pi^2 R^2} \quad \text{where } s_s = \text{mass of Sun}$$

or $$M_s = \frac{4\pi^2 R^3}{T^2 G}$$

or $$M_s = \frac{4\times9.87\times\left(1.5\times10^{11}\right)^3}{(365\times24\times60\times60)^2\times6.67\times10^{-11}} \text{ kg}$$

or $M_s = 2.0 \times 10^{30}$ kg.

$\therefore$ Mass of Sun = 2.0×10^{30} kg.

Q. 14. A saturn year is 29·5 times the Earth year. How far is the saturn from the Sun if the Earth is 1·5 × 10⁸ km away from the Sun ? [NCERT Ex., Q. 7.14, Page 142]

Ans. Here, $T_s = 29.5\, T_e$

$R_e = 1.5 \times 10^8$ km;

$R_s = ?$

Using the relation,

$$\frac{T_s^2}{R_s^3} = \frac{T_e^2}{R_e^3}$$

or $$R_s = R_e\left(\frac{T_s}{T_e}\right)^{2/3}$$

$$= 1.5 \times 10^8 \left[\frac{29.5\, T_e}{T_e}\right]^{2/3}$$

$$= 1.43 \times 10^9 \text{ km}$$

Q. 15. A body weighs 63 N on the surface of Earth. What is the gravitational force on it due to the Earth at a height equal to half the radius of Earth ? [NCERT Ex., Q. 7.15, Page 142]

Ans. Let h = height above Earth's surface = $\frac{R}{2}$

where, R = radius of Earth

Now, the acceleration due to gravity at a height 'h' above Earth's surface (g) is given by

$$g_h = g\left(1+\frac{h}{R}\right)^{-2}$$

Given, $$h = \frac{R}{2}$$

$\therefore$ $$g_h = g\left(1+\frac{R/2}{R}\right)^{-2}$$

or $\dfrac{g_h}{g} = \dfrac{1}{\left(1+\dfrac{1}{2}\right)^2} = \dfrac{1}{\left(\dfrac{3}{2}\right)^2}$

$= \left(\dfrac{2}{3}\right)^2 = \dfrac{4}{9}$

or $g_h = \dfrac{4}{9} \times g = \dfrac{4}{9} g$ ...(i)

Let m = mass of the body

If W and W_h be its weight at Earth's surface and at a height h above Earth's surface respectively, then

$W = mg = 63$ N (given)

and $W_h = mg_h = m \times \dfrac{4}{9} g = \dfrac{4}{9} mg$

or $W_s = \dfrac{4}{9} \times 63 = 28$ N

So, $W_h = 28$ N

Q. 16. Assuming the Earth to be a sphere of uniform mass density, how much would a body weight half way down to the centre of Earth, if it weighed 250 N on the surface ? [NCERT Ex., Q. 7.16, Page 142]

Ans. Suppose g, g_d be the acceleration due to gravity on Earth's surface and at a depth 'd', from surface respectively.

Also, suppose W and W_d be the weight of a body on Earth's surface and at depth 'd', respectively,

$\therefore$ $W = mg = 250$ N ...(i)

and $W_d = mg_d$ ...(ii)

Now, we know that

$g_d = g\left(1 - \dfrac{d}{R}\right)$ ...(iii)

Here, $d = \dfrac{R}{2}$, R = radius of Earth...(iv)

$\therefore$ From equations (iii) and (iv), we get

$g_d = g\left(1 - \dfrac{R/2}{R}\right)$

$= g\left(1 - \dfrac{1}{2}\right) = g \times \left(\dfrac{1}{2}\right)$

$= \dfrac{g}{2}$ ...(v)

$\therefore$ $W_d = mg_d$

$= m\dfrac{g}{2}$ [by using equation (v)]

$= \dfrac{1}{2} mg = \dfrac{1}{2} W$

$= \dfrac{1}{2} \times 250 = 125$ N.

$\therefore$ Weight of the body half way down to the centre of Earth = 125 N.

Q. 17. A rocket is fired vertically with a speed of 5 kms^{-1} from the Earth's surface. How far from the Earth does the rocket go before returning to the Earth? Mass of the Earth = $6{\cdot}0 \times 10^{24}$ kg, mean radius of Earth = 6.4×10^6 m, $G = 6.67 \times 10^{-11}$ Nm^2 kg^{-2}. [NCERT Ex., Q. 7.17, Page 143]

Ans. Suppose v be the initial speed of the rocket which reaches a height h above the surface of Earth where its velocity vanishes, i.e., becomes zero.

When m be the mass of the rocket, then its total energy at Earth's surface is

$K.E. + P.E. = \dfrac{1}{2} mv^2 - \dfrac{GMm}{R}$ ...(i)

where, M = Mass of Earth

R = Radius of Earth

G = Universal gravitational constant

At highest point,

$K.E. = 0$ ($\because$ Velocity = 0)

and $P.E. = -\dfrac{GMm}{R+h}$ ...(ii)

$\therefore$ Total energy of the rocket at a height h is given by

$= K.E. + P.E. = 0 + P.E.$

$= -\dfrac{GMm}{R+h}$ ...(iii)

From the law of conservation of energy.

$$\frac{1}{2}mv^2 - \frac{GMm}{R} = -\frac{GMm}{R+h}$$

$$\frac{1}{2}v^2 = \frac{GM}{R} - \frac{GM}{R+h}$$

$$= \frac{GM}{R}\left(1 - \frac{R}{R+h}\right) \quad \left(\because \frac{GM}{R^2} = g\right)$$

or $\dfrac{1}{2}v^2 = gR\left(\dfrac{R+h-R}{R+h}\right) = \dfrac{gR}{R+h} h$

or $2gRh = v^2(R + h)$

or $Rv^2 = 2ghR - v^2h = h(2gR - v^2)$

$\therefore$ $h = \dfrac{Rv^2}{2gR - v^2}$ ...(iv)

Given, $v = 5$ kms^{-1}

$= 5000$ ms^{-1} (given)

and $R = 6{\cdot}4 \times 10^6$ m.

Putting these values in eqn. (iv), we have

$\therefore$ $h = \dfrac{6.4 \times 10^6 \times (5 \times 10^3)^2}{2 \times 9.8 \times 6.4 \times 10^6 - (5 \times 10^3)^2}$

$= 1.6 \times 10^6$ m

$\therefore$ Distance from centre of Earth is given by

$= R + h = 6.4 \times 10^6 + 1.6 \times 10^6$

$= 8000$ km

Q. 18. The escape speed of a projectile on the earth's surface is 11.2 km S^{-1}. A body is projectile out with thrice this speed. What is the speed of the body for away from the earth? Ignore the presence of the sun and other places. [NCERT Ex., Q. 7.18, Page 143]

Ans. From principle of conservation of energy

$$\frac{1}{2}mv^2 = \frac{1}{2}mv_i^2 - \frac{1}{2}mv_e^2$$

or $$v = \sqrt{v_i^2 - v_e^2}$$

$$= \sqrt{(2v_e)^2 - v_e^2}$$

$$= \sqrt{3}\, v_e$$

$$= 1.732 \times 11.2 \text{ km/s}$$

$$[\because \sqrt{3} = 1.732]$$

$$= 31.68 \text{ km s}^{-1}.$$

Q. 19. A satellite orbits the Earth at a height of 400 km above the surface. How much energy must be expended to launch, the satellite out of the Earth's gravitational influence ?

Mass of the satellite = 200 kg; mass of the Earth = 6.0 × 10^{24} kg, radius of Earth = 6.4 × 10^6 m; G = 6.67 × 10^{-11} Nm^2-kg^{-2}. **[NCERT Ex., Q. 7.19, Page 143]**

Ans. Given:

$$M = 6 \times 10^{24} \text{ kg}$$

$$m = 200 \text{ kg}$$

$$R = 6.4 \times 10^6 \text{ m}$$

$$x = 0.4 \times 10^6 \text{ m}$$

Using, total energy of satellite in orbit,

$$E = -\frac{GMm}{2(R+x)}$$

we get $$E = -\frac{(6.67\times10^{-11})(6\times10^{24})200}{2(6.4\times10^6 + 0.4\times10^6)} \text{J}$$

$$= -\frac{6.67\times6\times2\times10^{15}}{2\times6.8\times10^6} \text{ J}$$

$$= -5.89 \times 10^9 \text{ J}$$

Energy required to send the satellite

$$= 5.9 \times 10^9 \text{ J}$$

Q. 20. Two stars each of one solar mass (= 2×10^{30} kg) are approaching each other for a head on collision. When they are at distance 10^9 km, their speeds are negligible. What is the speed with which they collide ? The radius of each star is 10^4 km. Assume the stars to remain undistorted until they collide. (Use the known value of G). **[NCERT Ex., Q. 7.20, Page 143]**

Ans. Mass of each star, $M = 2\times10^{30}$ kg

Initial distance between two stars, $r = 10^9$ km

$$= 10^{12} \text{ m}$$

Initial potential energy of the system = $\left(-\frac{GMm}{r}\right)$

Total kinetic energy of the system = $\frac{1}{2}Mv^2 + \frac{1}{2}Mv^2$

Where v is the speed of stars with which they collide. When the stars are about to collide the distance between their centres, $r' = 2R$, where R is their radius.

$\therefore$ Final potential energy of two stars = $-\frac{GMm}{2R}$

Since gain in $K.E$ = loss in $P.E$

$$\therefore Mv^2 = -\frac{GMM}{r} - \left(\frac{-GMM}{2R}\right) = \frac{-GMM}{r} + \frac{GMM}{2R}$$

$$2\times10^{30}v^2 = \frac{-6.67\times10^{-11}\times(2\times10^{30})^2}{10^{12}} + \frac{6.67\times10^{-11}\times(2\times10^{30})^2}{2\times10^7}$$

$$= -2.668\times10^{38} + 1.334\times10^{43}$$

$$= 1.334\times10^{43} J$$

$$\therefore \quad v = \sqrt{\frac{1.334\times10^{43}}{2\times10^{30}}} = \sqrt{0.66\times10^{13}} \text{ m/s}$$

$$= \sqrt{6.67\times10^{12}} = 2.583\times10^6 \text{ ms}^{-1}$$

Q. 21. Two heavy spheres each of mass 100 kg and radius 0.10 m are placed 1.0 m apart on a horizontal table. What is the gravitational force and potential at the mid point of the line joining the centres of the spheres. Is an object placed at the point is in equilibrium ? If so, is the equilibrium stable or unstable ?

[NCERT Ex., Q. 7.21, Page 143]

Ans. Here

$$G = 6.67 \times 10^{-11} \text{ Nm}^2 \text{ kg}^{-2}$$

$$M = 100 \text{ kg}$$

$$R = 0.1 \text{ m}$$

Distance between the two spheres d = 1.0 m

Suppose that the distance of either sphere from the mid point of the line joining their centre is r. Then

$$r = \frac{d}{2} = 0.5 \text{ m}.$$

The gravitational field at the mid point due to two spheres will be equal and opposite.

Hence, the resultant gravitational field at the mid point = 0

The gravitational potential at the mid point.

$$= \left(-\frac{GM}{r}\right)\times 2$$

$$= \frac{-6.67\times10^{-11}\times100\times2}{0.5} \text{ Jkg}$$

$$= -2.668 \times 10^{-8} \text{ Jkg}^{-1}$$

Any object placed at point x will be in equilibrium state, but the equilibrium is unstable. This is because any change in the position of the object will change the effecting force in that direction.

□□

MECHANICAL PROPERTIES OF SOLIDS

CHAPTER 8

Stress and Strain

➤ **Stress** is defined as the restoring force acting per unit area of a deformed body, *i.e.*,

$$\text{Stress} = \frac{\text{Restoring force}}{\text{Area}} = \frac{F}{A}$$

The S.I. unit of stress is N/m^2 and its dimensional formula = $[ML^{-1}T^{-2}]$. **Stress is a tensor quantity. Normal Stress** have following three types:

(a) Longitudinal stress: If a body changes its length under a deforming force and the stress is normal to the surface of the body then the stress is called longitudinal stress. The longitudinal stress can be a tensile stress or compression stress. The longitudinal stress produced because of increase in length of body under deforming force is known as **tensile stress.** The longitudinal stress produced due to decrease in length of body under a deforming force is known as **compression stress.**

(b) Volumetric stress: If a body changes its volume under a normal deforming force acting on every surface of the body, the stress set up in the body is volumetric stress.

(c) Tangential stress: It is also called shearing stress. When a deforming force applied tangentially to the surface of the body changes the shape of the body without changing its volume, the stress set up is known as tangential stress. The shape of the body changes or the body gets twisted due to tangential stress.

➤ **Strain** is defined as the ratio of change in configuration of the body because of a deforming force on it, to the original configuration of the body it means

$$\text{Strain} = \frac{\text{Change in configuration}}{\text{Original configuration}}$$

Scan to know more about this topic

Stress, strain Curve

Strain can be of following three types, depending upon the direction of force applied:

(a) **Longitudinal strain** $= \frac{\text{change in length}}{\text{original length}} = \frac{\Delta l}{l}$

(b) **Volumetric strain** $= \frac{\text{change of volume}}{\text{original volume}} \; \frac{\Delta V}{V}$

(c) Shearing strain is produced when the deforming force is applied parallel to the surface of a body and body changes its shape without changing its volume. Shearing strain is defined as the angle through which a vertical line perpendicular to the fixed surface gets rotated under the effect of a tangential deforming force.

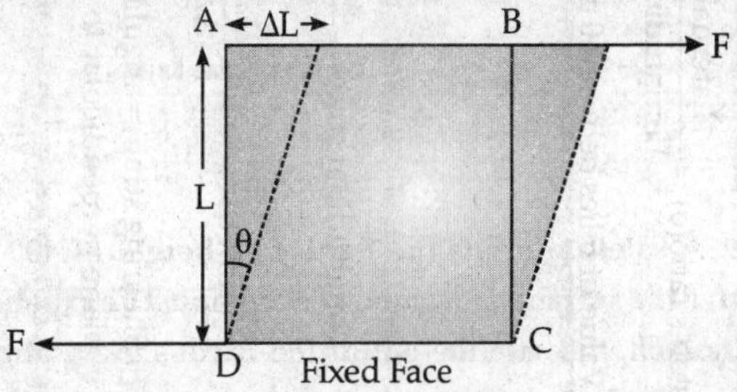

Shearing strain is also defined as the ratio of displacement of a surface (ΔL) under the tangential deforming force to the perpendicular distance (L) of the displaced surface from the fixed surface, *i.e.*,

$$\text{Shearing strain, } \theta = \frac{\Delta L}{L}$$

Strain has no units and dimensions.

(a) If a beam is bent, both compression strain as well as extension strain are produced.

Hooke's Law

➤ Hooke's law states that within elastic limit, stress is directly proportional to strain, i.e., Stress ∝ Strain.

Elastic Moduli

➤ **Modulus of elasticity or coefficient of elasticity (E)** of a body is defined as the ratio of stress to the corresponding strain produced, within the elastic limit, *i.e.*,

$$E = \frac{\text{Stress}}{\text{Strain}}$$

Modulus of elasticity is of three types:

(a) Young's modulus of elasticity (Y) is defined as the ratio of longitudinal stress to the longitudinal strain, within the elastic limit, *i.e.*,

$$Y = \frac{\text{Longitudinal stress}}{\text{Longitudinal strain}}$$

$$= \frac{F/A}{\Delta l / l} = \frac{F}{A} \times \frac{l}{\Delta l}$$

Scan to know more about this topic

Young's modulus of elasticity

Y is the property of solid material only. **Y** increases on mixing the impurity in the solid and decreases on increasing the temperature of the solid body.

(b) Bulk modulus of elasticity (K) is first defined by Maxwell. It is defined as the ratio of volume stress to the volumetric strain, within the elastic limit, *i.e.*,

$$K = -\frac{\text{Volume stress}}{\text{Volumetric strain}}$$

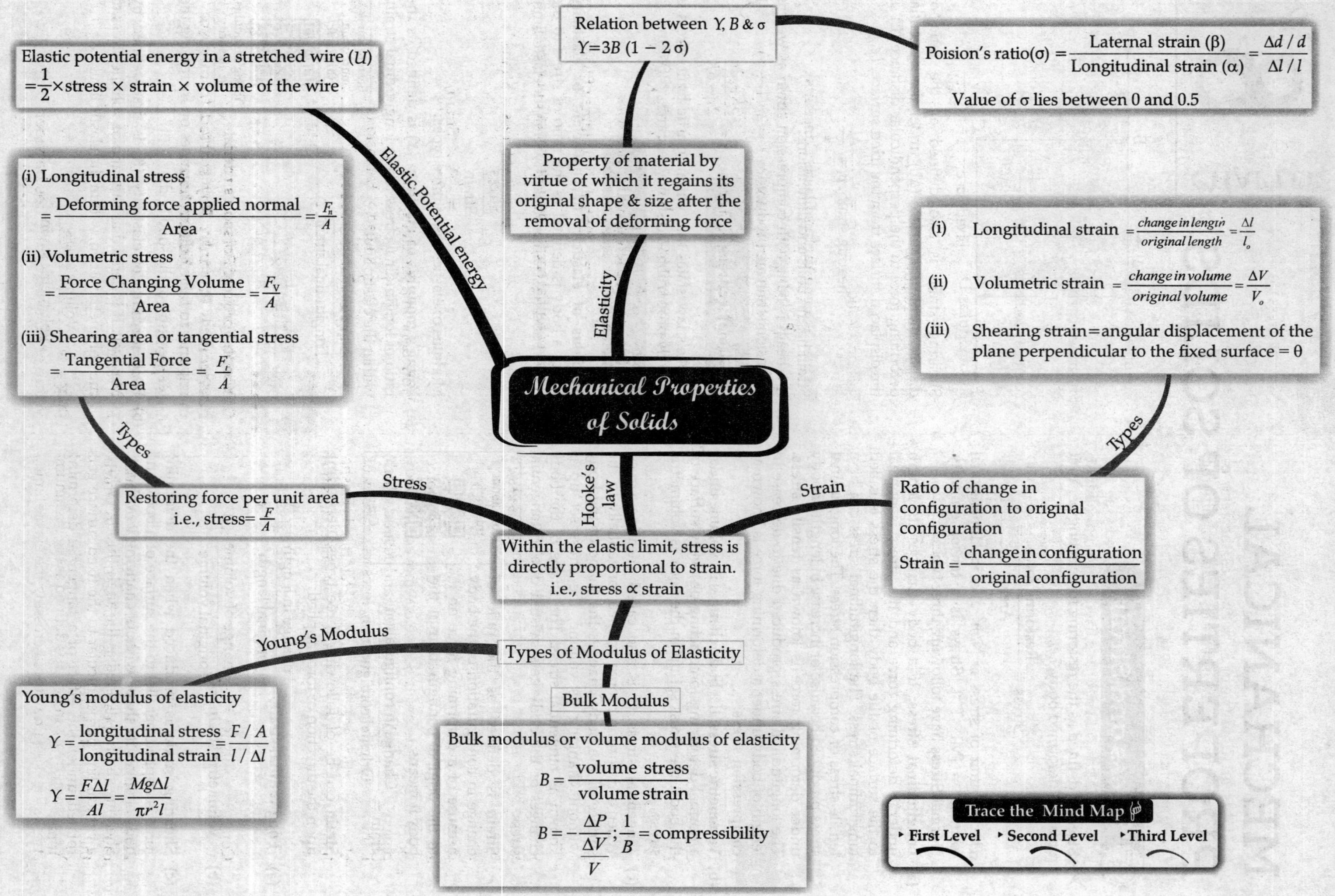
Mechanical Properties of Solids
Elasticity
Property of material by virtue of which it regains its original shape & size after the removal of deforming force
Relation between Y, B & σ
Y=3B (1 − 2σ)
Poision's ratio(σ) = Laternal strain (β) / Longitudinal strain (α) = Δd / d / Δl / l
Value of σ lies between 0 and 0.5
Elastic Potential energy
Elastic potential energy in a stretched wire (U) = 1/2 × stress × strain × volume of the wire
Hooke's law
Within the elastic limit, stress is directly proportional to strain. i.e., stress ∝ strain
Stress
Restoring force per unit area i.e., stress= F/A
Types
(i) Longitudinal stress = Deforming force applied normal / Area = Fn/A
(ii) Volumetric stress = Force Changing Volume / Area = FV/A
(iii) Shearing area or tangential stress = Tangential Force / Area = Ft/A
Strain
Ratio of change in configuration to original configuration
Strain = change in configuration / original configuration
Types
(i) Longitudinal strain = change in length / original length = Δl / lo
(ii) Volumetric strain = change in volume / original volume = ΔV / Vo
(iii) Shearing strain = angular displacement of the plane perpendicular to the fixed surface = θ
Types of Modulus of Elasticity
Young's Modulus
Young's modulus of elasticity
Y = longitudinal stress / longitudinal strain = F / A / l / Δl
Y = FΔl / Al = MgΔl / πr²l
Bulk Modulus
Bulk modulus or volume modulus of elasticity
B = volume stress / volume strain
B = −ΔP / (ΔV/V); 1/B = compressibility
Trace the Mind Map
First Level
Second Level
Third Level

$$K = \frac{P}{\frac{\Delta V}{V}} = -\frac{PV}{\Delta V}$$

K is the property for solids, liquids and gases.

- **Modulus of Rigidity** (η) is defined as the ratio of tangential stress to the shearing strain, within the elastic limit, *i.e.*,

$$\eta = \frac{\text{Tangential stress}}{\text{Shearing strain}} = \frac{F/A}{\theta} = \frac{F}{A\theta}$$

η is the characteristic of solid material only as the liquids and gases do not have fixed shape. η for liquid is zero.

- **Poisson's ratio** (σ). It is defined as the ratio of lateral strain to the longitudinal strain, *i.e.*,

Scan to know more about this topic

Poisson's ratio

$$\sigma = \frac{\text{Lateral strain}}{\text{Longitudinal strain}}$$

$$= \frac{\Delta D / D}{\Delta l / l} = -\frac{\Delta D.l}{D.\Delta l}$$

Numerically value of σ lies between –1 and $+\frac{1}{2}$ but practical value of σ lies between 0 and $+\frac{1}{2}$.

Key Words

- **Deforming force** is that force which when applied changes the configuration of the body.
- **Elasticity** is the property of the body by virtue of which the body regains its original configuration (length, volume or shape) when the deforming forces are removed.
- **Perfectly elastic body** is that body which perfectly regains its original form on removing the external deforming force from it, *e.g.*, quartz.
- **Plastic body** is that body which does not regain its original form at all on the removal of deforming force, howsoever small the deforming force may be, *e.g.*, putty and paraffin wax.
- **Elastic limit** is the upper limit of deforming force up to which if deforming force is removed, the body regains its original form completely and beyond which if the force is increased, the body loses its property of elasticity and it gets permanently deformed. Elastic limit is the property of a body whereas elasticity is the property of material of a body.
- **Compressibility** is defined as the reciprocal of bulk modulus of elasticity.

$$\text{Compressibility (c)} = \frac{1}{K} = -\frac{\Delta V}{PV}$$

- **Elastic fatigue** is the loss in strength of a material caused due to repeated alternating strains to which the material is subjected.
- Yield strength of a material is defined as the maximum stress it can sustain without crossing the elastic limit.

Key Formulae

- Normal stress (S) = F/A
- Breaking force = Breaking stress × area of cross-section
- Longitudinal strain = $\frac{\Delta l}{l}$
- Volumetric strain = $\frac{\Delta V}{V}$
- Shearing strain, $\theta = \frac{\Delta L}{L}$
- Young's modulus $Y = \frac{Fl}{A\Delta l}$
- Bulk modulus $K = -\frac{FV}{A\Delta V} = -P\frac{V}{\Delta V}$
- Modulus of Rigidity $\eta = \frac{FL}{A\Delta L}$
- Poisson's Ratio $\sigma = \frac{-\Delta D.l}{D.\Delta l}$
- **Relation Among Various Elastic Constants :**
  - **(i)** Relation between Y, K and σ, $Y = 3K(1 - 2\sigma)$
  - **(ii)** Relation between Y, η and σ, $Y = 2\eta(1 + \sigma)$
  - **(iii)** Relation between K, η and σ, $\sigma = \frac{3K - 2\eta}{2\eta + 6K}$
  - **(iv)** Relation between Y, K and η, $\frac{9}{Y} = \frac{1}{K} + \frac{3}{\eta}$
- Elastic potential energy in stretched wire,
  $U = \frac{1}{2} \times \text{Stress} \times \text{Strain} \times \text{Volume of wire}$
- Elastic potential energy per unit volume of wire,
  $u = \frac{1}{2} \times \text{Stress} \times \text{Strain} = \frac{1}{2} Y \times (\text{Strain})^2$
- Work done in a stretching wire
  $W = \frac{1}{2} \times \text{Load} \times \text{Extension}.$

Mnemonics

Concept: Value of Poisson's ratio.

Mnemonics: **P**riyanka **R**oy started from **zero** mark and ran for **half** an hour.

Interpretation:

P - Poisson's

R - Ratio

zero - 0

half - ½

Value of Poisson's ratio lies between 0 and ½.

NCERT CORNER

Q. 1. A steel wire of length 4.7 m and cross-section 3.0 × 10^5 m^2 stretches by the same amount as a copper wire of length 3.5 m and cross-section 4.0 × 10^{-5} m^2 under a given load. What is the ratio of the Young's modulus of steel to that of copper ? [NCERT Ex., Q. 8.1, Page 177]

Ans. Using the relation,

$$Y = \frac{Fl}{A\Delta l},$$

$$Y_S = \frac{Fl}{A\Delta l} = \frac{F \times 4.7}{(3 \times 10^{-5})\Delta l}$$

and
$$Y_C = \frac{Fl}{A\Delta l} = \frac{F \times 3.5}{(4 \times 10^{-5})\Delta l}$$

then
$$\frac{Y_S}{Y_C} = \frac{F \times 4.7}{(3 \times 10^{-5})\Delta l} \times \frac{(4 \times 10^{-5})\Delta l}{F \times 3.5}$$

$$= 1.79$$

Q. 2. Figure shows the strain-stress curve for a given material. What are (a) Young's modulus, and (b) approximate yield strength for this material ?

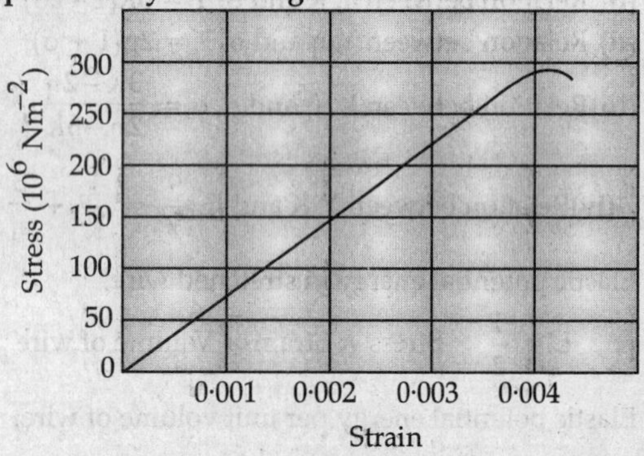

[NCERT Ex., Q. 8.2, Page 177]

Ans. From the graph for a stress of 150 × 10^6 Nm^{-2}, the strain is 0.002.

(a) Modulus of the material (Y) is given by

$$Y = \frac{150 \times 10^6}{0.002} = \frac{150 \times 10^6}{2 \times 10^{-3}}$$

$$= 75 \times 10^9 \text{ Nm}^{-2} = 7.5 \times 10^{10} \text{ Nm}^{-2}.$$

(b) Yield strength of a material is defined as the maximum stress it can sustain without crossing the elastic limit.

∴ From graph, the approximate yield strength of the given material

$$= 300 \times 10^6 \text{ Nm}^{-2} = 3 \times 10^8 \text{ Nm}^{-2}.$$

Q. 3. The stress-strain graphs for materials A and B are shown in figure. The graphs are drawn on the same scale.

(a) Which of the materials has the greater Young's modulus ?

(b) Which of the two is stronger material ?

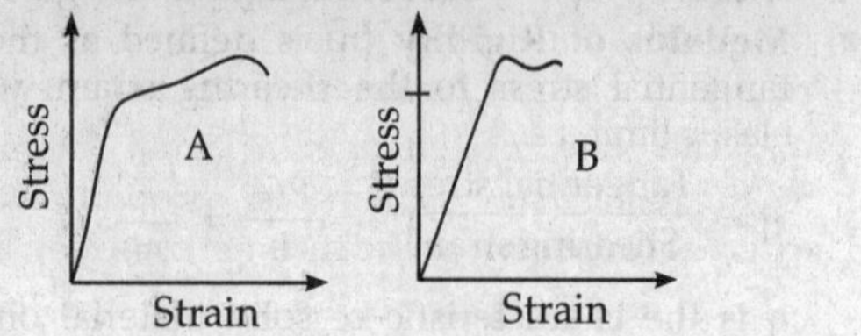

[NCERT Ex., Q. 8.3, Page 178]

Ans. (a) From graph it is clear that for a given strain, stress for A is more than that of B. Hence, Young's modulus (= stress/strain) is greater for *A* than that of *B*.

(b) A is stronger than B. Strength of a material is measured by the amount of stress required to cause fracture, corresponding to the point of fracture.

Q. 4. Read the following two statements below carefully and state, with reasons, if it is true or false:

(a) The Young's modulus of rubber is greater than that of steel.

(b) The stretching of a coil is determined by its shear modulus. [NCERT Ex., Q. 8.4, Page 178]

Ans. (a) Incorrect. This is because if steel and rubber wires of same length and area of cross-section are subjected to same deforming force, then the extension produced in steel is less than the extension produced in rubber, so $Y_s > Y_r$. In other words, for producing same strain in steel and rubber, more stress is required in case of steel.

(b) Correct. The reason is that when a coil spring is stretched, there is neither a change in the length of the coil (i.e., length of the wire forming the coil spring) nor a change in its volume. Since, the change takes place in the shape of the coil spring, its stretching is determined by its shear modulus.

Q. 5. Two wires of diameter 0.25 cm, one made of steel and other made of brass are loaded as shown in figure. The unloaded length of steel wire is 1.5 m and that of brass wire is 1.0 m. Compute the elongations of steel and brass wires. Young's modulus of steel and copper are respectively 2.0 × 10^{11} Pa and 0.91 × 10^{11} Pa. (1 Pa = 1 Nm^{-2}).

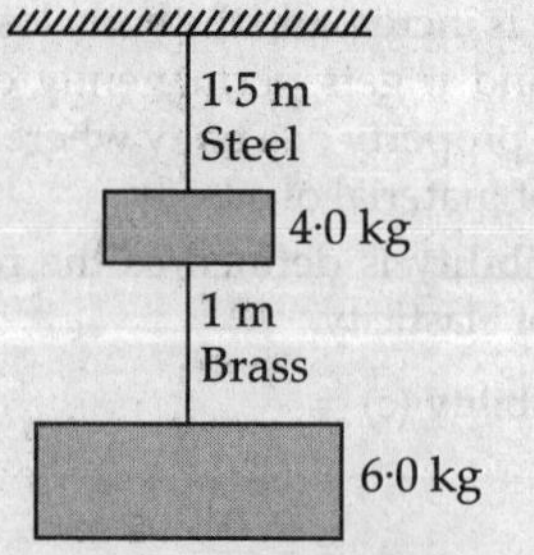

[NCERT Ex., Q. 8.5, Page 177]

Ans. For steel wire,

Total force, $F_1 = 4 + 6 = 10$ kgf

$= 10 \times 9.8$ N

$l_1 = 1.5$ m, $\Delta l_1 = ?$

$2r_1$ = Diameter of wire = 0.25 cm.

$$r_1 = \frac{0.25 \times 10^{-2}}{2} \text{ m}$$

$$= 0.125 \times 10^{-2} \text{ m}$$

$\therefore$ Area $A_1 = \pi r_1^2$.

Let Y_1 be the Young's modulus of steel wire,

Then $$Y_1 = \frac{F_1 / A_1}{\Delta l_1 / l_1}$$

or $$\Delta l_1 = \frac{F_1 l_1}{A_1 Y_1}$$

$$= \frac{(10 \times 9.8)(1.5) \times 7}{22 \times (0.125 \times 10^{-2})^2 \times 2 \times 10^{11}}$$

$$= 1.5 \times 10^{-4} \text{ m}.$$

In case of brass wire

$$F_2 = 6.0 \text{ kgf} = 6 \times 9.8 \text{ N}$$

$$Y_2 = 0.91 \times 10^{11} \text{ pa}$$

$$2r_2 = 0.25 \text{ cm}$$

$\therefore$ $$r_2 = \frac{0.25}{2} \text{ cm} = 0.125 \times 10^{-2} \text{ m}$$

$\therefore$ $$l_2 = 1.0 \text{ m}, \Delta l_2 = ?$$

$\therefore$ $$\Delta l_2 = \frac{F_2 l_2}{A_2 Y_2}$$

$$= \frac{(6 \times 9.8) \times 1.0 \times 7}{22 \times (0.125 \times 10^{-2})^2 \times 0.91 \times 10^{11}}$$

$$= 1.3 \times 10^{-4} \text{ m}.$$

Q. 6. The edge of an aluminium cube is 10 cm long. One face of the cube is firmly fixed to a vertical wall. A mass of 100 kg is then attached to the opposite face of the cube. The shear modulus of aluminium is 25 GPa. What is the vertical deflection of this face ?

[NCERT Ex., Q. 8.6, Page 178]

Ans. Given: Side of cube, $L = 10$ cm $= 0.1$ m

$\therefore$ A = area of the face (1)

$$= L \times L = L^2 = (0.1)^2$$

$$= 0.01 \text{ m}^2.$$

Mass attached to Face (1), $M = 100$ kg

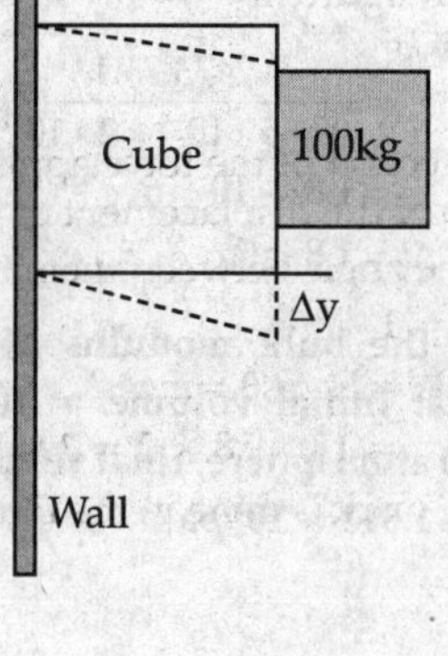

When F be the force on face (1) due to this mass. Then

$$F = Mg = 100 \times 9.8 \text{ N}.$$

$\therefore$ Shear stress on the face is given

$$= \frac{F}{A} = \frac{100 \times 9.8}{0.01} \text{ Nm}^{-2}$$

$$= 9.8 \times 10^4 \text{ Nm}^{-2}$$

Shear modulus of aluminium,

$$\eta = 25 \, GPa = 25 \times 10^9 \text{ Nm}^{-2}$$

Using the relation,

$$\eta = \frac{\text{Shearing stress}}{\text{Shearing strain}} \quad ...(1)$$

Suppose Δy = Vertical displacement of the face = ?

$\therefore$ Shearing strain,

$$\frac{\Delta y}{L} = \frac{\text{Shearing stress}}{\eta}$$

or $$\Delta y = \frac{\text{Shearing stress}}{\eta} \times L$$

$$= \frac{9.8 \times 10^4 \times 0.1}{25 \times 10^9}$$

or $$\Delta y = 0.0392 \times 10^{-5} \text{ m}$$

or $$= 3.92 \times 10^{-7} \text{ m}.$$

$$\approx 4 \times 10^{-7} \text{ m}$$

Q. 7. Four identical hollow cylindrical columns of steel support a big structure of mass 50,000 kg. The inner and outer radii of each column are 30 cm and 60 cm respectively. Assuming the load distribution to be uniform, calculate the compressional strain of each column. [NCERT Ex., Q. 8.7, Page 178]

Ans. Cross-sectional area of a column

$$= \pi (r_2^2 - r_1^2)$$

$$= \pi (0.6^2 - 0.3^2)$$

$$= 0.27\pi \text{ m}^2$$

Force on one column,

$$F = \frac{50000 \times 9.8}{4}$$

$$Y = \frac{F/A}{\Delta l / l}$$

Compressive strain

$$= \frac{\Delta l}{l} = \frac{F}{AY}$$

$$= \frac{50000 \times 9.8}{4(0.27\pi)(2 \times 10^{11})}$$

$$= 7.21 \times 10^{-7}.$$

Q. 8. A piece of copper having a rectangular cross-section of 15.2 mm × 19.1 mm is pulled in tension with 44,500N force, producing only elastic deformation. Calculate the resulting strain ? (Y for copper = 1.1×10^{11} Nm^{-2}.) [NCERT Ex., Q. 8.8, Page 178]

Ans. Given: $Y = 1.1 \times 10^{11}\ Nm^{-2}$

A = Area of cross-section
$= 15.2\ mm \times 19.1\ mm$
$= 15.2 \times 10^{-3}\ m \times 19.1 \times 10^{-3}\ m^2$

Force, $F = 44500\ N.$

$\therefore \quad Y = \dfrac{Stress}{Strain}$

or $\quad Strain = \dfrac{Stress}{Y} = \dfrac{F}{AY}$

or $\quad Strain = \dfrac{44500}{15.2 \times 19.1 \times 10^{-6} \times 1.1 \times 10^{11}}$

$= 1.39 \times 10^{-3}.$

Q. 9. A steel cable with a radius of 1.5 cm supports a chair lift at a ski area. If the maximum stress is not to exceed $10^8\ Nm^{-2}$, what is the maximum load the cable can support ? [NCERT Ex., Q. 8.9, Page 178]

Ans. Given: Radius of steel cable,

$r = 1.5\ cm = 1.5 \times 10^{-2}\ m.$

Maximum Stress $= 10^8\ Nm^{-2}.$

$\therefore$ Area of cross-section of cable

$A = \pi r^2 = \pi (1.5 \times 10^{-2})^2\ m^2$

Maximum load the cable can stand

= Maximum force

$$\text{Maximum stress} = \frac{\text{Maximum force}}{\text{Area of cross-section}}$$

or Maximum force = Maximum stress × Area of cross-section

or $\quad F_{max} = 10^8 \times \pi \times (1.5 \times 10^{-2})^2$

or $\quad F_{max} = 3.142 \times 2.25 \times 10^8 \times 10^{-4}\ N.$

or Maximum load the cable can withstand

$= 7.07 \times 10^4\ N.$

Q. 10. A rigid bar of mass 15 kg is supported symmetrically by three wires each 2 m long. Those at each end are of copper and the middle one is of iron. Determine the ratios of their diameters if each is to have the same tension. Given Young modulus of copper and iron are respectively $110 \times 10^9\ Nm^{-2}$ and $190 \times 10^9\ Nm^{-2}$.

[NCERT Ex., Q. 8.10, Page 178]

Ans. Suppose Y_1 and Y_2 be the Young's modulus of copper and iron wires respectively

$Y_1 = 110 \times 10^9\ Nm^{-2}$
$Y_2 = 190 \times 10^9\ Nm^{-2}$

Also suppose A_1 and A_2 be the areas of cross-section of copper and iron wires respectively. If d_1 and d_2 be their respective diameters.

Then $\quad A_1 = \pi d_1^2/4$

and $\quad A_2 = \pi d_2^2/4.$

$$\therefore \quad \frac{A_1}{A_2} = \frac{d_1^2}{d_2^2} = \left(\frac{d_1}{d_2}\right)^2$$

$L = 2\ m.$

Suppose Δl be the extension produced in each wire.
Suppose F = Tension produced in each wire

$\therefore$ Using relation,

$$Y = \frac{Stress}{Strain},$$

we get, Strain for copper wire $= \dfrac{F/A_1}{Y_1}$

and $\quad$ Strain for iron wire $= \dfrac{F/A^2}{Y_2}$

Since, the bar is supported symmetrically,
$\therefore$ The two strains are equal

$$\therefore \quad \frac{F}{A_1Y_1} = \frac{F}{A_2Y_2}$$

or $\quad A_1Y_1 = A_2Y_2$

$$\frac{A_1}{A_2} = \frac{Y_2}{Y_1}$$

$$\frac{\pi d_1^2/4}{\pi d_2^2/4} = \frac{Y_2}{Y_1}$$

$$\frac{d_1}{d_2} = \sqrt{\frac{Y_2}{Y_1}} = \sqrt{\frac{190 \times 10^9}{110 \times 10^9}}$$

$$= \sqrt{\frac{19}{11}} = \sqrt{1.73}$$

It means, $\quad \dfrac{d_1}{d_2} = 1.31$

or $\quad d_1 : d_2 = 1.31 : 1.$

Q. 11. A 14.5 kg mass, fastened to the end of a steel wire of unstretched length 1m, is whirled in a vertical circle with an angular velocity of 2 rev/s at the bottom of the circle. The cross-sectional area of the wire is 0.065 cm^2. Calculate the elongation of wire when the mass is at the lowest point of its path. $Y_{steel} = 2 \times 10^{11} N/m^2$

[NCERT Ex., Q. 8.11, Page 178]

Ans. Given: $m = 14.5\ kg,\ l = r = 1m$

$\omega = 2rps = 2 \times 2\pi\ rad/s$

$A = 0.065 \times 10^{-4}\ m^2$

Tension in wire at lowest position on vertical circle $= F = mg + mr\omega^2$

$$= 14.5 \times 9.8 + 14.5 \times 1 \times 4 \times \frac{22}{7} \times \frac{22}{7} \times 4$$

$= 142.1 + 2291.6$
$= 2433.7\ N$

$$Y = \frac{Fl}{A\Delta l}$$

or $\quad \Delta l = \dfrac{Yl}{AY}$

$$= \frac{2433.7 \times 1}{0.065 \times 10^{-4} \times 2 \times 10^{11}}$$

$= 1.87 \times 10^{-3}\ m$

$\Delta l = 1.87\ mm$

Q. 12. Compute the bulk modulus of water from the following data: Initial volume = 100 litre, pressure increase = 100 atmosphere, final volume = 100.5 litre (1 atmosphere = 1.013×10^5 pa).

Compare the bulk modulus of water with that of air (at constant temperature). Explain in simple terms why the ratio is so large. [NCERT Ex., Q. 8.12, Page 179]

Ans. Bulk Modulus,

$$B = \frac{-P}{\frac{\Delta V}{V}}$$

$$= P\frac{V}{\Delta V}$$

$$= \frac{100 \times 1.013 \times 10^5 \times 100 \times 10^{-3}}{0.5 \times 10^{-3}}$$

or $B_w = 2.026 \times 10^9$ Pa

Bulk Modulus of air, $B_A = 1.0 \times 10^5$ Pa

$$\therefore \frac{\text{Bulk Modulus of water, } B_w}{\text{Bulk Modulus of air, } B_A} = \frac{2.026 \times 10^9}{1.0 \times 10^5} = 2.026 \times 10^4$$

This ratio is too large because gases are more compressible than those of liquids. Interatomic forces are more strong in liquids than gases.

Q. 13. What is the density of water at a depth where pressure is 80.0 atm, given that its density at the surface is 1.03×10^3 kg m^{-3}? Compressibility of water is 45.8×10^{-11} Pa^{-1} and 1 atm = 1.03×10^5 Pa. [NCERT Ex., Q. 8.13, Page 179]

Ans. Compressibility $= \frac{1}{K} = (45.8 \times 10^{-11})$ Pa^{-1}

Pressure, $P = 80$ atm

$= 80 \times 1.013 \times 10^5$ Pa

Let change in volume,

$$\Delta V = \frac{M}{\rho} - \frac{M}{\rho_d} = M\left(\frac{1}{\rho} - \frac{1}{\rho_d}\right)$$

$\therefore$ Volumetric strain

$$= \frac{\Delta V}{V}$$

$$= M\left[\frac{1}{\rho} - \frac{1}{\rho_d}\right]\frac{\rho}{M} = 1 - \frac{\rho}{\rho_d}$$

where ρ is density of water at surface and ρ_d is the density of water at depth.

$$\frac{\Delta V}{V} = \frac{1}{K}$$

$$1 - \left(\frac{1.03 \times 10^3}{\rho_d}\right) = 80 \times 1.013 \times 10^5 \times 45.8 \times 10^{-11}$$

$$\rho_d = 1.034 \times 10^3 \text{ kgm}^{-3}.$$

Q. 14. Compute the fractional change in volume of a glass slab, when subjected to a hydraulic pressure of 10 atm. [NCERT Ex., Q. 8.14, Page 179]

Ans. Given: $P = 10$ atm

$= 10 \times 1.013 \times 10^5$ Pa

K for glass slab $= 37 \times 10^9$ Nm^{-2}.

Fractional change in volume of glass slab

$$= \frac{\Delta V}{V} = ?$$

From the relation $K = \frac{P}{\frac{\Delta V}{V}}$,

$$\frac{\Delta V}{V} = \frac{P}{K} = \frac{10 \times 1.013 \times 10^5}{37 \times 10^9}$$

$$= \frac{1.013}{37 \times 10^3} = 0.0274 \times 10^{-3}$$

$$= 2.74 \times 10^{-5}$$

$$\approx 0.003\%.$$

Q. 15. Determine the volume contraction of a solid copper cube, 10 cm on an edge, when subjected to a hydraulic pressure of 7×10^6 Pa. [NCERT Ex., Q. 8.15, Page 179]

Ans. Given: $L = 10$ cm $= 0.1$ m

K = bulk modulus of Cu

$= 140 \times 10^9$ Pa

$P = 7 \times 10^6$ Pa

ΔV = Volume contraction of solid copper cube = ?

$\therefore$ $V = L^3 = (0.1)^3 = 0.001$ m^3.

Using formula, $K = -\frac{P}{\left(\frac{\Delta V}{V}\right)}$

we get $\Delta V = -\frac{PV}{K} = \frac{7 \times 10^6 \times 0.001}{140 \times 10^9}$ m^3

$$= -\frac{1}{20} \times 10^{-6} \text{ m}^3$$

$$= -0.05 \times 10^{-6} \text{ m}^3$$

$$= -5 \times 10^{-2} \text{ cm}^3$$

Here, negative sign shows volume contraction.

Q. 16. How much should the pressure on a litre of water be changed to compress it by 0.10%. [NCERT Ex., Q. 8.16, Page 179]

Ans. Here $V = 1$ litre

$\Delta V = -0.10\%$ of V

$$= -\frac{0.10}{100} \times 1 = -\frac{1}{1000} \text{ litre}$$

Suppose ΔP = change in pressure required for compression of 1 litre of water.

K = bulk modulus of water $= 2.2 \times 10^9$ Nm^{-2}

From the relation

$$K = -\frac{P}{\left(\frac{\Delta V}{V}\right)}$$

we get $\Delta P = -K.\frac{\Delta V}{V}$

or $\Delta P = 2.2 \times 10^9 \times \frac{\left(\frac{1}{1000}\right)}{1}$

or $\Delta P = \frac{2.2 \times 10^9}{1000}$

$$= 2.2 \times 10^6 \text{ Nm}^{-2}.$$

MECHANICAL PROPERTIES OF FLUIDS

CHAPTER 9

Pressure

(i) Pressure is defined as the thrust acting per unit area of the surface in contact with liquid, i.e.,

$$P = \frac{\text{Thrust}(F)}{\text{Area}(A)} = \frac{F}{A} = h\rho g$$

(ii) Liquid pressure is independent of shape of the liquid surface as well as area of the liquid surface, but depends upon height of liquid column.

(iii) Total pressure at a depth h below liquid surface is $P = h\rho g + P_0$, where P_0 is the atmospheric pressure.

(iv) S.I. unit of pressure is Nm^{-2} or pascal (denoted by Pa) and its dimensional formula is $[ML^{-1}T^{-2}]$.

(v) Pressure is a scalar quantity because a liquid at rest exerts equal pressure in all directions at all points in the same horizontal plane.

➤ **Pascal's Law:** It states that if gravity effect is neglected, the pressure at every point of liquid in equilibrium of rest is same. Pascal's law also states that the increase in pressure at one point of the enclosed liquid in equilibrium of rest is transmitted equally to all other points of liquid provided the gravity effect is neglected.

Scan to know more about this topic

Application of Pascal's Law

➤ **Atmospheric pressure:**

(i) It is defined as the pressure exerted by atmosphere.

(ii) At S.T.P., the value of atmospheric pressure is 1.01×10^5 Nm^{-2} or 1.01×10^6 $dyne/cm^2$.

➤ **Archimedes' principle: It** states that when a body is immersed partly or wholly in a liquid at rest, it loses some of its weight, which is equal to the weight of the liquid displaced by the immersed part of the body.

Observed weight of body = True weight – Weight of liquid displaced.

If w is the observed weight of body of density ρ when immersed in a liquid of density σ, then

$$\begin{aligned} w &= Mg - mg \\ &= Ah\rho g - Ah\sigma g \\ &= Ahg(\rho - \sigma) \\ &= Ahg\rho\left(1 - \frac{\sigma}{\rho}\right) = W\left(1 - \frac{\sigma}{\rho}\right) \end{aligned}$$

∴ True weight, $$W = \frac{\text{apparent weight}}{(1 - \sigma/\rho)}$$

➤ **Laws of floatation:** It states that a body will float in a liquid if weight of the liquid displaced by the immersed part of the body is at least equal to or greater than the weight of the body.

(a) When true weight of the body $W > w$ (weight of the liquid displaced), the body will sink to the bottom of the liquid. It will be so when the density of solid body (ρ) is greater than the density of liquid (σ), i.e., $\rho > \sigma$.

(b) When $W < w$, the body will rise above the surface of liquid to such an extent that the weight of the liquid displaced by immersed part of the body (i.e., upward thrust) becomes greater than the weight of the body. The body then will float. In this case the density of solid body is less than the density of liquid, i.e., $\rho < \sigma$.

(c) When $W = w$, the body is at rest anywhere in the liquid. The body will float with its whole volume just immersed in the liquid. In this case the density of body is equal to density of liquid, i.e., $\rho = \sigma$.

There will be equilibrium of floating body when

(i) Weight of liquid displaced by the immersed part of body is equal to the weight of the body.

(ii) The centre of gravity of the body and the centre of buoyancy lie along the same vertical line.

(iii) If the centre of gravity of the body lies vertically below the meta centre then body is in stable equilibrium. The body will be in unstable equilibrium if centre of gravity lies vertically above the meta centre.

Surface Tension

➤ **Surface Tension:** It is the property of the liquid by virtue of which the free surface of the liquid at rest tends to have the minimum surface area and as such it behaves as if covered with a stretched membrane.

(a) Quantitatively, surface tension of a liquid is measured as the force acting per unit length of a line imagined to be drawn tangentially any where on the free surface of the liquid at rest. It acts at right angles to this line on both the sides and along the tangent to the liquid surface, i.e., $S = F/l$.

(b) Surface tension of a liquid is also defined as the amount of work done in increasing the free surface of liquid at rest by unity at constant temperature, i.e., $S = W/A$.

or $W = S \times A$ = Surface tension × Area of liquid surface formed.

(c) Surface tension is a molecular phenomenon and it arises due to electromagnetic forces. The explanation of surface tension was first given by Laplace.

(d) S.I. unit of surface tension is Nm^{-1} or Jm^{-2} and C.G.S. unit is $dyne\text{-}cm^{-1}$ or $erg\text{-}cm^{-2}$.

(e) Dimensional formula of surface tension = $[ML^0T^{-2}]$

(f) Surface tension is a scalar quantity as it has no specific direction for a given liquid.

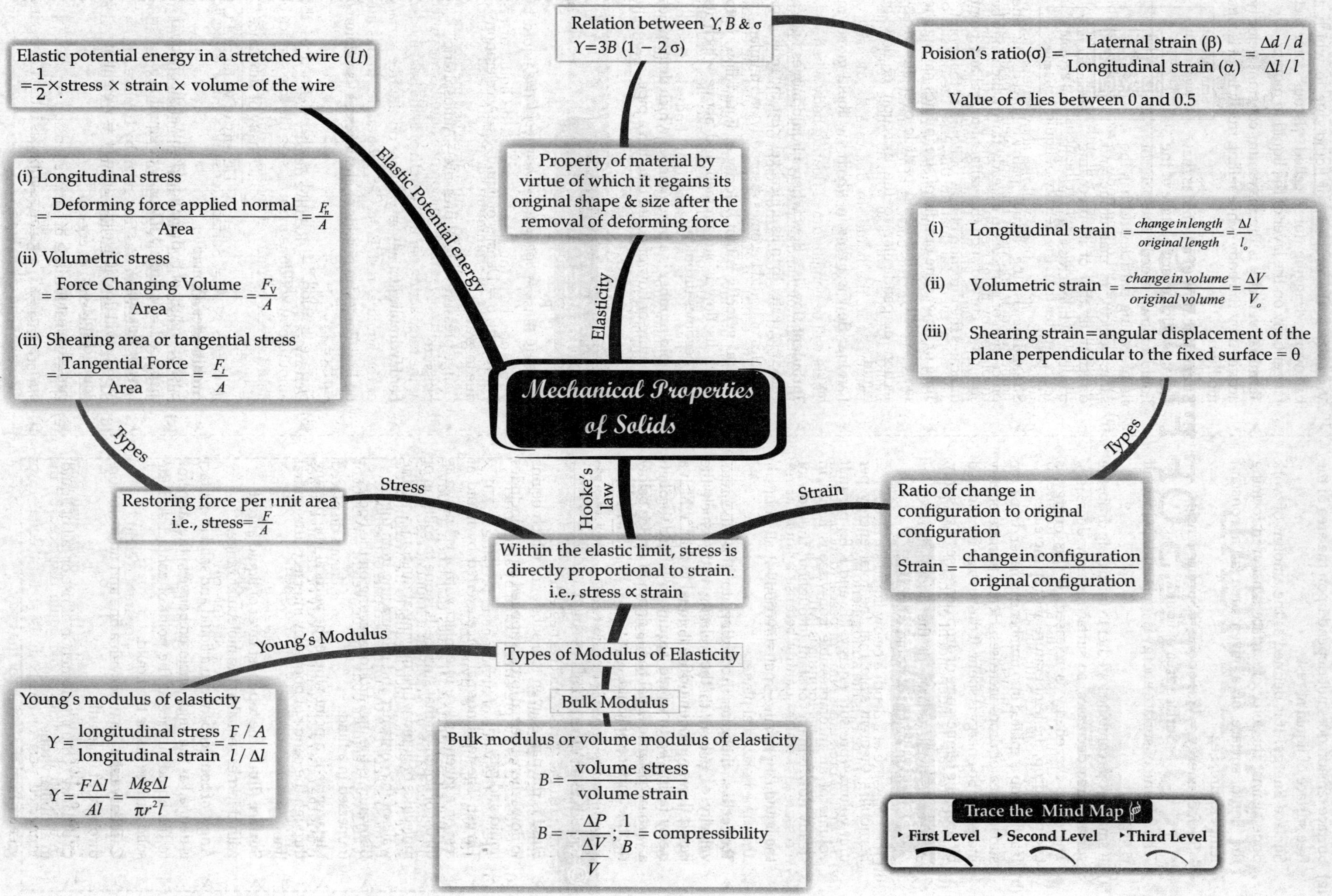
Mechanical Properties of Solids
Elasticity
Property of material by virtue of which it regains its original shape & size after the removal of deforming force
Relation between Y, B & σ
Y=3B (1 − 2σ)
Poision's ratio(σ) = Laternal strain (β) / Longitudinal strain (α) = Δd / d / Δl / l
Value of σ lies between 0 and 0.5
Elastic Potential energy
Elastic potential energy in a stretched wire (U) = 1/2 × stress × strain × volume of the wire
Stress
Restoring force per unit area i.e., stress= F/A
Types
(i) Longitudinal stress = Deforming force applied normal / Area = Fn/A
(ii) Volumetric stress = Force Changing Volume / Area = FV/A
(iii) Shearing area or tangential stress = Tangential Force / Area = Ft/A
Hooke's law
Within the elastic limit, stress is directly proportional to strain. i.e., stress ∝ strain
Strain
Ratio of change in configuration to original configuration
Strain = change in configuration / original configuration
Types
(i) Longitudinal strain = change in length / original length = Δl / lo
(ii) Volumetric strain = change in volume / original volume = ΔV / Vo
(iii) Shearing strain = angular displacement of the plane perpendicular to the fixed surface = θ
Types of Modulus of Elasticity
Young's Modulus
Young's modulus of elasticity
Y = longitudinal stress / longitudinal strain = F / A / l / Δl
Y = FΔl / Al = MgΔl / πr²l
Bulk Modulus
Bulk modulus or volume modulus of elasticity
B = volume stress / volume strain
B = − ΔP / (ΔV / V); 1/B = compressibility
Trace the Mind Map
First Level
Second Level
Third Level

(g) Surface tension does not depend upon the area of the free surface of liquid at rest.

- **Surface Energy: It** is defined as the amount of work done against the force of surface tension in forming the liquid surface of a given area at a constant temperature, i.e.,

  Surface energy = Work done = Surface tension × Surface area of liquid.

  The S.I. unit of surface energy is Joule and C.G.S. unit is erg.

(a) If small drops combine together to form a big drop, the surface area decreases, so surface energy decreases. Therefore the energy is released. If this energy is taken by drop, the temperature of drop increases.

(b) If a big drop is splitted into number of smaller drops, the surface area of drops increases. Hence, surface energy increases. So energy is spent. If this energy is pronated by drop, the temperature of drop decreases e.g., spray.

Bernoulli's Theorem

- Bernoulli's theorem state that the total energy per unit volume (pressure energy, P.E. and K.E.) per unit volume of an incompressible non-viscous liquid in steady flow remain constant throughout the flow of the liquid $P + \rho gh + \frac{1}{2}\rho v^2 = \text{constant}$.
- **Torricelli's theorem:** According to this theorem, velocity of efflux *i.e.,* the velocity with which the liquid flows out of an orifice is equal to that which a freely falling body would acquire in falling through a vertical distance equal to the depth of orifice below the free surface of liquid.

Key Words

- **Fluid** is the name given to a substance which begins to flow when external force is applied on it. It includes liquid and gas.
- **Thrust:** The total normal force exerted by liquid at rest on a given surface in contact with it is known as thrust of liquid on that surface. It is due to collision of molecules of liquid while moving at random, with the walls of the container and rebounding from them.
- **Buoyancy** is the upward force acting on the body immersed in a fluid.
- **Metacentre** is a point where the vertical line passing through the centre of buoyancy intersects the central line.
- **Surface film** is the top most layer of liquid at rest with thickness equal to the molecular range.
- **Angle of contact** between a liquid and solid in contact is defined as the angle enclosed between the tangents to the liquid surface at the point of contact and the solid surface inside the liquid.
- **Capillary tube** is a tube with a fine and uniform bore throughout its length.
- **Capillarity** is the phenomenon of rise or fall of liquid in a capillary tube.
- **Viscosity** is the property of liquid due to which a backward dragging force called viscous force act tangentially on the layer of the liquid in motion.
- **Terminal velocity** is the maximum constant velocity acquired by the body while falling freely in a viscous medium.
- **Streamline flow of a liquid** is that flow in which every particle of the liquid follows exactly the path of its preceding particle and has the same velocity in magnitude and direction as that of its preceding particle while crossing through that point.

Scan to know more about this topic

Streamline flow and Reynold's number

- **Streamline** is the actual path followed by the procession of particles in a steady flow which may be straight or curved such that tangent to it at any point indicates the direction of flow of liquid at that point.
- **Tube of flow** is the bundle of streamlines having the same velocity of the liquid particle over any cross-section perpendicular to the direction of flow of liquid.
- **Laminar flow** is a flow in which the liquid moves in layers.
- **Turbulent flow** is a flow when a liquid moves with a velocity greater than its critical velocity, the motion of particles of liquid becomes disorderly or irregular.
- **Critical velocity** is that velocity of liquid flow, upto which its flow is streamlined and above which its flow becomes turbulent.
- **Reynold number** is a pure number which determines the nature of flow of liquid through a pipe.

Key Formulae

- Pressure $= \frac{F}{A} = h\rho g$ *(due to h height of liquid)*

  h = height, ρ = Density of liquid, g = Acceleration due to gravity.
- Gauge pressure = Total pressure – Atmospheric pressure
- For Hydraulic lift; $\frac{F_1}{A_1} = \frac{F_2}{A_2}$

  F_1, F_2 = Forces on pistons of area of cross - sections A_1, A_2
- Density $= \frac{\text{Mass}}{\text{Volume}}$, Relative density

  $= \frac{\text{Density of substance}}{\text{Density of water at 4°C}}$
- **Archimedes' Principle:**

  Loss of weight of body in liquid = Weight of liquid displaced = Volume × Density of liquid × g
- **Law of floatation:**

  A body will float if, weight of body = Weight of liquid displaced.
- Surface tension, $S = F/l$
- Surface energy, E = Work done

- Work done, $W = S \times$ Increase in area
- Excess of pressure inside the liquid drop is

$$P = P_i - P_o = \frac{2S}{r};$$

P_i = Pressure inside bubble

- Excess of pressure inside the soap bubble is

$$P = P_i - P_o = \frac{4S}{r};$$

P_0 = Pressure outside bubble

- Total pressure in the air bubble at a depth h below the surface of liquid of density ρ is

$$P = P_o + h\rho g + \frac{2S}{r}$$

- Ascent/Decent Formula: $h = \frac{2S\cos\theta}{r\rho g}$

where, r = radius of capillary tube

ρ = density

S = Surface tension

θ = angle of contact

- **Newton's viscous drag force:** $F = \pm \eta A \frac{dv}{dx}$

η = coeff. of viscosity, A = area of layer of liquid, dv/dx = velocity gradient.

- **Poiseuille's Formula:** $V = \frac{\pi p r^4}{8\eta l}$

p = Pressure difference across length l of horizontal tube of radius r & V = volume.

Scan to know more about this topic

Bernoulli's principle and its applications

- **Stoke's Law:** $F = 6\pi\eta r v$
- **Terminal velocity:** $v = \frac{2r^2(\rho - \sigma)g}{9\eta}$

where, ρ = density of spherical body

σ = density of medium

r = radius of spherical body

η = coefficient of viscosity

- **Reynold's Number:** $R_N = \frac{\rho D v}{\eta}$

- **Bernoulli's Theorem:**

$$\frac{P}{\rho} + gh + \frac{1}{2}v^2 = \text{constant}$$

or $$\frac{P}{\rho g} + h + \frac{v^2}{2g} = \text{constant}$$

$\frac{P}{\rho}$ = pressure energy per unit mass

$\frac{P}{\rho g}$ = Pressure head, h = gravitational head

$gh = P.E.$ per unit mass

$\frac{v^2}{2g}$ = Velocity head

$\frac{1}{2}v^2 = K.E.$ per unit mass

Velocity of efflux: $v = \sqrt{2gh}$

Mnemonics

Concept: Excess pressure inside liquid drop, air bubble and soap bubble.

Mnemonics: Emily purchased two Swiss rolls for Lata didi and Amit bhaiya and four swiss rolls for Shanti bahin.

Interpretation:

E - Excess
P - pressure
T - Two
s - Surface tension
r - Radius
L - Liquid
d - drop
A - Air
b - bubble

Excess pressure in liquid drop and in air bubble are 2S/R.

f - four
s - Surface tension
r - Radius
S - soap
b - bubble

Excess pressure in soap bubble is 4S/R.

NCERT CORNER

Q. 1. Explain why

(a) The blood pressure in human is greater at the feet than at the brain.

(b) Atmospheric pressure at a height of about 6 km decreases to nearly half its value at the sea level, though the 'height' of the atmosphere is more than 100 km.

(c) Hydrostatic pressure is a scalar quantity even though pressure is force divided by area, and force is a vector. **[NCERT Ex., Q. 9.1, Page 199]**

Ans. (a) The height of the blood column in the human body is more at the feet than at the brain. That is why, the blood exerts more pressure at the feet than at the brain ($\because$ Pressure = $h\rho g$).

(b) The density of air is maximum near the surface of earth and decreases rapidly with height and at a height of about 6 km, it decreases to nearby half its value at the sea level. Beyond 6 km height the density of air decreases very slowly with height. Due to this reason the atmospheric pressure at the height of about 6 km decreases to nearly half of its value at sea level.

(c) Due to applied force on liquid, the pressure is transmitted equally in all directions inside the liquid. That is why there is no fixed direction for pressure due to liquid. Hence, hydrostatic pressure is scalar quantity.

Q. 2. Explain why

(a) The angle of contact of mercury with glass is obtuse, while that of water with glass is acute.

(b) Water on a clean glass surface tends to spread out while mercury on the same surface tends to form drops. (Put differently, water wets glass while mercury does not.)

(c) Surface tension of a liquid is independent of the area of the surface.

(d) Water with detergent dissolved in it should have small angles of contact.

(e) A drop of liquid under no external forces is always spherical in shape. [NCERT Ex., Q. 9.2, Page 199]

Ans. (a) The angle between the tangent to the liquid surface at the point of contact and the surface inside the liquid is called the angle of contact (θ), as shown in the given figure.

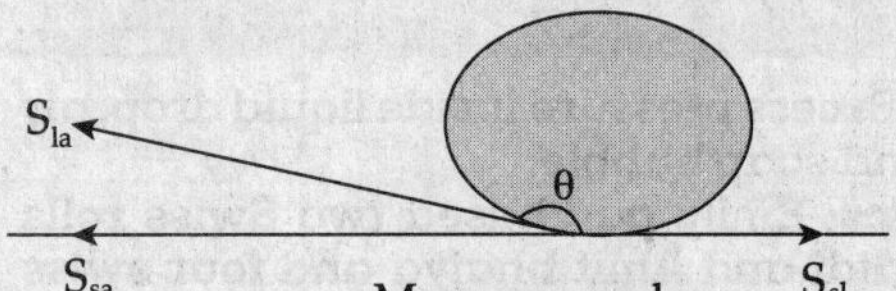

Mercury on glass

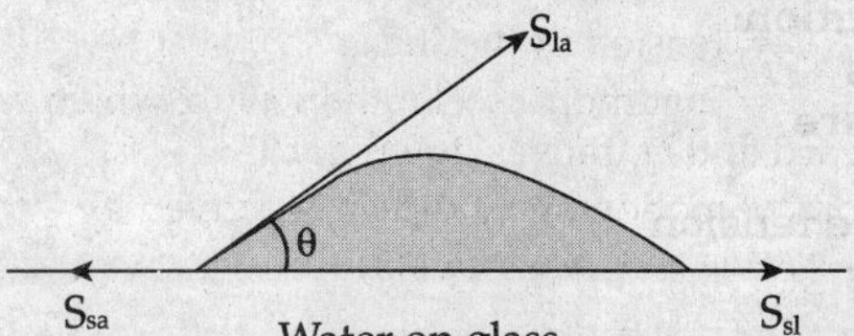

Water on glass

S_{la}, S_{sa}, and S_{sl} are the respective interfacial tensions between the liquid-air, solid-air, and

solid-liquid interfaces. At the line of contact, the surface forces between the three media must be in equilibrium, i.e.,

$$\cos\theta = \frac{S_{sa} - S_{sl}}{S_{la}}$$

The angle of contact θ, is obtuse if $S_{sa} < S_{sl}$ (as in the case of mercury on glass). This angle is acute if $S_{sa} < S_{sl}$ (as in the case of water on glass).

(b) Mercury molecules (which make an obtuse angle with glass) have a strong force of attraction between themselves and a weak force of attraction toward solids. Hence, they tend to form drops.

On the other hand, water molecules make acute angles with glass. They have a weak force of attraction between themselves and a strong force of attraction toward solids.

Hence, they tend to spread out.

(c) Surface tension is the force acting per unit length at the interface between the plane of a liquid and any other surface. This force is independent of the area of the liquid surface. Hence, surface tension is also independent of the area of the liquid surface.

(d) Water with detergent dissolved in it has small angles of contact (θ). This is because for a small θ, there is a fast capillary rise of the detergent in the cloth. The capillary rise of a liquid is directly proportional to the cosine of the angle of contact (θ). If θ is small, then cosθ will be large and the rise of the detergent water in the cloth will be fast.

(e) A liquid tends to acquire the minimum surface area because of the presence of surface tension. The surface area of a sphere is minimum for a given volume. Hence, under no external forces, liquid drops always take spherical shape.

Q. 3. Fill in the blanks using the words from the list appended with each statement:

(a) Surface tension of liquids generally _____ with temperature. (increases / decreases)

(b) Viscosity of gases _____ with temperature, whereas viscosity of liquids ______ with temperature. (increases / decreases)

(c) For solids with elastic modules of rigidity, the shearing force is proportional to ______ while for fluids it is proportional to ______. (shear strain / rate of shear strain)

(d) For a fluid in steady flow, the increases in flow speed at a construction follows form _____ while the decrease of pressure there follows from _____. (conservation of mass / Bernoulli's principle)

(e) For the model of a plane in a wind tunnel, turbulence occurs at a ______ speed than the critical speed for turbulence for an actual plane. (greater / smaller) [NCERT Ex., Q. 9.3, Page 200]

Ans. (a) decreases

(b) increases, decreases

(c) shear strain, rate of shear strain

(d) conservation of mass, Bernoulli's principle

(e) greater

Q. 4. Explain why:

(a) To keep a piece of paper horizontal, you should blow over, not under it.

(b) When we try to close a water tap with our fingers, fast jets of water gush through the openings between our fingers.

(c) The size of the needle of a syringe controls flow rate better than the thumb pressure exerted by a doctor while administering an injection.

(d) A fluid flowing out of a small hole in a vessel results in a backward thrust on the vessel.

(e) A spinning cricket ball in air does not follow a parabolic trajectory. [NCERT Ex., Q. 9.4, Page 200]

Ans. (a) When we blow over a piece of paper, velocity of air above the paper becomes more than that below it. Since, K.E. of air above the paper increases, so in accordance with Bernoulli's theorem for horizontal flow ($P + \frac{1}{2}\rho v^2$ = constant), its pressure energy and hence its pressure decreases. Because of greater value of pressure below the piece of paper it remains horizontal and does not fall.

While we blow under the paper, the pressure on the lower side decreases. The atmospheric pressure above the paper will therefore bend the paper downwards. So, the paper will not remain horizontal.

(b) This can be explained with the equation of continuity, i.e., $a_1v_1 = a_2v_2$. We try to close a water tap with our fingers, the area of cross-section of the outlet of water jet is reduced considerably as the openings between our fingers provide constriction (i.e., regions of smaller area). Hence, velocity of water increases greatly and fast jets of water come through the openings between our fingers.

(c) From Bernoulli's theorem, we know that

$$P + \frac{1}{2}\rho v^2 + \rho g h = \text{constant} \quad ...(i)$$

Here, the size of the needle controls the velocity of flow and the thumb pressure controls pressure.

Now P occurs with power 1 and velocity (v)occurs with power 2 in equation (i), therefore, the velocity has more influence. That is why the needle of syringe has a better control over the flow rate.

(d) If a fluid is flowing out of a small hole in a vessel, it acquires a large velocity and hence possesses large momentum. Since, no external force is acting on the system, a backward velocity must be attained by the vessel (according to the law of conservation of momentum). As a result of it, an impulse (backward thrust) is experienced by the vessel.

(e) This is because of Magnus effect. For a spinning ball the velocity of air at the top is higher than the velocity of air below the ball. So, according to Bernoulli's theorem, the pressure above the ball is less than the pressure below the ball. Thus there is a net upward force on the spinning ball, so the ball does not follow a curved path.

Q. 5. A 50 kg of girl wearing high heel shoes balances on a single heel. The heel is circular with a diameter 1.0 cm. What is the pressure exerted by the heel on the horizontal floor ? [NCERT Ex., Q. 9.5, Page 200]

Ans. $P = \frac{\text{Force}}{\text{Area}} = \frac{mg}{\pi(D/2)^2}$

$$= \frac{4mg}{\pi D^2}$$

$$= \frac{4\times 50\times 9.8}{\left(\frac{22}{7}\right)\times\left(10^{-2}\right)^2}$$

$$= 6.2 \times 10^6 \text{ Pa.}$$

Q. 6. Torricelli's barometer used mercury. Pascal duplicated it using French wine of density 984 kg m^{-3}. Determine the height of the wine column for normal atmospheric pressure. [NCERT Ex., Q. 9.6, Page 200]

Ans. $P = 0.76 \times (13.6 \times 10^3) \times 9.8 = h \times 984 \times 9.8$

or $$h = \frac{0.76\times 13.6\times 10^3\times 9.8}{984\times 9.8}$$

$$= 10.5 \text{ m}$$

Q. 7. A vertical offshore structure is built to withstand a maximum stress of 10^9 Pa. Is the structure suitable for putting up on top of an oil well in Bombay High? Take the depth of the sea to be roughly 3 km, and ignore the ocean currents. [NCERT Ex., Q. 9.7, Page 200]

Ans. Given: Maximum stress $= 10^9$ Pa

$h = 3$ km $= 3 \times 10^3$ m

$\rho_{water} = 10^3$ kg/m^3, $g = 9.8$ m/s^2.

This structure will be suitable, provided the pressure exerted by sea water is less than maximum stress if can bear.

Pressure due to sea water, $P = h\rho g$

$= 3 \times 10^3 \times 10^3 \times 9.8$

$= 2.94 \times 10^7$ Pa

The pressure of sea water is less than the maximum stress of 10^9Pa. So, the structure will be suitable for putting upon top of oil well.

Q. 8. A hydraulic automobile lift is designed to lift cars with a maximum mass of 3000 kg. The area of cross-section of the piston carrying the load is 425 cm^2. What maximum pressure would the smaller piston have to bear ? [NCERT Ex., Q. 9.8, Page 200]

Ans. Given: The maximum force which the bigger piston can bear,

$F = 3000$ kgf

$= 3000 \times 9.8$ N

Area of piston, $A = 425$ cm^2

$= 425 \times 10^{-4}$ m^2.

When P = maximum pressure on the bigger piston

Then $$P = \frac{F}{A} = \frac{3000\times 9.8}{425\times 10^{-4}}$$

$= 6.92 \times 10^5$ Pa

As the liquid transmits pressure equally in all directions, hence the maximum pressure the smaller piston would have to bear is 6.92×10^5 Pa.

Q. 9. A U-tube contains water and methylated spirit separated by mercury. The mercury columns in the two arms are in level with 10.0 cm of water in one arm and 12.5 cm of spirit in the other. What is the relative density of spirit ? [NCERT Ex., Q. 9.9, Page 200]

Ans. Since, the mercury columns in the two arms are at level

$$h_1\rho_1 g = h_2\rho_2 g$$

or $$\rho_2 = \frac{h_1\rho_1}{h_2}$$

Hence, here, $h_1 = 10$ cm, $h_2 = 12.5$ cm

and $\rho_1 = 1$ g cm^{-3}.

$$\rho_2 = \frac{10\times 1}{12.5} = 0.8 \text{ g cm}^{-3}.$$

Relative density of spirit = 0.8

Q. 10. In the previous problem, if 15.0 cm of water and spirit each are further poured into the respective arms of the tube, what is the difference in the levels of mercury in the two arms ? (Relative density of mercury = 13.6.) [NCERT Ex., Q. 9.10, Page 200]

Ans. Here, pressure exerted by (10 + 15 = 25 cm) of water column = pressure exerted by h cm of mercury column + pressure exerted by (12.5 + 15 = 27.5 cm) of spirit column.

i.e., $25 \times 1 \times g = h \times 13.6 \times g + 27.5 \times 0.8 \times g$

(Using $P = h\rho g$)

or $25 = 13.6\,h + 22$

$$\therefore \quad h = \frac{25-22}{13.6} = 0.22 \text{ cm.}$$

Q. 11. Can Bernoulli's equation be used to describe the flow of water through a rapid flow in a river ? Explain.

[NCERT Ex., Q. 9.11, Page 200]

Ans. No, Bernoulli's equation cannot be used to describe the rapid flow of water in a river (i.e., turbulent flow). This equation can be used for stream-line flow.

Q. 12. Does it matter if one uses gauge instead of absolute pressure in applying Bernoulli's equation?

[NCERT Ex., Q. 9.12, Page 200]

Ans. No, it does not matter if one uses gauge instead of absolute pressures in applying Bernoulli's equation, provided the atmospheric pressure at the two places of consideration are not different.

Q. 13. Glycerine flows steadily through a horizontal tube of length 1.5 m and radius 1.0 cm. If the amount of glycerine collected per second at one end is 4.0 × 10^{-3} kgs^{-1}, what is the pressure difference between the two ends of the tube ? (Density of glycerine = 1.3 × 10^3 kgm^{-3} and viscosity of glycerine = 0.83 Pa).

[NCERT Ex., Q. 9.13, Page 200]

Ans. Given: Radius, $r = 1.0 \text{ cm} = 10^{-2} \text{ m}$

Length of tube, $l = 1.5 \text{ m}$

Density of glycerine, $\rho = 1.3 \times 10^3 \text{ kg m}^{-3}$.

Mass of glycerine flowing per sec,

$M = 4 \times 10^{-3} \text{ kg s}^{-1}$

Viscosity of glycerine $\eta = 0.83$ Pa.

$= 0.83 \text{ Nm}^{-2}$ s.

Suppose P = pressure difference between two ends of the tube

Suppose V = Volume of glycerine flowing per sec.

$$= \frac{M}{\rho} = \frac{4 \times 10^{-3} \text{kgs}^{-1}}{1.3 \times 10^3 \text{kgm}^{-3}}$$

$$= \frac{4}{1.3} \times 10^{-6}$$

$$= 3.08 \times 10^{-6} \text{ m}^3 \text{ s}^{-1}$$

Now from Poiseuille's formula, we have

$$V = \frac{\pi p r^4}{8 \eta l}$$

or $$p = 8\eta l V / \pi r^4.$$

or $$p = \frac{8 \times 0.83 \times 1.5 \times \left(\frac{4}{1.3} \times 10^{-6}\right)}{3.142 \times \left(10^{-2}\right)^4}$$

$$= 9.7537 \times 10^2 \text{ Pa}$$

$$= 9.8 \times 10^2 \text{ Pa}$$

Q. 14. In a test experiment on a model aeroplane in a wind tunnel, the flow speeds on the upper and lower surface of the wing are 70 ms^{-1} and 63 ms^{-1} respectively. What is the lift on the wing if its area is 2.5 m^2. (Take the density of air to be 1.3 kg m^{-3}.)

[NCERT Ex., Q. 9.14, Page 200]

Ans. Here $\rho = 1.3 \text{ kgm}^{-3}$, $a = 2.5 \text{ m}^2$,

$v_1 = 70 \text{ ms}^{-1}$ and $v_2 = 63 \text{ ms}^{-1}$

Using Bernoulli's equation,

$$\frac{P_1}{\rho} + \frac{1}{2} v_1^2 = \frac{P_2}{\rho} + \frac{1}{2} v_2^2$$

$$(P_2 - P_1) = \frac{1}{2}(v_1^2 - v_2^2)\rho$$

$$= \frac{1}{2}[(70)^2 - (63)^2] \times 1.3$$

$$= 605.2 \text{ Nm}^{-2}.$$

Therefore lift on the wing

$$F = (P_2 - P_1) \times a = 605.2 \times 2.5$$

$$= 1513 \text{ N}$$

Q. 15. Figures (a) and (b) refer to the steady flow of a (non-viscous) liquid. Which of the two figures is incorrect ? Why ?

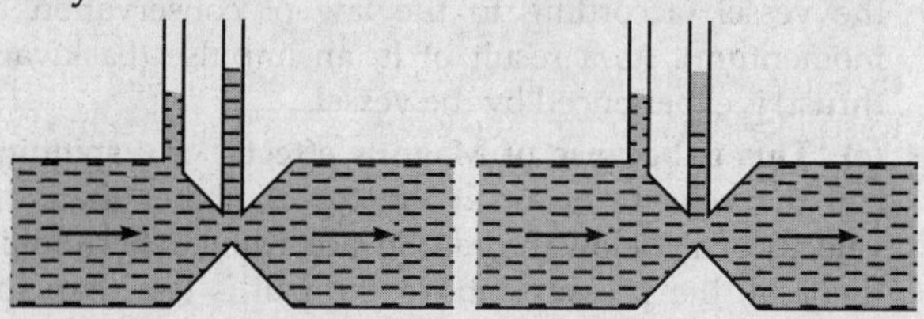

(a) (b)

[NCERT Ex., Q. 9.15, Page 200]

Ans. Figure (a) is incorrect. According to the equation of continuity aV = constant, where area of cross-section is less, flow is more. So, the velocity of liquid flow at a constriction of tube is more than other portion.

According to Bernoulli's theorem

$$P + \frac{1}{2}\rho v^2 = \text{constant}$$

So, where v is more, P is less.

Q. 16. The cylindrical tube of a spray pump has a cross-section of 8.0 cm^2 one end of which has 40 fine holes each of diameter 1.0 mm. If the liquid flow inside the tube is 1.5 m-min^{-1}, what is the speed of ejection of the liquid through the holes ?

[NCERT Ex., Q. 9.16, Page 201]

Ans. Here, $a_1 = 8 \text{ cm}^2 = 8 \times 10^{-4} \text{ m}^2$

$v_1 = 1.5 \text{ m min}^{-1}$

$= 0.025 \text{ ms}^{-1}$

Diameter of one hole, $d = 1 \text{ mm} = 10^{-3} \text{ m}$

$$\text{Area of hole} = \frac{\pi d^2}{4} = \frac{\pi \times \left(10^{-3}\right)^2}{4}$$

$$= \frac{\pi}{4} \times 10^{-6} \text{ m}^2$$

Therefore total cross-section of 40 holes

$$= \frac{\pi}{4} \times 10^{-6} \times 40 \text{ m}^2$$

If v_2 is the speed of ejection of the liquid through the hole

$$a_1v_1 = a_2v_2$$

$$v_2 = \frac{a_1v_1}{a_2} = \frac{8\times10^{-4}\times0.025}{\frac{\pi}{4}\times10^{-6}\times40}$$

$$= 0.637 \text{ m/s}$$

Q. 17. An U-shaped wire is dipped in a soap solution and removed. The thin soap film formed between the wire and the light slider supports a weight of 1.5 × 10⁻² N (which includes the small weight of the slider). The length of the slider is 30 cm. What is the surface tension of the film? [NCERT Ex., Q. 9.17, Page 201]

Ans. A soap film has two free surfaces, total length of the film to be supported, l = **2 × 30 cm**

$\Rightarrow$ l = 60 cm = 0.60 m

Suppose T = Surface tension of the film

When F = Total force on the slider due to surface tension.

Then $F = T \times 2l = T \times 0.6$ N,

$W = 1.5 \times 10^{-2}$ N.

In equilibrium position, the force F on the slider due to surface tension must be balanced by the weight (W) supported by the slider.

i.e., $F = W = mg$

or $T \times 0.6 = 1.5 \times 10^{-2}$

$$T = \frac{1.5\times10^{-2}}{0.6}$$

$$= 2.5 \times 10^{-2} \text{ Nm}^{-1}.$$

Q. 18. Figure (a) shows a thin liquid film supporting a small weight = 4.5 × 10⁻² N. What is the weight supported by a film of the same liquid at the same temperature in figure (b) and (c) ? Explain your answer physically.

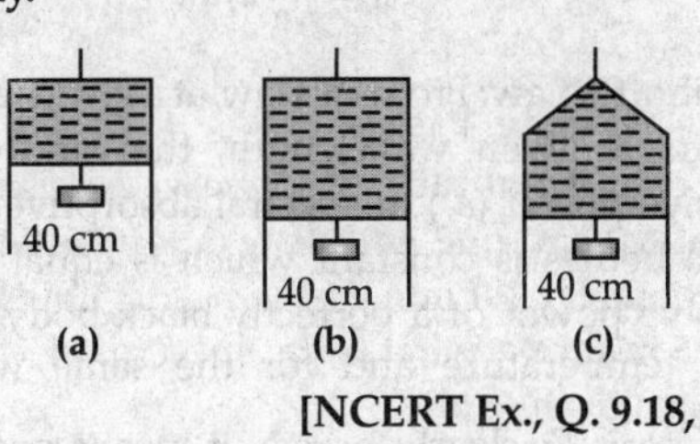

[NCERT Ex., Q. 9.18, Page 201]

Ans. Given: Length of the film supporting the weight

l = 40 cm = 0.4 m.

Total weight supported (i.e., force)

$= 4.5 \times 10^{-2}$ N.

T = surface tension = ?

The film has two free surfaces, so total length,

$L = 2l = 2 \times 0.4$ m.

$\therefore$ By formula $$T = \frac{\text{Force}}{\text{Length}} = \frac{4.5\times10^{-2}}{2\times0.4}$$

$$= 5.625 \times 10^{-2} \text{ Nm}^{-1}.$$

As the liquid is same for all the cases (a), (b) and (c) and temperature is also same, therefore surface tension for cases (b) and (c) will also be same,

i.e., 5.625×10^{-2} Nm^{-1}.

In Figure (b) and (c), the length of the film supporting the weight is also the same as that of (a), hence the total weight supported in each case is 4.5×10^{-2} N.

Q. 19. What is the pressure inside the drop of mercury of radius 3.00 mm at room temperature ? Surface tension of mercury at that temperature (20°C) is 4.65 × 10⁻¹ Nm⁻¹. The atmospheric pressure is 1.01 × 10⁵ Pa. Also give the excess pressure inside the drop. [NCERT Ex., Q. 9.19, Page 201]

Ans. Here, $S = 4.65 \times 10^{-1}$ Nm^{-1}

R = 3 mm

$= 3 \times 10^{-3}$ m

$P_{\text{outside}} = 1.01 \times 10^5$ Pa.

Using the relation,

$$\text{Excess pressure} = \frac{2S}{r},$$

$$= \frac{2\times4.65\times10^{-1}}{3\times10^{-3}}$$

$$= 310 \text{ Pa}$$

$$\text{Total pressure} = 1.01 \times 10^5 + 310$$

$$= 1.0131 \times 10^5 \text{ Pa}$$

Q. 20. What is the excess pressure inside a bubble of soap solution of radius 5.00 mm, given that the surface tension of soap solution at the temp. (20° C) is 2.50 × 10⁻² Nm⁻¹? If an air bubble of the same dimension were formed at a depth of 40.0 cm inside a container containing the soap solution (of relative density 1.20), what would be the pressure inside the bubble ? (1 atmospheric pressure is 1.0 × 10⁵ Pa.) [NCERT Ex., Q. 9.20, Page 201]

Ans. In case of soap bubble, excess pressure

$$= \frac{4S}{R} = \frac{4(2.5\times10^{-2})}{5\times10^{-3}}$$

$$= 20 \text{ Pa}$$

In case of air bubble, excess pressure

$$= \frac{2S}{R} = \frac{2(2.5\times10^{-2})}{5\times10^{-3}}$$

$$= 10 \text{ Pa}$$

P_{outside} = Pressure depth of 40 cm

= Atm. pressure + column pressure

$= (1.01 \times 10^5) + 0.4 \times 1.2 \times 10^3 \times 9.8$

$= 1.0570 \times 10^5 \text{ Pa} = 1.06 \times 10^5$Pa

Now, excess pressure $= P_{\text{inside}} - P_{\text{outisde}}$

$P_{\text{inside}} = P_{\text{outside}}$ + excess pressure

$= 1.06 \times 10^5 + 10$

$\approx 1.06 \times 10^5$ Pa

□□

THERMAL PROPERTIES OF MATTER

CHAPTER 10

Temperature and Heat

➤ **Four Scales of Temperature:**

S. No.	Scale	Ice point	Steam point	No. of divisions	Smallest division
1.	Centigrade scale	0°C	100°C	100	1°C
2.	Fahrenheit scale	32°F	212°F	180	1°F
3.	Thermodynamical scale or Absolute Kelvin scale	273 K	373 K	100	1 K

Thermal Expansion

➤ **Thermal Expansion of solids.:** It is the phenomenon of expansion of solids on heating. It is of three types:

(a) Linear Expansion: It is the increase in length of a solid on heating. α is called coefficient of linear expansion.

(b) Area Expansion: It is the increase in surface area of a solid on heating. β is called coefficient of area expansion.

(c) Volume Expansion: It is the increase in volume of a solid on heating. γ is called coefficient of volume expansion.

Scan to know more about this topic

Thermal expansion

➤ **Expansion of liquids:**

(a) Coefficient of real expansion of a liquid is defined as the real increase in volume of the liquid per unit original volume per °C rise in temperature. If γ_r is the coefficient of real expansion of a liquid, then

$$\gamma_r = \frac{\text{Real increase in volume}}{\text{Original volume} \times \text{Rise in temperature}}$$

(b) Coefficient of apparent expansion of a liquid is defined as the apparent increase in volume per unit original volume per °C rise in temperature. If γ_a is the coefficient of apparent expansion of a liquid, then

$$\gamma_a = \frac{\text{Apparent increase in volume}}{\text{Original volume} \times \text{Rise in temperature}}$$

Heat Transfer

➤ **Thermal Conductivity:**

(i) Coefficient of Thermal Conductivity: It is equal to rate of flow of heat per unit area per unit temperature gradient across the solid at steady state. It is represented by K and its value depends on nature of material of solid.

$$K = \frac{\Delta Q \Delta x}{\Delta T A}$$

$$K = \Delta Q, \text{ when } \left(\frac{\Delta x}{\Delta T}\right) = 1, A = 1$$

(ii) Thermal resistance corresponds to electrical resistance (V/*i*) and is given by the ratio of temperature difference and rate of flow of heat *i.e.,*

$$R_{Th} = \frac{T_1 - T_2}{dQ / dt} = \frac{x}{KA}$$

➤ **Total emittance or emissive power** of a body at a certain temperature is the total amount of thermal energy emitted per unit time per unit area of the body for all possible wavelengths. It is represented by *e*'.

$$e = \int_0^\infty e_\lambda d\lambda$$

Scan to know more about this topic

Thermal conductivity

➤ **Emissivity** (ε) of a body at a given temperature is the ratio of emissive power of the body (*e*) to the emissive power of perfectly black body (E) at that temperature,

i.e., $$\varepsilon = \frac{e}{E}$$

Similarly, we can define monochromatic absorptance or spectral absorptive power. Total absorptance or absorbing power

$$a = \int_0^\infty a_\lambda d\lambda$$

➤ **Kirchhoff's Law:** From this law, at a given temperature and for a given wavelength, the ratio of spectral emissive power (e_λ) to spectral absorptive power (a_λ) for all bodies is constant which is equal to spectral emissive power of a perfectly black body (E_λ) at the same temperature and for the same wavelength, i.e., $\frac{e_\lambda}{a_\lambda} = E_\lambda$ clearly, $e_\lambda \propto a_\lambda$ it means good emitters are good absorbers. The law implies that at a particular temperature, a body can absorb only those wavelengths, which it is capable of emitting.

➤ **Wien's law:** From this law, the wavelength (λ_m) corresponding to which energy emitted/sec/ unit area by a perfectly black body is maximum, is inversely proportional to the absolute temperature (T) of the black body.

$$\lambda_m \propto \frac{1}{T}$$

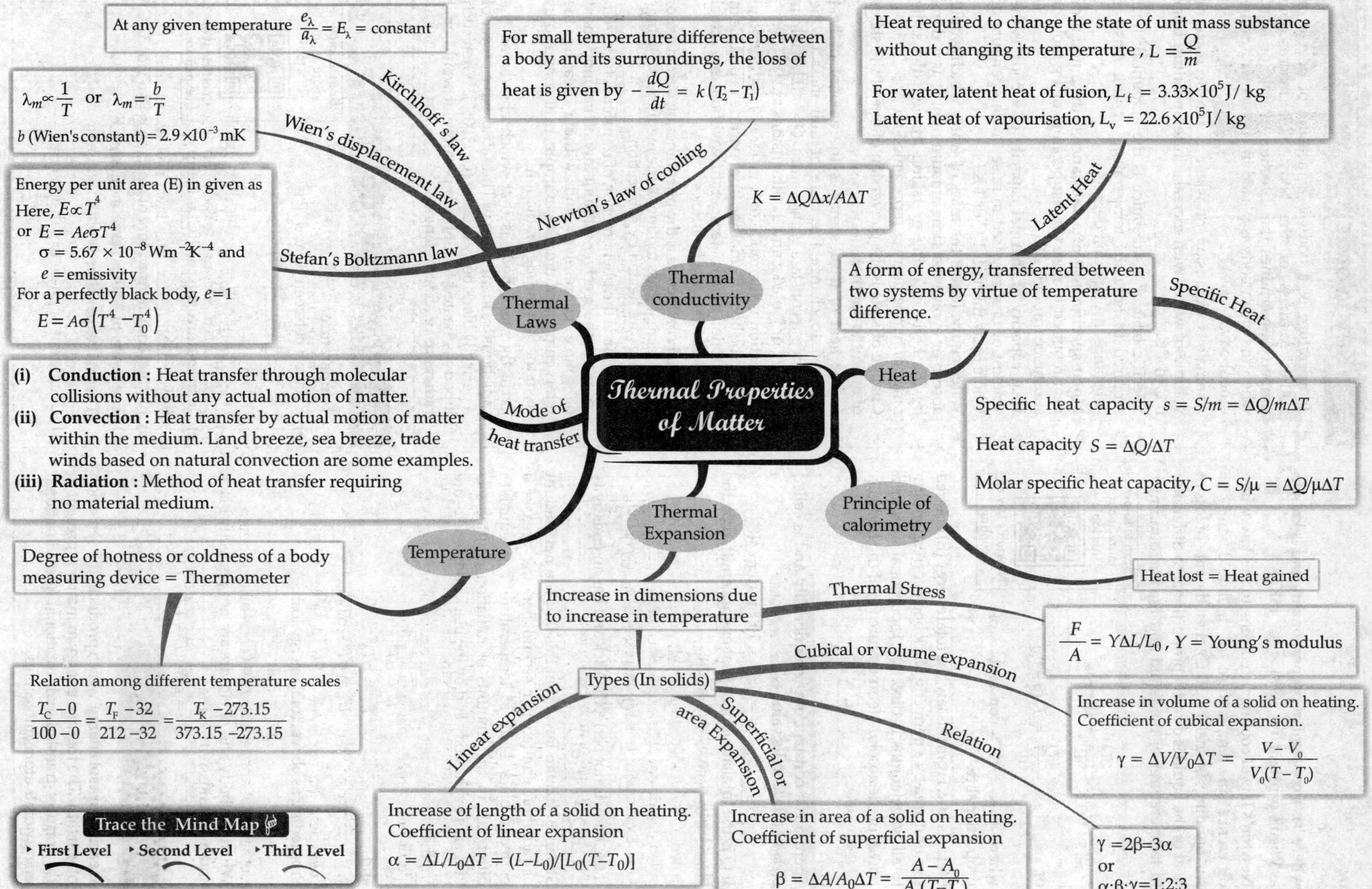
Thermal Properties of Matter
Thermal Laws
Kirchhoff's law
At any given temperature $\frac{e_\lambda}{a_\lambda} = E_\lambda$ = constant
Wien's displacement law
$\lambda_m \propto \frac{1}{T}$ or $\lambda_m = \frac{b}{T}$
b (Wien's constant) = 2.9×10^{-3} mK
Stefan's Boltzmann law
Energy per unit area (E) in given as
Here, $E \propto T^4$
or $E = Ae\sigma T^4$
$\sigma = 5.67 \times 10^{-8}$ Wm^{-2}K^{-4} and
e = emissivity
For a perfectly black body, e=1
$E = A\sigma\left(T^4 - T_0^4\right)$
Newton's law of cooling
For small temperature difference between a body and its surroundings, the loss of heat is given by $-\frac{dQ}{dt} = k(T_2 - T_1)$
Thermal conductivity
$K = \Delta Q \Delta x / A \Delta T$
Heat
A form of energy, transferred between two systems by virtue of temperature difference.
Latent Heat
Heat required to change the state of unit mass substance without changing its temperature, $L = \frac{Q}{m}$
For water, latent heat of fusion, $L_f = 3.33 \times 10^5$ J/ kg
Latent heat of vapourisation, $L_v = 22.6 \times 10^5$ J/ kg
Specific Heat
Specific heat capacity $s = S/m = \Delta Q/m\Delta T$
Heat capacity $S = \Delta Q/\Delta T$
Molar specific heat capacity, $C = S/\mu = \Delta Q/\mu\Delta T$
Mode of heat transfer
(i) Conduction : Heat transfer through molecular collisions without any actual motion of matter.
(ii) Convection : Heat transfer by actual motion of matter within the medium. Land breeze, sea breeze, trade winds based on natural convection are some examples.
(iii) Radiation : Method of heat transfer requiring no material medium.
Temperature
Degree of hotness or coldness of a body measuring device = Thermometer
Relation among different temperature scales
$\frac{T_C - 0}{100 - 0} = \frac{T_F - 32}{212 - 32} = \frac{T_K - 273.15}{373.15 - 273.15}$
Thermal Expansion
Increase in dimensions due to increase in temperature
Thermal Stress
$\frac{F}{A} = Y\Delta L/L_0$, Y = Young's modulus
Types (In solids)
Cubical or volume expansion
Increase in volume of a solid on heating. Coefficient of cubical expansion.
$\gamma = \Delta V/V_0\Delta T = \frac{V - V_0}{V_0(T - T_0)}$
Relation
$\gamma = 2\beta = 3\alpha$
or
$\alpha:\beta:\gamma = 1:2:3$
Superficial or area Expansion
Increase in area of a solid on heating. Coefficient of superficial expansion
$\beta = \Delta A/A_0\Delta T = \frac{A - A_0}{A_0(T - T_0)}$
Linear expansion
Increase of length of a solid on heating. Coefficient of linear expansion
$\alpha = \Delta L/L_0\Delta T = (L - L_0)/[L_0(T - T_0)]$
Principle of calorimetry
Heat lost = Heat gained
Trace the Mind Map
First Level
Second Level
Third Level

or, $$\lambda_m = \frac{b}{T}$$

where b is a constant of proportionality and is known as Wien's constant $b = 2.898 \times 10^{-3}$ mK.

- **Newton's law of cooling**: According to this law, when difference in temperature of a liquid and its surroundings is small (~ 30°C), then the rate of loss of heat of the liquid is directly proportional to difference in temperatures of the liquid and the surroundings, i.e.,

$$-\frac{dQ}{dt} \propto (\theta - \theta_0)$$

or, $$-\frac{dQ}{dt} = K(\theta - \theta_0)$$

where K is constant of proportionality.

Scan to know more about this topic

Newton's law of cooling

- **Stefan's law:** From this law, the total energy (E) emitted sec/ unit area by a perfectly black body corresponding to all wavelengths is directly proportional to fourth power of the absolute temperature (T) of the body *i.e.*

$$E \propto T^4$$

or, $$E = \sigma T^4$$

There σ is a constant of proportionality and is called *Stefan's constant*. Its value is

$$\sigma = 5.67 \times 10^{-8} \text{ watt m}^{-2}\text{K}^{-4}$$

If Q is the total amount of heat energy emitted by the black body, then by definition,

$$E = \frac{Q}{At}$$

$$\therefore \quad Q = At \times E = At\,(\sigma T^4)$$

If the body is not perfectly black and has an emissivity e, then $Q = eAt\,(\sigma T^4)$

- **Stefan Boltzman law:** From this law, the net amount of radiation emitted per second per unit area of a perfectly black body at temperature T is equal to difference in the amounts of radiation emitted/sec/ unit area by the body and by the black body enclosure at T_0.

$$\Rightarrow \quad E' = E - E_0$$

As $$E = \sigma T^4$$

and $$E_0 = \sigma T_0^4$$

$$\therefore \quad E' = \sigma T^4 - \sigma T_0^4 = \sigma(T^4 - T_0^4)$$

Proceeding as above, total energy lost

$$Q' = E'At = At\sigma\,(T^4 - T_0^4)$$

When the body and enclosure are not perfectly black and have emissivity ε, then

$$Q' = \varepsilon At\sigma(T^4 - T_0^4)$$

Key Words

- **Heat** is a form of energy, which produces the sensation of warmth. The thermal energy in matter is present in the form of translational, rotational and vibrational energy of its atoms/molecules.

Key Words

- **Temperature** of a body is a measure of degree of hotness/coldness of the body. This macroscopic property determines the direction of flow of heat, when the given body is placed in contact with some other body.
- Anomalous expansion of water is the decrease of volume of water with increase in temperature from 0°C to 4°C.
- **Specific heat of a substance** is the amount of heat required to raise the temperature of unit mass of substance through unit degree.
- **Molar specific heat of a substance** is the amount of heat required to raise the temperature of 1 g mole of substance through 1°C.
- **Heat capacity or thermal capacity** of a body is the amount of heat required to raise the temperature of whole body through 1°C or 1 K.
- **Water equivalent** is the mass of water which would absorb or evolve the same amount of heat as is done by the body in rising or falling through the same range of temperature & represented by W.
- **Change of state** is the conversion of one of the states of matter to another.
- **Latent heat** of a substance is the amount of heat required to change the state of unit mass of the substance at constant temperature ($Q = ML$). Its units are cal/g or joule/kg and its dimensions are $[L^2T^{-2}]$.
- **Conduction** is the mode of transfer of heat from one part of the body to another, from particle to particle in the direction of fall of temperature without any actual movement of heated particles.
- **Thermal convection** is the phenomenon of transfer of heat by actual mass motion of the medium. All liquids and gases are heated by convection.
- **Radiation** is the phenomenon of transfer of heat from source to the receiver without any actual movement of source or receiver and without heating the intervening medium. For example, heat comes to us from the Sun through radiation.
- **Perfectly black body** is that which absorbs all the radiations incident upon it. Thus absorptive power of a perfectly black body is unity (*i.e.*, 100%). When such a body is heated to high temperature, it would emit radiations of all wavelengths.

Key Formulae

- **Temperature**

(a) Relation between °C and °F is

$$\frac{C}{5} = \frac{F-32}{9}$$

(b) $T\,K = (t°C + 273)$ or $t°C = (T\,K - 273)$

(c) Temperature. diff. of 1°C = Temp. diff. of 1 K.

(d) Normal body temperature of a person is 98.6°F or 37°C.

(e) The temp. of – 40° is same in °C and °F.

Scan to know more about this topic

Coefficient of expansion

- **Thermal expansion**

(a) Coefficient of linear expansion $\alpha = \frac{\Delta L}{L\Delta T}$

Key Formulae

(b) Coefficient of Area expansion $\beta = \dfrac{\Delta S}{S(\Delta T)}$

(c) Coefficient of volume expansion $\gamma = \dfrac{\Delta V}{V(\Delta T)}$

(d) $\beta = 2\alpha$; $\gamma = 3\alpha$

(e) In liquids.

$\gamma_r = \gamma_a + \gamma_g$

where,

γ_r = Coefficient of real expansion of liquid

γ_a = Coefficient of apparent expansion of liquid

γ_g = Coefficient of expansion of vessel

- **Specific heat.** $\Delta Q = ms\Delta T$
- **Molar specific heat** $C = M \times s$
- **Latent heat** $\Delta Q = ML$, L = Latent heat
- **Specific heat of gases** $C_p - C_V = R$, Here $R = \dfrac{PV}{T}$
- Calorimetric principle: The heat lost by the hot body is equal to the heat gained by the colder body, provided no heat is allowed to escape to the surroundings.
- **Rate of conduction of Heat,** $\dfrac{\Delta Q}{\Delta t} = KA\dfrac{\Delta T}{\Delta x}$

Key Formulae

- **Thermal resistance,** $R_{Th} = \dfrac{T_1 - T_2}{dQ/dt}$
- **Emissive power,** $e' = \int_0^\infty e_\lambda d\lambda$
- **Emissivity,** $\varepsilon = \dfrac{e}{E}$

Mnemonics

Concept: Relation between coefficients of thermal expansion.

Mnemonics: **A**tal and **V**ikie stood **2nd** and **3rd** respectively in **last** exam.

Interpretation:

A - Areal thermal expansion

V - Volume thermal expansion

2nd - 2

3rd - 3

last - Linear thermal expansion

Coefficient of Areal Expansion = 2 × Coefficient linear expansion Coefficient of Volume Expansion = 3 × Coefficient linear expansion

NCERT CORNER

Q. 1. The triple points of neon and carbon dioxide are 24.57 K and 216.55 K respectively. Express these temperature on the Celsius and Fahrenheit scales.

[NCERT Ex., Q. 10.1, Page 223]

Ans. Relation between Kelvin and Celsius scale

$$T_C = T_K - 273.15$$

where T_C, T_K are temperatures in Celsius and Kelvin respectively.

For Neon: $T_C = 24.57 - 273.15 = -248.58°C$

For CO_2: $T_C = 216.55 - 273.15 = -56.60°C$

Relation between Kelvin and Fahrenheit

$$\frac{T_F - 32}{180} = \frac{T_K - 273.15}{100}$$

$$T_F = \frac{180}{100}(T_K - 273.15) + 32$$

For Neon: $T_F = \dfrac{180}{100}(24.57 - 273.15) + 32 = -415.44°F$

For CO_2: $T_F = \dfrac{180}{100}(216.55 - 273.15) + 32 = -69.88°F$

Q. 2. Two absolute scales A and B have triple points of water defined to be 200 A and 350 B. What is the relation between T_A and T_B?

[NCERT Ex., Q. 10.2, Page 223]

Ans. Given: Triple point of water = 200A = 350B = 273.16K

$\therefore$ $1A = \dfrac{273.16}{200}K$, $1B = \dfrac{273.16}{350}K$.

If T_A and T_B represent the triple point of water on scales A & B,

$$\frac{273.16}{200}T_A = \frac{273.16}{350}T_B$$

or $$\frac{T_A}{T_B} = \frac{200}{350} = \frac{4}{7}$$

$\therefore$ $$T_A = \frac{4}{7}T_B$$

Q. 3. The electrical resistance in ohms of a certain thermometer varies with temperature according to the approximate law:

$R = R_o [1 + \alpha(T - T_o)]$. The resistance is 101.6 Ω at the normal melting point of lead 600.5K. What is the temperature when the resistance is 123.4 Ω?

[NCERT Ex., Q. 10.3, Page 223]

Ans. $R_o = 101.6\ \Omega$, $T_o = 273.16$ K, $R_1 = 165.5\ \Omega$,

$T_1 = 600.5$ K, $R_2 = 123.4\ \Omega$,

As, $R = R_o [1 + \alpha(T - T_o)]$

$$165.5 = 101.6[1+\alpha(600.5-273.16)]$$

$$= 101.6[1+\alpha\times 327.34]$$

or $$\alpha = \frac{165.5-101.6}{101.6\times 327.34} \quad ...(1)$$

Also,

$$123.4 = 101.6[1+\alpha(T_2-273.16)]$$

$$123.4 = 101.6\left[1+\frac{63.9}{101.6\times 327.34}(T_2-273.16)\right]$$

[from (1) putting α]

$$\therefore T_2 = \frac{(123.4-101.6)\times 327.34}{63.9}+273.16$$

$$T_2 = 384.83\text{K}$$

Q. 4. Answer the following:

(a) The triple point of water is a standard fixed point in modern thermometer. Why ? What is wrong in taking melting point of ice and the boiling point of water as standard fixed points (as was originally done in Celsius scale) ?

(b) There were two fixed points in the original Celsius scale as mentioned above which were assigned the numbers 0°C and 100°C respectively. On the absolute scale one of the fixed points is the triple point of water, which on the Kelvin absolute scale is assigned the number 273.16 K. What is the other fixed point on this (Kelvin) Scale ?

(c) The absolute temperature (Kelvin scale) T is related to the temperature t_c on the Celsius scale by $t_c = T - 273.15$. Why do we have 273.15 in this relation and not 273.16 ?

(d) What is the temperature of triple point of water on an absolute scale whose unit interval size is equal to that of the Fahrenheit scale ?

[NCERT Ex., Q. 10.4, Page 223]

Ans. (a) This is because the triple point of water is unique condition of temperature and pressure, i.e., it occurs only at one particular set of values of pressure and temperature. Hence, it is easily reproducible. Hence it is used as a standard temperature in thermometry.

The melting point of ice and boiling point of water are pressure dependent which means they change with change in the value of pressure. They are also very sensitive to the dissolved impurities. Therefore these have been discarded as a reference point and triple of water has been taken as a fixed point.

(b) The 0 K or absolute zero itself is the other fixed point on the absolute scale of temperature. It corresponds to the temperature when the volume and pressure of a gas become zero.

(c) Triple point is 0.01°C and not 0°C. Thus to make a celsius degree equal to Kelvin degree 273.15 is assigned instead of 273.16. Moreover ice point on Kelvin scale is 273.15 K and the corresponding is point on celsius scale is 0°C which is clear from the relation, i.e., $t_c = T - 273.15$. When we have 273.16 instead of 273.15 in the above relation, then the ice point on celsius scale will be 0 which is not the case.

(d) The unit interval size of Fahrenheit scale is 212 – 32 = 180.

So, the required temperature of triple point of water =

$$T = \frac{273.16}{100} \times 180$$

$$= 491.69$$

Q. 5. Two ideal gas thermometers A and B use oxygen and hydrogen respectively. The following observations are made:

Temperature	Pressure thermometer A	Pressure thermometer B
Triple-point of water	1.250×10^5 Pa	0.200×10^5 Pa
Normal melting point of sulphur	1.797×10^5 Pa	0.287×10^5 Pa

(a) What is the absolute temperature of normal melting point of sulphur as read by thermometers A and B?

(b) What do you think is the reason behind the slight difference in answers of thermometers A and B? (The thermometers are not faulty). What further procedure is needed in the experiment to reduce the discrepancy between the two readings?

[NCERT Ex., Q. 10.5, Page 223]

Ans. (a) Triple point of water, $T = 273.16$ K

At this temperature, pressure in thermometer A, $P_A = 1.250 \times 10^5$ Pa

Let T_1 be the normal melting point of sulphur.

At this temperature, pressure in thermometer,

$P_1 = 1.797 \times 10^5$ Pa

According to Charles' law, we have the relation:

$$\frac{P_A}{T} = \frac{P_1}{T_1}$$

$$\therefore \quad T_1 = \frac{P_1 T}{P_A} = \frac{1.797\times 10^5 \times 273.16}{1.25\times 10^5}$$

$$= 392.69 \text{ K}$$

Therefore, the absolute temperature of the normal melting point of sulphur as read by thermometer A is 392.69 K.

At triple point 273.16 K, the pressure in thermometer B,

$P_B = 0.200 \times 10^5$ Pa

At temperature T_1, the pressure in thermometer B,

$P_2 = 0.287 \times 10^5$ Pa

According to Charles' law, we can write the relation:

$$\frac{P_B}{T} = \frac{P_2}{T_1}$$

$$\frac{0.200 \times 10^5}{273.16} = \frac{0.287 \times 10^5}{T_1}$$

$$\therefore \quad T_1 = \frac{0.287 \times 10^5}{0.200 \times 10^5} \times 273.16 = 391.98\,\text{K}$$

Therefore, the absolute temperature of the normal melting point of sulphur as read by thermometer B is 391.98 K.

(b) The oxygen and hydrogen gas present in thermometers A and B respectively are not perfect ideal gases. Hence, there is a slight difference between the readings of thermometers A and B.

To reduce the discrepancy between the two readings, the experiment should be carried under low pressure conditions. At low pressure, these gases behave as perfect ideal gases.

Q. 6. A steel tape 1m long is correctly calibrated for a temperature of 27.0°C. The length of a steel rod measured by this tape is found to be 63.0 cm on a hot day when the temperature is 45.0°C. What is the actual length of the steel rod on that day? What is the length of the same steel rod on a day when the temperature is 27.0°C? Coefficient of linear expansion of steel = 1.20 × 10^{-5} K^{-1}. [NCERT Ex., Q. 10.6, Page 224]

Ans. The length of the steel tape at temperature

$T = 27°C$, $l = 1$ m $= 100$ cm

At temperature $T_1 = 45°C$, the length of the steel rod, $l_1 = 63$ cm

Coefficient of linear expansion of steel, $\alpha = 1.20 \times 10^{-5}$ K^{-1}

Let l_2 be the actual length of the steel rod and l' be the length of the steel tape at 45°C.

$$l' = l + \alpha l\,(T_1 - T)$$

$$\therefore l' = 100 + 1.20 \times 10^{-5} \times 100(45 - 27)$$

$$= 100.0216 \text{ cm}$$

Hence, the actual length of the steel rod measured by the steel tape at 45°C can be calculated as:

$$l_2 = \frac{100.0216}{100} \times 63 = 63.0136 \text{ cm}.$$

Therefore, the actual length of the rod at 45.0°C is 63.0136 cm. Its length at 27.0°C is 63.0 cm.

Q. 7. A large steel wheel is to be fitted on a shaft of the same material. At 27°C, the outer diameter of the shaft is 8.70 cm and the diameter of the central hole in the wheel is 8.69 cm. The shaft cooled using 'dry ice'. At what temperature of the shaft does the wheel slip on the shaft? Assume the coefficient of linear expansion of the steel to be constant over the required temperature range.

$\alpha_{steel} = 1.20 \times 10^{-5} K^{-1}$.

[NCERT Ex., Q. 10.7, Page 224]

Ans. Suppose l_1 and l_2 be the outer diameter dimensions of a steel at temperatures T_1 and T_2 respectively.

Given $\alpha_{steel} = 1.20 \times 10^{-5} K^{-1}$.

$l_1 = 8.70$ cm

$l_2 = 8.69$ cm

$T_1 = 27°C = 273 + 27 = 300K$

$T_2 = ?$

When the steel shaft is cooled, its linear dimension, *i.e.*, its diameter decreases according to the formula.

$l_2 = l_1[1 + \alpha(T_2 - T_1)]$ ...(i)

When the shaft is cooled to temperature T_2 such that $l_2 = 8.69$ cm, the wheel can slip on the shaft.

$\therefore$ By putting all values in eq. (i), we get

$$8.69 = 8.70[1 + 1.20 \times 10^{-5}(T_2 - 300)]$$

or, $$T_2 - 300 = \frac{8.69 - 8.70}{8.70 \times 1.20 \times 10^{-5}}$$

$$= -95.78 \text{ K}$$

or, $$T_2 = 300 - 95.78 = 204.22 \text{ K}$$

$$= 204.22 - 273.15$$

$$= -68.93°C$$

$$\therefore \quad T_2 = -69°C.$$

Q. 8. A hole is drilled in a Cu sheet. The diameter of the hole is 4.24 cm at 27°C. What is the change in diameter of the hole when the sheet is heated to 227°C ? (Coefficient of linear expansion of Cu = 1.7 × 10^{-5} $°C^{-1}$.) [NCERT Ex., Q. 10.8, Page 224]

Ans. Using, $S_2 = S_1(1 + \beta\Delta T)$ when

$$S_1 = \frac{\pi d_1^2}{4}$$

$$= \frac{\pi}{4}(4.24)^2$$

$$= \pi \times 4.494 \text{ cm}^2$$

$$\Delta T = 227 - 27$$

$$= 200°C$$

$$\beta = 2\alpha$$

$$= 2 \times 1.7 \times 10^{-5}\,°C^{-1}.$$

we get, $$S_2 = (\pi \times 4.94)\,[1 + (2 \times 1.7 \times 10^{-5})(200)]$$

$$= \pi \times 4.525 \text{ cm}^2$$

or $$\frac{\pi d_2^2}{4} = \pi \times 4.525$$

or $$d_2 = \sqrt{4 \times 4.525} = 4.254 \text{ cm}$$

Change in diameter $= d_2 - d_1$

$= 4.254 - 4.24 = 0.014$ cm

Q. 9 A brass wire 1.8 m long at 27°C is held tight with little tension between two rigid supports. If the wire is cooled to a temperature of – 39°C. What is the tension developed in the wire, if its diameter is 2.0 m ?

[NCERT Ex., Q. 10.9, Page 224]

Ans. Here, $l_1 = 1.8$ m,

$\Delta T = (-39) - 27$

$= -66°C$

$\alpha = 2 \times 10^{-5}\,°C^{-1}$

$l_2 = l_1(1 + \alpha\Delta T)$

$= 1.8[1 + (2 \times 10^{-5})(-66)]$

$= 1.798$ m

Change in length $= 1.8 - 1.798$

$= 0.002$ m

Here $A = \frac{\pi d^2}{4} = \frac{\pi}{4}(2 \times 10^{-3})^2$

$= 3.14 \times 10^{-6}\ m^2$

$Y = \frac{F}{A} \times \frac{l}{\Delta l}$

or, $F = \frac{YA\Delta l}{l}$

$= (0.91 \times 10^{11}) \times (3.14 \times 10^{-6}) \times \left(\frac{0.002}{1.8}\right)$

$= 3.81 \times 10^2$ N

Q. 10. A brass rod of length 50 cm and diameter 3.0 mm is joined to a steel rod of the same length and diameter, what is the change in length of the combined rod at 250°C, if the original lengths are at 40.0°C ? Is there a 'thermal stress' developed at the junction ? The ends of the rod are free to expand.

[NCERT Ex., Q. 10.10, Page 224]

Ans. For brass rod $l_2 = l_1(1 + \alpha\Delta T)$,

$l_2 = 50[1 + (2 \times 10^{-5})(250 - 40)]$

$= 50.21$ cm

For steel Rod $l_2' = l_1'(1 + \alpha\Delta T')$,

$l_2' = 50[1 + (1.2 \times 10^{-5})(250 - 240)]$

$= 50.126$ cm

Combined length $= 50.21 + 50.126$

$= 100.336$

Change in combined length at 250°C

$= 100.336 - 100$

$= 0.336$ cm

Since, the rods are free to expend at both ends, no thermal stress is developed at the junction.

Q. 11. The coefficient of volume expansion of glycerine is 49 × 10^{-5} °C^{-1}. What is the fractional change in its density for a 30°C rise in temperature ?

[NCERT Ex., Q. 10.11, Page 224]

Ans. Here, $\Delta T = 30°C$

and $\gamma = 49 \times 10^{-5}\ °C^{-1}$

$V = V_0[1 + \gamma\Delta T)$,

we get $V = V_0[1 + (49 \times 10^{-5})(30)]$

$= 1.015\ V_0$

Initial density, $\rho_0 = \frac{m}{V_0}$

Final density, $\rho = \frac{m}{V} = \frac{m}{1.015V_0} = \frac{\rho_0}{1.015}$

$= 0.986\ \rho_0$

Fractional change in density

$= \frac{\rho_0 - \rho}{\rho_0} = \frac{\rho_0 0.986\rho_0}{\rho_0} = 0.014$

$= 0.014$

Q. 12. A 10 kW drilling machine is used to drill a bore in a small aluminium block of mass 8.0 kg. How much is the rise in temperature of the block in 2.5 min, assuming 50% of power is used up heating the machine itself or lost to the surrounding ? (Specific heat of aluminium = 0.91 Jg^{-1}°C^{-1}.) **[NCERT Ex., Q. 10.12, Page 224]**

Ans. Here $t = 2.5\ min = 2.5 \times 60 = 150\ s$

and $P = 10^4$ W

Energy used in drilling

$Q' = P \times t$

$= 10^4 \times 150 = 1.5 \times 10^6$ J

Useful energy $Q = Q' \times \frac{50}{100} = \frac{1.5 \times 10^6 \times 50}{100}$

$= 7.5 \times 10^5$ J

Using $Q = mc\Delta T$,

$7.5 \times 10^5 = 8 \times 0.91 \times 10^3\ \Delta T$

$7.5 \times 10^5 = 7.28 \times 10^3\ \Delta T$

$\therefore \Delta T = \frac{7.5 \times 10^5}{7.28 \times 10^3} = 103°C$

Q. 13. A copper block of mass 2.5 kg is heated in a furnace to a temperature of 500°C and then placed on a large ice block. What is the maximum amount of ice that can melt? (Specific heat of Copper = 0.39 J/g°C, Latent heat of fusion of water = 335 J/g.)

[NCERT Ex., Q. 10.13, Page 224]

Ans. Here $M = 2.5$ kg, $\Delta t = 500°C$

and $c = 0.39 \times 10^3\ Jkg^{-1}\ °C^{-1}$

Using $Q = Mc\Delta t$,

Heat absorbed by Cu block,

$Q = 2.5 \times 0.39 \times 10^3 \times 500$ J

Heat absorbed by the ice block to melt,

$Q = ML$

$= M \times 335 \times 10^3$ J

Then $(3.35 \times 10^3)\ M = 2.5 \times 0.39 \times 10^3 \times 500$

$M = \frac{2.5 \times 0.39 \times 10^3 \times 500}{335 \times 10^3}$

$= 1.455$ kg

Q. 14. In an experiment on the specific heat of a metal, a 0.20 kg block of the metal at 150°C is dropped in Cu calorimeter of water equivalent 0.025 kg containing 150 cm³ of water at 27°C. The final temperature is 40°C. Compute the specific heat of the metal.

[NCERT Ex., Q. 10.14, Page 224]

Ans. Here $T_1 = 150°C$,

$T_2 = 27°C$

and $T = 40°C$

$M_1 = 0.20$ kg

and $W = 0.25$ kg

Volume of water in calorimeter

$= 150\ cm^3$

$= 150 \times 10^{-6}\ m^3$

Mass of water in calorimeter,

$M_2 = (150 \times 10^{-6}) \times 10^3$

$= 150 \times 10^{-3}$ kg

Using,

Heat gained = Heat Lost

$(M_2 + W)\ c_2(T - T_2) = M_1c_1(T_1 - T)$

$$(150 \times 10^{-3} + 0.025) \times (4.2 \times 10^{-3})(40 - 20) = 0.20c_1(150 - 40)$$

or $9.55 \times 10^{-3} = 22c_1$

$$c_1 = 434 \text{ J kg}^{-1}\,°\text{C}^{-1}$$

Q. 15. Given below are observations on molar specific heats at room temperature of some common gases.

Gas	Molar specific heat (C_v) (cal mol^{-1}) K^{-1}
Hydrogen	4.87
Nitrogen	4.97
Oxygen	5.02
Nitric oxide	4.99
Carbon monoxide	5.01
Chlorine	6.17

The measured molar specific heats of these gases are markedly different from those for monatomic gases. Typically, molar specific heat of a monatomic gas is 2.92 cal/mol K. Explain this difference. What can you infer from the somewhat larger (than the rest) value for chlorine? [NCERT Ex., Q. 10.15, Page 224]

Ans. The gases listed in the given table are diatomic. Besides the translational degree of freedom, they have other degrees of freedom.

Heat must be supplied to increase the temperature of these gases. This increases the average energy of all the modes of motion. Hence, the molar specific heat of diatomic gases is more than that of monatomic gases.

If only rotational mode of motion is considered, then the molar specific heat of a diatomic gas $= \frac{5}{2}R$

$$= \frac{5}{2} \times 1.98 = 4.95 \text{ cal mol}^{-1}\text{K}^{-1}$$

With the exception of chlorine, all the observations in the given table agree with $\left(\frac{5}{2}R\right)$

This is because at room temperature, chlorine also has vibrational modes of motion besides rotational and translational modes of motion.

Q. 16. A child running a temperature of 101 °F is given an antipyrin (i.e. a medicine that lowers fever) which causes an increase in the rate of evaporation of sweat from his body. If the fever is brought down to 98 °F in 20 min, what is the average rate of extra evaporation caused, by the drug? Assume the evaporation mechanism to be the only way by which heat is lost. The mass of the child is 30 kg. The specific heat of human body is approximately the same as that of water, and latent heat of evaporation of water at that temperature is about 580 cal g^{-1}.

[NCERT Ex., Q. 10.16, Page 225]

Ans. Initial temperature of the body of the child, $T_1 = 101°\text{F}$

Final temperature of the body of the child, $T_2 = 98°\text{F}$.

Change in temperature, $\Delta T = \left[(101 - 98) \times \frac{5}{9}\right]°C$

Time taken to reduce the temperature, $t = 20$ min

Mass of the child, m = 30 kg

Specific heat of the human body = Specific heat of water = c = 1000 cal / kg / °C

Latent heat of evaporation of water, $L = 580$ cal g^{-1}

The heat lost by the child is given as:

$$\Delta Q = mc\Delta T$$

$$= 30 \times 1000 \times (101 - 98) \times \frac{5}{9}$$

$$= 50000 \text{ cal}$$

Let m_1 be the mass of the water evaporated from the child's body in 20 min.

Loss of heat through water is given by:

$$\Delta Q = m_1 L$$

$$\therefore m_1 = \frac{\Delta Q}{L}$$

$$= \frac{50000}{580} = 86.2\text{g}$$

$\therefore$ Average rate of extra evaporation caused by the drug

$$= \frac{m_1}{t}$$

$$= \frac{86.2}{20} = 4.3\text{g / min}$$

Q. 17. A 'thermocol' icebox is a cheap and efficient method for storing small quantities of cooked food in summer in particular. A cubical icebox of side 30 cm has a thickness of 5.0 cm. If 4.0 kg of ice is put in the box, estimate the amount of ice remaining after 6 h. The outside temperature is 45 °C, and co-efficient of thermal conductivity of thermocol is 0.01 $J\,s^{-1}m^{-1}K^{-1}$. [Heat of fusion of water = 335 × 10^3 $J\,kg^{-1}$]

[NCERT Ex., Q. 10.17, Page 225]

Ans. Side of the given cubical ice box, $s = 30\ cm = 0.3\ m$

Thickness of the ice box, $l = 5.0\ cm = 0.05\ m$

Mass of ice kept in the ice box, $m = 4$ kg

Time gap, $t = 6\ h = 6 \times 60 \times 60s$

Outside temperature, $T = 45°\text{C}$

Coefficient of thermal conductivity of thermocol, $K = 0.01 J s^{-1} m^{-1} K^{-1}$

Heat of fusion of water, $L = 3\,35 \times 10^3\ J\,kg^{-1}$

Let m′ be the total amount of ice that melts in 6 h.

The amount of heat lost:

$$Q = \frac{KA(T_1 - T_2)t}{l}$$

where, A = Surface area of the box = $6s^2$

$$= 6 \times (0.3)^2$$

$$= 0.54\ m^3$$

$$Q = \frac{0.01 \times 0.54 \times (45) \times 6 \times 60 \times 60}{0.05}$$

$$= 104976J$$

Also, $Q = m'L$ [m' = amount of ice melt]

$$\therefore m' = \frac{Q}{L}$$

$$= \frac{104976}{335 \times 10^3} = 0.313.\text{ kg}$$

Mass of ice left = 4 – 0.313 = 3.687 kg

Hence, the amount of ice remaining after 6 h is 3.687 kg

Q. 18. A brass boiler has a base area 0.15 m^2 and thickness 1.0 cm. It boils water at the rate of 6.0 kg min^{-1} when placed on a gas stove. Estimate the temperature of the part of the flame in contact with the boiler. (Thermal conductivity of brass = 109 Js^{-1} m^{-1} °C^{-1}, heat of vaporisation of water = 2256 × 10^3 J kg^{-1}.)

[NCERT Ex., Q. 10.18, Page 225]

Ans. Using

$$\frac{Q}{t} = \frac{KA(T_1 - T_2)}{d},$$

we get $$\frac{Q}{t} = \frac{109 \times 0.15}{10^{-2}}(T_1 - 100)$$

$$= 1635(T_1 - 100)$$

Also $$\frac{Q}{t} = \frac{ML}{t}$$

$$= \frac{6}{60} \times 2256 \times 10^3$$

i.e., $$1635(T_1 - 100) = \frac{6}{60} \times 2256 \times 10^3$$

$$T_1 = \frac{100 \times 2256}{1655} + 100$$

$$= 236.31°C.$$

Q. 19. Explain why:

(a) a body with large reflectivity is a poor emitter

(b) a brass tumbler feels much colder than a wooden tray on a chilly day

(c) an optical pyrometer (for measuring high temperatures) calibrated for an ideal black body radiation gives too low a value for the temperature of a red hot iron piece in the open, but gives a correct value for the temperature when the same piece is in the furnace

(d) the earth without its atmosphere would be inhospitably cold

(e) heating systems based on circulation of steam are more efficient in warming a building than those based on circulation of hot water.

[NCERT Ex., Q. 10.19, Page 225]

Ans. (a) A body which has large reflectivity is a poor absorber of heat. So, it is poor emitter of heat also.

(b) When a brass tumbler or a wooden tray is touched on a chilly day heat flows from body to the brass tumbler or the wooden tray. Brass being a good conductor of heat good amount of heat from our body and we feel colder. Wood being a bad conductor of heat not much amount of heat flow from our body and we do not feel that much cold.

(c) When the red hot iron is in furnace then the energy radiated = $E_1 = \sigma T_4$

When it is brought outside the energy radiated is $E_2 = \sigma (T_4 - T_0^4)$

So, the pyrometer shows low value for the temperature in the open.

(d) Atmosphere traps the heat reaching earth from sun. In absence of atmosphere, almost the total heat reaching earth will be reflected back. So, the earth will be inhospitably cold.

(e) Steam at 100°C contains 2.27 × 10^6 J amount of heat (as latent heat) per kg more than water at 100°C. So, steam is more efficient in warming than water.

Q. 20. A body cools from 80 °C to 50 °C in 5 minutes. Calculate the time it takes to cool from 60 °C to 30 °C. The temperature of the surroundings is 20 °C.

[NCERT Ex., Q. 10.20, Page 225]

Ans. In 1st case:

Initial temperature = T_i = 80°C

Final temperature = T_f = 50°C

Surrounding temperature = T_0 = 20°C

Time = t = 5 minutes

Applying Newton's law of cooling,

$$\frac{dT}{dt} = K\left[\frac{T_i + T_f}{2} - T_0\right]$$

or, $$\frac{(80 - 50)}{5} = K\left[\frac{80 + 50}{5} - 20\right]$$

$$\therefore \quad K = \frac{2}{25}$$

In 2nd case:

Initial temperature = T_i = 60°C

Final temperature = T_f = 30°C

Surrounding temperature = T_0 = 20°C

Time = t

Applying Newton's law of cooling,

$$\frac{dT}{dt} = K\left[\frac{T_i + T_f}{2} - T_0\right]$$

or, $$\frac{(60 - 30)}{t} = \left(\frac{2}{15}\right) \times \left[\frac{60 + 30}{2} - 20\right]$$

$$\therefore \quad t = 9 \text{ minutes}$$

CHAPTER 11

THERMODYNAMICS

Thermal Equilibrium

- **Thermodynamics:** Thermodynamics is the branch of physics that deals with the concepts of heat and temperature and the inter-conversion of heat and other forms of energy. Thermodynamics is a macroscopic science. It deals with bulk systems and does not go into the molecular constitution of matter.
- **Thermal equilibrium:** A system is in equilibrium if the macroscopic variables (pressure, volume, temperature, mass and composition) those characterise the system do not change with time.
- **Adiabatic wall:** Adiabatic wall is an insulating wall that does not allow flow of energy (heat) from one to another.
- **Diathermic wall:** Diathermic wall is a conducting wall that allows flow of energy (heat) from one to another.

Zeroth Law of Thermodynamics

- Two systems in thermal equilibrium with a third system separately are in thermal equilibrium with each other.
- **Internal energy:** Every bulk system consists of a large number of molecules. Internal energy is the sum of the kinetic energies and potential energies of these molecules.
- **Equivalence of work and heat:** Work is a form of heat energy. 4.18×10^3 Joule of work is equivalent to 1 kilocalorie of heat.

$$W = JQ$$

J is the mechanical equivalent of heat.
- **Sign convention of heat:**

(i) Negative when heat is given from a system to its surroundings.

(ii) Positive when heat is taken from the surroundings by the system.

First Law of Thermodynamics

- If an amount of heat ΔQ is given to a system, a part of it is increases the internal energy ΔU of the system and the rest is utilized in doing work ΔW by the system.

$$\Delta Q = \Delta U + \Delta W$$

- **In cyclic process:** In cyclic process, a system is taken from one initial state to other different states and finally brought back to its initial state.

So, there is no change in internal energy i.e.

$$\Delta U = 0$$

So, $\Delta Q = \Delta W$

- **In isobaric process:** In isobaric process the pressure remains constant.

Work done $= \Delta W = P\Delta V$

So, $\Delta Q = \Delta U + P\Delta V$

- **In isochoric process:** In isochoric process the volume remains constant.

So, work done $= \Delta W = P\Delta V = 0$

So, $\Delta Q = \Delta U$

- In isothermal process: In isothermal process the temperature remains constant.

$$\Delta Q = \Delta U + \Delta W$$

(For ideal gas, the internal energy depends on temperature only. As temperature is constant, then $\Delta U = 0$.

So, $\Delta Q = \Delta W$)

- In adiabatic process: In adiabatic process heat neither enters nor leaves the system.

Hence, $\Delta Q = 0$

So, $\Delta U = -\Delta W$

Thermodynamic Processes

(a) Isothermal process, where the temperature remains constant. The pressure and volume of a given mass of gas changes.

Essential conditions:

(i) Walls of container must be perfectly conducting.

(ii) Changes must be slow.

Isothermal process obeys Boyle's law i.e., PV = constant.

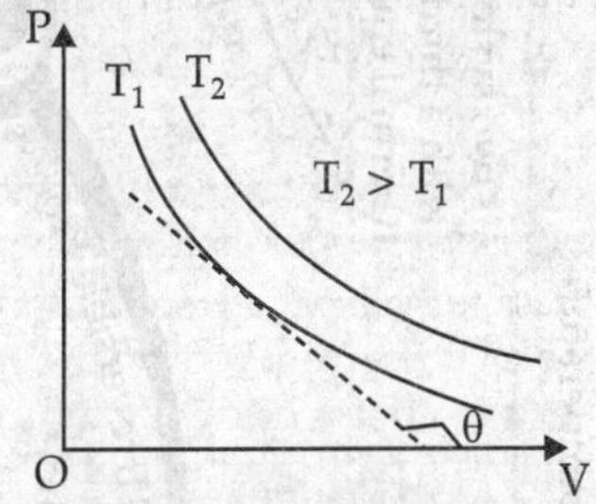

Variation of P with V at constant temperature is represented by Isothermal curves.

Slope of an isothermal graph is negative.

(b) Adiabatic process, where the heat content of a gaseous system remains constant. The pressure and volume of given mass of gas change with consequent change in temperature.

Essential conditions are:

(i) Walls of container must be perfectly insulating.

(ii) Changes must be sudden.

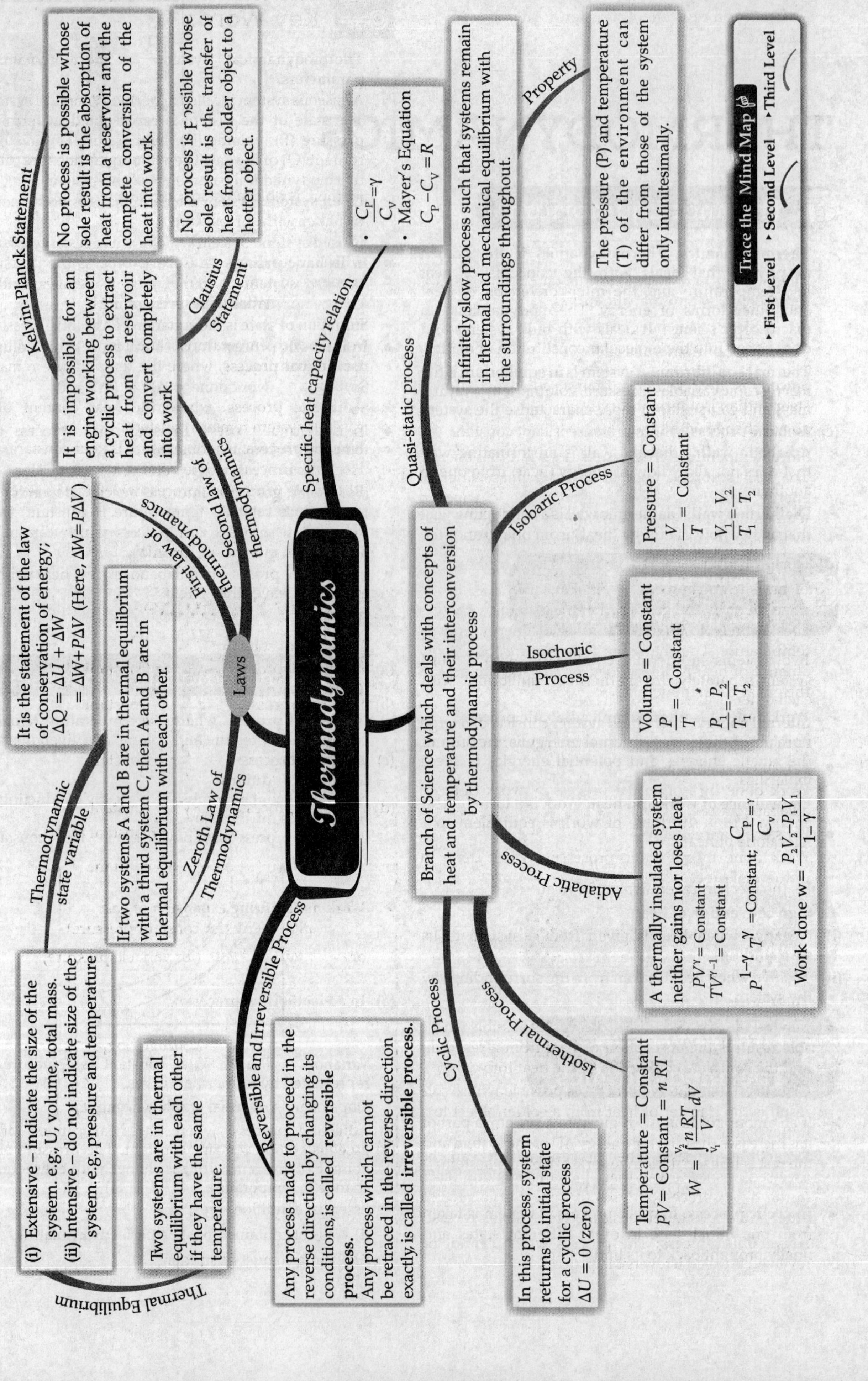
Thermodynamics
Laws
First law of thermodynamics
It is the statement of the law of conservation of energy; $\Delta Q = \Delta U + \Delta W$ $= \Delta W + P\Delta V$ (Here, $\Delta W = P\Delta V$)
Second law of thermodynamics
Kelvin-Planck Statement
It is impossible for an engine working between a cyclic process to extract heat from a reservoir and convert completely into work.
No process is possible whose sole result is the absorption of heat from a reservoir and the complete conversion of the heat into work.
Clausius Statement
No process is possible whose sole result is the transfer of heat from a colder object to a hotter object.
Zeroth Law of Thermodynamics
If two systems A and B are in thermal equilibrium with a third system C, then A and B are in thermal equilibrium with each other.
Thermodynamic state variable
(i) Extensive – indicate the size of the system. e.g., U, volume, total mass.
(ii) Intensive – do not indicate size of the system. e.g., pressure and temperature
Thermal Equilibrium
Two systems are in thermal equilibrium with each other if they have the same temperature.
Reversible and Irreversible Process
Any process made to proceed in the reverse direction by changing its conditions, is called **reversible process.**
Any process which cannot be retraced in the reverse direction exactly, is called **irreversible process.**
Specific heat capacity relation
• $\frac{C_P}{C_V} = \gamma$
• Mayer's Equation $C_P - C_V = R$
Quasi-static process
Infinitely slow process such that systems remain in thermal and mechanical equilibrium with the surroundings throughout.
Property
The pressure (P) and temperature (T) of the environment can differ from those of the system only infinitesimally.
Branch of Science which deals with concepts of heat and temperature and their interconversion by thermodynamic process
Isobaric Process
Pressure = Constant
$\frac{V}{T}$ = Constant
$\frac{V_1}{T_1} = \frac{V_2}{T_2}$
Isochoric Process
Volume = Constant
$\frac{P}{T}$ = Constant
$\frac{P_1}{T_1} = \frac{P_2}{T_2}$
Adiabatic Process
A thermally insulated system neither gains nor loses heat
PV^{γ} = Constant
$TV^{\gamma-1}$ = Constant
$P^{1-\gamma} T^{\gamma}$ = Constant; $\frac{C_P}{C_V} = \gamma$
Work done $w = \frac{P_2V_2 - P_1V_1}{1-\gamma}$
Isothermal Process
Temperature = Constant
PV = Constant = $n RT$
$W = \int_{V_1}^{V_2} \frac{n RT}{V} dV$
Cyclic Process
In this process, system returns to initial state for a cyclic process $\Delta U = 0$ (zero)
Trace the Mind Map
First Level
Second Level
Third Level

Adiabatic process obeys Poission's law i.e., PV^{γ} = constant.

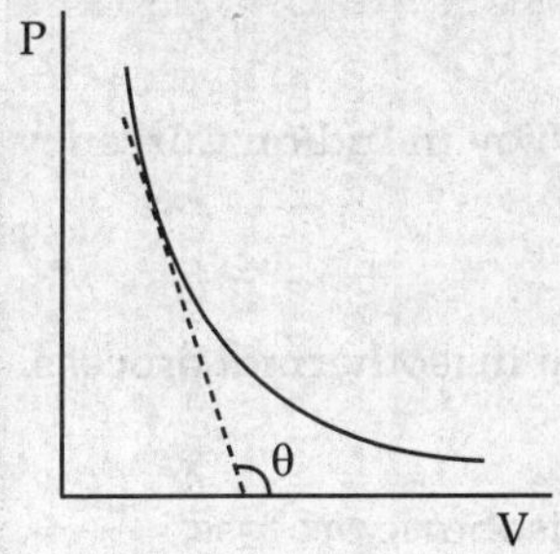

The variation of P with V at constant heat content is represented by an Adiabatic curve.

$$\frac{\text{Slope of adiabatic curve}}{\text{Slope of isothermal curve}} = \gamma$$

Since, γ is always greater than 1, adiabatic curve is steeper than isothermal curve.

(c) Isobaric process, where pressure is kept constant.

Since, temperature changes, so does internal energy. The heat absorbed goes partly to increase internal energy and partly to do work. The change in temperature for a given amount of heat is determined by the specific heat of the gas at constant pressure.

(d) Isochoric process, where volume is kept constant.

In an isochoric process, V is constant. No work is done on or by the gas. The heat absorbed by the gas goes entirely to change its internal energy and its temperature. The change in temperature for a given amount of heat is determined by the specific heat of the gas at constant volume.

➢ **Work done in isothermal and adiabatic process:**

Area under the curve is the measurement of work done.

- For same expansion,
  Work done by isothermal process > work done in adiabatic process.
- For same compression:
  Work done by adiabatic process > work done in isothermal process.

Second Law of Thermodynamics

There are two statements:

- Kelvin-Planck statement: No process is possible whose sole result is the absorption of heat from a reservoir and the complete conversion of the heat into work.
- Clausius statement: No process is possible whose sole result is the transfer of heat from a colder object to a hotter object.

➢ **Reversible process:** The process which can be reversed in such a way that all changes taking place in the direct process are exactly repeated in reverse order and opposite sense is called reversible process.

➢ **Irreversible process:** The process which cannot be reversed is called irreversible process.

Key Words

➢ **Thermodynamical system & thermodynamical parameters.**
A gaseous system is called a thermodynamical system. The state of the system is represented in terms of pressure (P), volume (V), temperature (T) and heat content (Q) of the gas. These four quantities are called thermodynamical parameters of the system.

➢ **Open system:** System which exchanges both energy & matter with surroundings.

➢ **Closed system:** System which exchanges only energy with surroundings.

➢ **Isolated system:** System which Exchanges neither energy nor matter with surroundings.

➢ **Equation of state** is the equation connecting pressure, volume and temperature of the gas.

➢ **Isothermal process,** where the temperature remains constant.

➢ **Adiabatic process,** where the heat content of a gaseous system remains constant.

➢ **Isobaric process,** where pressure is kept constant.

➢ **Isochoric process,** where volume is kept constant.

➢ **Reversible process** is a process which can be reversed back to initial state.

➢ **Irreversible process** is a process which cannot be traced back in opposite direction.

Key Formulae

➢ **Equation of state for:**

(a) Isothermal process: PV = Constant.

(b) Isobaric process: $\frac{V}{T}$ = Constant.

(c) Isochoric process: $\frac{P}{T}$ = Constant.

(d) Adiabatic process: PV^{γ} = constant;
$TV^{\gamma-1}$ = constant and
$\frac{P^{\gamma-1}}{T^{\gamma}}$ = constant.

➢ **Work done during expansion of gas:**

$dW = PdV$ (for constant pressure)

or $W = \int_{V_1}^{V_2} PdV$ (for variable pressure)

(a) In an isothermal process:

$$W = 2.3026\, RT \log_{10}\left(\frac{V_2}{V_1}\right)$$

$$W = 2.3026\, RT \log_{10}\left(\frac{P_1}{P_2}\right)$$

(b) In an adiabatic process:

$$W = \frac{R}{1-\gamma}(T_2 - T_1)$$

$$= \frac{1}{1-\gamma}(P_2V_2 - P_1V_1)$$

Mnemonics

➤ **Concept:** Four thermodynamic processes.

➤ **Mnemonics:** Today Income **T**ax was **p**aid in **I**ndian **B**ank by **V**ijoy in **I**ndian **C**urrency, **ad**jacent to **N**ational **h**ighway.

Interpretation:

T → temperature is constant
I → Iso
T → Thermal
} Temperature remains constant in isothermal process.

P → pressure
I → Iso
B → baric
} Pressure remains constant in isobaric process.

V → volume
I → Iso
C → Choric
} Volume remain constant in isochoric process.

Ad → adiabatic
N → No
h → heat transfer
} No heat transfer between system and surrounding takes place in adiabatic process.

NCERT CORNER

Q. 1. A geyser heats water flowing at the rate of 3 litres per minute from 27°C to 77°C. If the geyser operates on a gas burner, what is the rate of consumption of the fuel if its heating of combustion is 4.0×10^4 J/g ?

[NCERT Ex., Q. 11.1, Page 242]

Ans. The mass of water flowing per unit time

$= 3000$ g per min.

$= \frac{3000}{60} = 50$ g/s

$= \frac{50}{1000}$ kg/s

Heat required to heat this water from 27°C to 77°C

$= mc\,\Delta T$

$= \frac{50}{1000} \times 4.2 \times 10^3 \times 50$ J/s

$= 1.05 \times 10^4$ J/s

Heat generated by the combustion of 1 g of fuel

$= 4.0 \times 10^4$ J

∴ Fuel required per second

$= \frac{1.05 \times 10^4}{4.0 \times 10^4}$

$= 0.2625$ g

Fuel required to be burnt per min.

$= 0.2625 \times 60 = 15.75$ g

Q. 2. What amount of heat must be supplied to 2.0×10^{-2} kg of nitrogen (at room temperature) to raise its temperature by 45°C at constant pressure ? (Molecular mass of $N_2 = 28$, $R = 8.3$ J mol^{-1} K^{-1})

[NCERT Ex., Q. 11.2, Page 242]

Ans. Mass of nitrogen, $m = 2 \times 10^{-2}$ kg $= 20$ g

Rise in temperature. $\Delta T = 45$°C

Molecular mass of N_2, $M = 28$

Universal gas constant, $R = 8.3$ J mol^{-1} K^{-1}

Number of moles, $n = m/M$

$= (2 \times 10^{-2} \times 10^3) / 28$

$= 0.714$

Molar specific heat at constant pressure for nitrogen, $C_p = (7/2)R$

$= (7/2) \times 8.3$

$= 29.05$ J mol^{-1} K^{-1}

The total amount of heat to be supplied is given by the relation:

$\Delta Q = nCp\,\Delta T$

$= 0.714 \times 29.05 \times 45$

$= 933.38$ J

Therefore, the amount of heat to be supplied is 933. 38 J

Q. 3. Explain why

(a) Two bodies at different temperatures T_1 and T_2, if brought in thermal contact do not necessarily settle to the mean temperature $(T_1 + T_2) / 2$?

(b) The coolant in a chemical or a nuclear plant (i.e., the liquid used to prevent the different parts of a plant from getting too hot) should have high specific heat. Comment

(c) Air pressure in a car tyre increases during driving. Why?

(d) The climate of a harbour town is more temperate than that of a town in a desert at the same latitude. Why?

[NCERT Ex., Q. 11.3, Page 242]

Ans. (a) When two bodies at different temperatures T_1 and T_2 are brought in thermal contact, heat flows from the body at higher temperature to the body at lower temperature till equilibrium is achieved, i.e., the temperatures of both the bodies becomes equal. The equilibrium temperature becomes equal to the mean temperature $(T_1 + T_2) / 2$ only when thermal capacities of the two bodies are equal.

(b) The coolant in a chemical or nuclear plant should have a high specific heat. This is because higher the specific heat of the coolant, higher is its heat-absorbing capacity and vice-versa. So, it absorbs more heat for 1 degree rise of temperature. Hence, cooling is better.

(c) When the car is in motion, the temperature of air inside the tyre increases due to motion of the air molecules. According to Charles's law, pressure is directly proportional to the temperature, $P \propto T$. Hence, if the temperature inside a tyre increases, then the air pressure inside the tyre will also increase.

(d) A harbour town has a more temperate climate than a town located in a dessert at the same latitude. This is because in a harbour town, the relative humidity is more than in a desert town.

Q. 4. A cylinder with a movable piston contains 3 moles of hydrogen at constant temperature and pressure. The walls of a cylinder are made up of a heat insulator, and the piston is insulated by having a pile of sand on it. By what factor does the pressure of a gas increases if the gas is compressed to half its original volume ? [NCERT Ex., Q. 11.4, Page 242]

Ans. Since, the process is adiabatic

$$P_1V_1^\gamma = P_2V_2^\gamma$$

$\therefore$

But $$\frac{V_1}{V_2} = \frac{2}{1}$$

$$\gamma = 7/5 \text{ for hydrogen}$$

$\therefore$ Factor by which the pressure of the gas increases

or $$\frac{P_2}{P_1} = \left(\frac{V_1}{V_2}\right)^\gamma$$

$$\frac{P_2}{P_1} = \left(\frac{2}{1}\right)^\gamma = (2)^{7/5}$$

so, $$P_2 = 2^{7/5}\,P_1 = 2.64\,P_1$$

Q. 5. In changing the state of a gas adiabatically from an equilibrium state A to another equilibrium state B, an amount of work equal to 22.3 J is done on the system. If the gas is taken from state B to A via a process in which the net heat absorbed by the system is 9.35 cal, how much is the net work done by the system in the later case ? (Take 1 cal = 4.19 J)

[NCERT Ex., Q. 11.5, Page 242]

Ans. Since, the system is going from A to B and then back to A, it is undergoing a cyclic change. Now in cyclic change there is no change in internal energy ($\Delta U = 0$). From first law of thermodynamic.

$$\Delta Q = \Delta U + \Delta W$$

For first case, $$\Delta U = 22.3\text{ J}$$

$$[\therefore \Delta Q = 0, \Delta W = -22.3\text{ J}]$$

In the second case, $\Delta Q = 9.35$ cal

$$= 9.35 \times 4.19 = 39.18\text{ J}$$

$$\Delta W = ?$$

As, $$\Delta U + \Delta W = \Delta Q$$

$$\Delta W = \Delta Q - \Delta U$$

$$= 39.18 - 22.3$$

$$= 16.9\text{ J}$$

Q. 6. Two cylinders A and B of equal capacity are connected to each other via a stopcock. A contains a gas at standard temperature and pressure. B is completely evacuated. The entire system is thermally insulated. The stopcock is suddenly opened. Answer the following:

(a) What is the final pressure of the gas in A and B ?

(b) What is change in the internal energy of the gas ?

(c) What is the change in the temperature of the gas ?

(d) Do the intermediate states of the system (before setting to the final equilibrium state) lie on its P–V–T surface ? [NCERT Ex., Q. 11.6, Page 242]

Ans. (a) The gas would rush from A to B. Now the volume becomes double.

So, the pressure becomes half. Earlier pressure was 1 atmosphere. So, the present pressure will be 0.5 atmosphere.

(b) The change in internal energy of the gas will be zero. (if gas is ideal)

(c) The change in temperature will be zero.

(d) Since the process is rapid, the intermediate states are not equilibrium states and hence do not satisfy the gas equation. So, the intermediate states of the system do not lie on the P–V–T surface.

Q. 7. An electric heater supplies heat to a system at a rate of 100W. If system performs work at a rate of 75 joules per second. At what rate is the internal energy increasing? [NCERT Ex., Q. 11.7, Page 242]

Ans. Heat supplied to the system at the rate of 100 W

Heat supplied, $Q = 100$ J/s

The system performs work at a rate of 75 J/s

Therefore, work done, $W = 75$ J/s

From the 1st law of thermodynamics

$$Q = U + W$$

$$100 = U + 75$$

$$U = 100 - 75 = 25\text{ J/s} = 25\text{ W}$$

Therefore, the internal is increasing at the rate of 25 W.

Q. 8. A thermodynamic system is taken from an original state to an intermediate state by the linear process shown in figure.

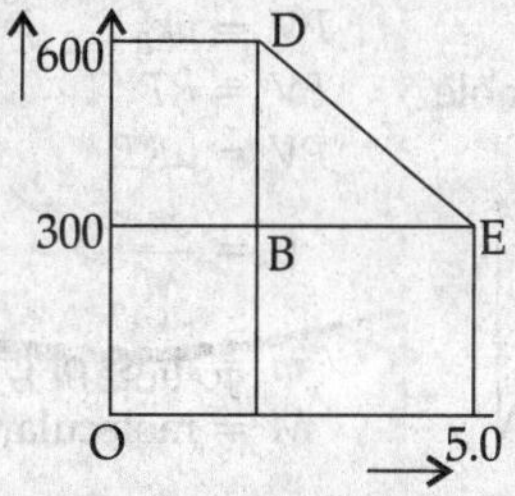

Its volume is then reduced to the original value from E to F by an isobaric process. Calculate the total work done by the gas from D to E to F.

[NCERT Ex., Q. 11.8, Page 242]

Ans. Total work done by the gas from D to E to F = Area of ΔDEF

$$\text{Area of } \Delta DEF = \frac{1}{2} \times DE \times EF$$

Where, DF = Change in pressure

$= 600\text{ N/m}^2 - 300\text{N/m}^2$

$= 300\text{ N/m}^2$

FE = Change in volume

$= 5.0\text{ m}^3 - 2.0\text{ m}^3$

$= 3.0\text{ m}^3$

$$\text{Area of } \Delta DEF = \frac{1}{2} \times 300 \times 3 = 450\text{ J}$$

Therefore, the total work done by the gas from D to E to F is 450J.

□□

CHAPTER 12

KINETIC THEORY

Behaviour of Gases

➤ **Ideal Gases:**

(a) Strictly obeys gas laws, like Boyle's law, Charles's law etc.

(b) The size of the gas molecules is almost zero and the volume of the gas molecule is also almost zero.

(c) There is no force of attraction or repulsion amongst the molecules.

(d) Collisions between molecules are perfectly elastic.

➤ **Equation of state of Ideal gas:**

(a) **From Boyel's law:** $P_1V_1 = P_2V_2$

(b) **From Charles' law:** $\frac{V_1}{T_1} = \frac{V_2}{T_2}$

(c) **Combining Charles' and Boyel's law:** $\frac{P_1V_1}{T_1} = \frac{P_2V_2}{T_2}$

or $PV = KT$

K is a proportionality constant.

Again, $K = nk_B$

Where n = number of molecules

K_B = Boltzmann constant

$\therefore \quad PV = nk_B T$

For 1 gram mole, $PV = RT$

For μ mole, $PV = \mu RT$

Where $\mu = \frac{m}{M}$

m = mass of gas sample

M = molecular weight

$\therefore \quad PV = \frac{m}{M}RT$

Scan to know more about this topic

Ideal gas equation

Number of molecules in 1 mole (i.e., M gram) gas = Avogadro number (N)

So, number of moles in m gram gas $= \frac{Nm}{M}$

So, $\frac{m}{M} = \frac{n}{M}$

$\therefore \quad PV = \frac{n}{N}RT$

Value of $R = 8.31$ J mol$^{-1}K^{-1}$

Value of $k = 1.38 \times 10^{-23}$ J K^{-1}

➤ **Assumptions of Kinetic Theory of Gases:**

(a) A gas consists of a very large number of molecules which are perfectly elastic spheres and are identical in all respects for a given gas and are different for different gases.

(b) The molecules of a gas are in a state of continuous, rapid and random motion.

(c) The volume occupied by the molecules is negligible in comparison to the volume of the gas.

(d) The molecules do not exert any force of attraction or repulsion on each other, except during collision.

(e) The collisions of the molecules with themselves and with the walls of the vessel are perfectly elastic.

(f) Molecular density is uniform throughout the gas.

(g) A molecule moves along a straight line between two successive collisions.

(h) The collisions are almost instantaneous.

➤ **Brownian Motion:** It is defined as continuous zig-zag motion of particles of macroscopic size (10^{-5} to 10^{-6} m) suspended in fluid.

Brownian motion increases:

(a) When size of suspended object increases.

(b) When density of fluid is decreases.

(c) When temperature of medium increases.

(d) When viscosity of medium decreases.

➤ **Pressure of an ideal gas:**

Pressure exerted by an ideal gas is equal to two third of its translational kinetic energy per unit volume.

$$P = \frac{2}{3}E = \frac{1}{3}\frac{mn}{V}\overline{v^2} = \frac{1}{3}\rho\overline{v^2}$$

Where, $\overline{v^2}$ = mean square velocity of the molecules

mn = Mass of the whole gas

V = Volume of the gas

ρ = Density of gas

➤ **Root mean square speed**

Root mean square speed of the molecules is defined as the square root of the mean of the squares of speed of all the gas molecules.

$$v_{rms} = \sqrt{\overline{v^2}} = \sqrt{\frac{v_1^2 + v_2^2 + v_3^2 + \ldots + v_n^2}{n}}$$

Since, pressure of a gas $= P = \frac{1}{3}\rho\overline{v^2}$

$$\therefore \quad v_{rms} = \sqrt{\frac{3P}{\rho}}$$

➤ **Interpretation of temperature:**

The root mean square speed of the molecules of a gas is directly proportional to the square root of absolute temperature of gas.

$$\therefore \quad v_{rms} = \sqrt{\frac{3RT}{M}}$$

$$v_{rms} \propto \sqrt{T}$$

When $T = 0$, $v_{rms} = 0$

So, absolute temperature is the temperature at which the motion of the molecules of the gas becomes zero and no temperature below absolute zero is possible.

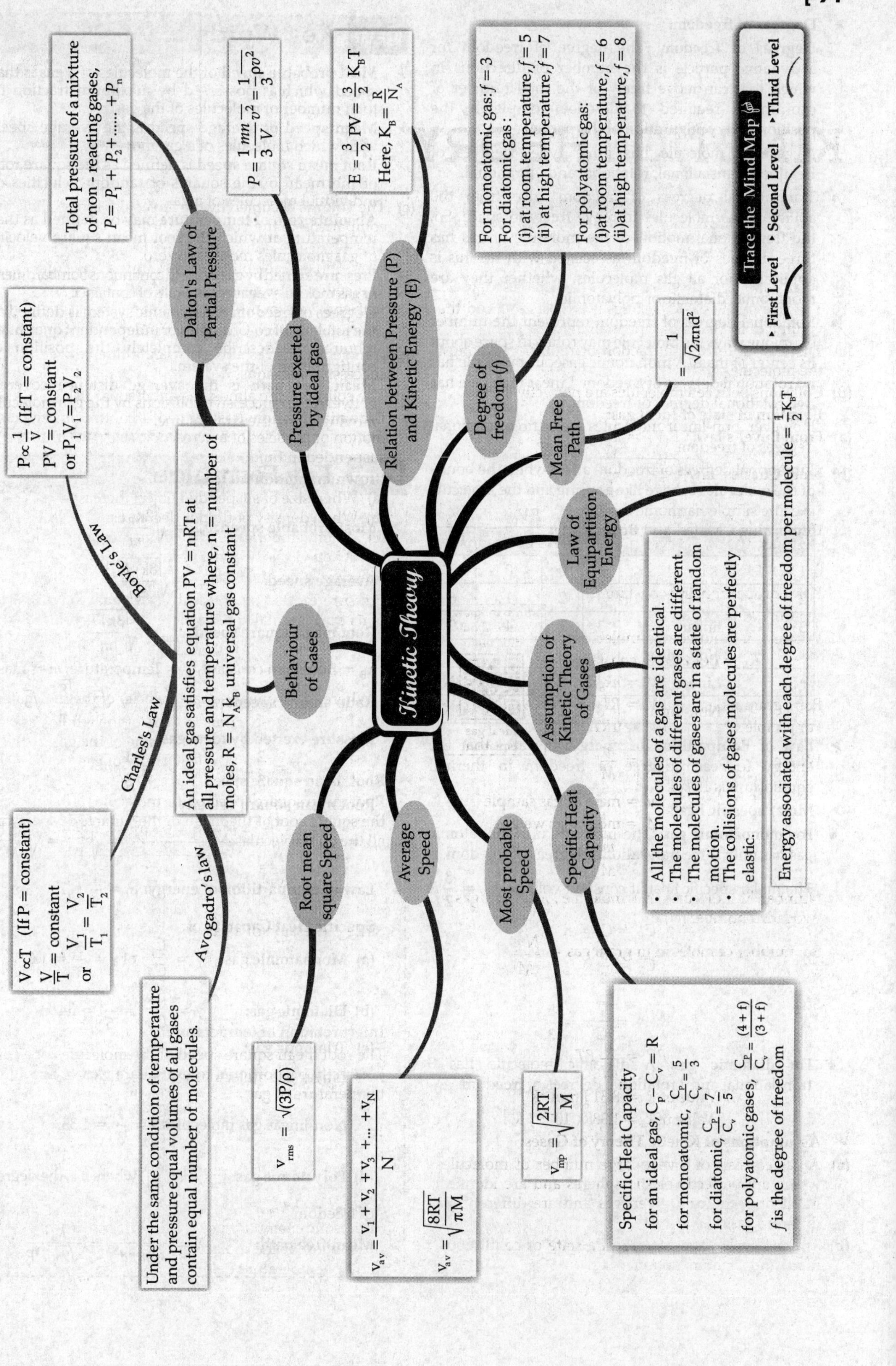

Kinetic Theory
Behaviour of Gases
An ideal gas satisfies equation PV = nRT at all pressure and temperature where, n = number of moles, $R = N_A k_B$ universal gas constant
Boyle's Law
$P \propto \frac{1}{V}$ (If T = constant)
PV = constant
or $P_1V_1 = P_2V_2$
Charles's Law
$V \propto T$ (If P = constant)
$\frac{V}{T}$ = constant
or $\frac{V_1}{T_1} = \frac{V_2}{T_2}$
Avogadro's law
Under the same condition of temperature and pressure equal volumes of all gases contain equal number of molecules.
Dalton's Law of Partial Pressure
Total pressure of a mixture of non - reacting gases, $P = P_1 + P_2 + ... + P_n$
Pressure exerted by ideal gas
$P = \frac{1}{3}\frac{mn}{V}\overline{v^2} = \frac{1}{3}\rho\overline{v^2}$
Relation between Pressure (P) and Kinetic Energy (E)
$E = \frac{3}{2}PV = \frac{3}{2}K_BT$
Here, $K_B = \frac{R}{N_A}$
Degree of freedom (f)
For monoatomic gas: f = 3
For diatomic gas :
(i) at room temperature, f = 5
(ii) at high temperature, f = 7
For polyatomic gas:
(i)at room temperature, f = 6
(ii)at high temperature, f = 8
Mean Free Path
$= \frac{1}{\sqrt{2}\pi nd^2}$
Law of Equipartition Energy
Energy associated with each degree of freedom per molecule $= \frac{1}{2}K_BT$
Assumption of Kinetic Theory of Gases
• All the molecules of a gas are identical.
• The molecules of different gases are different.
• The molecules of gases are in a state of random motion.
• The collisions of gases molecules are perfectly elastic.
Specific Heat Capacity
Specific Heat Capacity
for an ideal gas, $C_P - C_V = R$
for monoatomic, $\frac{C_P}{C_V} = \frac{5}{3}$
for diatomic $\frac{C_P}{C_V} = \frac{7}{5}$
for polyatomic gases, $\frac{C_P}{C_V} = \frac{(4+f)}{(3+f)}$
f is the degree of freedom
Most probable Speed
$v_{mp} = \sqrt{\frac{2RT}{M}}$
Average Speed
$v_{av} = \frac{v_1 + v_2 + v_3 + ... + v_N}{N}$
$v_{av} = \sqrt{\frac{8RT}{\pi M}}$
Root mean square Speed
$v_{rms} = \sqrt{(3P/\rho)}$
Trace the Mind Map
First Level
Second Level
Third Level

➤ **Degrees of freedom:**

Degrees of freedom: The degree of freedom for a dynamic particle is the number of directions in which that can move freely or the total number of coordinates required to describe completely the position and configuration of the particle.

A gaseous molecule has three types degrees of freedom: translational, rotational and vibrational.

- Translational degrees of freedom arise from the ability of gas molecules to move freely in space. So, the translational motion of the molecule of gas has three degrees of freedom associated with it. This is applicable for all gas molecules, whether they are monatomic, diatomic or polyatomic,
- Rotational degrees of freedom represent the number of unique ways the molecule may rotate in space about its center of mass. A monatomic gaseous molecule has no rotational degrees of freedom. Linear molecule has two rotational degrees of freedom.

  However, non-linear molecules have three rotational degrees of freedom.
- Vibrational degrees of freedom arises when the bonds of the molecules behave like a spring and the molecule execute simple harmonic motion.

Atomicity		Degrees of freedom			
1		3	0	0	3
2		3	2	1	6
3	linear	3	2	4	9
	Non-linear	3	3	3	9
N	Linear	3	2	3N - 5	3N
	Non-linear	3	3	3N - 6	3N

➤ **Law of Equipartition of energy:** It states that the energy for each degree of freedom in thermal equilibrium is 12 k_BT.

➤ **Molar specific heat:**

- **For monoatomic gas:** The molecule of a monatomic gas has only three translational degrees of freedom.

The molar specific heat at constant volume, $C_V = \frac{3}{2}R$

$$C_P = C_V = R$$

$$\therefore \quad C_P = \frac{3}{2}R$$

$$\therefore \quad \gamma = \frac{C_P}{C_V} = \frac{5}{3}$$

- **For diatomic gas:** A diatomic molecule has 3 translational and 2 rotational degrees of freedom.

$$C_V = \frac{5}{2}R$$

$$C_P - C_V = R$$

$$\therefore \quad C_P = \frac{7}{2}R$$

$$\therefore \quad \gamma = \frac{C_P}{C_V} = \frac{9}{7}$$

Key Words

➤ **Most probable speed** of the molecules of a gas is that speed which is possessed by maximum fraction of total number of molecules of the gas.

➤ **Mean speed or average speed** is the average speed with which molecules of a gas move.

➤ **Root mean square speed** is defined as the square root of the mean of the squares of random velocities of individual molecules of a gas.

➤ **Absolute zero of temperature** may be defined as that temperature at which the root mean square velocity of gas molecules reduces to zero.

➤ **Pressure** exerted by gas is due to continuous bombardment of gas molecules against the walls of container.

➤ **Degrees of freedom** of a dynamic system is defined as the total no. of co-ordinates or independent quantities required to describe completely the position & configuration of the system.

➤ **Mean free path** is the average distance covered between two successive collisions by the gas molecule moving along the straight line.

Key Formulae

➤ **Most probable speed:** $c_{mp} = \sqrt{\frac{2k_BT}{m}}$

➤ **Average speed:** $c_{av} = \sqrt{\frac{8k_BT}{\pi m}}$

➤ **Root mean square speed:** $c_{rms} = \sqrt{\frac{3k_BT}{m}}$

k_B = Boltzman constant, T = Temperature, m = mass

➤ **Ratio among speeds:** $c_{mp}: c_{av}: c_{rms} = \sqrt{2} : \sqrt{\frac{8}{\pi}} : \sqrt{3}$

➤ **Pressure exerted by ideal gas:**

$$P = \frac{2}{3}E = \frac{1}{3}\frac{mn}{V}\overline{v^2} = \frac{1}{3}\rho\overline{v^2}$$

➤ **Root mean square velocity:**

$$v_{rms} = \sqrt{\overline{v^2}} = \sqrt{\frac{v_1^2 + v_2^2 + v_3^2 + ... + v_n^2}{n}} = \sqrt{\frac{3P}{\rho}} = \sqrt{\frac{3RT}{M}}$$

➤ **Law of equipartition of energy:** $E_t = \frac{1}{2} k_BT$

➤ **Specific Heat Capacity of:**

(a) Monoatomic gas: $\gamma = \frac{C_P}{C_V}$ or $\gamma = \frac{5}{3} = 1.67$

(b) Diatomic gas: $\gamma = \frac{C_P}{C_V} = \frac{7}{5} = 1.4$

(c) Triatomic gas:

Linear gas molecules $\gamma = \frac{9}{7} = 1.28$

Non-linear gas molecules $\gamma = \frac{4}{3} = 1.33$.

(d) Polyatomic gas: $\gamma = \left(1+\frac{2}{n}\right)$, where n is the degree of freedom

➤ **Mean free path:** $\lambda = \frac{1}{\sqrt{2}n\pi d^2} = \frac{k_BT}{\sqrt{2}\pi d^2 P}$

Mnemonics

Concept: Degrees of freedom.

Mnemonics: Baa Baa Black Sheep
Have you any wool?
Yes, sir, **Mom** has **3** bags full.
Dadi needs **5** bags **n**ormally rule.
Papa keeps **6** bags normal rule.
Papa Dadi each needs **2** bags more
High **c**old whenever, be very sure.

Interpretation: Mom has **3** bags full → Degrees of freedom of Monoatomic gas is 3.

Dadi needs **5** bags **n**ormally cool
Degrees of freedom of diatomic gas at normat → (room) temperature is 5.

Papa keeps **6** bags **n**ormal rule → Degrees of freedom of Polyatomic gas at normal (room) temperature is 6.

Papa, **Dadi** each needs **2** bags more → Degrees of freedom of Polyatomic gas at high temperature is 6 + 2 = 8.

High cold whenever, be very sure → Degrees of freedom of Diatomic gas at high temperature is 5 + 2 = 7.

NCERT CORNER

Q. 1. Estimate the fraction of molecular volume to the actual volume occupied by oxygen gas at STP. Take the diameter of an oxygen molecule to be 3Å.

[NCERT Ex. Q. 12.1, Page 257]

Ans. Given: diameter, $d = 3\text{Å}, r = \frac{d}{2} = 1.5\text{Å}$

$$= 1.5 \times 10^{-8} \text{ cm}$$

Molecular volume $V = \frac{4}{3}\pi r^3 N$

(Here, N = Avogadro's number)

$$= \frac{4}{3} \times \frac{22}{7} \times (1.5 \times 10^{-8})^3 \times (6.023 \times 10^{23})$$

$$= 8.52 \text{ cc}$$

Let V′ be actual volume occupied by 1 mole of O_2 at STP = 22400cc.

$$\therefore \frac{V}{V'} = \frac{8.52}{22400} = 3.8 \times 10^{-4}$$

Q. 2. Molar volume is the volume occupied by 1 mol of any (ideal) gas at standard temperature and pressure (STP: 1 atm pressure, 0°C). Show that it is 22.4 litres.

[NCERT Ex. Q. 12.2, Page 257]

Ans. Here, n = 1 mol, T = 273 K, R = 8.31 J/mole/K.

P = 1 atm = 0.76 m of Hg

$= 0.76 \times 9.8 \times 13.6 \times 10^3 \text{ N/m}^2$

Using the relation $PV = nRT$,

or, $V = \frac{nRT}{P}$

$$= \frac{1 \times 8.31 \times 273}{0.76 \times 9.8 \times (13.6 \times 10^3)}$$

$$= 22.4 \times 10^{-3} \text{ m}^3$$

$$= 22.4 \text{ lit.}$$

Q. 3. Figure shows plot of PV/T versus P for 1.00×10^{-3} kg of oxygen gas at two different temperatures.

(a) What does the dotted line signify ?

(b) Which is true: $T_1 > T_2$ or $T_1 < T_2$?

(c) What is the value of $\frac{PV}{T}$ where the curves meet on the y-axis ?

(d) If we obtained similar plots for $1{\cdot}00 \times 10^{-3}$ kg of hydrogen, would we get the same value of PV/T at the point where the curves meet on the Y-axis ? If not, what mass of hydrogen yields the same value of PV/T (for low pressure high temperature region of the plot) ? [Molecular mass of hydrogen (H_2) = 2.02 u, of O_2 = 32.0 u, R = 8.31 mol^{-1}K^{-1}.]

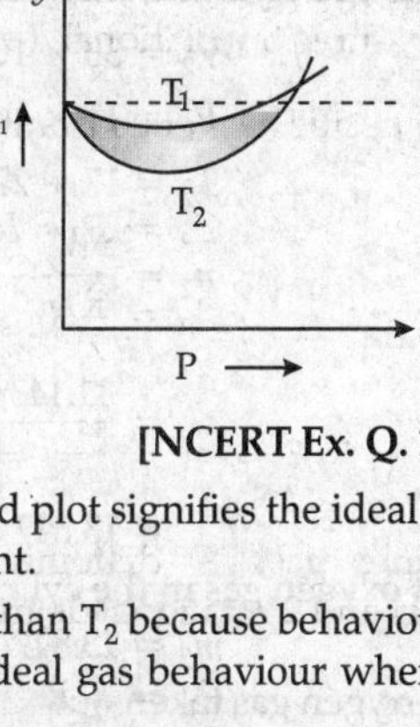

[NCERT Ex. Q. 12.3, Page 257]

Ans. **(a)** The dotted plot signifies the ideal gas behaviour as PV/T = constant.

(b) T_1 is greater than T_2 because behaviour of a real gas approaches the ideal gas behaviour when temperature is increased.

(c) Here, $\frac{PV}{T} = nR = \frac{8.31}{(32 \times 10^{-3})} \times 1 \times 10^{-3}$

$$= 0.26 \text{ JK}^{-1}$$

($\because R = 8.31 \text{ Jmol}^{-1}\text{K}^{-1}$, $O_2 = 32 \times 10^{-3}$ kg and mass of O_2 is given as 1×10^{-3} kg)

(d) No, this is because PV/T depends upon the volume of gas and volume of equal masses of different gases are different. For hydrogen

$$\frac{PV}{T} = \frac{8.31\times10^{-3}}{2.02\times10^{-3}} = 4{\cdot}11\ JK^{-1}$$

The value is not same.

Mass of hydrogen for same value of this term $\frac{PV}{T}$, i.e., $0{\cdot}26\ JK^{-1}$ is given by,

$$= \frac{2.02\times10^{-3}}{8.31} \times 0.26 = 6.32 \times 10^{-5}\ kg$$

Q. 4. An oxygen cylinder of volume 30 litres has an initial gauge pressure of 15 atm and a temperature of 27°C. After some oxygen is withdrawn from the cylinder, the gauge pressure drops to 11 atm and its temperature drops to 17°C. Estimate the mass of oxygen taken out of the cylinder. [NCERT Ex. Q. 12.4, Page 258]

Ans. Initially in the oxygen cylinder

$$V_1 = 30 \text{ litres} = 30 \times 10^{-3}\ m^3$$

$$P_1 = 15 \text{ atm} = 15 \times 1{\cdot}01 \times 10^5 \text{ Pa.}$$

$$T_1 = 27 + 273 = 300\ K$$

If the cylinder contains n_1 mole of oxygen gas then

$$P_1V_1 = n_1RT_1$$

or

$$n_1 = \frac{P_1V_1}{RT_1} = \frac{15\times1.01\times10^5\times30\times10^{-3}}{8.3\times300} = 18.253$$

For oxygen, molecular weight $M = 32$ g

Initial mass of cylinder $m_1 = n_1M = 18{\cdot}253 \times 32 = 584{\cdot}1$ g

Finally in the oxygen cylinder, let n_2 moles of oxygen be left

$$V_2 = 30 \times 10^{-3}\ m^3$$

$$P_2 = 11 \times 1.01 \times 10^5 \text{ Pa.}$$

$$T_2 = 17 + 273 = 290\ K.$$

Now,

$$n_2 = \frac{P_2V_2}{RT_2} = \frac{11.143\times10^5\times30\times10^{-3}}{8.3\times290} = 13.847$$

Final mass of oxygen gas in the cylinder

$$m_2 = 13.847 \times 32 = 443.1\ g$$

Mass of the oxygen gas taken out

$$= m_1 - m_2 = 584.1 - 443.1 = 141.0\ g$$

Q. 5. An air bubble of volume 1.0 cm³ rises from the bottom of a lake 40 m deep at a temperature of 12°C. To what volume does it grow when it reaches the surface, which is at a temperature of 35°C ? (Given, 1 atm = 1·01 × 10⁵ Pa) [NCERT Ex. Q. 12.5, Page 258]

Ans. When the air bubble is at 40 m depth, then

$$V_1 = 1.0\ cm^3 = 1.0 \times 10^{-6}\ m^3$$

$$T_1 = 12°C = 12 + 273 = 285\ K$$

$$P_1 = 1 \text{ atm} + h\rho g = 1.01 \times 10^5 + 40 \times 10^3 \times 9{\cdot}8 = 4{,}93{,}000 \text{ Pa}$$

When the air bubble reaches at the surface of lake, then

$$V_2 = ?$$

$$T_2 = 35°C = 35 + 273K = 308\ K$$

$$P_2 = 1 \text{ atm} = 1{\cdot}01 \times 10^5 \text{ Pa}$$

Now

$$\frac{P_1V_1}{T_1} = \frac{P_2V_2}{T_2}$$

or

$$V_2 = \frac{P_1V_1T_2}{T_1P_2}$$

$$V_2 = \frac{493000\times1.0\times10^{-6}\times308}{285\times1.01\times10^5} = 5.275 \times 10^{-6}\ m^3.$$

Q. 6. Estimate the total number of air molecules (inclusive of oxygen, nitrogen, water vapour and other constituents) in a room of capacity 25.0 m³ at a temperature of 27°C and 1 atm pressure. [NCERT Ex. Q. 12.6, Page 258]

Ans. Here,

$$P = 1 \text{ atm} = 1.01 \times 10^5 \text{ Pa}$$

$$V = 25\ m^3$$

$$k_B = (1.38 \times 10^{-23})\ J/K$$

$$T = 273 + 27 = 300\ K$$

Using, $PV = nk_BT$, we get

$$n = \frac{PV}{k_BT} = \frac{(1.01\times10^5)(25)}{(1.38\times10^{-23})(300)} = 6.1 \times 10^{26}.$$

Q. 7. Estimate the average thermal energy of a helium atom at (i) room temperature (27°C), (ii) the temperature on the surface of the sun (6000 K), (iii) temperature of 10 million kelvin (the typical care temperature in the case of star). [NCERT Ex. Q. 12.7, Page 258]

Ans. (i)

$$K.E._{avg} = \frac{3}{2}kT = \frac{3}{2}(1.38 \times 10^{-23})(27 + 273) = 6.21 \times 10^{-21}\ J$$

(ii)

$$K.E.'_{avg} = \frac{3}{2}kT' = \frac{3}{2}(1.38 \times 10^{-23}) \times 6000 = 1.242 \times 10^{-19}\ J$$

(iii)

$$K.E.''_{avg} = \frac{3}{2}kT'' = \frac{3}{2}(1.38 \times 10^{-23}) \times 10^7 = 2.07 \times 10^{-16}\ J$$

Q. 8. Three vessels of equal capacity have gases at the same temperature and pressure. The first vessel contains neon (monoatomic), the second contains chlorine (diatomic), and the third contains uranium hexafluoride (polyatomic). Do the vessels contains equal number of respective molecules ? Is the root mean square speed of molecules the same in the three cases ? If not, in which case is v_{rms} the largest ?

[NCERT Ex. Q. 12.8, Page 258]

Ans. (a) Yes, because according to Avogadro's hypothesis, equal volume of all the gases have same number of molecules under the condition of same temperature and pressure.

(b) Using $v_{rms} = \sqrt{\dfrac{3kT}{m}}$, we get $v_{rms} \propto \dfrac{1}{\sqrt{m}}$, i.e., v_{rms} will not be same in the three cases because it depends upon mass of the gas. It will be the largest for neon.

Q. 9. At what temperature is the root mean square speed of an atom in an argon gas cylinder equal to the r.m.s. speed of a helium gas atom at –20°C ? (Atomic mass of Ar = 39.9 u and that of He = 4.0 u.)

[NCERT Ex. Q. 12.9, Page 258]

Ans. R.M.S. speed of argon at temperature T

$$v = \sqrt{\frac{3RT}{M}} = \sqrt{\frac{3RT}{39.9}}$$

R.M.S. for helium at temperature – 20°C or 253K is

$$v' = \sqrt{\frac{3R\times 253}{4.0}}$$

But $\quad v = v'$ (given)

$$\sqrt{\frac{3RT}{39.9}} = \sqrt{\frac{3R\times 253}{4.0}}$$

or
$$\frac{T}{39.9} = \frac{253}{4.0}$$

$$T = 2523.7\text{K}.$$

Q. 10. Estimate the mean free path and collision frequency of nitrogen molecule in a cylinder containing nitrogen at 2.0 atm and temperature 17°C. Take the radius of a nitrogen molecule to be roughly 1.0 Å. Compare the collision time with the time the molecule moves freely between two successive collisions. (Molecular mass of N_2 = 28.0 u). [NCERT Ex. Q. 12.10, Page 258]

Ans. From Maxwell's correction, the mean free path (λ) of a gas molecule is given by

$$\lambda = \frac{1}{\sqrt{2}\pi n d^2}$$

where $\quad d$ = diameter of a molecule.

and
$$n = \frac{N}{V} = \frac{\text{Number of molecules}}{\text{Volume of gas}}$$

At 2 atm pressure, the volume of the gas of mass M is given by $V = \dfrac{RT}{P}$, T = 273 + 17 = 290 K.

$$\therefore \quad n = \frac{N}{V} = \frac{NP}{RT} \quad \text{(i)}$$

Now given: $N = 6.023 \times 10^{23}$ mole^{-1}

$P = 2$ atm $= 2 \times 1.013 \times 10^5$ Nm^{-2}.

$R = 8.3$ JK^{-1} mol^{-1}.

From equ (i)

$$n = \frac{6.023\times 10^{23} \times 2\times 1.013\times 10^5}{8.3\times 290} = 5.07 \times 10^{25}$$

Here, $\quad r = 1\text{Å} = 1 \times 10^{-10}$ m

So, $\quad d = 2r = 2 \times 10^{-10}$ m

Mean free path,

$$\lambda = \frac{1}{\sqrt{2}\times 3.142\times (2\times 10^{-10})^2 \times 5.07\times 10^{25}} = 1.0 \times 10^{-7} \text{ m}$$

The *r.m.s.* velocity is given by

$$c = \sqrt{\frac{3RT}{M}}$$

Putting $R = 8.31$ Jmol^{-1} K^{-1}, $T = 290$ K,

$M = 28 \times 10^{-3}$ kg/mol

In equation (i),

$$c = \sqrt{\frac{3\times 8.31\times 290}{28\times 10^{-3}}} = 5.08 \times 10^2 \text{ ms}^{-1} = 5.10 \times 10^2 \text{ ms}^{-1}.$$

∴ Collision frequency (ν) is given by

$$\nu = \frac{c}{\lambda} = \frac{5.1\times 10^2}{1.0\times 10^{-7}} = 5.1 \times 10^9 \text{ s}^{-1}.$$

Suppose τ be the time between two successive collisions,

$$\therefore \quad \tau = \frac{\lambda}{c} = \frac{1.0\times 10^{-7}\text{ m}}{5.1\times 10^2\text{ ms}^{-1}} = 2{\cdot}0 \times 10^{-10} \text{ s.} \quad \text{(ii)}$$

Also suppose t = time taken for the collision.

$$\therefore \quad t = \frac{d}{c} = \frac{2\times 10^{-10}}{5.10\times 10^2} = 4 \times 10^{-13} \text{ s} \quad \text{(iii)}$$

(ii)/(iii) gives
$$\frac{\tau}{t} = \frac{2.0\times 10^{-10}\text{ s}}{4\times 10^{-13}\text{ s}} = 500$$

or τ = 500 t, i.e., the time taken between successive collisions is 500 times the time taken for a collision to take place, i.e., the two molecules are in contact. This shows that the molecule in a gas moves nearly free for most of the time.

CHAPTER 13

OSCILLATIONS

- **Harmonic Oscillations:** Those oscillations which can be expressed in terms of single harmonic function. *i.e.,* (sine function or cosine function).

$$y = a\sin \omega t \text{ or } y = a\cos \omega t.$$

- **Non-Harmonic Oscillations:** Those oscillations which cannot be expressed in terms of single harmonic function i.e.,

$$y = a\sin \omega t + b\sin 2\omega t.$$

- **Periodic Functions:** Those functions which are used to represent periodic motion i.e.,

$$f(t) = f(t + T) = f(t + 2T).$$

sine & cosine functions are periodic functions.

- **Phase:** Phase of vibrating particle at any instant is a physical quantity which completely expresses the position and direction of motion of particle at that instant with respect to its mean position.
- **Some Facts:**

(a) In oscillatory motion, the phase of a vibrating particle is the argument of sine or cosine function involved to represent the generalised equation of motion of the vibrating particle.

(b) When the displacement of the particle executing a vibratory motion is represented by $y = a\sin(\omega t + \phi)$, then $(\omega t + \phi)$ is called phase of the vibrating particle.

(c) ϕ is called the initial phase of the vibrating particle.

- **Simple Harmonic Motion:** It is a special type of periodic motion, in which a particle moves to and fro repeatedly about a mean (i.e., equilibrium) position under a restoring force, which is always directed towards the mean position and whose magnitude at any instant is directly proportional to the displacement of the particle from the mean (i.e., equilibrium) position at that instant, i.e.,

Scan to know more about this topic

Simple harmonic motion

$$F = -ky$$

where k is known as force constant. Here negative sign represent that the restoring force (F) is always directed towards the mean position.

- **Geometrical interpretation of S.H.M.:** S.H.M. is defined as the projection of a uniform circular motion on any diameter of a circle of reference.

(a) S.H.M. may be linear and angular S.H.M.

(b) The linear S.H.M. is always along a straight line about a fixed point on a line, whereas the angular S.H.M. is always along an arc of a circle about a fixed point on the arc.

(c) The linear S.H.M. is controlled by force law, where $F = -ky$, where k is the restoring force constant, *i.e.,* force per unit displacement.

(d) The angular S.H.M. is controlled by torque law, where $\tau = -C\theta$, where C is the restoring torque constant, *i.e.,* restoring torque per unit twist.

- **Characteristics of S.H.M.:**

(a) Displacement: The displacement of a particle executing linear S.H.M. at an instant is defined as the distance of the particle from the mean position at that instant.

(b) Velocity: is defined as the time rate of change of the displacement of the particle at the given instant.

(c) Amplitude: The maximum displacement on either side of mean position.

(d) Acceleration: It is defined as the time rate of change of the velocity of the particle at the given instant.

(e) Time Period: It is defined as the time taken by the particle executing S.H.M. to complete one vibration.

- **Restoring Force & Force Constant:** Force constant is the force required to give unit displacement to the body.

$F = -ky$ Here, k is force constant.

- **Simple Pendulum:** It is most common example of S.H.M. An ideal simple pendulum consists of a heavy point mass body suspended by a weightless inextensible and perfectly flexible string from a rigid support about which it is free to oscillate.

$$\text{Time period, } = 2\pi\sqrt{\frac{l}{g}}$$

- **Energy of S.H.M:** A particle executing S.H.M. possesses two types of energy:

(a) Potential Energy: This energy is on account of the displacement of the particle from its mean position.

(b) Kinetic Energy: This energy is on account of the velocity of the particle.

Key Words

- **Periodic motion:** The motion which is identically repeated after a fixed interval of time.
- **Oscillatory motion or vibratory motion:** The motion in which a body moves to and fro or back and forth repeatedly about a fixed point (called mean position), in a definite interval of time.

Some terms related to periodic motion:

Time period: It is the least interval of the time after which the periodic motion of a body repeats itself.

Frequency: It is defined as the no. of periodic motions executed by the body per second.

Angular frequency: It is equal to the product of frequency of the body with factor 2π. *i.e.,* $\omega = 2\pi\nu$.

Displacement: It is the change in position under consideration with time in a periodic motion.

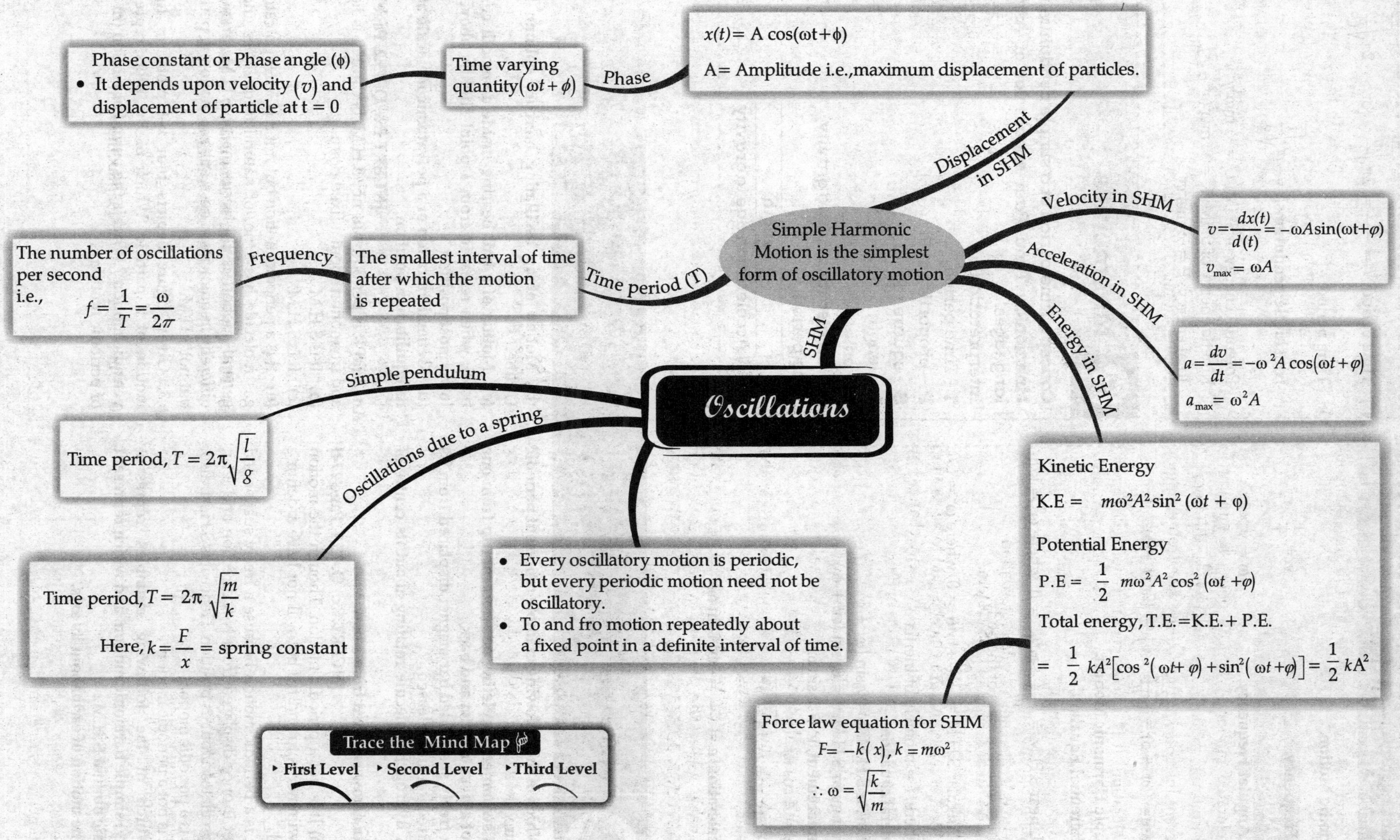
Oscillations
SHM
Simple Harmonic Motion is the simplest form of oscillatory motion
Displacement in SHM
x(t)= A cos(ωt+ϕ)
A= Amplitude i.e.,maximum displacement of particles.
Phase
Time varying quantity(ωt + ϕ)
Phase constant or Phase angle (ϕ)
• It depends upon velocity (v) and displacement of particle at t = 0
Time period (T)
The smallest interval of time after which the motion is repeated
Frequency
The number of oscillations per second i.e., f = 1/T = ω/2π
Velocity in SHM
v = dx(t)/d(t) = −ωAsin(ωt+φ)
v_max = ωA
Acceleration in SHM
a = dv/dt = −ω²A cos(ωt+φ)
a_max = ω²A
Energy in SHM
Kinetic Energy
K.E = mω²A² sin² (ωt + φ)
Potential Energy
P.E = 1/2 mω²A² cos² (ωt + φ)
Total energy, T.E.=K.E.+ P.E.
= 1/2 kA²[cos²(ωt+ φ) + sin²(ωt + φ)] = 1/2 kA²
Force law equation for SHM
F= −k(x), k = mω²
∴ ω = √(k/m)
• Every oscillatory motion is periodic, but every periodic motion need not be oscillatory.
• To and fro motion repeatedly about a fixed point in a definite interval of time.
Simple pendulum
Time period, T = 2π√(l/g)
Oscillations due to a spring
Time period, T = 2π √(m/k)
Here, k = F/x = spring constant
Trace the Mind Map
First Level
Second Level
Third Level

Key Formulae

➤ **Periodic Motion.**

(a) Frequency, $\nu = \frac{1}{T}$

(b) Angular Frequency, $\omega = \nu \times 2\pi$

or $\omega = \frac{2\pi}{T}$

➤ Phase= $(\omega t + \phi) = \left(\frac{2\pi t}{T} + \phi\right) = (2\pi\nu t + \phi)$

➤ **Simple Harmonic Motion:**

(a) Differential Equation,

(i) Linear S.H.M.= $\frac{d^2y}{dt^2} + \omega^2 y = 0$, where $\omega^2 = k/m$,

here, m is the mass of the body

(ii) Angular S.H.M.= $\frac{d^2\theta}{dt^2} + \omega^2\theta = 0$, where $\omega^2 = C/I$,

here, I = moment of inertia

(b) General *equation*—

(i) Linear S.H.M. $y = y_0 \sin(\omega t + \phi)$

(ii) Angular S.H.M. $\theta = \theta_0 \sin(\omega t + \phi_0)$

(c) Displacement, $y = A \sin \omega t$ or $y = A \cos \omega t$

(d) Velocity, $v = \omega\sqrt{A^2 - y^2}$

(e) Acceleration, $a = \frac{dv}{dt} = -\omega^2 A \sin \omega t$

(f) Time Period, $T = \frac{2\pi}{\omega} = 2\pi\sqrt{\frac{m}{k}}$ or $2\pi\sqrt{\frac{I}{C}}$

➤ **Time period:**

For simple pendulum $T = 2\pi\sqrt{\frac{l}{g}}$

Potential energy of SHM: $U = \frac{1}{2} m\omega^2 y^2$

Kinetic energy of SHM: $K = \frac{1}{2} m\omega^2(a^2 - y^2)$

Total energy: $E = \frac{1}{2} m\omega^2 a^2$

Mnemonics

Concept: Time period of a simple pendulum.

Mnemonics: Tanu Paul speaks lot of Asian languages.

Interpretation:

T - Time period

P - proportional to

S - square root of

L - length

O - on

A - acceleration due to gravity

Time period

$\propto \sqrt{\frac{\text{Length}}{\text{Acceleration due to gravity}}}$

NCERT CORNER

Q. 1. Which of the following example represent periodic motion:

(a) A swimmer completing one (return) trip from one bank of a river to other and back,

(b) A freely suspended bar magnet displaced from its N-S direction and released,

(c) A hydrogen molecule rotating about its centre of mass.

(d) An arrow released from a bow.

[NCERT Ex., Q. 13.1, Page 274]

Ans. (a) It is not a periodic motion. Though the motion of a swimmer is to and fro but will not have a definite period.

(b) It is a periodic motion because a freely suspended magnet if once displaced from N-S direction and let it go, it oscillates about its position. Hence it is S.H.M. also.

(c) It is a periodic motion.

(d) It is not a periodic motion.

Q. 2. Which of the following examples represent (nearly) simple harmonic motion, and which represent periodic but not S.H.M.:

(a) The motion of earthabout its axis.

(b) Motion of an oscillating mercury column in a U-tube.

(c) Motion of a ball bearing inside a smooth curved bowl, when released from a point slightly above the lowermost position.

(d) General vibration of a polyatomic molecule about its equilibrium position.

[NCERT Ex., Q. 13.2, Page 274]

Ans. (a) It is periodic but not S.H.M. because it is not to and fro motion about a fixed point.

(b) It is S.H.M.

(c) It is S.H.M.

(d) It is a periodic motion but not S.H.M. A polyatomic gas molecule has a no. of natural frequencies and its general motion is the resultant of S.H.M. of no. of different frequencies. The resultant motion is periodic but not S.H.M.

Q. 3. Given figure depicts four *x–t* plots for linear motion of a particle. Which of the plots represent periodic motion ? What is the period of motion (in case of periodic motion) ?

(a) 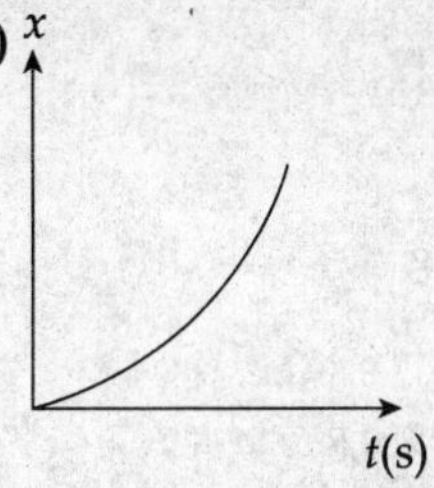

(b) 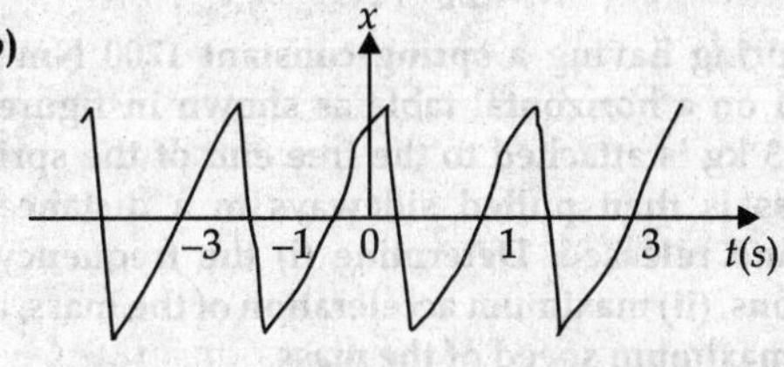

(c) 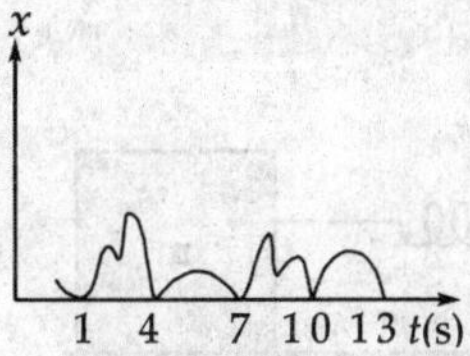

(d) 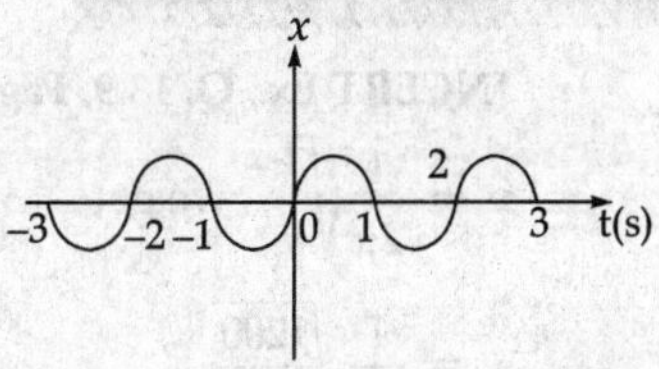

[NCERT Ex., Q. 13.3, Page 274]

Ans. **(a)** This figure does not represent periodic motion as the motion neither repeats nor comes to mean position.

(b) This figure represents periodic motion with period equal to 2 s.

(c) This figure does not represents periodic motion because it does not repeat identically.

(d) This figure represents periodic motion having period equal to 2 s.

Q. 4. Which of the following functions of time represent (a) simple harmonic, (b) periodic but not simple harmonic, and (c) non-periodic motion ? (Give the time period for each case of periodic motion, ω is any positive constant.)

(a) $\sin \omega t - \cos \omega t$

(b) $\sin^3 \omega t$

(c) $3\cos\left(\frac{\pi}{4} - 2\omega t\right)$

(d) $\cos \omega t + \cos 3\omega t + \cos 5\omega t$

(e) $e^{-\omega^2 t^2}$

(f) $1 + \omega t + \omega^2 t^2$ **[NCERT Ex., Q. 13.4, Page 275]**

Ans. The function will represent a periodic motion, if it is identically repeated after a fixed interval of time and will represent S.H.M. if it can be written uniquely in the form of $A\cos\left(\frac{2\pi t}{T} + \phi\right)$ or $A\sin\left(\frac{2\pi t}{T} + \phi\right)$, where T is the time period.

(a) $\sin \omega t - \cos \omega t = \sqrt{2}\left[\frac{1}{\sqrt{2}}\sin \omega t - \frac{1}{\sqrt{2}}\cos \omega t\right]$

$$= \sqrt{2}\left[\sin \omega t \cos\frac{\pi}{4} - \cos \omega t \sin\frac{\pi}{4}\right]$$

$$= \sqrt{2}\sin\left(\omega t - \frac{\pi}{4}\right)$$

It is a S.H.M. and its Time period is $2\pi/\omega$.

(b) $\sin^3 \omega t = \frac{1}{4}[3\sin \omega t - \sin 3\omega t]$

Here, each term $\sin \omega t$ and $\sin 3\omega t$ individually represents S.H.M. But (ii) which is the outcome of the superposition of two S.H.Ms. will only be periodic but not S.H.M. Its time period is $2\pi/\omega$.

(c) $3\cos\left(\frac{\pi}{4} - 2\omega t\right) = 3\cos\left(2\omega t - \frac{\pi}{4}\right)$

$[\because \cos(-\theta) = \cos\theta]$

Clearly it represents S.H.M. and its time period is $2\pi/2\omega$ *i.e.*, π/ω.

(d) $\cos \omega t + \cos 3\omega t + \cos 5\omega t$. Each is a SHM. But superposition of three SHMs is not a SHM. It is periodic. The time period is LCM of the periods of the three SHMs i.e., $\frac{2\pi}{\omega}$.

(e) $e^{-\omega^2 t^2}$: it is an exponential function which never repeats itself. Therefore, it represents non-periodic motion.

(f) $1 + \omega t + \omega^2 t^2$ represents non-periodic motion.

Q. 5. A particle is in linear S.H.M. between two points, A and B, 10 cm apart. Take the direction from A to B as the positive direction and give the signs of velocity, acceleration and force on the particle when it is :

(a) at the end A,

(b) at the end B,

(c) at the mid point of AB going towards A,

(d) at 2 cm away from B going towards A,

(e) at 3 cm away from A going towards B, and

(f) at 4 cm away from A going towards A.

[NCERT Ex., Q. 13.5, Page 275]

Ans. **(a) End A:** Velocity = 0; acceleration +*ve*, force +*ve*.

(b) End B: Velocity = 0; acceleration – *ve*; force – *ve*.

(c) Velocity – *ve*; acceleration = 0, force = 0 [mean position].

(d) Velocity – *ve*; acceleration = – *ve*; force – *ve*.

(e) Velocity + *ve*; acceleration + *ve*; force + *ve*

(f) Velocity – *ve*; acceleration + *ve*; force + *ve*.

Q. 6. Which of the following relationships between the acceleration a and the displacement x of a particle involve S.H.M.

(a) $a = 0.7x$ **(b) $a = -200x^2$**

(c) $a = -10x$ **(d) $a = 100x^3$.**

[NCERT Ex., Q. 13.6, Page 275]

Ans. **(c)** As we know $a = -kx$. Hence, option (C) satisfies the SHM.

Q. 7. The motion of particle executing SHM is described by the displacement function –

$$x(t) = A\cos(\omega t + \phi)$$

If the initial (t=0) position of the particle is 1 cm and the initial velocity is ω cm/s, what are its amplitude and initial phase angle? The angular frequency of the particle is πs^{-1}. If instead of the cosine function, we choose the sine function to describe the SHM: $x = B\sin(\omega t + \alpha)$, what are the amplitude and initial

phase of the particle with the above initial conditions ?
[NCERT Ex., Q. 13.7, Page 275]

Ans. Given:

$t = 0, x = 1$ cm, $v = \omega$ cm/s, $\omega = \pi$ s^{-1}.

$$x(t) = A\cos(\omega t + \phi)$$

or $$1 = A\cos(\pi \times 0 + \phi)$$
$$= A\cos\phi = 1 \quad \text{(i)}$$

Velocity, $$v = \frac{dx}{dt} = -A\omega\sin(\omega t + \phi)$$

or $$\omega = -A\omega\sin(\pi \times 0 + \phi)$$
$$1 = -A\sin\phi \text{ or } A\sin\phi = -1 \quad \text{(ii)}$$

Squaring the eq^n.(s) (i) & (ii), then adding –
$$A^2(\cos^2\phi + \sin^2\phi) = 1 + 1 = 2$$
$$A^2 = 2 \text{ or } A = \sqrt{2}\text{ cm}$$

Now, Dividing eq^n. (ii) by eq^n. (i).
$$\tan\phi = -1$$
$$\phi = -\frac{\pi}{4} \text{ or } \frac{3\pi}{4}$$

If we choose sine function instead of cosine function, then,
$$x(t) = B\sin(\omega t + \alpha) \quad \text{(iii)}$$
$$x = 1\text{cm}$$
or $$1 = B\sin(0 + \alpha)$$
$$B\sin\alpha = 1 \quad \text{(iv)}$$

Velocity,
$$v(t) = \frac{dx(t)}{dt} = B\omega\cos(\omega t + \alpha) \quad \text{[using (iii)]}$$

At $t = 0$, $v(t) = \omega$cm/s
$$\omega = +B\omega\cos(0 + \alpha)$$
$$B\cos\alpha = +1 \quad \text{(v)}$$

Squaring (iv) & (v), then adding –
$$B^2\sin^2\alpha + B^2\cos^2\alpha = 1 + 1$$
or, $$B^2(\sin^2\alpha + \cos^2\alpha) = 2$$
$\therefore$ $$B = \pm\sqrt{2}\text{ cm}$$

Hence, amplitude of motion$= \sqrt{2}$ cm.

Now, Dividing equation (iv) by (v),
$$\frac{B\sin\alpha}{B\cos\alpha} = \frac{1}{1} \text{ or, } \tan\alpha = 1 \text{ or, } \alpha = \frac{\pi}{4} \text{ or } \frac{5\pi}{4}$$

Q. 8. A spring balance has a scale that reads from 0 to 50 kg. The length of the scale is 20cm. A body suspended from this balance, when displaced and released, oscillates with a period of 0.6 s, what is the weight of the body? [NCERT Ex., Q. 13.8, Page 275]

Ans. Given: mass, m = 50 kg,

maximum extension, y = 20 – 0 = 20 cm
= 0.2 m

Time, t = 0.6 s.

Force, F = mg = 50 × 9.8 N

$\therefore$ $$k = \frac{F}{y} = \frac{50 \times 9.8}{0.2} = 2450 \text{ N/m.}$$

Now, $$T = 2\pi\sqrt{\frac{m}{k}} \text{ or } m = \frac{T^2 k}{4\pi^2}$$
$$m = \frac{(0.6)^2 \times 2450}{4 \times (3.14)^2} = 22.36\text{kg}$$

so, weight of the body = mg
= 22.36 × 9.8
W = 219.1 N.

Q. 9. A spring having a spring constant 1200 Nm^{-1} is mounted on a horizontal table as shown in figure. A mass of 3 kg is attached to the free end of the spring. The mass is then pulled sideways to a distance of 2.0 cm and released. Determine (i) the frequency of oscillations, (ii) maximum acceleration of the mass, and (iii) the maximum speed of the mass.

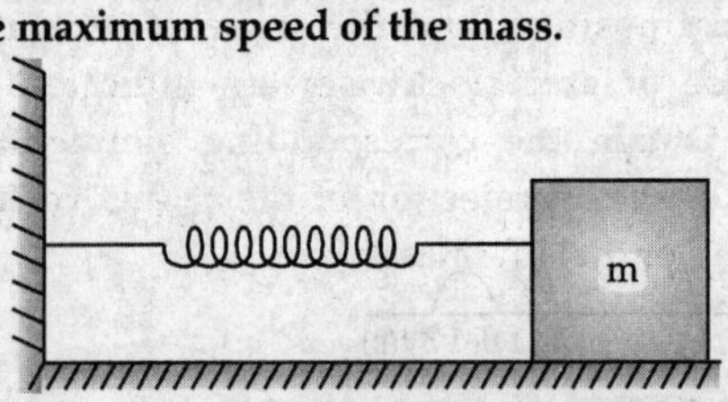

[NCERT Ex., Q. 13.9, Page 275]

Ans. (i) Using, $$\nu = \frac{1}{2\pi}\sqrt{\frac{k}{m}}, \text{ we get}$$
$$\nu = \frac{1}{2\pi}\sqrt{\frac{1200}{3}}$$
$$= 3.18 \text{ s}^{-1}$$

(ii) Maximum acceleration = $r\omega^2$
= $r(2\pi\nu)^2$
= $4\pi^2\nu^2 r$
= $4\pi^2$ (3.18)^2 × 0.02
= 7.98 ms^{-2}

(iii) Maximum speed = $r\omega$
= $r2\pi\nu$
= 2π × 3.18 × 0.02
= 0.4 ms^{-1}.

Q. 10. In the above question, let us take the position of mass when the spring is in natural length, i.e, unstretched as x = 0, and the direction from left to right as the positive direction of x-axis, Given x as a function of time t for the oscillating mass if at the moment we start the stop watch (t = 0), the mass is:

(a) at the mean position,

(b) at the maximum stretched position, and

(c) at the maximum compressed position.

In what way do these functions for S.H.M. differ from each other, in frequency, in amplitude or the initial phase ? [NCERT Ex., Q. 13.10, Page 276]

Ans. (a) When t = 0, the mass is at mean position.

Using, $x = r\sin(\omega t + \phi)$,
$$\omega = 2\pi f$$
$$= \sqrt{\frac{k}{m}} = \sqrt{\frac{1200}{3}}$$
$$= 20 \text{ rad s}^{-1}.$$

We get $x = r\sin(20 \times t + 0)$

$= 2\sin 20t$

(b) at $t = 0$, mass is at extreme stretched position.

Then, $x = 2\sin\left(20 \times t + \frac{\pi}{2}\right)$

$= 2\cos 20t$

(c) at $t = 0$, mass is at extreme compressed position

Then $x = 2\sin\left(20 \times t + \frac{3\pi}{2}\right)$

$= -2\cos 20t.$

These functions differ in initial phase.

Q. 11. Figure below corresponds to two circular motions. The radius of the circle, the period of revolution, the initial position, and the sense of revolution (*i.e.*, clockwise or anti clockwise) are indicated on each figure. Obtain the corresponding simple harmonic motion of the *x*-projection of the radius vector of the revolving particle P, in each case.

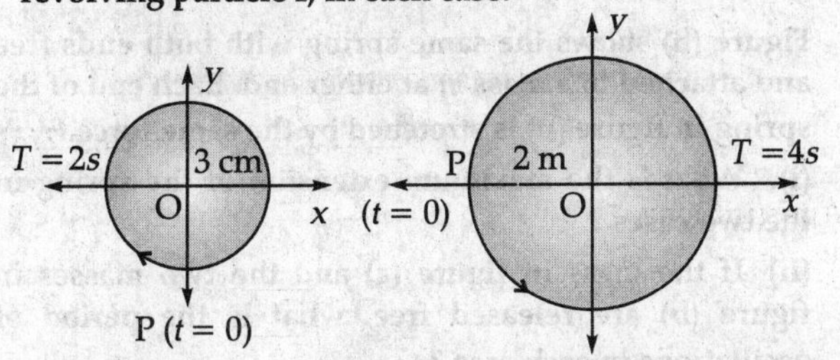

[NCERT Ex., Q. 13.11, Page 276]

Ans. (a) Here, at $t = 0$, OP makes an angle $\frac{\pi}{2}$ with *x*-axis. As motion is clockwise, so $\phi = \frac{+\pi}{2}$ radian. So, the *x*-projection of OP at time t will give us the equation of S.H.M. given by.

$$x = A\cos\left(\frac{2\pi t}{T} + \phi\right)$$

$$= 3\cos\left(\frac{2\pi t}{T} + \frac{\pi}{2}\right)$$

$(\because A = 3 \text{ cm}, T = 2 \text{ s})$

or $x = 3\cos\left(\pi + \frac{\pi}{2}\right)$

$x = -3\sin \pi t$ (*x* is in cm)

$\therefore$ *x* $= -3\sin \pi t$ *which is the equation of S.H.M.*

(b) Here $T = 4$ s, $A = 2$ m

At $t = 0$, OP makes an angle π with the positive direction of *x*-axis, *i.e.*, $\phi = +\pi$.

Hence, the x-projection of OP at time *t* will give us the equation of S.H.M.

as: $x = A\cos\left(\frac{2\pi}{T} + \phi\right)$

$= 2\cos\left(\frac{2\pi}{T} + \pi\right)$

$= -2\cos\left(\frac{\pi}{2}t\right)$

or $x = -2\cos\left(\frac{\pi}{2}t\right)$ (m).

which is the equation of S.H.M.

Q. 12. Plot the corresponding reference circle for each of the following simple harmonic motions. Indicate the initial ($t = 0$) position of the particle, the radius of the circle and the angular speed of the rotating particle. For simplicity, the sense of rotation may be fixed to be anti-clockwise in every case:

(*x* is in cm and *t* is in s).

(a) $x = -2\sin\left(3t + \frac{\pi}{3}\right)$

(b) $x = \cos\left(\frac{\pi}{6} - t\right)$

(c) $x = 3\sin\left(2\pi t + \frac{\pi}{4}\right)$

(d) $x = 2\cos \pi t$ **[NCERT Ex., Q. 13.12, Page 276]**

Ans. (a)

$$x = -2\sin\left(3t + \frac{\pi}{3}\right) = 2\cos\left(3t + \frac{\pi}{3} + \frac{\pi}{2}\right) = 2\cos\left(3t + \frac{5\pi}{6}\right)$$

Comparing with standard SHM equation, $x = A\cos\left(\frac{2\pi}{T}t + \phi\right)$

$\therefore$ Amplitude, $A = 2$ cm

Phase angle, $\phi = \frac{5\pi}{6} = 150°$

Angular velocity, $\omega = \frac{2\pi}{T} = 3$ rad/s

Corresponding reference circle is –

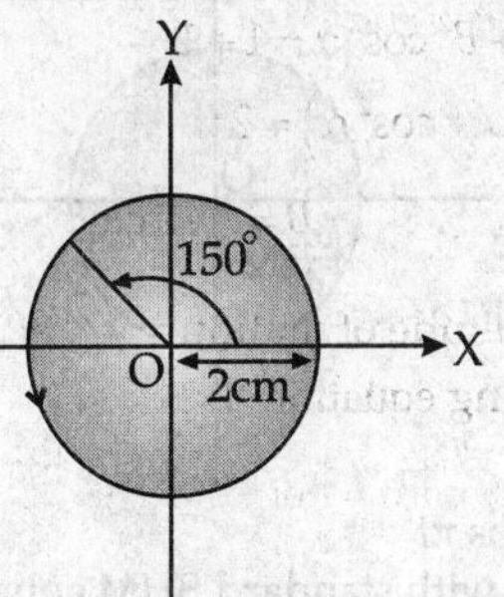

(b) $x = \cos\left(\frac{\pi}{6} - t\right)$

$x = \cos\left(t - \frac{\pi}{6}\right)$ $[\because \cos(-\theta) = \cos\theta]$

Comparing with standard SHM equation,

$x = A\cos\left(\frac{2\pi}{T}t + \phi\right)$,

$\therefore$ Amplitude, $A = 1$

Phase angle, $\phi = \frac{-\pi}{6} = -30°$

Angular velocity, $\omega = \frac{2\pi}{T} = 1\,\text{rad/s}$.

Corresponding reference circle is –

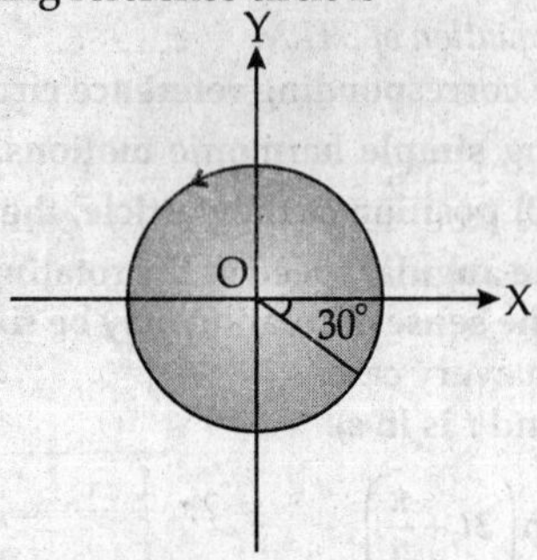

(c) $x = 3\sin\left(2\pi t + \frac{\pi}{4}\right)$

$x = -3\cos\left[\left(2\pi t + \frac{\pi}{4}\right) + \frac{\pi}{2}\right]$ $\left[\because \cos\left(\frac{\pi}{2} + \theta\right) = -\sin\theta\right]$

or $x = -3\cos\left(2\pi t + \frac{3\pi}{4}\right)$

Comparing with standard SHM equation, $x = A\cos\left(\frac{2\pi}{T}t + \phi\right)$

Amplitude, $A = 3$ cm

Phase angle, $\phi = \frac{3\pi}{4} = 135°$

Angular velocity, $\omega = \frac{2\pi}{T} = 2\pi$ rad/s

Corresponding reference circle is

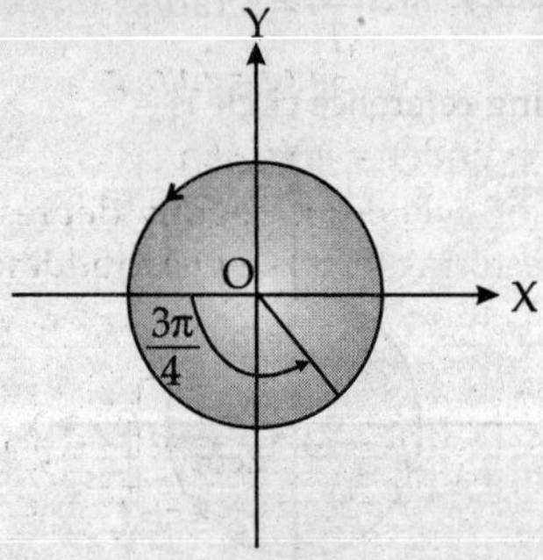

(d) $x = 2\cos \pi t$

Comparing with standard SHM equation

$\therefore$ Amplitude, $A = 2$ cm

Phase angle, $\phi = 0$

Angular velocity, $\omega = \pi\,\text{rad/s}$.

Corresponding reference circle is –

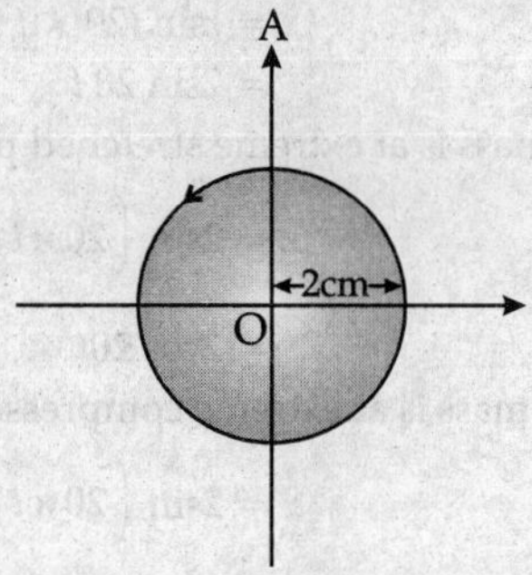

Q. 13. Figure (a) shows a spring of force constant k clamped rigidly at one end and a mass m attached to its free end. A force applied at the free end stretches the spring.

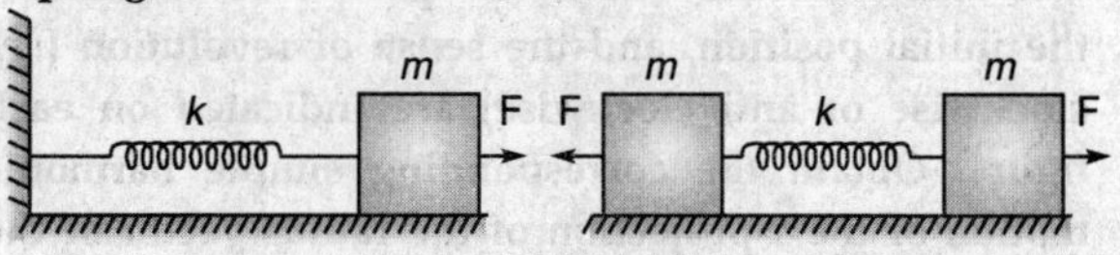

(a) (b)

Figure (b) shows the same spring with both ends free and attached to a mass m at either end. Each end of the spring in figure (b) is stretched by the same force F.

(i) What is the maximum extension of the spring in the two cases ?

(ii) If the mass in figure (a) and the two masses in figure (b) are released free, what is the period of oscillations in each case ?

[NCERT Ex., Q. 13.13, Page 276]

Ans. (i) (a) Using $F = ky$,

The maximum extension,

$$y = \frac{F}{k}$$

(b) Here, the springs have no rigid support, so, each mass behaves as a support for the spring against force applied on the other end.

$\therefore$ Maximum extension,

$$y = \frac{F}{k}$$

(ii) (a) Here, time period,

$$T = 2\pi\sqrt{\frac{m}{k}}$$

(b) In figure (b), we have a two body system of spring constant k and reduced mass,

$$m' = \frac{m \times m}{m + m} = \frac{m}{2}$$

Inertia factor = $m/2$

Spring factor = k

$$\therefore \quad T = 2\pi\sqrt{\frac{m}{2k}}$$

Q. 14. The piston in the cylinder head of a locomotive has a stroke (twice the amplitude) of 1.0 m. If the piston moves with S.H.M. with an angular frequency of 200 rad/min. What is its maximum speed ?

[NCERT Ex., Q. 13.14, Page 277]

Ans. Given, $a = \frac{1}{2} m$, $\omega = 200$ rad/min.

$$v_{max} = a\omega = \frac{1}{2} \times 200$$

$$= 100 \text{ m/min.}$$

Q. 15. The acceleration due to gravity on the surface of Moon is 1.7 ms^{-2}. What is the time period of a simple pendulum on the surface of Moon if its time period on the surface of Earth is 3.5 s?

(g on the surface of Earth is 9.8 ms^{-2})

[NCERT Ex., Q. 13.15, Page 277]

Ans. Acceleration due to gravity on the surface of Moon, $g_m = 1.7$ ms^{-2}

Acceleration due to gravity on the surface of Earth, g_e = 9.8 ms^{-2}

Time period of a simple pendulum on Earth $T_e = 3.5$s

$$T_e = 2\pi\sqrt{\frac{l}{g_e}}$$

Where,

l is the length of the pendulum

$$\therefore \quad l = \frac{T_e^2}{4 \times (3.14)^2} \times g_e$$

$$= \frac{(3.5)^2}{4 \times (3.14)^2} \times 9.8 \text{ m}$$

The length of pendulum remains constant.

On Moon's surface, time period, $T_m = 2\pi\sqrt{\frac{l}{gm}}$

$$T_m = 2\pi\sqrt{\frac{(3-5)^2 \times 9.8}{4 \times (3.14)^2 \times 1.7}} = 8.4s$$

Hence, the period of the simple pendulum on the surface of Moon is 8.4s.

Q. 16. A simple pendulum of length l and having a bob of mass M is suspended in a car. The car is moving on a circular track of radius R with a uniform speed v. If the pendulum makes small oscillations in a radial direction about its equilibrium position, what will be its time period ? [NCERT Ex., Q. 13.16, Page 277]

Ans. As the pendulum is oscillating in the radial direction, it is acted upon by an additional acceleration equal to the centripetal acceleration of the car on the circular track of radius R, *i.e.*, v^2/R where v = uniform speed of the car. So, there are two accelerations acting on the pendulum in mutually perpendicular directions. *i.e.*,

(i) acceleration due to gravity (g)

(ii) a_c = centripetal acceleration (v^2/R)

When a be the resultant acceleration of the pendulum, then

$$a = \sqrt{g^2 + a_c^2}$$

$$a = \sqrt{g^2 + \left(\frac{v^2}{R}\right)^2}$$

$$a = \sqrt{g^2 + \frac{v^4}{R^2}}$$

When T be the time period of oscillation of the pendulum, then

$$T = 2\pi\sqrt{\frac{l}{a}}$$

$$= 2\pi\sqrt{\frac{l}{\sqrt{g^2 + \frac{v^4}{R^2}}}}$$

$$\therefore \quad T = 2\pi\sqrt{\frac{l}{\left(g^2 + \frac{v^4}{R^2}\right)^{\frac{1}{2}}}}$$

Q. 17. A cylindrical piece of cork of base area A and height h floats in a liquid of density ρ_l. The cork is depressed slightly and then released. Show that the cork oscillates up and down simple harmonically with a period $T = 2\pi\sqrt{\frac{h\rho}{\rho_l g}}$

Where ρ is the density of cork. (Ignore damping due to viscosity of the liquid).[NCERT Ex., Q. 13.17, Page 277]

Ans. Let height of cylinder be y inside the liquid (Initially in equilibrium).

Then, weight of the cylinder = upthrust due to liquid displaced

$$\therefore Ah\pi g = Ay\rho_l g$$

Mass of the cylinder = $m = Ah\rho$

When cork of cylinder is slightly depressed by x and released, a restoring force is equal to additional upthrust, acts on it.

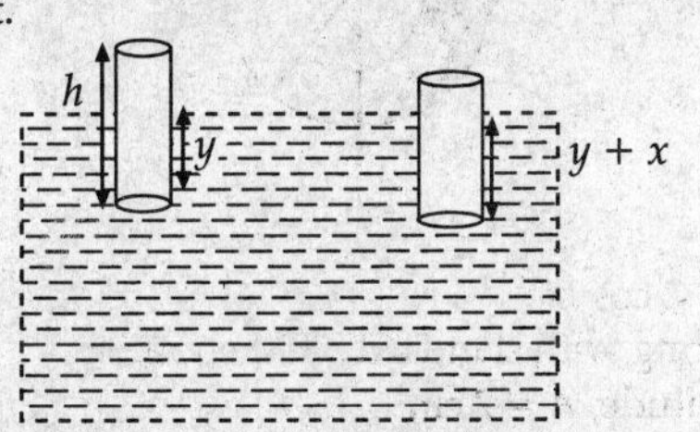

Upthrust = $F = \rho_l (y + x) Ag$

$$\text{Restoring force} = -(F - mg)$$
$$= -[(\rho_l \times (y + x) Ag) - \rho_l Ayg]$$
$$= -\rho_l Agx$$
$$= -kx \quad \text{(where } k = \rho_l Ag\text{)}$$

So, the cork exhibits a SHM.

$$\text{Time period} = T = 2\pi\sqrt{\left(\frac{m}{k}\right)}$$

or

$$T = 2\pi\sqrt{\left(\frac{\rho Ah}{\rho_1 Ag}\right)}$$

Q. 18. One end of a U-tube containing mercury is connected to a suction pump and the other end to atmosphere. A small pressure difference is maintained between the two columns. Show that, when the suction pump is removed, the liquid column of mercury in the U-tube executes simple harmonic motion.

[NCERT Ex., Q. 13.18, Page 277]

Ans. The suction pump creates the pressure difference. Hence mercury rises in one limb of the U-tube. When it is removed a net force acts on the mercury column due to the difference in levels of mercury in the two limbs and therefore the mercury column executes S.H.M. which can be explained as follows:

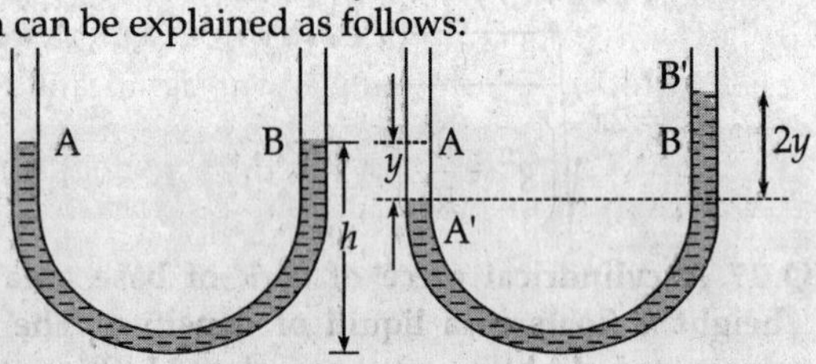

The mercury contained in a vertical U-tube upto the level A and B in its two limbs.

Suppose ρ = density of the mercury.

L = Total length of the mercury column in both the limbs.

A = internal cross-sectional area of U-tube.

m = mass of mercury in U-tube = $LA\rho$.

Suppose the mercury be depressed in left limb to A′ by a small distance y, then it rises by the same amount in the right limb to position B′.

$\therefore$ Difference in levels in the two limbs = $A'B' = 2y$.

$\therefore$ Volume of mercury contained in the column of length $2y = A \times 2y$

$$\therefore \qquad m = A \times 2y \times \rho.$$

When W = weight of liquid contained in the column of length 2y.

Then $\qquad W = mg = A \times 2y \times \rho \times g.$ ½

This weight produced the restoring force (F) which tends to bring back the mercury to its equilibrium position.

$$F = -2\,Ay\rho g = -(2A\rho g)y$$

When a = acceleration produced in the liquid column, Then

$$a = \frac{F}{m} = -\frac{(2A\rho g)y}{LA\rho}$$

or

$$a = -\frac{2\rho yg}{L\rho} = -\frac{2\rho g}{2h\rho}y \qquad \text{...(i)}$$

$$(\because L = 2h)$$

where h = height of mercury in each limb. Now from (i) it is clear that $a \propto y$ and $-ve$ sign shows that it acts opposite to y, so the motion of mercury in U-tube is simple harmonic in nature having time period (T) given by

$$T = 2\pi\sqrt{\frac{y}{a}} = 2\pi\sqrt{\frac{2h\rho}{2\rho g}}$$

$$= 2\pi\sqrt{\frac{h\rho}{\rho g}}$$

$$T = 2\pi\sqrt{\frac{h}{g}}$$

□□

CHAPTER 14

WAVES

Waves and Wave Motion

➢ **Wave motion** is a kind of disturbance which travels through a medium on account of repeated periodic vibrations of the particles of the medium about their mean position.

Scan to know more about this topic

Simple harmonic motion

- **The medium** for wave propagation should have three properties:
  (a) elasticity
  (b) inertia
  (c) minimum frictional resistance.

➢ **Kinds of waves:**

(i) Mechanical waves or elastic waves: The waves which require a material medium for propagation. Example: sound waves, waves on the surface of water, waves on strings.

(ii) Electromagnetic waves: The waves which require no medium for propagation. Example: light waves, radio waves.

(iii) Longitudinal waves: In which particles vibrate in the direction of propagation of waves. Longitudinal waves travel through a medium in the form of compressions and rarefactions involving changes in pressure and volume and can travel in all modes and cannot be polarised. The medium required must possess elasticity of volume. Example: Sound waves in air are longitudinal.

(iv) Transverse waves: In which particles vibrate in a direction perpendicular to the direction of propagation of waves. Transverse waves travel through a medium in the form of crests and troughs involving changes in shape can travel in solid and liquid and can be polarised. The medium required must possess elasticity of shape. Example: Vibrations in strings

(v) Matter waves: These waves are associated with constituents of matter - electrons, protons, neutrons, atoms and molecules. Those arise in quantum mechanical description of nature.

(vi) Capillary waves and gravity waves: The waves on the surface of water are of two kinds: capillary waves and gravity waves.

Ripple wave: These are ripples of fairly short wavelength—not more than a few centimetre—and the restoring force that produces them is the surface tension of water.

Gravity waves: These are have wavelengths typically ranging from several metres to several hundred meters. The restoring force that produces these waves is the pull of gravity, which tends to keep the water surface at its lowest level.

➢ **Laplace correction:** According to Laplace, the changes in pressure & volume of a gas, when sound waves propagate through it are not isothermal but it is adiabatic. since,

(a) Velocity of sound in gas is quite large.

(b) A gas is bad conductor of heat.

$\therefore$ Velocity of sound, $v = \sqrt{\frac{B_a}{\rho}}$

B_a = Bulk modulus = γP, ρ = density of gas

Principle of Superposition of Waves

(a) According to this principle, overlapping waves add algebraically to produce a resultant wave or a net wave.

or

When any number of waves meet simultaneously at a point in a medium, the net displacement at a given time is the algebraic sum of displacements due to each wave at that time.

i.e., $y = y_1 + y_2 + \ldots\ldots + y_n$

Important phenomenon related to Superposition of waves:

(i) Stationary waves: When two identical transverse or longitudinal progressive waves travel in a bounded medium with same speed but in opposite directions, then by their superposition a new type of wave is produced which appears stationary in the medium. This is known as stationary or standing wave.

(ii) Beats: When two sound waves of nearly equal frequencies superimpose, the intensity of the resultant wave increases and decreases alternately with time. Then phenomenon is known as beats.

(iii) Interference of waves: When two waves of same frequency travel in a medium simultaneously in the same direction, then due to their superposition, the resultant intensity at any point of the medium becomes different from the sum of the intensities of the two waves. At some pints the intensity of resultant wave is very large while at some other points it is very low or zero. This phenomenon is known as interference.

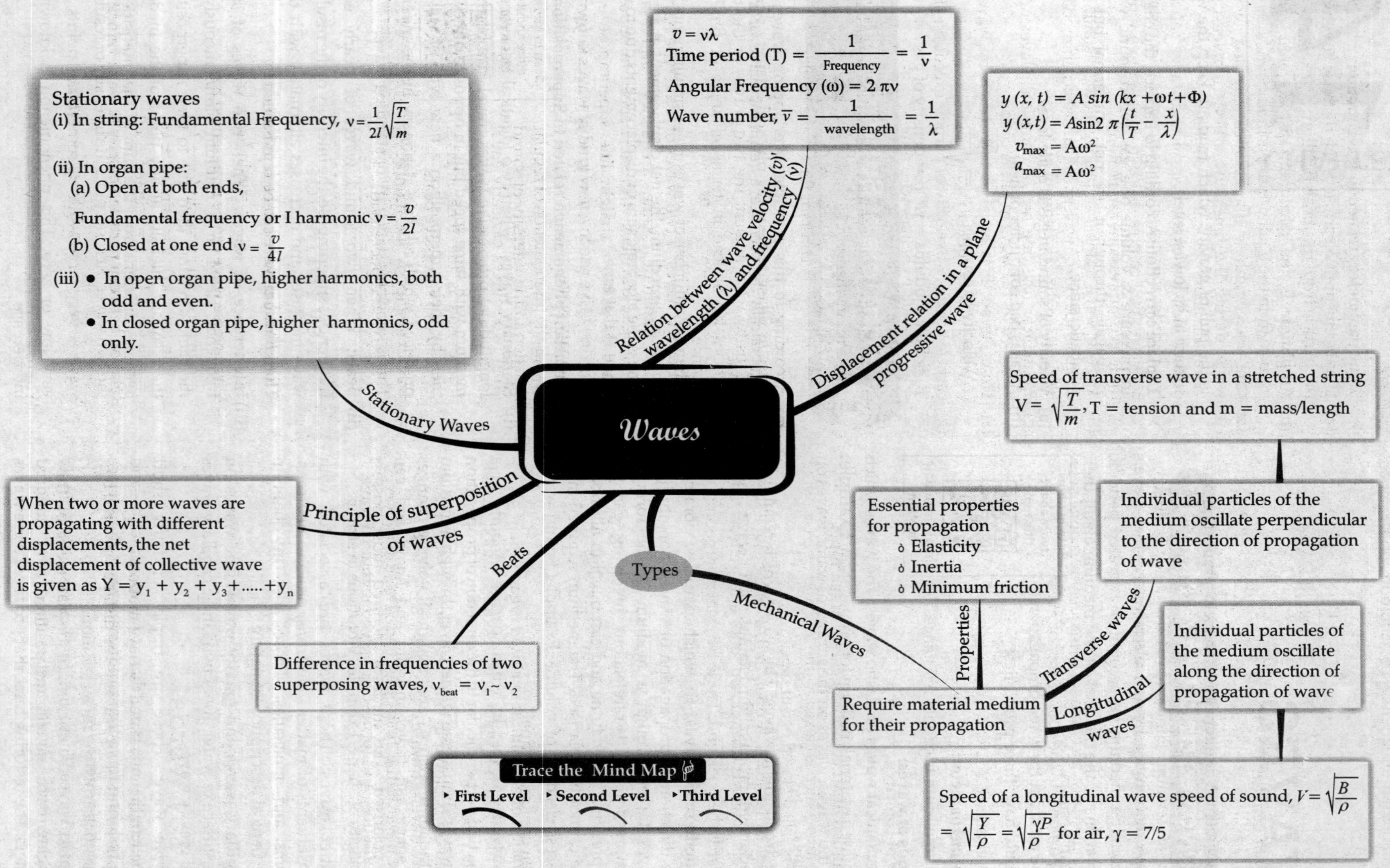
Waves
Relation between wave velocity (v) wavelength (λ) and frequency (ν)
$v = \nu\lambda$
Time period (T) = $\frac{1}{\text{Frequency}} = \frac{1}{\nu}$
Angular Frequency (ω) = $2\pi\nu$
Wave number, $\bar{v} = \frac{1}{\text{wavelength}} = \frac{1}{\lambda}$
Displacement relation in a plane progressive wave
$y(x, t) = A \sin (kx + \omega t + \Phi)$
$y(x,t) = A \sin 2\pi\left(\frac{t}{T} - \frac{x}{\lambda}\right)$
$v_{max} = A\omega^2$
$a_{max} = A\omega^2$
Stationary Waves
Stationary waves
(i) In string: Fundamental Frequency, $\nu = \frac{1}{2l}\sqrt{\frac{T}{m}}$
(ii) In organ pipe:
(a) Open at both ends,
Fundamental frequency or I harmonic $\nu = \frac{v}{2l}$
(b) Closed at one end $\nu = \frac{v}{4l}$
(iii) • In open organ pipe, higher harmonics, both odd and even.
• In closed organ pipe, higher harmonics, odd only.
Principle of superposition of waves
When two or more waves are propagating with different displacements, the net displacement of collective wave is given as $Y = y_1 + y_2 + y_3 + ... + y_n$
Beats
Difference in frequencies of two superposing waves, $\nu_{beat} = \nu_1 \sim \nu_2$
Types
Mechanical Waves
Require material medium for their propagation
Properties
Essential properties for propagation
Elasticity
Inertia
Minimum friction
Transverse waves
Individual particles of the medium oscillate perpendicular to the direction of propagation of wave
Speed of transverse wave in a stretched string
$V = \sqrt{\frac{T}{m}}$, T = tension and m = mass/length
Longitudinal waves
Individual particles of the medium oscillate along the direction of propagation of wave
Speed of a longitudinal wave speed of sound, $V = \sqrt{\frac{B}{\rho}} = \sqrt{\frac{Y}{\rho}} = \sqrt{\frac{\gamma P}{\rho}}$ for air, $\gamma = 7/5$
Trace the Mind Map
First Level
Second Level
Third Level

- **Laws of Vibrations of Stretched Strings.**

Fundamental Frequency of vibration of stretched string

$$\nu = \frac{1}{2L}\sqrt{\frac{T}{m}} = \frac{1}{LD}\sqrt{\frac{T}{\pi\rho}}$$

(a) Law of Length: $\nu \propto \frac{1}{L}$

Fundamental frequency is inversely proportional to length.

(b) Law of Tension: Fundamental frequency is directly proportional to square root of tension. *i.e.,*

$$\nu \propto \sqrt{T}$$

(c) Law of Mass: Fundamental frequency is inversely proportional to the square root of mass:

$$\nu \propto \frac{1}{\sqrt{m}}$$

(d) Law of Diameter: $\nu \propto \frac{1}{D}$

(e) Law of Density: $\nu \propto \frac{1}{\sqrt{\rho}}$

- **Vibration of air column in closed organ pipe:**

The tube which is closed at one end and open at other end is called closed organ pipe.

When air is blown at open end, a longitudinal wave travels towards the closed end and reflects back towards the open end. These two waves superimpose and form stationary longitudinal wave.

$$\lambda = \frac{4L}{2m-1}$$

$$\nu = \frac{v}{4L} \times (2m-1)$$

where $m = 1, 2, 3, 4$.......

- **Vibration of air column in closed organ pipe:**

The tube which is open at both ends is called closed organ pipe.

When air is blown at one open end, a longitudinal wave travels towards the other end and reflects back towards the first open end. These two waves superimpose and form stationary longitudinal wave.

$$\lambda = \frac{2l}{m}$$

$$\nu = \frac{v}{2L} \times m$$

where $m = 1, 2, 3, 4$.......

Key Words

- **Some parameters related to wave motion**

(a) Displacement of a particle is the distance covered by the particle from the mean position.

(b) Amplitude is the maximum displacement of the particle from the equilibrium position.

Key Words

- **Some parameters related to wave motion**

(a) Displacement of a particle is the distance covered by the particle from the mean position.

(b) Amplitude is the maximum displacement of the particle from the equilibrium position.

(c) One wavelength is the distance travelled by the wave, during the time the particle completes one vibration about its mean position. We may also define, one wavelength = smallest distance between two particles vibrating in the same phase = distance between the centres of two consecutive crests/troughs/compressions/rarefactions.

(d) Angular wave number or propagation constant: It is 2π times the no. of waves that can be accommodated per unit length. It is denoted by K.

(e) Frequency: It is the no. of complete wavelengths traversed by the wave in one second.

(f) Time period: It is equal to time taken by wave to travel a distance equal to wavelength.

(g) Particle velocity = velocity of particle executing SHM $= \frac{dx}{dt}$. Its value changes with time.

(h) Wave velocity is the velocity with which disturbance travels in the medium.

$$v = n\lambda = \frac{\lambda}{T} = \text{constant for a wave motion.}$$

- **Phase or phase angle** is the physical quantity which tells us by what amount the two waves or the two particles lag or lead in terms of angle or time or distance.
- **Stationary Waves:** If two waves of same type having same amplitude, same frequency and same wavelength, travelling with same speed in opposite directions along a straight line superimpose each other, they give rise to a new kind of waves known as stationary wave.
- **Beats** is the phenomenon of regular variation in the intensity of sound when two sources of nearly equal frequencies are sounded together.

Scan to know more about this topic

Stationary waves

(i) Beat period is the time interval between two successive beats.

(ii) Beat frequency is the number of beats produced per second.

Key Formulae

- **A longitudinal wave** can be represented by

$$x = a\sin(\omega t \pm kx)$$

A transverse wave can be represented by

$y = a\sin(\omega t \pm kz)$; $y = a\sin(\omega t \pm kx)$

$z = a\sin(\omega t \pm kx)$; $z = a\sin(\omega t \pm ky)$

$x = a\sin(\omega t \pm ky)$; $x = a\sin(\omega t \pm kz)$

- **Relation between particle velocity & wave velocity.**

$$u(x, t) = -v\frac{}{dx}[y(x, t)]$$

Where u = particle velocity, v = wave velocity.

Key Formulae

- **Particle Acceleration:**

$$a(x, t) = -(2\pi\nu)^2 y = -\omega^2 y.$$

- **Plane progressive wave:**

(a) Standard Equations $y = r\sin\left[\frac{2\pi t}{T} - \frac{2\pi x}{\lambda}\right]$

or $y = r\cos\left[\frac{2\pi t}{T} - \frac{2\pi x}{\lambda}\right]$

where y = displacement, r = amplitude, T = time period, λ = wavelength, x = starting distance of wave from origin.

(b) Angular frequency: $\omega = \frac{2\pi}{T}$

(c) Propagation constant: $k = \frac{2\pi}{\lambda}$

(d) Velocity of wave: $v = \nu\lambda = \frac{\lambda}{T}$

(e) Velocity of particle: $u = \frac{dy}{dt}$, $u_{max} = r\omega$

(f) Acceleration of particle: $a = \frac{d^2y}{dt^2}$, $a_{max} = -\omega^2 r$

(g) Phase: For wave $y(x, t) = a\sin(kx - \omega t + \phi)$

Phase $= (kx - \omega t + \phi)$

- **Equation of stationary wave:**

When incident wave: $y_1 = A\sin\frac{2\pi}{\lambda}(vt - x)$ and

Reflected wave: $y_2 = A\sin\frac{2\pi}{\lambda}(vt - x)$

Then the standing wave: $y = 2A\sin\frac{2\pi}{\lambda}vt\cos\frac{2\pi}{\lambda}x$

Key Formulae

- **Normal modes of vibration of strings:**

(a) Frequency of fundamental tone: $\nu_0 = \frac{1}{2l}\sqrt{\frac{T}{m}}$

(b) 1st overtone or 2nd harmonic: $\nu_1 = 2\nu_0$

(c) 2nd overtone or 3rd harmonic: $\nu_2 = 3\nu_0$

- **Organ Pipes:**

(a) Closed organ pipe:

(i) Fundamental note $\nu_0 = \frac{v}{4L}$

(ii) 1st overtone or 3rd harmonic $\nu_1 = 3\nu_0$

(iii) 2nd overtone or 5th harmonic $\nu_2 = 5\nu_0$

(b) Open organ pipe:

(i) Fundamental note $\nu_1 = \frac{v}{2L}$

(ii) 1st overtone or 2nd harmonic $\nu_1 = 2\nu_0$

(iii) 2nd overtone or 3rd harmonic $\nu_2 = 3\nu_0$

- **Beats:** Beat frequency $n_1 - n_2$ or $n_2 - n_1$

Mnemonics

Concept: Transverse and longitudinal wave.

Mnemonics: **T**eacher **P**unished **l**azy **d**og.

Interpretation:

T - Transverse wave

P - perpendicular to direction of propagation

L - Longitudinal wave

D - direction of propagation

If constituents of the medium oscillate perpendicular to the direction of wave propagation, we call the wave a transverse wave. If constituents of the medium oscillate along the direction of wave propagation, we call the wave a longitudinal wave.

NCERT CORNER

Q. 1. A string of mass 2.5 kg is under a tension of 200 N. The length of the stretched string is 20.0 m. If the transverse jerk is struck at one end of the string, how long does the disturbance take to reach the other end ?

[NCERT Ex., Q. 14.1, Page 297]

Ans. Using $v = \sqrt{\frac{T}{m}}$

Putting, $m = \frac{2.5}{20} = 0.125 \text{ kgm}^{-1}, T = 200 \text{ N},$

$$v = \sqrt{\frac{200}{0.125}} = 40 \text{ ms}^{-1}$$

Time, $t = \frac{l}{v} = \frac{20}{40} = 0.5 \text{ s}$

Q. 2. A stone dropped from the top of a tower of height 300 m high splashes into the water of a pond near the base of the tower. When is the splash heard at the top given that the speed of sound in air is 340 ms⁻¹ ? (g = 9.8 ms⁻²)

[NCERT Ex., Q. 14.2, Page 297]

Ans. Let total time $t = t_1 + t_2$, where t_1 is the time taken by the stone to reach the surface of water and t_2 is the time taken by sound to reach the top.

Calculation of t_1:

Using $s = ut_1 + \frac{1}{2}at_1^2$

Putting, $u = 0, a = g = 9.8 \text{ ms}^{-2}$

and $s = 300$ m,

$$300 = \frac{1}{2} \times 9.8 \times t_1^2$$

or $t_1 = 7.8255$ s

Calculation of t_2:

Using $$v = \frac{s}{t_2},$$

$$t_2 = \frac{s}{v} = \frac{300}{340} = 0.88 \text{ s}$$

$$t = t_1 + t_2 = 7.82 + 0.88 = 8.70 \text{ s}$$

Q. 3. A steel wire has a length of 12.0 m and a mass of 2.10 kg. What should be the tension in the wire so that speed of a transverse wave on the wire equals the speed of sound in dry air at 20°C = 343 ms^{-1}

Ans. Using $$v = \sqrt{\frac{T}{m}}$$

we have $$T = v^2 m$$

where, m is mass per unit length

Now $$m = \frac{M}{l} = \frac{2{\cdot}1}{12}$$

$$= 0.175 \text{ kg m}^{-1}$$

and $$v = 343 \text{ ms}^{-1}$$

we get $T = (343)^2 \times 0.175 = 20588.6 = 2.06 \times 10^4$ N

Q. 4. Use the formula $v = \sqrt{\frac{\gamma P}{\rho}}$ to explain why the speed of sound in air:

(a) is independent of pressure.

(b) increases with temperature.

(c) increases with humidity.

Ans. (a) The formula for velocity of sound in air is given by.

$$v = \sqrt{\frac{\gamma P}{\rho}} \quad ..(1)$$

where γ = constant for a given gas, i.e., air

ρ = density of the gas

From gas equation, $PV = RT$

or $$P = \frac{RT}{V} \quad ...(2)$$

$\therefore$ From equation (1) and (2),

$$v = \sqrt{\frac{\gamma RT}{\rho V}} = \sqrt{\frac{\gamma RT}{M}} \quad ...(3)$$

where $\rho V = M$ = molecular weight of air or gas.

For a given gas, M = constant

R is also constant.

When T = constant, then from equation (3), we conclude that v is independent of the pressure of air (gas) if temperature remains constant.

(b) Effect of temperature:

From eqn. (3) $$\sqrt{\frac{\gamma RT}{M}}$$

Since, γ, R and M are constants, so

$$v \propto \sqrt{T}$$

It means velocity of sound in a gas is directly proportional to the square root of its temperature, hence we conclude that the velocity of sound in air increases with increase in temperature.

(c) Effect of humidity: The presence of water vapours in air changes the density of air, thus the velocity of sound changes with humidity of air.

Let ρ_m = density of moist air

ρ_d = density of dry air

v_m = velocity of sound in moist air

v_d = velocity of sound in dry air

From eqn. (1) $$v = \sqrt{\frac{\gamma P}{\rho}},$$

In moist air, $$v_m = \sqrt{\frac{\gamma P}{\rho_m}} \quad ..(4)$$

In dry air, $$v_d = \sqrt{\frac{\gamma \rho}{\rho_d}} \quad ..(5)$$

Dividing equation (4) by equation (5),

$$\frac{v_m}{v_d} = \sqrt{\frac{\rho_d}{\rho_m}} \quad ...(6)$$

Also we know that density of moist air is less than the density of dry air. It means dry air is heavier than moist air. so

$$\rho_m < \rho_d$$

or $$\frac{\rho_d}{\rho_m} > 1 \quad ..(iv)$$

$\therefore$ from equation (6)

$$\frac{v_m}{v_d} > 1$$

$\therefore$ $$v_m > v_d$$

It means speed of sound increases with humidity.

Q. 5. You have learnt, that a travelling wave in one dimension is represented by a function $y = f(x, t)$, where x and t must appear in the combination $(x - vt)$ or $(x + vt)$, i.e., $y = f(x \pm vt)$. Is the converse true ? That is, does every function of $(x - vt)$ or $(x + vt)$ represent a travelling wave ? Examine, if the following function for y can possibly represent a travelling wave:

(a) $(x - vt)^2$ **(b)** $\log\left[\frac{x+vt}{x_0}\right]$

(c) $\frac{1}{x+vt}$

[NCERT Ex., Q. 14.5, Page 298]

Ans. No, the converse is not true. The basic requirement for a wave function to represent a travelling wave is that for all values of x and t, wave function must have a finite value.

Out of the given functions for y only (c) satisfies this condition. The other functions cannot represent a travelling wave as the necessary condition is not satisfied by these functions.

Q. 6. A bat emits ultrasonic sound of frequency 1000 kHz in air. If the sound meets a water surface, what is the wavelength of (a) the reflected sound, (b) the transmitted sound ? Speed of sound in air is 340 ms^{-1} and in water 1,486 ms^{-1}.

[NCERT Ex., Q. 14.6, Page 298]

Ans. (a) The reflected sound:

Using $v = \frac{\lambda}{T} = \lambda \nu$

$$\lambda = \frac{v}{\nu} = \frac{340}{10^6} = 3.4 \times 10^{-4}\text{ m}$$

(b)The transmitted sound:

Here, $\lambda' = \frac{1486}{10^6} = 1.486 \times 10^{-3}\text{ m}$

Q. 7. A hospital uses an ultrasonic scanner to locate tumours in a tissue. What is the wave length of sound in the tissue in which the speed of sound is 1.7 kms^{-1} ? The operating frequency of the scanner is 4.2 MHz.

Ans. Using $\lambda = \frac{v}{\nu}$,

or $\lambda = \frac{1.7 \times 10^3}{4.2 \times 10^6}$

$= 0.405 \times 10^{-3}$ m.

Q. 8. A transverse harmonic wave on a string is described by $y(x, t) = 3.0 \sin(36t + 0.018x + \pi/4)$ where x and y are in cm and t in sec. The positive direction of x is from left to right.

(a) Is this a travelling wave or a stationary wave? If it is travelling, what are the speed and direction of its propagation ?

(b) What are its amplitude and frequency ?

(c) What is the initial phase at the origin ?

(d) What is the least distance between two successive crests in the wave ? [NCERT Ex., Q. 14.8, Page 298]

Ans. Here $y(x, t) = 3\sin(36t + 0.018x + \pi/4)$

$= 3\sin[0.018(2000t + x) + \pi/4]$

Comparing with standard equation

$$y(x, t) = r \sin\left[\frac{2\pi}{\lambda}(vt + x) + \phi\right]$$

It is observed that the given equation represents a travelling waveform right to left.

(a) Here, $v = 2000\text{ cms}^{-1}$

(b) $r = 3$ cm

Also, $\frac{2\pi}{\lambda} = 0.018$

or $\lambda = \frac{2\pi}{0.018}$ cm

Using $v = \lambda\nu$,

$$\nu = \frac{v}{\lambda} = \frac{2000}{2\pi} \times 0.018 = 5.73\text{ s}^{-1}$$

(c) Initial phase at origin, $\phi = \frac{\pi}{4}$ radian

(d) Distance between successive crests

$$= \lambda = \frac{2\pi}{0.018}$$

$= 349$ cm $= 3.49$ m

Q. 9. For the wave described in the above question plot the displacement (y) versus (t) graphs for $x = 0, 2$ and 4 cm. What are the shapes of these graphs ? In which aspects does the oscillatory motion in travelling waves differ from one point to another : amplitude, frequency or phase?

Ans. $y(x, t) = 3.0 \sin\left(36t + 0.018x + \frac{\pi}{4}\right)$

When $x = 0$,

$$y(0, t) = 3.0 \sin\left(36t + \frac{\pi}{4}\right)$$

Initial displacement $= y(0, 0) = 3.0 \sin\frac{\pi}{4} = \frac{3}{\sqrt{2}}$

$= 2.121$ cm

When $x = 2$,

$$y(2, t) = 3.0 \sin\left(36t + 0.036 + \frac{\pi}{4}\right)$$

Initial displacement $= y(2, 0) = 3.0 \sin\left(0.036 + \frac{\pi}{4}\right)$

$= 2.122$ cm

When $x = 4$,

$$y(2, t) = 3.0 \sin\left(36t + 0.072 + \frac{\pi}{4}\right)$$

Initial displacement $= y(4,0) = 3.0\sin\left(0.072 + \frac{\pi}{4}\right)$

$= 2.124$ cm

All the three graphs are sine graphs. All are having same amplitude (3 cm) and same frequency $\left(\frac{2\pi}{36} = \frac{\pi}{18}\frac{\text{rad}}{\text{s}}\right)$. Graphs differ in initial phase.

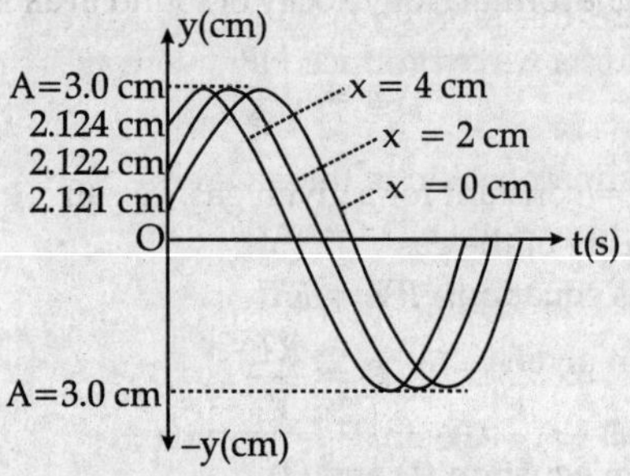

Q. 10. For the travelling harmonic wave $y(x, t) = 2.0 \cos 2\pi[10t - 0.0080x + 0.35]$ where x and y are in cm and t in s. Calculate the phase difference between oscillatory motion of two points separated by a distance of (a) 4 m, (b) 0.5 m, (c) $\lambda/2$ (d) $3\lambda/4$. [NCERT Ex., Q. 14.10, Page 298]

Ans. Here

$y = 2\cos 2\pi(10t - 0.0080x + 0.35)$

$= 2\cos[2\pi(10t - 0.0080x) + 2\pi(0.35)]$

$$= 2\cos\left[2\pi \times 0.0080\left(\frac{10}{0.0080}t - x\right) + 2\pi \times 0.35\right]$$

Standard equation for a travelling wave is

$$y = r\cos\left[\frac{2\pi}{\lambda}(vt - x) + \phi\right]$$

Here $\varphi = \frac{2\pi}{\lambda}x = 2\pi \times 0.008x$

$$\left[\because \frac{1}{\lambda} = 0.008\text{cm}\right]$$

(a) when $x = 4$ m = 400 cm,
$\varphi = 2\pi \times 0.008 \times 400$
$= 6.4\pi$ rad

(b) when $x = 0.5$ m = 50 cm,
$\varphi = 2\pi \times 0.008 \times 50$
$= 0.8\pi$ rad

(c) when $x = \frac{\lambda}{2}$, $\varphi = \frac{2\pi}{\lambda} \times \frac{\lambda}{2} = \pi$ rad

(d) when $x = \frac{3}{4}\lambda$, $\varphi = \frac{2\pi}{\lambda} \times \frac{3\lambda}{4} = \frac{3\pi}{2}$ rad

Q. 11. The transverse displacement of a string (clamped at its both ends) is given by

$$y(x,t) = 0.06\sin\left(\frac{2\pi}{3}x\right)\cos(120\ \pi t)$$

Where x and y are in m and t in s. The length of the string is 1.5 m and its mass is 3.0×10^{-2} kg.
Answer the following:
(a) Does the function represent a travelling wave or a stationary wave?
(b) Interpret the wave as a superposition of two waves travelling in opposite directions. What is the wavelength, frequency, and speed of each wave?
(c) Determine the tension in the string.

Ans. (a) Given: $y(x,t) = 0.06\sin\left(\frac{2\pi}{3}x\right)\cos(120\pi t)$

It is same as the equation for stationary wave-
$$y(x, t) = 2a\sin kx\cos\omega t$$

Therefore, this represents stationary wave.
(b) Standing wave produced by two waves-
$$y(x, t) = 2a\sin kx\cos\omega t$$

Due to superposition of these waves-
$$y_1(x,t) = a\sin(\omega t - kx)$$
$$y_2(x,t) = a\sin(\omega t + kx)$$

Equation given-
$$y(x,t) = 0.06\sin\left(\frac{2\pi x}{3}\right)\cos(120\pi t)$$

So, $k = \frac{2\pi}{\lambda} = \frac{2\pi}{3} \therefore \lambda = 3$ m
$\omega = 120\pi$ rad/s
$\omega = 2\pi\nu$ or $\nu = \frac{\omega}{2\pi} = \frac{120\pi}{2\pi}$
$\therefore$ $\nu = 60$ Hz

(c) Speed of wave, $v = \nu\lambda$
= 60 x3
= 180 m/s

$2a = 0.06$ or $a = 0.03$m

$$\therefore\ y_1 = 0.03\sin\left(120\pi t - \frac{2\pi}{3}x\right)$$
$$y_2 = 0.03\sin\left(120\pi t + \frac{2\pi}{3}x\right)$$

Wave's speed = 180 m/s
Mass per unit length

$$\mu = \frac{m}{l}$$
$$= \frac{3.0}{1.5} \times 10^{-2}\ \text{Kg m}^{-1}$$
$$= 2 \times 10^{-2}\ \text{Kg m}^{-1}$$

Therefore, $T = v^2\mu$
$T = (180)^2 \times 2 \times 10^{-2}$
Tension, $T = 648$ N

Q. 12. For the wave on a string described in above question do all the points on the string oscillate with the same (i) (a) frequency, (b) phase, (c) amplitude? Explain your answers. (ii) What is the amplitude of a point 0.375 m away from one end?
[NCERT Ex., Q. 14.12, Page 299]

Ans. (i) Transverse Displacement is-
$$y(x,t) = 0.06\sin\frac{2\pi}{3}x\cos 120\pi t$$

(a) Yes, cos 120 πt represents its frequency, as this function does not depend on x, so oscillation's frequency of all points on the string is same.
(b) Yes, phase of all points on string is same. except at nodes.
(c) As amplitude depends on x, it will not be same at all points on the string.
(ii) Now, amplitude at a point-0.375 m away from one end-
$$a = 0.06\sin\frac{2\pi}{3} \times 0.375$$
$$= 0.06\sin 0.7854$$
$$= 0.06 \times 0.707$$
$$a = 0.042\ \text{m}$$

Q. 13. Given below are some functions of x and t to represent the displacement (transverse or longitudinal) of an elastic wave. State which of these represent
(i) a travelling wave,
(ii) a stationary wave, or
(iii) none of all ?
(a) $y = 2\cos(3x)\sin(10t)$
(b) $y = 2\sqrt{x - vt}$
(c) $y = 3\sin(5x - 0.5t) + 4\cos(5x - 0.5t)$
(d) $y = \cos x\sin t + \cos 2x\sin 2t$
[NCERT Ex., Q. 14.13, Page 299]

Ans. (a) It represents a stationary wave in harmonic functions of x and t are contained separately in the equation.
(b) It cannot represent any type of wave.
(c) It represents a progressive travelling harmonic wave.
(d) This equation is sum of two functions each representing a stationary wave. Therefore, it represents superposition of two stationary waves.

Q. 14. A wire stretched between two rigid supports vibrates in its fundamental mode with a frequency 45 Hz. The mass of the wire is 3.5×10^{-2} kg and its linear density is 4.0×10^{-2} kg m^{-1}. What is
(a) the speed of a transverse wave on the string, and
(b) the tension in the string ?
[NCERT Ex., Q. 14.14, Page 299]

Ans. Using $l = \frac{M}{m} = \frac{3.5 \times 10^{-2}}{4 \times 10^{-2}}$
$= 0.875$ m

(a) In fundamental mode,

$$l = \frac{\lambda}{2}$$

or $\lambda = 2l = 2 \times 0.875 = 1.75$ m

Velocity $= f\lambda = 45 \times 1.75 = 78.75$ ms^{-1}

(b) $v = \sqrt{T/m}$

or, $T = v^2 m = (78.75)^2 \times 4 \times 10^{-2}$

≈ 248 N.

Q. 15. A 1 metre long tube open at one end, with a movable piston at other end, shows resonance with a fixed frequency source (a tuning fork of frequency 340 Hz) when the tube length is 25.5 cm or 79.3 cm. Estimate the speed of sound in air at the temperature of the experiment. The edge effects may be neglected.

[NCERT Ex., Q. 14.15, Page 299]

Ans. For the fundamental tone in a closed organ pipe,

$$\frac{\lambda_0}{4} = L = 25.5 \text{ cm}$$

$\therefore$ $\lambda_0 = 102$ cm $= 1.02$ m

Frequency $= v = 340$ Hz

$\therefore$ Velocity of sound $= v\lambda_0$

$= 340 \times 1.02$

$= 346.8$ ms^{-1}

Q. 16. A steel rod 100 cm long is clamped at its middle. The fundamental frequency of longitudinal vibrations of the rod are given to be 2.53 kHz. What is the speed of sound in steel ? [NCERT Ex., Q. 14.16, Page 299]

Ans. When a rod clamped in the middle it has anti-nodes (A) at its ends and node (N) at the point of clamping. In fundamental mode, so the length of the rod is

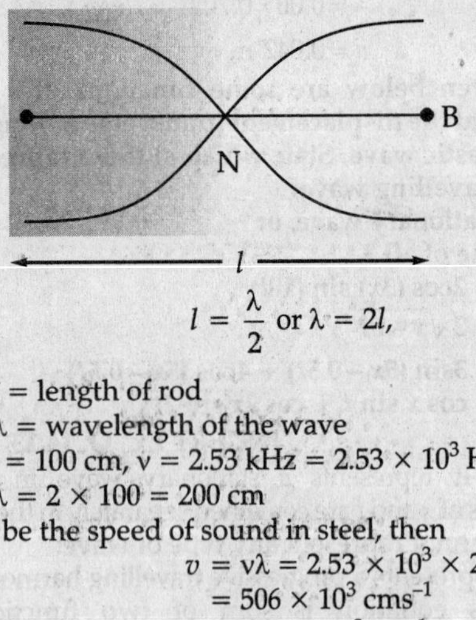

$$l = \frac{\lambda}{2} \text{ or } \lambda = 2l,$$

where l = length of rod

and λ = wavelength of the wave

Given: $l = 100$ cm, $\nu = 2.53$ kHz $= 2.53 \times 10^3$ Hz

$\therefore$ $\lambda = 2 \times 100 = 200$ cm

When v be the speed of sound in steel, then

$v = \nu\lambda = 2.53 \times 10^3 \times 200$

$= 506 \times 10^3$ cms^{-1}

$v = 5.06 \times 10^3$ ms^{-1}

Q. 17. A pipe 20 cm long is closed at one end. Which harmonic mode of the pipe is resonantly excited by a 430 Hz source? Will the same source be in resonance with the pipe if both ends are open? (speed of sound in air is 340 ms^{-1}). [NCERT Ex., Q. 14.17, Page 299]

Ans. Given: Pipe's length, $l = 20$ cm

$= 0.2$ m

frequency, $\nu = 430$ Hz

speed of sound $= 340$ m/s

For closed pipe, fundamental frequency,

$$\nu_1 = \frac{v}{4l}$$

$$= \frac{340}{4 \times 0.2}$$

$= 425$ Hz

Hence, fundamental frequency will resonate with the source. For open pipe, fundamental frequency,

$$\nu_2 = \frac{v}{2l}$$

$$= \frac{340}{2 \times 0.2}$$

$= 850$ Hz

Then, there will be no resonance.

Q. 18. Two sitar strings A and B playing the note '*Ga*' are slightly out of tune and produce beats of frequency 6 Hz. The tension in the string A is slightly reduced and the beat frequency is found to reduce to 3 Hz. If the original frequency of A is 324 Hz, what is the frequency of B? [NCERT Ex., Q. 14.18, Page 299]

Ans. Let ν_A, ν_B be frequency of A and B respectively

$$\nu_A - \nu_B = \pm 6$$

or $\nu_B = \nu_A \pm 6 = 324 \pm 6$

$\nu_B = 330$ or 318 Hz

When tension is reduced, frequency also decreases-

$$\nu \propto \sqrt{T}$$

$\therefore$ No. of Beats also decreases

Hence, $\nu_B = 324 - 6 = 318$ Hz

Q. 19. Explain why (or how):

(a) in a sound wave, a displacement node is a pressure antinode and vice versa.

(b) bats can ascertain distances, directions, nature, and sizes of the obstacles without any "eyes".

(c) a violin note and sitar note may have the same frequency, yet we can distinguish between the two notes.

(d) solids can support both longitudinal and transverse waves, but only longitudinal waves can propagate in gases, and

(e) the shape of a pulse gets distorted during propagation in a dispersive medium.

[NCERT Ex., Q. 14.19, Page 299]

Ans. (a) Displacement node is a point of zero displacement, so pressure is maximum at this point where as on anti-nodes the reverse happens, hence it is a pressure antinode.

(b) Bats produce and detect ultrasonic waves and emit sound of frequencies between 20-100 KHz for this purpose, hence they developed 'Echo-location' system.

(c) Because nature of waveforms and presence of overtones are different in the given two cases.

(d) Gases cannot sustain shearing stress as in case of transverse wave propagation, the medium must have property of sustaining shearing. So gases cannot support transverse wave propagation.

(e) This is the property of dispersive medium that waves of different wave length travel with different speeds in different directions or with different velocities. Thus, when sound pulse (a combination of waves of different wavelengths) travels through it, gets distorted.